CONSENSUS AND CONFLICT

CONSENSUS AND CONFLICT
Essays in Political Sociology

SEYMOUR MARTIN LIPSET

Transaction Books
New Brunswick (U.S.A.) and Oxford (U.K.)

To the Memory of Stein Rokkan,
Friend and Colleague.
We shall never know his equal in intellect, energy, and helpfulness to
others.

———◇———

Library of Congress Catalog Number: 85-1038
ISBN: 0-88738-051-4 (cloth), 0-88738-608-3 (paper)
Printed in the United States of America

Library of Congress Cataloging in Publication Data

Lipset, Seymour Martin.
  Consensus and conflict

  Bibliography: p.
  1. Political sociology—Addresses, essays, lectures.
2. Consensus (Social sciences)—Addresses, essays,
lectures.   3. Social conflict—Addresses, essays,
lectures.   I. Title.
JA76.L547   1985   306′.2   85-1038
ISBN 0-88738-051-4
ISBN 0-88738-608-3 (pbk.)

Contents

List of Tables and Figures

Acknowledgments

The author gratefully acknowledges the following publishers and publications for permission to use copyrighted material:

1. "Social Structure and Social Change," in Peter Blau (ed.), *Approaches to the Study of Social Structures* (New York: Free Press, 1975), pp. 172–209.

2. "Social Class," in David Sills (ed.), *International Encyclopedia of the Social Sciences* (New York: Macmillan, 1968), Vol. XV, pp. 296–316.

3. " 'The End of Ideology' and the Ideology of Intellectuals," in Joseph Ben David and Terry Clark (eds.), *Culture and Its Creators* (Chicago: University of Chicago Press, 1977), pp. 15–42.

4. (with Stein Rokkan) "Cleavage Structures, Party Systems and Voter Alignments: An Introduction," in Seymour M. Lipset and Stein Rokkan (eds.), *Party Systems and Voter Alignments: Cross-National Perspectives* (New York: Free Press, 1967), pp. 1–64.

5. "The Industrial Proletariat in Comparative Perspective," in Jan F. Triska and Charles Gati (eds.), *Blue Collar Workers in Eastern Europe* (London: Allen & Unwin, 1981), pp. 1–29.

6. "Radicalism or Reformism: The Sources of Working-Class Politics," *American Political Science Review* 77 (March 1983): pp. 1–18.

7. "The Revolt Against Modernity," in Per Torsvik (ed.), *Mobilization, Center-Periphery Structures and Nation Building* (Bergen, Norway: Universitets Forlaget, 1981), pp. 451–500.

8. Chapter 8 is an amalgam of various articles, analyzing violence and extremism in the context of studies of American values and structures in my earlier work. See "On the Politics of Conscience and Extreme Commitment," *Encounter* (August 1968), pp. 68–71; "The Paradox of American Politics," *The Public Interest* 41 (Fall 1975): 142–165; and (with Carl Sheingold) "Values and Political Structures: An Interpretation of the Sources of Extremism and Violence in American Society," in W.J. Crotty (ed.),

Assassinations and Political Order (New York: Harper & Row, 1971), pp. 388–414.

9. ''Predicting the Future of Post-Industrial Society: Can We Do It?'' in S.M. Lipset (ed.), *The Third Century: America as a Post-Industrial Society* (Stanford, Calif.: The Hoover Institution Press, 1979), pp. 1–35.

Introduction

This book is the second volume of essays which I have published. The first, *Revolution and Counterrevolution*, contains articles that essentially build on and extend themes developed in two earlier books, *Political Man* and *The First New Nation*, analyses of the social requisites of democratic society, studies of party conflict, perceived as "the democratic class struggle" both in world comparative and American terms, and comparisons of social structures and values in Latin America, Canada, and the United States.

The articles contained here, as the title indicates, deal with social and political conflict and, to a lesser extent, with the way in which value systems and political institutions serve to maintain order and consensus. The first three chapters seek in different ways to demonstrate that the differences between conflict and consensus paradigms—emphasized by some who classify themselves as in the "conflict school"—are greatly exaggerated. All complex societies are characterized by a high degree of internal tension and conflict, but consensual institutions and values are necessary conditions for their persistence. Hence, any effort to deal with political or social systems must treat conflict and consensus.

Exponents of the conflict paradigm have criticized efforts to specify the common values of societies as ideologically linked approaches that serve to reduce awareness of the variations in intrasocietal interest or contradictions that result in conflict.

Such judgments are factually incorrect. As one who has been defined and criticized by conflict theorists as an adherent of the so-called consensus school, I would note that most of my political sociology has dealt with conflict and change, not with consensus and integration. I have studied radical change-oriented movements of the Left and Right, trade unions, party conflict as a form of class conflict, and the role of students and intellectuals as agents of change. In the first section of this book I discuss the ways other social scientists who are classified as consensual have dealt with social change and conflict.

Conflict school theorists reject the assumption of national value systems. They also do not agree with the functionalist thesis that systems of inequality, of social stratification, rest in large part on agreement within societies about the relative standing of positions, statuses, or roles. To specify common

1

national values, it is necessary to view them in comparative perspective, to recognize the differences among Americans, English, French, and so on. On a number of occasions Margaret Mead argued that for the purposes of comparative analysis, a "sample" of one is permissible, since all individuals reared and living within distinct cultures reflect the unique values of their society or subgroup.[1] An example of the way an outsider, even from a closely related culture, can be sensitive to the special values of a neighboring nation has been written by a Canadian scholar, Sacvan Bercovitch, in reporting on his reaction to the United States during the conflict-ridden 1960s:

> My first encounter with American consensus was in the late sixties, when I crossed the border into the United States and found myself inside the myth of America. Not of North America, for the myth stopped short of the Canadian and Mexican borders, but of a country that despite its arbitrary frontiers, despite its bewildering mix of race and creed, could believe in something called the True America, and could invest that patent fiction with all the moral and emotional appeal of a religious symbol. . . . Here was the Jewish anarchist Paul Goodman berating the Midwest for abandoning the promise; here, the descendant of American slaves, Martin Luther King, denouncing injustice as a violation of the American way; here, an endless debate about national destiny, . . . conservatives scavenging for un-Americans, New Left historians recalling the country to its sacred mission.
>
> Nothing in my Canadian background had prepared me for that spectacle. . . . It gave me something of an anthropologist's sense of wonder at the symbols of the tribe. . . . To a Canadian skeptic, a gentile in God's country . . . [here was] a pluralistic, pragmatic people . . . bound together by an ideological consensus.
>
> Let me repeat that mundane phrase: *ideological consensus*. For it wasn't the idea of exceptionalism that I discovered in '68. . . . It was a hundred sects and factions, each apparently different from the others, yet all celebrating the same mission. . . . Ideology in this sense is perhaps a narrower concept than those usually associated with "America," but a more helpful one. It speaks of the day-to-day *uses* of myth. . . . Thus, although the consensus I refer to is not a measure of what census-takers call society, and although its function has been to mystify or mask social realities, nonetheless it denotes something equally "real": a system of values, symbols, and beliefs, and a series of rituals designed to keep the system going.[2]

The notion that there is an American value system that differs from those of other countries, including even Canada, is not of course a discovery of Mr. Bercovitch or of conservative writers. Almost a century ago, another comparison of the United States and Canada by a European visitor to both countries explained the lower level of development in Canada by reference to the differences in the values of the two countries, with Canada's still resembling those of Europe. Friedrich Engels argued that Canada required an infusion of the "spirit of the Americans," of "Yankee blood," in order to grow economically.[3] Socialist and Communist analysts such as Antonio Gramsci, Leon Samson, Gunnar Myrdal, and Michael Harrington have pointed to the general acceptance of Americanism, of the American Creed, and agreement on its content in their efforts to account for political behavior in this country.[4] But as Bercovitch emphasizes, such consensus does not prevent conflict; it may be the very stuff which defines the issues Americans fight about. Samson argued in the 1930s, and Harrington voiced agreement with him in the 1970s, citing Marx for justification, that socialists had failed in the United States in large part because they presented their case in European rather than American terms.

To emphasize the existence of common value systems clearly does not imply a low level of internal conflict. Values which are accepted throughout a society may in fact generate intense struggles, revolutionary and deviant behavior. The logic that a system of stratification requires consensus about the legitimacy of inequality, while *at the same time* inequality stimulates protest, revolt, and class consciousness among the underprivileged is developed in chapter 2. Here I would only note the obvious point that without agreement that more money, power, status is better than less, people would not be motivated to try for various positions or conform to the rules defining success in the eyes of significant others. At the same time, since to be lowly is worse, and exposes those who are to real punishment, to social rejection, the less privileged resent their position and either try to improve it individually or to join with others to change the social arrangements that are responsible for their inferiority. As Robert K. Merton has noted, the emphasis in America on success, on getting ahead, is related both to high crime rates and forms of rebellion.[5]

The debate over the emphasis on conflict or consensus has in many ways been a disguise for an argument over Marxist and non-Marxist "mainstream," particularly functionalist, approaches to social science. Marxism with its focus on class conflict and structural contradiction as the engines of change is perceived as diametrically opposite to functionalism with its supposedly conservative assumption that whatever is is necessary, that the interdependent links among institutions and practices mean that the social consequences of planned social change are unpredictable, and often disastrous. A stress on consensus and order is seen as inherent in functionalism.

Such arguments ignore the fact that Marx's methodological approach was basically functionalist and he was concerned with the mechanisms which sustain consensus. As noted in chapter 1, the well-known British Marxist historian Eric Hobsbawm points out that Marx was an early, if not the first, functionalist. More recently, following a visit to America, British Marxist sociologist Kenneth Thompson complains that American sociologists are responsible for "a serious distortion" of Marxism when they collapse it "into an amorphous conflict paradigm." He contends they ignore the fact that the strength of "Marxist contributions to sociology lies in the fact that their analyses . . . address questions of social order *and* social change . . . that Althusser and Gramsci were just as interested in the ways in which social order is produced and reproduced as were Durkheim and Talcott Parsons."[6]

Ironically, as indicated in chapter 1, Parsons devoted much of his attention to the problem of order because he assumed with Hobbes that disorder and conflict are inherent in the human condition. Marx, on the other hand, assumed that stability is the normal condition of society, since the institutional system, including mechanisms of socialization and opinion formation, is functionally related to the hegemony of the dominant class. Marx took order for granted and sought to explain conflict and change; Parsons took disorder—conflict—for granted and sought to explain consensus and stability.

A detailed analysis of the convergence between the approaches to conflict and consensus of Marxists and of mainstream sociologists from Comte through Durkheim and Parsons may be found in a recent book by Thomas Bernard, *The Consensus-Conflict Debate*. As he notes:

> Sociological consensus theories assume there will always be a great many conflicts between human beings because the source of these conflicts is in human nature. The hypothetical "utopian" society does not resolve the conflicts per se but rather strengthens social bonds to control their overt expression.
>
> In radical theories, the source of the conflict is said to be in socioeconomic relations, not in human nature, and the "utopian" societies are seen as resolving the conflicts by changing *the relations*.[7]

The same institutions may be seen as sources of integration and/or of conflict. Thus trade unions and political parties are clearly agents of conflict with groups representing other classes and interests. But they are also mediating structures, which as Tocqueville noted, serve the function of binding individuals to the larger society. Unorganized individuals are potentially a greater source of support for revolutionary and extremist forces of the Left or Right than are those who belong to groups organized for conflict. Successful revolutionary movements have been much more prevalent in authoritarian repressive societies than in democratic ones. This is the point Herbert Marcuse was trying to emphasize by his phrase "repressive tolerance." From a revolutionary point of view, a democratic order is almost impossible to overthrow precisely because it accepts conflict as legitimate and necessary, and provides its citizens with the opportunity to join and support groups which fight for diverse interests and values.

This thesis was elaborated earlier by a dedicated revolutionary. Writing in 1907, Lenin suggested that the weakness of socialism in America stemmed from the fact that the United States had "the most firmly established democratic system in the world," that there were no "big, nation-wide democratic tasks facing the proletariat." Five years later he noted that one of the principal causes of the "strength of bourgeois labor policy in . . . America is the long-standing political liberty."[8]

Much as I do in the first three chapters of this book, Bernard, in his review of the literature on the abundant debate among consensus and conflict theorists, functionalists, Weberians, and Marxists, concludes that his analysis "has demonstrated that the areas of agreement among them are more extensive than the areas of disagreement." He then goes on to ask why the debate has generated so much heat when the theories have "so much in common." And he makes the paradoxical suggestion that the intensity validates the generalization derived from Simmel and Coser that "the closer the relationship, the more intense the conflict."[9]

As noted earlier, the essays in this book reflect my concerns with the theoretical controversies between Marxism and functionalism, radical and mainstream sociology, as well as my continued effort to analyze political and class conflicts. The chapters in Part I, "Social Structure and Social Change," "Social Stratification and Social-Class Analysis," and "A Concept and Its History: The End of Ideology," point out the congruence in analyses of social structure and change, social class and stratification, and changes in ideology among exponents of Marxist, Weberian, and functionalist schools. They do not say that different conceptual frameworks yield similar hypotheses or research findings, but that serious social scientists of diverse theoretical persuasions tend to find comparable answers to similar questions.

The five chapters in Part II, "Cleavage Structures, Party Systems and Voter Alignments," "The Industrial Proletariat and the Intelligentsia in Comparative Perspective," "Radicalism or Reformism: The Sources of Working-Class Politics," "The Revolt against Modernity," and "Values and Political Structure: Moralism, Movements, and Violence" are more empirical in content, seeking to explain political phenomena. Chapter 4, the longest one in the book, written in collaboration with the late Stein Rokkan, elaborates on a theoretical framework derived from Talcott Parsons, seeking to bring some conceptual order to the analysis of the diverse political party systems which emerged in the Western world in the past century. The other chapters deal with parties and social movements in historical and comparative perspective. The final one in this section, chapter 8, treats some paradoxes of American politics, linking them to the ways in which American values differ from those in other nations. The last section, which contains one chapter, "The Limits of Social Science," is designed to emphasize the historical character of macroscopic analysis, that the multivariate complexity of human society limits the ability of social science to anticipate social outcomes.

All these chapters have appeared in print. Chapter 2, "Social Stratification and Social-Class Analysis," is also in my earlier collection of essays *Revolution and Counterrevolution*, while chapter 3, "A Concept and Its History: The End of Ideology," was reprinted at the end of the updated 1981 edition of my book *Political Man*. I have included them here because together with chapter 1 they form a coherent unit dealing with theoretical convergences.

Since I believe that one of the purposes of bringing these essays together is to permit readers to evaluate the validity and usefulness of my analyses over a 17-year period, I have not tried to revise or update them. I have, however, edited them to eliminate duplication, which inevitably is present among articles dealing with similar issues, and to delete references to the contents of books in chapters originally written as introductions to edited volumes. I would also note that chapter 8, "Values and Political Structure: Moralism, Movements, and Violence," is an amalgamation of three articles, which so overlap that I felt they had to be combined.

Although I have resisted the impulse to make changes in light of subsequent events, I cannot refrain from noting that the division within the Democratic Party in the 1984 nomination contest adds another case to my analysis of postindustrial politics as presented in chapter 5. The Hart-Mondale contest continued the pattern set in 1952 when Adlai Stevenson, who openly rejected New Deal economic class and welfare state politics in favor of environmentalism, a higher culture, and dovish internationalism, was opposed by Estes Kefauver running as a New Deal Populist, and appealing to class resentments. Stevenson set the tone for the new "postmaterialist" politics and became the beloved candidate of the intelligentsia, of the Yuppies (the young urban professionals). It is interesting to note that in an interview in 1978, Gary Hart, who had been George McGovern's campaign manager in 1972, said that he was attracted to McGovern in 1970, because he saw him "as part of the Gene McCarthy, Adlai Stevenson, Eleanor Roosevelt, Kennedy wing" of the Democratic party.[10] Conversely, there is a direct line of continuity in leadership of the New Deal economic issue oriented, more hawkish, labor-based wing from Kefauver through Humphrey, Henry Jackson, and Mondale.

Three articles in this volume are linked to my good friend Stein Rokkan. Chapter 4 was written together with him during a semester he spent in 1964-65 at Berkeley, where I was then teaching. Chapter 6 was initially presented as the first Stein Rokkan memorial lecture at a meeting of the European Consortium for Political Research in Aahrus, Denmark, in 1981, and chapter 7 was published in a *Festschrift* to his memory. Stein Rokkan was the giant of comparative political sociology in the postwar world. Much of the systematic collaboration that developed among scholars in diverse countries owes its intellectual and organizational existence to Rokkan's energy and dedication. He played a decisive role in the development of the International Political

Science Association, the International Social Science Council, the Research Committee on Political Sociology, and the European Consortium. As his many friends well know, Stein gave a considerable amount of his time to such organizations. Coming from a small country, Norway, he felt the need to visit with scholars and teach graduate students in many countries. Although these activities inevitably affected the time available for his own research and writing, he was a very productive scholar. His intellectual activities set a model both on the theoretical and empirical levels for studies of democratic political systems. That there are many books and articles dealing with almost all the stable democracies which address similar concerns within a common conceptual framework reflects Stein's influence. The dedication of this book to his memory expresses my deep obligation to him, intellectually and personally. I miss him.

I would like to express my indebtedness to Ronit Bogler, James Scamanaci, and Janet Shaw for their assistance in helping to prepare these essays for publication. Their efforts were invaluable in screening out duplications and strengthening references.

Notes

1. See Margaret Mead, "Introduction," in Margaret Mead and Rhoda Metraux (eds.), *The Study of Culture at a Distance* (Chicago: University of Chicago Press, 1953), pp. 41–49.
2. Sacvan Bercovitch, "The Rites of Assent: Rhetoric, Ritual, and the Ideology of American Consensus," in Sam B. Girgus (ed.), *The American Self: Myth, Ideology and Popular Culture* (Albuquerque: University of New Mexico Press, 1981), pp. 5–6 (emphases in original).
3. Engels to Sorge, 10 September 1888, in Karl Marx and Friedrich Engels, *Letters to Americans* (New York: International Publishers, 1935), p. 204. For comparable comments on other countries by Marx and Engels see S.M. Lipset, "Racial and Ethnic Tensions in the Third World," in W. Scott Thompson (ed.), *The Third World: Premises of U.S. Policy* (San Francisco: Institute for Contemporary Studies, 1978), pp. 137–39.
4. See my discussion of their writings in S.M. Lipset, "Why No Socialism in the United States?" in S. Bialer and S. Sluzar (eds.), *Sources of Contemporary Radicalism*, Vol. 1 (Boulder, Colo.: Westview, 1977), pp. 72–79.
5. Robert K. Merton, *Social Theory and Social Structure* (Glencoe, Ill.: Free Press, 1957), pp. 162–69.
6. Kenneth Thompson, "Marxism without Tears," in the *Times Higher Education Supplement*, 8 June 1984, p. 14 (emphasis in original).
7. Thomas J. Bernard, *The Consensus-Conflict Debate* (New York: Columbia University Press, 1983), p. 194.

8. V.I. Lenin, *On Britain* (Moscow: Foreign Languages Publishing House, n.d.), p. 51; and V.I. Lenin, *Collected Works*, Vol. 36 (Moscow: Progress Publishers, 1966), p. 215.
9. Bernard, *The Consensus-Conflict Debate*, p. 214. The quote is from Lewis Coser, *The Functions of Social Conflict* (New York: Free Press, 1956), pp. 67–72, who in turn was citing Georg Simmel, *Conflict and the Web of Group Affiliations* (New York: Free Press, 1955), pp. 33–35.
10. Molly Ivins, "Gary Hart: Heir Presumptive?" *Politics Today* 6 (January/February 1979): 37.

PART I

ANALYTIC CONVERGENCES

1

Social Structure and Social Change

Sociological analysis, particularly in its functionalist form, has been frequently criticized by extramural as well as intramural critics for its emphasis on explaining (and hence supposedly justifying) the stability of social systems, while neglecting the forces making for breakdowns and change. The focus by functionalists on "values" as distinct from "interests" seems to the critics to result in an underestimation of the inherent forces for social conflict among those having different interests.

The very concept of social structure, which is basic to all forms of sociological analysis, also appears to confirm the image of sociological preoccupation with statics in that the term as used by many sociologists refers to stable interrelations among parts of a system, e.g., the relation between a husband and wife or between workers and employers. As Max Weber emphasized, such relationships always involve "at least a minimum of mutual orientation" of the actors involved.

> The "meaning" relevant in this context is always a case of the meaning imputed . . . in a given concrete case, on the average, or in a theoretically formulated pure type. Even in cases of such forms of social organization as a state, church, association, or marriage, the social relationship consists exclusively in the fact that there has existed, exists, or will exist a probability of action in some definite way appropriate to this meaning. . . . A "state," for example, ceases to exist in a sociologically relevant sense whenever there is no longer a probability that certain kinds of meaningfully oriented social action will take place.[1]

Basically, when we say that groups or systems have an organization or structure we refer to standardized normative patterns, rights, rules of behavior, and the like. Consequently, at the core of sociological analysis is a concern with norms, with expected patterns of behavior held in the minds of individuals. The sociologist, therefore, is concerned with all that sustains or undermines norms, including deviance, innovation, and rebellion.

This chapter starts with an effort to clarify some misconceptions about the structural-functionalist analysis of social change and suggests a considerable overlap in its approach with that of Marxism. It then deals with the way functionalists have dealt with value-induced tensions, interest-conflict, and coercion in the analysis of stratification as a source of instability and change. Finally, Weber's and Mannheim's concepts of different forms of "rationality" are used to help account for the expression of political conflict in contemporary society.

Functionalist Analysis of Social Change

There can be little doubt that, as contrasted with Marxist analysis, with its predominant interest in change and conflict, functionalist sociology has devoted much more of its theoretical energies to explaining social order—the ways in which society is held together. Yet any paradigm for social analysis that ignores change, revolutions, and breakdowns would be unrealistic, just as is a framework that sees society predominantly in terms of Hobbesian conflict. Sociology has had to deal with both stable patterns and instability. The three main theoretical approaches to social stratification—Marxian, Weberian, and Durkheimian (functionalist)—have sought to account for the existence and persistence of inequality, while assuming that a form of "alienation" is inherent in all stratification systems. To put it in other words, each theory implies that systems of hierarchical inequality contain both stabilizing and destabilizing mechanisms, as discussed in the next chapter. Similarly, it may be noted that studies which focus on conflict have contributed to the analysis of cohesion, as Lewis Coser has demonstrated.[2] Alvin and Helen Gouldner have noted the importance of the "line of analysis stemming largely from the pioneering work of . . . Georg Simmel . . . as amplified and developed by Robert Dubin, Lewis Coser, Max Gluckman, and others" which stresses the integrative consequences of conflict.[3]

Marxist analysis shares with functionalism the assumption that social systems "constantly tend to an equilibrium . . . [which, however,] is exercised, only in the shape of a reaction against the constant upsetting of this equilibrium."[4] Talcott Parsons also has emphasized the "precarious" nature of the equilibrium and notes "that breakdown of equilibrium is scientifically as important a phenomenon as its preservation."[5]

Pierre Van den Berghe, in fact, sees the basis for a rapprochement between functionalism and Marxism because "both theories are fundamentally based on an equilibrium model."[6] There can be little doubt that Robert Friedrichs is correct when he stresses that "contrary to the impression of most American sociologists, Marx's stance . . . is at a number of points startlingly congruent with system theory as we have come to know it in Western sociology."[7] A number of Marxist scholars have emphasized the same point. Thus Pradeep Bandyopadhyay, writing in the oldest Marxist scholarly magazine in the English language, *Science and Society*, observes that "Marxian sociology is often just as concerned [as functionalism] with the analysis of system, structure and equilibrium."[8] Writing from inside the Communist world, Steiner and Schkaratan note that with all its deficiencies from a Marxist point of view, Parsons's "functional system theory is preferable to most of the other mentioned [Western sociological] concepts because it tries to understand the social structure as a social organism."[9]

The Polish sociologist Sztompka also concludes "that there is a *fundamental affinity* between Marxism and functionalism," as both are variants of the same "systemic-functional methodological approach."[10]

Perhaps the most succinct discussion of Marxism as a variant of structural-functional theories with "good claims to be the first of them" has been presented by E. J. Hobsbawm, the leading Marxist historian in the English-speaking world.[11] Although written in the context of elaborating the differences between Marxism and other forms of functional analysis, Hobsbawm's comments are worth quoting at length since they may serve as a point of comparison with more "academic" approaches:

> [Marxism] implies the analysis of the structure and functioning of . . . [social] systems as entities maintaining themselves, in their relations both with the outside environment—non-human and human—and in their internal relationships. Marxism is far from the only structural-functionalist theory of society, though it has good claims to be the first of them, but it differs from most others in two respects. First it insists on a hierarchy of social phenomena (e.g. "basis" and "superstructure") and second, on the existence within any society of internal tensions ("contradictions") which counteract the tendency of the system to maintain itself as a going concern. (It need hardly be said that the "basis" consists not of technology or economics, but "the totality of these relations of production," i.e. social organization in its broadest sense as applied to a given level of the material forces of production.)
>
> The importance of these peculiarities of Marxism is in the field of history, for it is they which allow it to explain—unlike other structural-functional models of society—why and how societies change and transform themselves; in other words, the facts of social evolution. . . . Human societies must, if they are to persist, be capable of managing themselves successfully, and therefore all existing ones must be functionally adequate; if not they would have become extinct. . . . The point here is not that it is illegitimate to develop separate analysis models for the static and the dynamic, such as Marx's schemas of simple and extended reproduction, but that historical enquiry makes it desirable for these different models to be connected.
>
> The point about . . . internal contradictions is, that they cannot be defined simply as "disfunctional" except on the assumption that stability and permanence are the norm, and change the exception. . . . It is rather that, as is now

recognized much more widely than before among social anthropologists, a structural model envisaging only the maintenance of a system is inadequate. It is the simultaneous existence of stabilizing and disruptive elements which such a model must reflect. And it is this which the Marxist model—though not the vulgar-Marxist versions of it—has been based on.

Such a dual (dialectical) model is difficult to set up and use, for in practice the temptation is great to operate it, according to taste or occasion, either as a model of stable functionalism or as one of revolutionary change; whereas the interesting thing about it is, that it is both. It is equally important that internal tensions may sometimes be reabsorbed into a self-stabilizing model by feeding them back as functional stabilizers, and that sometimes they cannot. Class conflict can be regulated through a sort of safety-valve, as in so many riots of urban plebians in preindustrial cities, or institutionalized as "rituals of rebellion" (to use Max Gluckman's illuminating phrase) or in other ways; but sometimes it cannot. The state will normally legitimize the social order by controlling class conflict within a stable framework of institutions and values, ostensibly standing above and outside them (the remote king as "fountain of justice"), and in doing so perpetuate a society which would otherwise be riven asunder by its internal tensions. This is indeed the classical Marxist theory of its origin and function, as expounded in *Origin of the Family*. Yet there are situations when it loses this function.

Difficult though it may be, social scientists of various kinds . . . have begun to approach the construction of models of equilibria based on tension or conflict, and in so doing draw nearer to Marxism.[12]

Most sociologists understand that propensity for change is as much an inherent component of human society as are the stabilizing factors.[13] Talcott Parsons has pointed out that "there is a certain falsity in the dilemma between 'static' and 'dynamic' emphases. If theory is *good* theory, whichever type of problem it tackles most directly, there is no reason whatever to believe that it will not be equally applicable to the problems of change and to those of process within a stabilized system."[14] More recently, he has emphasized that "the reason for insistence on the importance of keeping the concepts of structure and process and of stability and change analytically distinct is not a predilection in favor of one or the other item in each pair, but in favor of orderly procedure in scientific analysis."[15] Eisenstadt has summarized the position of functionalist sociologists as insisting that change is inherent in all social systems "because of basic problems to which there is no overall continuous solution. These problems include uncertainties of socialization, perennial scarcity of resources relative to individual aspirations, and contrasting types of social organization or principles of social organization (e.g., *Gemeinschaft* vs. *Gesellschaft*) within the society."[16]

If we look at the main approach of functionalist sociology in dealing with social change, it turns out to be the dialectic notion of contradiction. As Robert Merton has pointed out the "key concept bridging the gap between statics and dynamics in functional theory is that of strain, tension, contradiction, or discrepancy between the component elements of social and cultural structure.''[17] David Lockwood also notes that ''the idea of structural contradictions is central to the functionalist view of change.''[18] Gideon Sjoberg calls attention to the ''presence of 'contradictory functional requirements'— inferred from contradictory structural arrangements'' and insists that ''a dialectical theory of change, to be meaningful, must be set within a structural-functional framework.'' Sjoberg notes that Parsons's pattern variable analyses implicity assume ''inherent contradictions within systems.''[19] Parsons himself explicitly discusses the ''serious strains and inconsistencies in the value-implementation of any complex social system.''[20] As Lewis Feuer has noted, ''Parsonian 'inconsistencies' have some resemblance to Marxian 'contradictions.' ''[21] Gouldner also points up similarities between Marxian and functional analysis, in the way each has applied the ''principle of functional reciprocity'' to account for change, as a breakdown in ''reciprocal functional interchanges'' among structures results in contradictions and reduces their ability to persist.[22] ''Hence,'' correctly notes Robert Nisbet, ''the incessant search by the functionalist for the specific type of strain and stress that tend naturally to inhere in a given social system.''[23]

Surprising as it may seem to those who would emphasize the theoretical differences among schools of sociology, functionalist analysis shares with Marxist thought Hegel's insight that all social systems inherently contain contradictions, the resolution of which presses for social change.[24] As Demerath has stressed, the gap between functionalist and Marxist analyses of change ''is not as wide as is customarily assumed.''[25] The British radical sociologist, Dick Atkinson, also emphasizes that ''even in the field of social change Parsons, Marx, and those whom their interpretations influence . . . show crucial similarities.''[26] He points out that the main variation in the structural analyses of the two men flows from differing initial assumptions concerning human nature. ''Marx felt it was basically cooperative, rational, self-controlling. Parsons, following Hobbes and Durkheim, felt it was in competition with itself and implied conflict in social relationships generally. . . . Parsons and Marx were consequently faced with a similar problem. For Marx, the question became: how is conflict possible when man is rational and cooperative? For Parsons, the question became: how is order possible when man is basically destructive and competitive?''[27]

A similar point has been made by the French-Canadian sociologist Guy Rocher, who stresses that Parsons has devoted so much of his writing to an analysis of the sources of social stability because of his ''perpetual astonishment at the existence of *order*,'' an orientation which resulted in his wrongly gaining a ''reputation as a social conservative interested only in maintaining the *status quo*. . . . [His critics] *forget that for Parsons, order appears less as a fact than as a problem. . . .* What is most surprising is not that there are conflicts and struggles, but that in spite of the sources of breakdown, some order persists. . . . [For Parsons] order cannot be taken for granted, but must be explained.''[28]

Atkinson, who focuses on the logical similarity in Marx's and Parsons's analyses of conflict and order, concludes that ''it should not be a source of surprise that each man arrived at similar solutions.''[29] He emphasizes that both reject the Kantian and liberal concept of ''free and rational choice.'' Each stresses the ways in which the objective tensions associated with the ''actor's structural position (for Parsons the 'status' position, for Marx his class position)'' may produce normative conflict. The essential difference between them is that the ''norms'' which for Parsons are ''placed between [the] actor and the goal internalized within the actor are predominantly placed by Marx in the external situation itself.''[30] But Marx is forced ''to begin to offer an explicitly normative explanation at the theoretical level when action is not based on full awareness or when rationality is seen as constraint.'' In seeking to explain ''false consciousness,'' Marx poses a ''rigid and overtly normative structure between the actor and his false, irrational values as a means of explaining those 'false' values and rational actions.''[31] Atkinson concludes that Parsons reaches ''exactly the same methodological position which Marx arrives at with the crucial aid of 'false-consciousness.' For Parsons, empirical deviance from the theoretically expected is to be explained in terms of a theoretical concept of 'deviance,''' seen as a consequence of exposure to conflicting sets of normative ''expectations such that complete fulfillment of both is realistically impossible.''[32] On the most universal level, as W. E. Moore has emphasized, for the functionalist such pressures for change lie ''in a universal feature of human societies which in its most general form may be stated as the lack of close correspondence between the 'ideal' and the 'actual.'''[33]

It should be noted that while Parsons emphasizes the impact of normative contradictions which help produce ''a set of alienative motivational orientations,'' the source of the breakdown in support for the dominant ideologies lies in structural changes which upset a given equilibrium. Thus to ''account for the existence of widespread alienative motivation is scarcely a problem in any society which has been undergoing a very rapid process of industrialization.''[34] And in discussing the dynamics of social change in *The Social System*, Parsons begins with an analysis of the ''repercussions of the changes introduced by scientific and technological advance,'' first with respect to their effect on the creation of new roles and obsolescence of old ones, and second with concomitant changes in the character of instrumental organizations. Both changes produce large-scale alienation, as well as defensive behavior by those with "a strong vested interest in their ways of doing things." Such changes in turn may be linked to shifts in cultural and ideological expressions.[35]

In tandem with a Marxist approach, Parsons notes that to analyze the way in which such technological changes "will affect the total society over a long period . . . , the *only* way to proceed outside of sheer 'intuition' is to attempt to trace meticulously the repercussions of the changes through the various parts of the system, and back again to the locus of the original changes." Any given society responds by adjustments designed to maintain "a relatively precarious state of moving equilibrium." But this equilibrium

> can break down in either of two main directions, both of which if they occur should be interpreted as consequences of the fact that strain in certain parts of the system has mounted to points which cannot be coped with short of major alterations of the moving equilibrium state. One of these centers on the mounting resistance of the "vested interests" elements to further change, so that the essential process itself is finally choked off and the society stabilized on a traditionalistic basis. This, fundamentally, seems to be what happened to the society of later Mediterranean antiquity partly at least under the influence of Christianity. The other direction is that of mounting strain in "progressive" sectors so that a radically alienated revolutionary movement develops.[36]

Parsons notes that both processes "are continually occurring in sub-sectors of our society."[37] As Devereux emphasizes, Parsons's concern with equilibrium reflects "the view that society represents a veritable powder keg of conflicting forces. . . . That any sort of equilibrium is achieved at all, as it evidently is in most societies most of the time, thus represents for Parsons something both of miracle and challenge."[38]

Amitai Etzioni has effectively summarized the normative functionalist analysis of change:

> A societal structure is, thus, to be viewed . . . as a temporary form reflecting the past actions of conforming and deviating member-units and internal and external elites, and as a base line for future interaction among these actors within the environmental limits. Societal structures are expected to be continually restructured or transformed; it is an exception rather than the rule when the relations among the units, supra-units, and elites are so balanced as to cause a forward and backward "swinging" of a pattern as if it were the focal point of a stable equilibrium. This concept of structure assumes that *the extent and intensity of deviance will be greater, the less the patterns of the distributive structure and the political organization parallel the patterns prescribed by the symbolic-normative system.* Moreover, even when this parallelism is maximal, a built-in strain is to be expected; differences between the symbolic-normative and asset facets of society are never completely resolved because the symbolic-normative systems tend to be relatively more integrated than the asset bases. This is the case because societal assets must provide for a multitude of partially

incompatible functions, and because nonsymbolic elements are more scarce than symbols. Additional societal strains are generated by differences in the distributive patterns of the various kinds of assets which create stratification imbalances.[39]

The convergence on structural contradiction as a main source of destabilization and social change does not, of course, explain the breakdown of specific systems or catalytic events which seemingly gives rise to drastic or revolutionary changes. Most social analysts from Marx to Parsons have pointed to the fact that social systems are able to endure chronic serious contradictions or sources of strain without breaking down or making major adjustments to alleviate the tension. The identification of structural contradictions no more permits an analyst to predict the direction and ultimate outcome of the changes which may occur than does the existence of large-scale poverty, racism, or other form of exploitation indicate that a mass protest movement will occur. Tension-ridden social systems may collapse and retrogress, as occurred with the Roman Empire; they may provide the motivation for support for successful revolutionary movements; they may readjust their internal relations to reduce the strain without experiencing fundamental systemic change; or they may simply continue to go on without any significant adjustments because of given power relationships or absence of bases for alternative structural relationships. Marx, for example, emphasized that "no social order ever perishes before all the productive forces for which there is room in it have developed."[40] And Trotsky argued, in seeking to explain the reemergence of a sharply stratified society in the Soviet Union, that Marx had anticipated that efforts to create socialism, except under conditions of extremely high productivity in which all could enjoy material wealth and total freedom from disagreeable work, would break down. He quoted Marx to the effect that "a development of the productive forces is the absolutely necessary practical premise [of Communism], because without it want is generalized, and with want the struggle for necessities begins again, and that means that all the old crap must revive."[41]

Specific major structural changes and successful social movements usually occur as a result of the cumulation of a variety of developments or events, the occurrence of which may in some cases even be fortuitous.[42] Parsons has emphasized the need to distinguish "sources of change which are external to the society from those which are internal."[43] In many cases, the decisive catalytic thrust which made possible or required system change was provided by external forces or events. The barbarian invasions of the Roman Empire which undermined that society occurred, according to the quantitative studies of Frederick Teggart, as a response to climatic changes in central Asia which gave rise to migrations and invasion of Europe.[44]

The most comprehensive effort to codify the important determinants of collective efforts at social change has been formulated by Neil Smelser. These include: "(1) Structural conduciveness . . .; (2) Structural strain . . .; (3) Growth and spread of generalized belief . . .; (4) Precipitating factors . . .; (5) Mobilization of participants for action . . .; (6) The operation of social control. . . ."[45] Although Smelser is a functionalist theorist and a student and disciple of Talcott Parsons, it should be noted that all six of the factors he classified may be found scattered in the writings of Marx and Lenin in their discussions of the conditions for the emergence of revolutionary movements.

The methodological convergence in the analyses of social change in various theoretical approaches is not new. Eisenstadt emphasizes that the "founding fathers," such as Durkheim and Weber, shared with Marx and his followers an insistence that social systems are characterized by "contradictions." "Both Durkheim and Weber saw many contradictions inherent in the very nature of the human condition in society in general, and saw them articulated with increasing sharpness in the developments of the modern order in particular." He argues that the "bourgeois" fathers were far less "optimistic" than Marx and other chiliastic revolutionary thinkers about the possibility of ever ending the processes of basic social change, i.e., tensions and contradictions, for they "stressed the ubiquity and continuity of tensions between the creative and restrictive aspects of modern life, of potential contradictions between liberty and rationality, between these on the one hand and justice and solidarity on the other."[46]

In pointing out the similarities in varying sociological approaches to change, social structure, and inequality, it is not my intention to argue that the theoretical (or political) differences are minimal, or to deny that varying theoretical emphases result in quite disparate analyses of comparable phenomena. Quite the contrary. In the following chapter these theoretical differences are brought into sharp relief in the discussion of social class analysis.[47]

As a final note on the congruence among the varying approaches to social change between normative functionalism and structural Marxism, it is important to recognize that functionalists from Durkheim to Parsons have shared with Marxism a commitment to an evolutionary approach.[48] At the heart of the analysis of the former has been an emphasis on structural differentiation as the source of the change. For Durkheim "the focus of structural differentiation is economic organization." As Robert Bellah has summarized Durkheim's analysis, "as size and dynamic density increase, competition between unspecialized units engaged in the same activities increases. Structural differentiation is then seen as an adaptive response to this increased competition."[49]

Parsons, of course, though also stressing structural differentiation, does not share the emphasis of Durkheim and Marx on the primary role of any one factor such as the economic in social change, but as Gouldner has argued, the

> divergence between [the] analytic models . . . is not so radical as is often assumed. . . . It may be that the distinction between social theories has not so much been between system and factor theories, but rather between overt and covert factor theories, or between implicit and explicit system theories. . . . It may be . . . that earlier functionalists neglected the problem of weighting system parts, because they lacked the mathematical tools requisite for a rigorous resolution of the problem. Today, however, mathematical and statistical developments may be on the verge of making this possible.[50]

To illustrate the way in which an emphasis on the normative concept of social structure has resulted in an understanding of the way in which normative "contradictions" facilitate social change, I would like to discuss two examples: first, social stratification and, second, different systems of rationality, *Wertrationalität* and *Zweckrationalität*. The first of these topics deals briefly with the factor which has been traditionally emphasized by all major schools of sociological thought to interpret conflict and protest in industrial society, while the second treats in more detail recent efforts to account for the use of new sources of tensions and rebellion in "postindustrial" society.

Social Stratification

The assumptions about value consensus with respect to stratification imply that hierarchical systems are inherently contradictory, that their very existence produces the conditions for deviance and rebellion, for both moderate and revolutionary social change. The conviction that a stratified social structure is inherently unstable may, of course, be found in the great precursor of modern French functionalist thought from whom Durkheim drew many of his insights, Alexis de Tocqueville. Though insisting on the necessity of inequality and of hereditary privilege, as conditions for liberty and social leadership, Tocqueville also concluded that endemic to stratification was rejection of inequality by the underprivileged. "There is, in fact, a manly and lawful passion for equality that incites men to wish all to be powerful and honored . . . which impels the weak to attempt to lower the powerful to their own level and reduces men to prefer equality in slavery to inequality with freedom."[51] Tocqueville went on to generalize: "Remove the secondary causes that have produced the great convulsions of the world and you will almost always find the principle of inequality at the bottom."[52]

Tocqueville's emphasis on the omnipresence of both inequality and rejection of hierarchy points up the sources of the inherent "contradictions" in the values of complex social systems. Thus, all social systems lay down assorted ends or goals, as part of the cultural structure, and a set of socially structured means or prescribed behaviors that may be legitimately used to attain them, which are often rooted in institutions.[53]

Most functionalists assume that differentiated rewards are assigned to various positions to encourage people to seek to achieve the diverse positions necessary in a complex society.[54] Given this assumption, any system of stratification requires a general set of ideological justifications, which explain and propagate the system of inequality, to induce men to accept as legitimate the fact of their own inequality. But it is logically doubtful, as Tocqueville argued, that the socially inferior can ever totally accept the propriety of their position. The generally accepted sociological assumption that individuals seek to maximize the esteem in which they are held implies that those who are in low-valued positions experience such disesteem as punishment. Consequently, there is an inherent tension (contradiction) between the need to maximize esteem and the requirements of a stratified system.

Different societies, of course, have varied in the severity of such tensions. Durkheim assumed that they were less in preindustrial societies with overt ascriptive positions. These systems prescribed varying sets of goals for different strata, so that those belonging to ascribed lower strata could obtain a sense of self-respect within their own ascriptive group. In many cultures, transvaluational religious beliefs which identify poverty with virtue and reward in the hereafter appear to have relieved some of these tensions. Societies, however, which justify inequality on meritocratic grounds and which encourage people to seek to "get ahead" serve to exacerbate the contradiction between the values of hierarchy and self-esteem.

Durkheim's account of what Merton has called the "seeming contradictions between cultural goals and socially restricted access to these goals" is a key aspect of the theory of social change and stratification that is inherent in functionalism.[55] Since no complex society can achieve a complete balance between its emphases on ends and means, stratification systems always generate pressure on individuals and strata to deviate systematically from the cultural prescriptions of the society. The relations between approved goals and prescribed means, as analyzed by Merton and others, create a variety of strains fostering change, a subject discussed in more detail in chapter 2.

In stressing the relevance of the Durkheim-Merton emphasis on the congruity or discongruity of the relationship between means and ends in producing conformity or "aberrant behavior" it is not my intention to suggest that the ultimate stability or instability of a society is primarily a function of the degree of satisfaction or frustration engendered. Reinhard Bendix and I noted the fallacy of such assumptions a number of years ago in our introduction to the first edition of *Class, Status and Power*:

> The stability or instability of a society cannot be judged by the degree of satisfaction or frustration which it engenders. The fact that European feudalism or the Indian caste system have persisted for centuries does not prove that a majority of the people living in these societies were adjusted to their position within them. In feudal Europe there were many peasants who ran away to join so-called robber bands, and who revolted against the local manorial lords. The prolonged existence of feudalism may not have been due primarily to the stability of this social structure, to the degree of satisfaction with which each individual enjoyed his privileges and bore his burdens, but rather to the fact that the isolated peasant-rebels had no means of organizing a successful revolution. A society is characterized not only by the facts of social stratification, but also by a system of power-relations between conflicting social groups. Hence the fact that a dominant social group possesses most of the power in a society may be a more important reason for the apparent stability of that society than the fact that people accept privileges and burdens which are theirs by virtue of their social and economic position.
>
> Of course, "power" refers to more than control over the instrumentalities of coercion. It refers to all the means by which an individual or a group of individuals can exert a controlling influence over others. Perhaps one of the most effective means of exercising power has been the doctrine that the poor are worthy and will be rewarded in the next world. At times this doctrine probably helped to stabilize the society by making it psychologically easier to be content with a low social position. At such times it would have been plausible to conclude that the society was "in equilibrium" and that each individual was more or less content to play his "social role." But the same doctrine has also been used to challenge the established order by claiming that the poor were more virtuous and deserving than the rich, that poverty made legitimate the protest of the poor against the prevailing order. The fact that the same doctrine could be made to serve such conflicting purposes illustrates that the study of stratification cannot be safely premised on any theory which rests on the assumption either of stability or of change.[56]

Our emphasis on the role of power or coercion is congruent with that of exponents of normative functionalism. Thus, as Gouldner notes, Durkheim argued that the system of stratification "offends the moral expectations of people in contemporary cultures, because it constrains to an unequal exchange of goods and services. The exploitation thus rendered possible by notable power disparities among the contracting parties conduces to a sense of injustice which has socially unstabilizing consequences. Thus, almost surprisingly, both Durkheim and Marx converge on a concept of 'exploitation' as a contributant to current social instabilities."[57]

Less surprising, since he drew on both Durkheim and Marx, Talcott Parsons's analysis also converges with theirs. In his earliest major work, *The Structure of Social Action*, Parsons criticized "the great majority of liberal economists," arguing that "it must be sharply emphasized that considerations of the logical simplicity of a system of economic theory that excludes coercion should not be allowed to obscure the enormous empirical importance of coercion in actual economic life."[58] He noted that "Weber is not subject to this criticism. He had a deep, almost tragic, consciousness of the importance of coercion in human affairs." A decade later, in discussing "Social Classes and Class Conflict," Parsons not only stressed the "arrogance" of the successful and the "resentment" of the "losers" in the stratification system, but reiterated, first, that a system of hierarchical "organization means that there must be an important part played by discipline and authority," second, that there is "a general tendency for the strategically placed, the powerful, to exploit the weaker or less favorably placed," and third, that there "will tend to be a differentiation of attitude systems, of ideologies, and of definitions of the situation to a greater or less degree around the structure of the occupational system and of other components of the instrumental complex, such as the relation to markets and profits. . . . A leading modern example is the opposing ideologies of business and labor groups in modern industrial society."[59] And more recently, in discussing "political power" on an abstract level, Parsons emphasized that an understanding of both the consensual and the coercive aspects are essential to an analysis of the role of power.[60] He treats power not only as involving legitimation, but notes that the capacity of the system "to secure performance of binding obligations" implies that "in case of recalcitrance there is a presumption of enforcement by negative situational sanctions."[61]

> Legitimation is, therefore, in power systems, the factor that is parallel to confidence in mutual acceptability and stability of the monetary unit in monetary systems.
>
> Questioning the legitimacy of the possession and use of power leads to resort to progressively more "secure" means of gaining compliance. These must be progressively more effective "intrinsically." . . . Furthermore, insofar as they are intrinsically effective, legitimacy becomes a progressively less important factor of their effectiveness—at the end of this series lies resort, first to various types of coercion, eventually to the use of force as the most intrinsically effective of all means of coercion.[62]

Value Rationality

The functionalist analysis of the tensions inherent in systems of stratification assumes a fundamental "contradiction" posed by the scarcity of means available for the attainment of generally accepted goals, a dilemma present in many areas of life. In a different context, Max Weber and Karl Mannheim posited the existence of a basic social tension between the emphasis on one or the other, found in the conflicting implications for action of the two forms of rationality, *Wertrationalität*, or "substantive rationality," involving conscious judgments about goals or ultimate values and *Zweckrationalität*, or "functional rationality," referring to means "to attain the given goal."[63] Societies, in other words, require ultimate values which are believed in, independently of prospects for actual achievement. But they also require people to be instrumentally rational, that is, to choose effective means for attaining given ends.

The tension between the two sorts of rationality is built into the whole structure of social action. A society cannot maintain its pursuit of rational means-ends relationships, except in the context of a set of absolute values which anchor and direct the search for means. Yet a passionate commitment to absolute ends must break down. Weber traced the secularization of Protestantism, the rise of *Zweckrationalität* in the West, to its tremendous commitment to certain absolute values. Trying, as Calvinism did, to see every action as a means to some higher end required tremendous zeal which had to recede.[64] But the routinization of charismatic *Wertrationalität* ultimately leaves a gap in the motivational system which legitimates functionally rational action and encourages the emergence of new forms of charismatic rationality.

As Anthony Giddens indicates, Weber's analysis of the basic contradictions of capitalist society rests on a similar logic. Modern capitalism emphasizes the "values of efficiency or productivity" which, however, "contravene some of the most distinctive values of western civilization, such as those which emphasize the importance of individual creativity and autonomy of action. . . . In this sense, western society can be said to be founded upon an intrinsic antimony between formal [functional] and substantive rationality which, according to Weber's analysis of modern capitalism, cannot be resolved."[65]

Talcott Parsons, building on Weber's analysis, noted the inherent conflict between those committed to a "plurality of legitimate directions of value achievement," hence seeing action as determined by "interest," and those who orient "action to a specific value, e.g., salvation, which is absolute in the sense that all other potential values become significant only as means and conditions, possible aids or hindrances, to the attainment of this central value."[66] Derivative from the former, *Zweckrationalität* is an emphasis on the "ethics of responsibility," the recognition that the means used shape the ends which are achieved. Conversely, an emphasis on *Wertrationalität* is more likely to result in a commitment to the "ethics of absolute ends."[67] The two orientations in their pure form, as Weber indicated, are inherent in the structural situations of different groups whose outlooks are "fundamentally differing and irreconcilably opposed" to each other.[68]

These varying *Weltanschauungen* have been used since the time of the ancient Greeks to account for conflict between the generations concerning the pace of directed social change. Thus Aristotle noted that youth are more disposed to emphasize what would later be called *Wertrationalität* and the "ethic of absolute ends," while older age cohorts are disposed to *Zweckrationalität* and "the ethic of responsibility." As he put it 2,500 years ago: "[Youth] have exalted notions, because they have not yet been humbled by life or learnt its necessary limitations; moreover their hopeful disposition makes them think themselves equal to great things—and that means having exalted notions. They would always rather do noble deeds than useful ones; their lives are regulated more by moral feeling than by reasoning."[69]

These distinctions have continued to be cited by contemporary analysts of politics to explain the differential age base of "extreme" and "moderate" political forces, i.e., the fact that movements of the extreme right and left draw heavily from the young. As I noted in an earlier publication:

> It is the essence of extremism in politics to eliminate restraint, to conceptualize the struggle as one between absolute good versus absolute evil, thereby justifying the use of any tactics. . . . And the greater propensity of youth for the "ethic of absolute ends" as distinct from the "ethic of responsibility" . . . is another way of saying that youth politics are more likely to reflect impulse than restraint. It also is another way of indicating that youth are more prone to favor change, reform, radicalism of all varieties, than older people. Youth-based movements, therefore, whether of the left or right, should have major elements in common.[70]

The assumption that youth, particularly those defined in a marginal status as students or adolescents, between childhood and adulthood, will be disposed toward *Wertrationalität* has seemingly been confirmed by their disproportionate participation in revolutionary movements, from Luther's religious rebellion through the events leading up to the American Revolution, the Revolution of 1848, the assorted French and Russian revolutionary movements of the nineteenth century, others in various colonial and less developed nations, and in the fascist movements of the 1920s and 1930s. These clearly indicate that much of what we have seen in the expressive styles of radical student activists is not new but is rooted in the processes Aristotle described.[71]

Various developments in the contemporary world may be analyzed in terms of shifting commitments to the two forms of rationality. Writing at the end of the 1920s, Karl Mannheim anticipated that existent political and intellectual trends would result in a decline within industrial society of the ideological and utopian impulses (*Wertrationalität*), as total doctrines (*Weltanschau-*

ungen) were reduced to partial pragmatic ones (*Zweckrationalität*).[72] The renewed tensions between the two forms of rationality have been described by Eisenstadt and Bell as a source of "intergenerational conflicts and intellectual antinomianism" in the context of specific developments in modern society. As Eisenstadt notes, these

> are rooted in the contradiction between the "liberating" or creative potential given in the extension of substantive rationality as against the potential for constriction and compulsion inherent in the organizational extension of functional rationality, which can be most clearly seen in the growing tendencies to bureaucratization inherent in modern societies. This contradiction—which has sometimes been seen as parallel to that between the liberating power of charisma as against the more constrictive tendencies of the process of its routinization—is not abated by the fact that very often it is the very extension of substantive rationality (as evident, for example, in the broadening of the political community, or in the extension of scientific knowledge) that creates the conditions for the intensification of the more constrictive tendencies inherent in extension of functional rationality in almost all spheres of human endeavor and of social life.[73]

The spread of contemporary youth rebellion is in part a consequence of the contradiction between the widespread diffusion of the goal of freedom as an absolute value and the emergence of "a new type of social alienation focused not only around the feeling of being lost in a maze of large-scale, anonymous organizations and frameworks, but also around the possibility of the loss of the meaning of participation in these political and national centers." In other words, substantive and functional rationality in modern society have produced ultimate goals for a good society and means to sustain the social order which are sharply divergent. The basic contradiction between a superordinate emphasis on a free, egalitarian, and participant society as ideal and the constraints derivative from the bureaucratic hierarchical organization as means is inherent in the economic growth of modern industrial society. This tension makes for intense frustration, particularly among the educated young, who must accept the charismatic *Wertrationalität* of the social order. And Eisenstadt has argued that it is no accident that the university has become the symbol of the strain, charged with hypocrisy. "The choice of the university as the object of . . . attack rather emphasizes the denial that the existing order can realize these basic premises of modernity: to establish and maintain an order that could do justice to the claims to creativity and participation in the broader social order."[74] Hence the generational attack is directed against the basic values of modernism concentrated in academe, an antinomian rejection of science and reason.

The tension between *Wertrationalität* and *Zweckrationalität*, between substantive and functional rationality, is in many ways at the heart of Daniel

Bell's analysis of the basic contradictions of postindustrial society. As he sees it, antinomian attitudes have repeatedly appeared among the culture creators reflecting their desire to reduce or abolish restraints "to attain some form of ecstasy." As such, they are in sharp opposition to the means orientation of the workaday world, "the economy, technology, and occupational system . . . [which] is rooted in functional rationality and efficiency . . . shaped by the principle of calculation, the rationalization of work and of time, and a linear sense of progress."[75] The "adversary culture" of the intellectuals, their opposition to the basic values and institutions of the owners and controllers of industry and politics in capitalist and post-capitalist societies, is inherent in the nature of their work, the emphasis on creativity, originality, and "break-throughs."[76] It is interesting to note that Max Weber, writing soon after World War I, anticipated the desire of many intellectuals to find some form of ecstasy in a period characterized "by rationalization and intellectualization and, above all, by the 'disenchantment of the world.' " Faced with "disen-chantment," with the absence of charismatic *Wertrationalität*, some will shift their value emphasis "into the transcendental realm of mystic life or into the brotherliness of direct and personal human relations." They may try "intel-lectually to construe new religions without a new and genuine prophecy," which can only result in "miserable monstrosities. And academic prophecy, finally, will create only fanatical sects but never a genuine community." For Weber, the most ethical reaction for the intellectual "who cannot bear the fate of the times" is to return to traditional religion. "In my eyes, such religious return stands higher than the academic prophecy, which does not realize that in the lecture-rooms of the university no other virtue holds but plain intellectual integrity."[77]

A few years later, Karl Mannheim, in the same essay in which he anticipated the decline of ideology and utopia, noted the difficulty of living in "congru-ence with the realities of . . . a world, utterly without any transcendent element, either in the form of a utopia or an ideology."[78] He foretold the rise of an emphasis on "'genuineness' and 'frankness' in place of the old ideals." And like Weber before him, Mannheim predicted that it would be "the socially unattached intellectuals . . . even more than now in increasing proportions recruited from all social strata rather than merely from the more privileged ones" who, unable to accommodate to a situation without ideo-logical conflict, will seek "to reach out beyond that tensionless situation."[79]

The decline in *Wertrationalität* in the economy and polity has become an increasing source of strain and instability in modern society, as the numbers, prestige, and influence of those involved in intellectually related institutions increase sharply, as the system becomes increasingly dependent on facilities and trained manpower able to operate complex technology and to innovate in research and development. Although, as Bell notes, the countercultural life-styles stemming from the antinomian tendencies fostered by the intellectuals and students are absorbed within the market economy of western society, "the cultural chic of 'modernism' . . . retains its subversive thrust however much it is absorbed by the system."[80]

The extent to which these cultural contradictions become the source of social change in advanced industrial or postindustrial society may be seen in the inversion of past class relationships with respect to propensity to protest. Traditional class theory, congruent with Marxist analysis, suggests that opposition to the status quo comes primarily from the ranks of the underprivileged, because they are oppressed. This generalization has held up in most societies. Insofar as the predominant political issue has been the existing distribution of privileges, the redistributionist or egalitarian movements have been supported by the poorer strata and by those subject to discrimination because of ascriptive traits.

This relationship, however, does not hold up within the intellectual community, nor with respect to movements and tendencies that reflect antinomian values, seeking to break down restraint and to reject functional rationality. A variety of surveys of opinion and behavior among those engaged in intellectually related work find that the more socially critical, those more rejective of the status quo, are more likely to come from the more successful, those who are regarded by their peers as the most creative. Within the academy, those most involved in research activities, who publish more, who are in the more prestigious universities, are more disposed to a critical *Weltanschauung*. Those more engaged in transmitting culture, i.e., teaching, as distinct from creating, tend to be more conservative, even though they are found disproportionately at the less distinguished institutions, receive less pay, and experience more onerous working conditions. Those academics involved in disciplines concerned with "basic" research or the creative arts are much more disposed to favor the "adversary culture" than professors dealing with the more applied professional fields.[81] A survey of the opinions of 110 American intellectuals, judged as eminent by their peers, reports that they are somewhat to the left of the elite academics, who in turn are the most socially critical within the university world.[82] Similar findings have been published with respect to the media. The more prestigious the newspaper or broadcast medium, the more liberal its editors, culture critics, or reporters.[83] A survey of over 500 leaders of American life in business, labor, government, politics, voluntary associations, government (civil service), and the mass media conducted in 1971–72 found that the latter—publishers, editors, TV executives, and columnists—were more liberal in their view than all other groups on foreign policy and social issues. Solid majorities of the "media leaders" supported the youth rebellion and lacked confidence in the leaders of major institutions and the operation of the political system.[84] These studies confirm

Bell's generalization that the "new class, which dominates the media and the culture, thinks of itself less as radical than 'liberal,' yet its values centered on 'personal freedom,' are profoundly anti-bourgeois."[85]

The preference of the intellectual elite for antinomian socially critical and countercultural values is related to the differences in social outlook among university students. As a myriad of empirical surveys have demonstrated, anti-system politics and countercultural life styles have appealed disproportionately to the more affluent students in the more academically selective institutions and in the liberal arts, particularly the social sciences and humanities, as distinct from less well-to-do students in the more vocationally oriented schools and subjects.[86]

There is some evidence to suggest that the values stemming from the intellectual and university community, transmitted through the elite media, are also affecting the orientations of many employed in bureaucratic executive levels of government and industry, where more are working "in professional than in line executive capacities."[87] Public opinion analyst Louis Harris reports that interview surveys of such elite groups indicate "that the professionals felt much more beholden to their outside discipline—whether it be systems engineering, teaching, scientific research, or other professional ties— than to the particular company or institution they worked for." On a variety of issues bearing on changing moral attitudes, black equality, and the Vietnam War, "the burgeoning professional group, now a majority of those in the $15,000 and up group" were much more likely to support change than the line executives, or those with incomes under $5,000 a year, the most conservative of all on these issues. The "new professionals, who had as a group incomes higher than the line executives, were the most dedicated to changing the system."[88]

A similar basis for the divisions within the European elite has been noted by the British Marxist, E. J. Hobsbawm. The intellectually oriented professionals

> are more numerous, since both the growth of scientific technology and the expansion of the tertiary sector of the economy (including administration and communications) require them in much larger numbers than before. They are technically proletarianized, in as much as the bulk of them are no longer "free professionals" or private entrepreneurs but salaried employees. . . . They are recognizable by specific attitudes . . . ; e.g., reading the *Guardian* rather than the *Daily Telegraph*, and being relatively impervious to the sales appeals of status symbols as against *Which*-type [Consumers Union] criteria. Politically the bulk of this stratum . . . is probably today left of centre in western countries.[89]

In discussing France, Hobsbawm points out that the 1968 general strike was militantly backed by "the research-and-development types, the laboratory and design departments and the communicators . . . whereas the administrators, executives, sales departments, etc. remained on the side of management.''

More generally, similar findings have been reported for entire populations (see chapter 4). The political scientist Ronald Inglehart, using survey data from a number of North Atlantic countries, has differentiated between materialist and postmaterialist values, which in many ways correspond to functional and substantive rationality, and turn out to correlate with political orientations, though not with the traditional class correlates of party choice. Materialist values emphasize "economic and physical security" (*Zweck-rationalität*, while "Post-Materialist values emphasize individual self-expression and achieving a more participant, less hierarchical society" (*Wert-rationalität*). And though adherents of the latter are the most change-oriented in contemporary society, "Materialists tend to be recruited from lower income groups, which traditionally have supported the Left—while the Post-Materialists come mainly from middle class families."[90]

Inglehart's research has been repeated in Japan by Joji Watanuki with somewhat similar results. "Postindustrial" values are weaker there than in various European countries, possibly reflecting the fact that Japan has only recently fully entered the stage of a developed industrial society. But, as in Europe and the United States, these values found their strongest support in Japan among "the younger and the more educated."[91]

In Germany, as a detailed analysis by Erwin Scheuch shows, blue-collar workers oriented toward materialistic gains have become much more positive in their attitudes toward the sociopolitical system from the late 1960s on. Conversely, however, the better educated, those in high white-collar occupations, reveal a steady decline in trust in the system. A sizable percentage of the latter have moved to the left in their voting preferences. The rise of a significant New Left type left-wing within the Social Democratic party during this period is based on the entrance of well-educated young people and women, largely from affluent backgrounds, into the party.[92]

Not surprising, as Erik Allardt demonstrates, Scandinavia exhibits the same pattern. In Denmark, Norway, and Sweden, the Social Democrats continue to secure their electoral support largely from the working class, with little "upper-class" backing. Parties to their left, mainly reflecting New Left tendencies, derive a considerable part of their growing vote from the "upper" and "new middle" classes. In Denmark, for example, "it appears that 14 percent of the Danish upper class voted for some of the parties left of the Social Democrats while only 2 percent voted for the Social Democrats."[93]

Inglehart suggests that the basis of political cleavage in the emerging post-industrial society will differ from that of industrial society. The latter has emphasized economic or interest conflict, linked in Weberian terms of *Zweck-rationalität*, while the new type emphasizes the more intangible values of participation and freedom from restraint and reveals "a relative *aversion* to traditional bureaucratic institutions."[94] As one would expect, they are to be found most commonly among young well-educated relatively affluent people.

The variations between materialist and post-materialist orientations are difficult to sort out in contemporary politics because they are linked to two different forms of "leftist" orientations, which still may be found within the same movements. The traditional Left of industrial society has "sought change in the direction of economic equality above all—even, if necessary, by means of increased governmental interference with the liberty of the individual. . . . The Industrial Left has generally accepted a considerable degree of organizational discipline and hierarchy as necessary for effective political change and economic progress." The postindustrial Left, reflecting the emerging values of a new type of society, found more prevalently among intellectuals, those employed in the knowledge-related and opinion-forming occupations, and the better-educated young, "is distinguished by an emphasis on the self-development of the individual—even, if necessary at the cost of further economic expansion. . . . The Post-Industrial Left tends to give a relatively low priority to economic growth. . . . Suspicious of the State, they are far more sympathetic to both individualism *and* communalism than to the norms of rational bureaucracy. For the individual is, in part, that which he is born."[95]

Inglehart finds that in countries in which parties with a New Left coloration have contested national elections, individuals classified as postmaterialists on the basis of their attitudes, are much more likely to back New Left than traditional left parties, findings which are congruent with the research on student activism.[96] Thus though Inglehart is apparently unaware of the linkages between his own concepts and those of Weber, Mannheim, Parsons, and Eisenstadt (he derives much of his approach from Bell), his comparative analysis of attitudes and electoral behavior sustain their assumptions that the basic tensions between the values of *Wertrationalität* and *Zweckrationalität* constitute a major social contradiction which fosters social change.

The postindustrial leftists are the real revolutionaries of modern society precisely because they have rejected functional rationality and adhere to the "ethic of ultimate ends." As Weber noted well over half a century ago in prescient words which describe developments within the contemporary New Left: "In the world of realities, as a rule, we encounter the ever-renewed experience that the adherent of an ethic of ultimate ends suddenly turns into a chiliastic prophet. Those, for example, who have preached 'love against violence' now call for the use of force for the *last* violent deed, which would lead to a state of affairs in which *all* violence is annihilated."[97]

These value conflicts are rooted in the twin developments of modern society noted earlier, the steady growth of bureaucracy with its accompanying emphasis on hierarchy and restraints and the increase in the demand for participation, free choice, equality, and creativity inherent in greater numbers exposed to higher levels of education, the situation of the studentry, the freedom from economic necessity. As Eisenstadt puts it,

> the most important constrictions on such freedom and creativity—and hence also the most important sources of change, instability and alienation in societies in general and in modern societies in particular—are rooted in the contradiction between the structural implications of the types of rationality. . . . [T]hese constrictions are rooted in the contradiction between the "liberating" or creative potential given in the extension of substantive rationality as against the potential for constriction and compulsion inherent in modern societies. This contradiction . . . has sometimes been seen as parallel to that between the liberating power of charisma as against the more constrictive tendencies of the process of its routinization.[98]

Lest this line of analysis be dismissed as another effort to deny or to challenge a materialistic or structural analysis of change by normative functionalists, let me close my discussion of the contradictions implied by the need for the two forms of rationality by noting with the radical sociologist Richard Flacks the congruence between this body of analysis "by 'bourgeois' social analysts" and that of assorted "radical intellectuals. . . [who] perceive that this situation might have revolutionary implications—that the emergence of a post-industrial system represents the final realization of capitalism and hence its demise."[99] Summing up the analyses of a number of neo-Marxist analysts, including his own trenchant one, Flacks notes that the opposition to a post-industrial capitalist society comes to a considerable extent from *"those whose social position is already post-industrial*—who have been able to aspire to be able to make a life outside of the goods producing sector— i.e., in the production and distribution of knowledge, culture and human services, or as free persons—and those whose needs in a material sense have been satiated by the existing system."[100] And this movement projects a new *Wertrationalität*,

> a vision of a society in which the *primary vocational activities* would be focused around the production and distribution of knowledge and art, around the provision of a vast array of human services, and around collective efforts to create maximally beneficial communal and natural environments. . . . It is a *culture* which values cooperation and love over competition and dominance, self-expression over self-denial, equality over materially-based status differentiation. It is a quest for a *political order* in which the nation-state is replaced by self-governing communities.[101]

In short, what Flacks anticipates is the dominance of *Wertrationalität* over *Zweckrationalität*, the triumph of antinomian values; and he and other New Leftists locate the support for these trends in the same liberated privileged elements of postindustrial society as the "bourgeois" social analysts. Where most of the neo-Marxists differ, however, is in their insistence that at the heart of the revolution of postindustrial society is a "new working-class," 'who support change because they are subject to economic and bureaucratic constraints, a hypothesis which seeks " 'to save' the Marxist concept of social change."[102] In fact, however, as Flacks, who knows the relevant empirical data, has also noted, the heart of the "adversary culture" comes from the most successful and socially privileged elements among the "new class." The differences in the analyses of social change in postindustrial society between the "bourgeois" and the "neo-Marxist" analysts are minimal.

Conclusion

Sociology in the 1960s witnessed a breakdown in consensus about what the discipline is all about, particularly as to appropriate theoretical and methodological approaches. Norman Birnbaum suggested that "at the moment, . . . sociology presents the appearance of chaos, an intellectual tower of Babel."[103] The Dutch sociologist C. J. Lammers noted in less dramatic language that a multiplicity of paradigms had become the "natural state" of the field.[104]

This situation is quite different from the one which existed a decade earlier when agreement appeared to exist concerning the basic approaches and methodologies of the discipline. Donald MacRae in introducing a book on *Modern Social Theory* noted that its author, Percy Cohen, had demonstrated that "a unity" in sociological analysis "which is not merely manufactured but genuine is possible and, indeed, is largely achieved," and it may lead to "a comparatively long period of quiet, logical refinement and cleaning-up operations. . . . This book is fortunate in its timing, both because of that unification of theory to which it contributes, and because of the lull that must for some time be expected and in which the newest generation of sociologists can and will be educated."[105] C. Wright Mills stood out almost alone among the prominent figures in the field as a critic of the dominant orientations. Writings concerned with what has come to be called the "sociology of sociology" were almost nonexistent.[106]

The change which occurred during the late sixties was, of course, closely related to the revival of left-wing activist concerns within intellectualdom generally, but particularly within the academy. It resulted in heightened levels of politically related conflicts, especially within the social sciences. A comparative study of the political life of American academic discipline associations by Ira Wessler found that the social sciences have been by far the most engaged. All of them passed political resolutions dealing with the Vietnam war and other social issues during the late 1960s. Political caucuses were organized in each. By contrast, almost no political resolutions were passed by the various natural science associations between 1965 and 1971, and radical caucuses were largely absent from them, with the single exception of the physicists. The humanists were somewhat more politically involved than the scientists, largely within the American Philosophical Association, the Modern Languages Association, and the American Historical Association.[107] Wessler contends that the strong commitment of social scientists to political activism follows from the influence of three basic and widely noted factors: "[that] their subject matter is basically connected with values . . . , [that] social scientists constantly participate in value laden situations and . . . [that] social scientists are essentially activated to contribute to human welfare."[108] To these may be added the related factor derivative from analyses of the Carnegie Commission's surveys of faculty and student opinion, that the subject matter of the social sciences attracts individuals committed to socially critical views both as undergraduates and graduate students and that the differences among the disciplines evidenced by the behavior of the professional societies are already evident in the attitudes of students and young faculty.[109]

But if the social sciences as a group are more disposed to liberal-left views than other segments of academe, the available data, drawn from surveys of students and faculty, indicate that sociology is the most left of all. Hence, it is not surprising that, during a period of intense politicization, the sociological community has been most exposed to political differences of opinion. As Ladd and I suggested, "perhaps the reason that there is so much literature in sociology attacking other sociologists for their alleged 'conservatism' is that the left is more heavily represented in this field than in any other, and that within a 'left' discipline (as within a radical political party) the question of who is the 'most revolutionary' becomes salient."[110]

But if the stronger left disposition largely accounts for the "Babel" in the field, for the fact that sociologists recently have emphasized the implications of differences among them, rather than seeking to find bases for theoretical agreement, as in most other fields, studies of the opinions of sociologists do not bear out the assumption of some critics that theoretical divergencies are related to sharp variations in orientations toward social change or even social reform. Thus depth interviews with "30 outstanding sociologists" at seven major American universities, conducted in 1963–64 by a Yugoslav Marxist sociologist, Mihailo Popovich, reported that when asked "which problems are among the most important in contemporary sociology," more (10) mentioned "social change" than any other issues, while "social problems of economic development" was in second place (5). When asked about the relationship of Marxism to other sociological approaches, the majority indicated that there is a considerable overlap in approach and concerns. As Popovich commented, "it is a significant fact that almost all of the interviewed sociologists think that there are some 'common points' between Marxist theory and non-Marxist sociological theories. These common points concern not only certain categories or principles, but also some problems. As is pointed out above, problems of social change and economic development are mentioned as *the* important issues of modern sociology."[111] The findings of this set of interviews with leading sociologists in 1963–64, before the wave of intense activism of the 1960s began, were reiterated in the largest single survey of sociological opinion based on over 3,000 questionnaire responses conducted in 1964 by Alvin Gouldner and his then doctoral student J. T. Sprehe.[112] This study found that as a group sociologists are disposed to the left and favor major social changes. As of 1964, race relations was perceived as the most pressing issue of concern by sociologists, followed by unemployment, mental health, and urban problems. Three-fifths thought that "Many modern institutions are deeply unstable and tensionful." Over three-quarters of those sampled indicated that "Basic Change in Structure and Values" of American society was necessary to solve its major problems. Since, as Gouldner has indicated, the great majority (82.4 percent) also favored functional analysis, this meant that they did not see any incompatibility between that theoretical orientation and the need for "basic change." In line with Popovich's interviews, and other surveys, the Gouldner-Sprehe data indicated that the more prestigeful the sociologist, the more he published, and the more involved he was in extramurally financed research activities, the more likely was he to support a more change-oriented view, to identify with sociology's playing a role in "solving society's problems," and to reject a value-free approach.[113]

Further evidence that support for a functional approach to sociological analysis is compatible with a commitment to radical social change may be found in a survey of Japanese sociologists. This study indicated that most sociologists voted for the left-wing Marxist Socialist party, with the Communists receiving the next highest support. Only one in 10 voted for the "bourgeois" Liberal Democrats, the majority party in the country, while less than 10 percent chose the pro–Western Democratic Socialists. Yet these predominantly radical Japanese scholars, when asked to name non-Japanese sociologists worthy of considerable attention, listed Talcott Parsons more frequently than anyone else (24 percent), with Robert Merton in second place (19 percent). Endorsements of Parsons and Merton and for Marxist parties were inversely related with age. The younger the Japanese sociologist, the more likely he was to mention Parsons and Merton and to vote for the Marxist left.[114]

Analysis of the way in which different schools of sociology approach the study of social structure and social change, as well as surveys of the professional opinions and sociopolitical values of sociologists, suggests a considerable basis for convergence or, if one prefers a dialectical term, synthesis, among divergent orientations rather than dissensus within the field. In a recent evaluation of the discipline, S. N. Eisenstadt has noted the "growing convergence and potentially constructive mutual impingement of the different approaches in contemporary sociology . . . on several levels." These include both "conceptual convergence" with respect to a "similar range of concepts such as roles, resources, rewards," and various other terms, and in

> the basic assumptions of each approach—the existence of division of labor and systematic organization; of groups and societies; the pursuance by individuals of various goals—both 'private' and institutionalized in social interaction; the importance of symbolic models of orientation in the patterning of such behavior and organization, the importance of the meaningful definition of the situation by those participating in it; the existence of some eco-systemic organizations— seem to have been accepted as evolutionary universals of any human society, by almost all these approaches.[115]

His conclusions are reinforced by the recent work of the Polish theorist, Piotr Sztompka, who notes that in Eastern Europe, "The concepts of system, structure, function, relationship, interaction, organization, etc., acquired a central place in Marxist sociology."[116]

Although Alvin Gouldner has strongly criticized academic sociology's emphasis on "continuity, cumulation, codification, convergence," as reflecting "the joyless prescriptions of a structuralizing methodology," he has also suggested that "not despite, but because of" its approach, it has "focused attention on some of the new sources and sites of social change in the modern social world."[117]

> For example, and to be provocatively invidious about it, it was not the Marxists but Talcott Parsons and other functionalists who early spotted the importance of the emerging "youth culture," and at least lifted it out as an object for attention. It was the academic sociologists, not the Marxists, in the United States who helped many to get their first concrete picture of how Blacks and other subjugated groups live, and who contributed to such practical political developments as the Supreme Court's desegregation decision. It is the ethnography of conventional academic sociologists that has also given us the best picture of the emerging psychedelic and drug cultures, which are hardening the separation and conflict of generations.[118]

The limitations of an ideological emphasis on the sources of different paradigmatic orientations in sociology may also be illustrated by noting the methodological and conceptual similarities between the Parsonian structural approach—included its efforts to find universal rules, the functional prerequisites of human society—and those of a number of contemporary western radical social theorists. In discussing critical theory in Germany, Rolf Klima points out its current leading spokesman, Jürgen Habermas, "has been trying all along to give Parsonian functionalism a hermeneutic-dialectic reinterpretation."[119] George Lichtheim and Harold Bershady note "that Louis Althusser, the French Marxist, defines certain of the theoretical tasks of structural Marxism in similar ways" to Parsons, a fact which also leads him and his followers to be criticized for their "a-historicism."[120] And Bershady emphasizes that "if Marxism is not merely historicism . . . Parsons's epistomological enterprise is not nearly as anti-Marxist as has been made out."[121] Noam Chomsky has argued the case for an ahistorical structuralism, for looking for the structural limitations of the forms of human organization, in even stronger terms than Althusser, Parsons, or Lévy-Strauss.[122] In the *New Left Review*, Chomsky recommended that social science follow the model he has developed for linguistics of looking for the universal aspects of social structure, those that underlie and limit the nature of all social systems—feudalism, capitalism, and socialism.

> As a linguist I am interested in the fact that English and Japanese are rather minor modifications of a basic pattern. . . . Now it is possible to carry out this study as a linguist because we can move up to a level of abstraction from which we can survey a vast class of possible systems and ask how the existing human linguistic systems fit into this class. And I think we will discover that they fit into a very narrow part of it. A serious study of morals or of social systems would attempt the same thing. It would ask itself what kinds of social system are conceivable. Then it would ask itself what kinds have actually been realized in history and it would ask how these came into existence, given the range of possibilities that exist at some moment of economic and cultural development. Then, having reached that point, the next question is whether the range of social systems that human beings have constructed is broad or narrow, what is its scope, what are its potentialities, are there kinds of social systems human beings could not possibly construct and so on. We have not really begun this kind of investigation. Hence it is only a guess when I say that the range of possible social systems may turn out to be very narrow. Of course, there is an enormous human significance in living in one social system rather than another. . . . But that is a different question from asking which kinds of social organizations are possible for human beings and which kinds are not.[123]

Clearly the larger goal which Chomsky sets for the social sciences is almost identical with that which Parsons has attempted. As Bershady stresses, "the analogy between Parsons's and Chomsky's endeavors should help elicit the fact that the endeavor itself need not be associated necessarily with any specific 'sentiments' or 'metaphysical' assumptions," or, it may be added, a lack of interest in the sources of social change and conflict.[124]

These conclusions point up the criticisms of Polish sociologist Stefan Nowak, who, in challenging "recent discussions about the 'conservative assumptions' of functionalism" notes that "the critics of functionalism failed to perceive that it has such conservative implications—for conservatives only.'' And Nowak goes on (italics supplied) to ''defend . . . the *general problem area of functionalism*, which stresses the importance of looking for the social functions of different cultural patterns and institutions, and leaves (or should leave) open the problem of acceptance of the functions and of various kinds of social equilibrium. The conclusions to be drawn as to the appropriate *social actions* must be based on the confrontation of these empirically assessed functions with different human values.''[125]

In suggesting that a genuine basis for synthesis and intellectual cooperation exists among sociologists with varying theoretical orientations, it is not my intention to imply that sociology is approaching a state of agreement about a theoretical paradigm, or that criticism of the approach or research of any given school or sociologist is bad for the discipline. The contrary is true with respect to both points. Efforts to understand the basis for theoretical and empirical disagreements are necessary for the progress of any field of inquiry. But it does little good to conduct such critical analyses in the spirit of ideological controversy, one which assumes that to ''reveal'' the underlying political assumptions says anything about the validity or usefulness of a given work: Sociology is a discipline concerned with stability and change.

Notes

1. Max Weber, *Economy and Society* (New York: Bedminster Press, 1968), p. 27.
2. Lewis A. Coser, *The Functions of Social Conflict* (New York: Free Press, 1956).
3. Alvin W. Gouldner and Helen P. Gouldner, *Modern Sociology: An Invitation to the Study of Human Interaction* (New York: Harcourt, Brace & World, 1963), p. 596.
4. Karl Marx, *Capital*, vol. 1 (Moscow: Foreign Languages Publishing House, 1959), pp. 355–56; Nikolai Bukharin, *Historical Materialism: A System of Sociology* (New York: International Publishers, 1925), pp. 72–79.
5. Talcott Parsons, ''The Point of View of the Author,'' in Max Black (ed.), *The Social Theories of Talcott Parsons* (Englewood Cliffs: Prentice-Hall, 1961), p. 338.
6. Pierre Van den Berghe, ''Dialectic and Functionalism: Toward a Theoretical Synthesis,'' *American Sociological Review* 28 (October 1963): 705.
7. Robert W. Friedrichs, *A Sociology of Sociology* (New York: Free Press, 1970), p. 262.
8. Pradeep Bandyopadhyay, ''One Sociology or Many: Some Issues in Radical Sociology,'' *Science and Society* 35 (Spring 1971): 19.
9. Helmut Steiner and Owesj I. Schkaratan, ''The Analysis of Society as a System and Its Social Structure,'' (paper presented at the Research Committee of Social Stratification and Social Mobility, 7th World Congress of Sociology, Varna, Bulgaria, 1970), p. 3.
10. Piotr Sztompka, *System and Function: Toward a Theory of Society* (New York: Academic Press, 1974), pp. 169–70, 177–78.

11. E. G. Hobsbawm, "Karl Marx's Contribution to Historiography," in Robin Blackburn (ed.), *Ideology in Social Science* (New York: Vintage, 1973), p. 273.
12. Ibid., pp. 273–74, 276, 277, 279–80, 281.
13. Wilbert E. Moore, "A Reconsideration of Theories of Social Change," *American Sociological Review* 25 (December 1960): 810–18; Van den Berghe, "Dialectic and Functionalism"; Robin Williams, Jr., "Some Further Comments on Chronic Controversies," *American Journal of Sociology* 71 (May 1966): 717–21.
14. Talcott Parsons, *The Social System* (New York: Free Press, 1951), p. 535.
15. Talcott Parsons, "A Functionalist Theory of Change," in Amitai Etzioni and Eva Etzioni (eds.), *Social Change* (New York: Basic Books, 1964), p. 84.
16. S. N. Eisenstadt, "Institutionalization and Change," *American Sociological Review* 29 (April 1964): 235.
17. Robert K. Merton, *Social Theory and Social Structure* (New York: Free Press, 1957), p. 122.
18. David Lockwood, "Social Integration and System Integration," G. K. Zollschan and W. Hirsch (eds.), *Explorations in Social Change* (Boston: Houghton Mifflin, 1964), p. 250.
19. Gideon Sjoberg, "Contradictory Functional Requirements and Social Systems," in N. J. Demerath III and R. A. Peterson (eds.), *System, Change and Conflict* (New York: Free Press, 1967), pp. 339, 341–42.
20. Parsons, *The Social System*, p. 522.
21. Lewis S. Feuer, "The Social Theories of Talcott Parsons: A Critical Examination," *The Journal of Philosophy* 59 (March 1962): 191.
22. Alvin W. Gouldner, "Reciprocity and Autonomy in Functional Theory," in Llewellyn Gross (ed.), *Symposium on Sociological Theory* (Evanston: Row, Peterson, 1959), p. 249. "The principle of reciprocity enters Marx's theoretical analysis in peripheral but central ways; it is most importantly implicated in his concept of 'exploitation'; . . . If one puts aside Marx's moral condemnations of exploitation and considers only its sociological substance, it is clear that it refers to a breakdown in reciprocal functionality." Ibid., p. 267.
23. Robert Nisbet, *Social Change and History* (New York: Oxford University Press, 1969), p. 236.
24. "The notion of intrinsic contradictions within the social order has been the mainstay of Marxist types of explanations." Lewis Coser, *Continuities in the Study of Social Conflict* (New York: Free Press, 1967), p. 141.
25. N. J. Demerath III, "Synecdoche and Structural-Functionalism," in N. J. Demerath III and R. A. Peterson (eds.), *System, Change and Conflict* (New York: Free Press, 1967), p. 515.
26. Dick Atkinson, *Orthodox Consensus and Radical Alternative* (London: Heinemann, 1971), p. 124.
27. Ibid., p. 109.
28. Guy Rocher, *Talcott Parsons et la Sociologie Americaine* (Paris: Presses Universitaires de France, 1972), pp. 51–52.
29. Atkinson, *Orthodox Consensus*, p. 109.
30. Ibid., p. 112.
31. Ibid., p. 112.
32. Ibid. p. 120. Parsons, *The Social System*, p. 280.
33. Wilbert E. Moore, *Social Change* (Englewood Cliffs: Prentice-Hall, 1963), p. 20.

34. Parsons, *The Social System*, p. 523.

35. Ibid., pp. 505–20.

36. Ibid., pp. 519–20.

37. Ibid., p. 520.

38. Edward C. Devereux, Jr., "Parsons' Sociological Theory," in Max Black (ed.), *The Social Theories of Talcott Parsons* (Englewood Cliffs: Prentice-Hall, 1961), pp. 33–34.

39. Amitai Etzioni, *The Active Society* (New York: Free Press, 1968), p. 329, italics added.

40. Karl Marx, "Preface to a Contribution to the Critique of Political Economy," in Karl Marx, *Selected Works,* vol. 1 (New York: International Publishers, 1936), pp. 356–57.

41. Leon Trotsky, *The Revolution Betrayed* (Garden City: Doubleday, Doran, 1937), p. 56.

42. Robert M. MacIver, *Social Causation* (Boston: Ginn, 1942), pp. 251–65; Gunnar Myrdal, *An American Dilemma* (New York: Harper & Brothers, 1944), pp. 1065–70; Etzioni, *The Active Society*, pp. 387–427.

43. Rocher, *Talcott Parsons*, p. 98.

44. Frederick J. Teggart, *Rome and China: A Study of Correlations in Historical Events* (Berkeley: University of California Press, 1939).

45. Neil Smelser, *Theory of Collective Behavior* (London: Routledge & Kegan Paul, 1962), pp. 15–18.

46. S. N. Eisenstadt, *Tradition, Change and Modernity* (New York: Wiley, 1973), p. 7. For a discussion of the possibilities of the emergence of a social system without contradictions see "A Concept and Its History: The End of Ideology," chapter 3 in this volume.

47. See also Coser's statements: "Marx's stress on the function of social interests in the historical process can serve as a counter argument to those who claim that a functional orientation precludes concern with power and social change." Gouldner also has emphasized that Marx and Engels, as well as latter-day Marxists such as Bukharin, "were deeply concerned about system analysis." Conversely, Gouldner notes that Durkheim stressed that the "exploitation . . . rendered possible by power discrepancies . . . conduces to a sense of injustice which has socially unstabilizing consequences" and to end these he advocated the abolition of the "institution of inheritance." Charles Loomis effectively pointed up some of the similarities in approach when he presented a number of graduate students in sociology with a number of quotations from Marx dealing with system and function and asked them to choose from a list of names the author of the quotations. Almost all of them selected Parsons, not Marx. Coser, *Study of Social Conflict*, p. 138; Gouldner, "Functional Theory," pp. 269–70; Alvin W. Gouldner, *For Sociology* (New York: Free Press, 1973), p. 386; Charles P. Loomis, "In Praise of Conflict and Its Resolution," *American Sociological Review* 32 (December, 1967): 876.

48. Van den Berghe, "Dialectic and Functionalism"; Talcott Parsons, *Societies: Evolutionary and Comparative Perspectives* (Englewood Cliffs: Prentice-Hall, 1966); Robert A. Nisbet, "Developmentalism: A Critical Analysis," in John C. McKinney and Edward A. Tiryakian (eds.), *Theoretical Sociology* (New York: Appleton-Century-Crofts, 1970), pp. 193–96.

49. Robert Bellah, "Durkheim and History," in W. J. Cahnman and A. Boskoff (eds.), *Sociology and History* (New York: Free Press, 1964), p. 90. For a general

discussion of Durkheim's theory of "structural differentiation," see also Leo Schnore, "Social Morphology and Human Ecology," *American Journal of Sociology* 63 (May 1958): 620–34. Ruschemeyer has stressed the links between Marx's and Durkheim's analyses of differentiation. Dietrich Ruschemeyer, "Reflections on Structural Differentiation," *Zeitschrift fur Soziologie* 3 (June 1974): 279–94.

50. Gouldner, "Functional Theory," pp. 265–66.
51. Alexis de Tocqueville, *Democracy in America* (New York: Vintage, 1954), p. 56; Robert A. Nisbet, *The Sociological Tradition* (New York: Basic Books, 1966), pp. 183–95; Lee Benson, "Group Cohesion and Social and Ideological Conflict," *American Behavioral Scientist* 16 (May/June 1973): 751–53.
52. Tocqueville, *Democracy*, p. 266. See also Irving M. Zeitlin, *Liberty, Equality and Revolution in Alexis de Tocqueville* (Boston: Little, Brown, 1971), pp. 40–42.
53. "Cultural structure may be defined as that organized set of normative values governing behavior which is common to members of a designated society or group" in Merton, *Social Theory*, pp. 162–64; Talcott Parsons, Robert F. Bales and Edward A. Shils, *Working Papers on the Theory of Action* (New York: Free Press, 1953), pp. 67–78; Emile Durkheim, *Suicide: A Study in Sociology* (New York: Free Press, 1951), pp. 246–57.
54. Kingsley Davis and Wilbert E. Moore, "Some Principles of Stratification," *American Sociological Review* 10 (April 1945): 242–49.
55. Merton, *Social Theory*, p. 123.
56. Reinhard Bendix and S. M. Lipset (eds.), *Class, Status and Power: A Reader in Social Stratification* (Glencoe: Free Press, 1953), p. 13.
57. Gouldner, *For Sociology*, p. 386.
58. Talcott Parsons, *The Structure of Social Action* (New York: McGraw-Hill, 1937; New York: Free Press, 1949), p. 658.
59. Talcott Parsons, *Essays in Sociological Theory* (New York: Free Press, 1954), pp. 330–31. In commenting on this analysis, the radical British sociologist Dick Atkinson notes Parsons's emphasis on the inevitability of interest conflicts inherent in role differentiation in complex society as part of his "continuing concern for aspects of conflict." (Atkinson, *Orthodox Consensus*, p. 24). The French leftist sociologist Alain Touraine has also written approvingly of this discussion of Parsons and stresses that he has been "wrongly accused of being only interested in consensus and social equilibrium." Alain Touraine, *Post-Industrial Society* (New York: Random House, 1971), p. 76.
60. Talcott Parsons, *Politics and Social Structure* (New York: Free Press, 1969), p. 353.
61. Ibid., p. 361.
62. Ibid., p. 362. Jessop notes that Parsons "seems to recognize that values and stratification are maintained primarily by a dominant class in arguing that differentiation and adaptive upgrading make it increasingly difficult to maintain a class system in which one class is excluded from full membership in the societal community by another, superior class." Bob Jessop, *Social Order, Reform and Revolution* (London: Macmillan, 1972), p. 42.
63. Weber, *Economy and Society*, pp. 24–26; Max Weber, *The Theory of Social and Economic Organization*, Talcott Parsons (ed.), (New York: Oxford University Press, 1947), pp. 115–18; Max Weber, *On Charisma and Institution Building* (Chicago: University of Chicago Press, 1968), pp. 6–7; Karl Mann-

heim, *Man and Society in an Age of Reconstruction* (New York: Harcourt, Brace, 1950), pp. 51–60.

64. Ann Swidler, "The Concept of Rationality in the Work of Max Weber," *Sociological Inquiry* 43 (Spring 1973): 38–41.

65. Anthony Giddens, *Capitalism and Modern Social Theory* (Cambridge: Cambridge University Press, 1971), p. 184.

66. Parsons, *Structure of Social Action*, pp. 643, 653.

67. Max Weber, in *From Max Weber: Essays in Sociology*, H. H. Gerth and C. Wright Mills (eds.) (New York: Oxford University Press, 1946), pp. 117–22.

68. Ibid., p. 120.

69. Aristotle, *The Basic Works of Aristotle* (New York: Random House, 1941), p. 1404.

70. Seymour Martin Lipset, *Rebellion in the University* (Boston: Little, Brown, 1972), p. 120.

71. Seymour Martin Lipset (ed.), *Student Politics* (New York: Basic Books, 1967), pp. 3–53; S. M. Lipset and Philip Altbach (eds.), *Students in Revolt* (Boston: Houghton Mifflin, 1969), pp. v–vii; Lipset, *Rebellion*, pp. 23–30, 127.

72. Karl Mannheim, *Ideology and Utopia* (New York: Harcourt, Brace, 1949), pp. 222–36.

73. Eisenstadt, *Tradition, Change and Modernity*, pp. 250–51.

74. Ibid., p. 249.

75. Daniel Bell, *The Coming of Post-Industrial Society* (New York: Basic Books, 1973), pp. 477–78.

76. S. M. Lipset and Richard B. Dobson, "The Intellectual as Critic and Rebel: With Special Reference to the United States and the Soviet Union," *Daedalus* 10 (Summer 1972): 137–98.

77. Weber, *From Max Weber*, p. 155.

78. Mannheim, *Ideology and Utopia*, pp. 230–31.

79. Ibid., pp. 232–33.

80. Bell, *Post-Industrial Society*, p. 479. See also Lionel Trilling, *Beyond Culture* (New York: Viking, 1965), pp. xii–xiii.

81. S. M. Lipset, "Academia and Politics in America," in T. J. Nossiter et al. (eds.), *Imagination and Precision in the Social Sciences* (London: Faber, 1972); Lipset and Dobson, "Intellectual as Critic"; Everett C. Ladd, Jr. and S. M. Lipset, *The Divided Academy: The Politics of Academe* (New York: McGraw-Hill, 1975).

82. Charles Kadushin, *American Intellectual Elite* (Boston: Little, Brown, 1974).

83. J. W. C. Johnstone, E. J. Slawski, and W. W. Bowman, "The Professional Values of American Newsmen," *Public Opinion Quarterly* 36 (Winter 1972–73): 522–40; United Church of Christ, News Release on Harris Poll Survey of Culture Critics (16 March 1970). More recent analyses of elite newsreporters and television producers report similar findings. See Robert S. Lichter and Stanley Rothman, "Media and the Business Elites," *Public Opinion* 4 (October/November 1981): 42–46, and Linda S. Lichter, Robert S. Lichter, and Stanley Rothman, "Hollywood and America: The Odd Couple," *Public Opinion* 5 (December/January 1983): 54–58.

84. Allen H. Barton, *The Limits of Consensus among American Leaders* (Preliminary report of the American Leadership Study, Bureau of Applied Research, Columbia University, 1973).

85. Bell, *Post-Industrial Society*, pp. 479–80.

86. Lipset, *Rebellion*, pp. 80–113.

87. Louis Harris, *The Anguish of Change* (New York: W. W. Norton, 1973), p. 45.

88. Ibid., pp. 45–47.

89. E. G. Hobsbawm, *Revolutionaries* (London: Weidenfeld & Nicholson, 1973), pp. 258–59.

90. Ronald Inglehart, "Industrial, Pre-Industrial and Post-Industrial Political Cleavages in Western Europe and the United States," (Paper prepared for the 1973 meeting of the American Political Science Association, September 4–8; Ronald Inglehart, "The Silent Revolution in Europe: Intergenerational Change in Post-Industrial Societies," *American Political Science Review* 65 (December 1971): 991–1017. Statistical data from American opinion surveys demonstrating the same point may be found in Harris, *Anguish of Change*, pp. 36–41.

91. Joji Watanuki, "Report of Governability of Democracy Task Force (Japan)," (Paper prepared for the Trilateral Commission, Tokyo, 15 January 1975).

92. Erwin Scheuch, "Die politischen und sozialen Aurwirkungen der Wirtshaftskrise," (Expert Opinion Report prepared for the Chancellor's Office, Bonn, 30 December 1974).

93. Erik Allardt, "A Comparative Study of Need-Satisfaction, Alienation and Discontent in the Scandinavian Countries," (Paper presented at the conference on Recent Political Trends in the Scandinavian Countries, Washington D.C., American Enterprise Institute, 10–11 February 1975), pp. 47–48.

94. Inglehart, "Political Cleavages," p. 12.

95. Ibid., pp. 69–70.

96. Ibid., p. 72.

97. Weber, *From Max Weber*, p. 122.

98. Eisenstadt, *Tradition, Change and Modernity*, p. 250.

99. Richard Flacks, "On the New Working Class and Strategies for Social Change," in Philip G. Altbach and R. S. Laufer (eds.), *The New Pilgrims* (New York: McKay, 1972), p. 86.

100. Ibid., p. 88.

101. Ibid., pp. 89–90. See also Touraine, *Post-Industrial Society*; A. Gorz, *Reforme et Revolution* (Paris: Seuil, 1969); J. Rowntree and M. Rowntree. "Youth as Class," *Our Generation* 6 (1968): 155–90.

102. Bell, *Post-Industrial Society*, pp. 39–40.

103. Norman Birnbaum, *Toward A Critical Sociology* (New York: Oxford University Press, 1971), p. 230.

104. Cornelius J. Lammers, "Mono- and polyparadigmatic developments in natural and social sciences," in Richard Whitley (ed.), *Social Processes of Scientific Development* (London: Routledge & Kegan Paul, 1974), pp. 123–47.

105. Donald MacRae, "Introduction," in Percy Cohen, *Modern Social Theory* (New York: Basic Books, 1968), pp. vii–viii. It should be noted that MacRae deplored this possibility and voiced the "hope" that it would not occur because of the weaknesses in the unified theory.

106. C. Wright Mills, *The Sociological Imagination* (New York: Oxford University Press, 1959).

107. Ira E. Wessler, "The Political Resolutions of American Learned Societies," (Ph.D. diss., New York University, 1973), pp. 214–47.

108. Ibid., p. 412.

109. Ladd and Lipset, *The Divided Academy*.

110. S. M. Lipset and E. C. Ladd, Jr., "The Politics of American Sociologists," in Robert K. Merton et al. (eds.), *Varieties of Political Expression in Sociology* (Chicago: University of Chicago Press, 1972), p. 95.

111. M. Popovich, "What American Sociologists Think about Their Science and Its Problems," *American Sociologist* 1 (May 1966): 135.

112. Alvin W. Gouldner and J. T. Sprehe, "Sociologists Look at Themselves," *Trans-Action* 2 (May/June 1965): 42–44.

113. J. T. Sprehe, "The Climate of Opinion in Sociology: A Study of the Professional Value and Belief Systems of Sociologists," (Ph.D. diss., Washington University, St. Louis, 1967).

114. H. Suzuki, *The Urban World* (Tokyo: Seishin Shobo, 1970), pp. 368, 383.

115. S. N. Eisenstadt, "Some Reflections on the 'Crisis' in Sociology," *Sociologische gids* 4 (July/August 1973): 260–61.

116. Sztompka, *System and Function*, p. 177.

117. Alvin W. Gouldner, *The Coming Crisis of Western Sociology* (New York: Basic Books, 1970), pp. 265, 17–18.

118. Alvin W. Gouldner, "Toward a Radical Reconstruction of Sociology," *Social Policy* 1 (May/June 1970): 21.

119. Rolf Klima, "Theoretical Pluralism, Methodological Dissension and the Role of the Sociologist," *Social Science Information* 11 (1972): 80.

120. George Lichtheim, "A New Twist in the Dialectic," *New York Review of Books* 12 (30 January 1969): 33–38.

121. Harold J. Bershady, *Ideology and Social Knowledge* (New York: Wiley, 1973), p. 133.

122. Ibid., pp. 14–19.

123. Noam Chomsky, "Linguistics and Politics," *New Left Review* 57 (September/October 1969): 32.

124. Bershady, *Ideology and Social Knowledge*, p. 16.

125. Stefan Nowak, "Empirical Knowledge and Social Values in the Cumulative Development of Sociology," (Revision of paper prepared for the Round Table "Is There a Crisis in Sociology?" at the 8th World Congress of Sociology, Toronto, August 1974).

2

Social Stratification and Social-Class Analysis

Concern with social class and social stratification is as old as social thought. The ancient Greek philosophers were extremely conscious of the effects of stratification, and propositions about stratification may be found throughout many of the writings of Aristotle and Plato. Thus Aristotle, in discussing the conditions for different types of political organization, suggested in essence that constitutional government—limitation on the powers of the political elite—is most likely to be found in societies with large middle classes, while city-states characterized by large lower classes and small middle and upper classes would be more likely to be governed as dictatorships based on mass support, or as oligarchies. This general approach has been elaborated in contemporary studies of the social requisites of democracy. Plato, in the *Republic*, discussed the conditions for a genuine equalitarian communist society and suggested that the family is the key support of inequality—that is, of social stratification. His argument, which is still followed by many contemporary sociologists, was that individuals are motivated to secure for other family members, for whom they feel affection, any privileges that they themselves enjoy. Hence, in every society there is a built-in pressure to institutionalize inequality by making it hereditary. Plato argued that the only way to create a communist society would be to take children away from their parents and to have the state raise them, so as to eliminate the tendency toward inherited social privilege.

Most of contemporary sociological theory and research on social class, however, does not stem from the Greeks. The emphasis of the Enlightenment on the possibility of social laws and of their discovery through observation and comparative study must be taken as one of the principal methodological breakthroughs. Institutional regularities, such as those governing class, status, and political relationships, became objects of disinterested inquiry as things in themselves, thus reversing the notion, dominant in the Middle Ages, that the temporal sphere was nothing more than an auxiliary part of the supernatural plan, subject to the principles of natural law.

45

The Enlightenment served to erase the assumptions about hierarchy, class, and intergroup relationships that stemmed from the medieval model of an organic Christian civilization. Thus, the basis was being laid for a science of society.

But it was Karl Marx, more than anyone else, who carried this scientific perspective into the study of social class, even going so far as to derive his idea of class from what he called the scientific laws of history. He then not only accepted the premise that social phenomena possess their own laws, but also set out to discover the underlying variables and how they are expressed under differing historical conditions. Thus, if one were to award the title of father of the study of social class to any individual, it would have to be to Marx. He made class the central aspect of his analysis of society and of his theory of social change. Though most latter-day sociologists have disagreed with many, if not most, of Marx's assumptions about stratification, may of the non-Marxist or anti-Marxist ideas on the subject have come about in reaction to Marx's original formulations.

This does not mean, of course, that there were not other important eighteenth-century and nineteenth-century figures who used stratification concepts in a sophisticated manner. Marx obviously was a child of his times; many of his ideas, sometimes in almost identical form, can be found in the writings of others. The Marxist formulation, laid down in the chapter "Social Classes" in *Capital*,[1] that there are three major economic classes in modern society—landlords receiving rent, capitalists profit, and workers wages—is derived directly from Ricardo's *Principles*, published in 1817, a work that also presented the labor theory of value.[2] Adam Smith's great book, *The Wealth of Nations*, is an important work for the study of stratification, as are other writings of the school of Scottish philosophers of his day.[3] The American founding fathers contended that all complex societies are stratified and that there is an inherent basis of conflict among groups with diverse economic and class interests. Various American Marxist groups have, in fact, sought to legitimate Marxist doctrine as compatible with classic American thought by pointing to the similarities between the ideas presented in No. 10 of *The Federalist Papers* and various writings of Marx.[4] However, these precursors of Marxism influenced sociology primarily through their influence on Marx himself. It was he who formulated the theory of class so powerfully that he defined the terms of the argument for later sociological thinkers.

Types of Theoretical Approach

Approaches to the fact of social inequality have differed in the extent to which they emphasize change or stability in social systems. These differences in theoretical orientation have to a considerable extent reflected political differences. Reformists or radicals have seen reactions against social inequality and social class differences as sources of social change, which they are inclined to favor. Theorists with more conservative political tastes have justified aspects of the existing order of trying to show the functions performed by hierarchy in all social systems. Concern with social change has generally been associated with interest in social classes, that is, groups within stratified collectivities that are said to act politically as agents of change. Those stressing the functional basis of inequality have been interested in social stratification and in the purposes served by differential rewards, particularly in prestige, for various positions in social systems.

Those using the concept of social class to interpret the dynamics of social change have assumed that the creation of new occupational or economic roles has often resulted in the emergence of groups that initially were outside the traditional hierarchical system. As these new groups attempt to stabilize their position within society, they come into conflict with older, privileged strata whose status, economic resources, or power they challenge. The new groups also often develop sets of values, both secular and religious, that enhance their position by undermining the stability of the prior value system and the structure of privilege it justified. Thus historical change is viewed basically as a consequence of the rise of new classes and the downfall of old ones; it is assumed that complex social systems are inherently unstable and that conflicts stemming from inequality cause pressure for changes in the system.

In contrast, functional theorists have assumed that social systems must be treated as if they were in equilibrium. From this point of view, it is necessary to relate the various attributes of the social hierarchy to the conditions for social stability. Class, therefore, has been seen by these theorists not as an intervening variable in the process of social change but, rather, as a set of institutions that provide some of the conditions necessary for the operation of a complex society. These conditions, basically, amount to the need for a system of differentiated rewards as a means of institutionalizing the division of labor: differentiation by status and income is posited as a necessary part of the system of motivation required to place individuals in the various positions that must be filled if society is to operate.

The interest of students of social change in why men rebel, why they want change, has led to an emphasis within the tradition of class analysis on the way in which inequality frustrates men and leads them to reject the *status quo*. Functional analysts, on the other hand, are much more concerned with how the social system gets men to conform, to seek and remain in various positions in society, including ones that are poorly rewarded or require onerous work. The former, in other words, often ask how systems of stratification are undermined; the latter seek to know how and why they hold together.

It is important to note that while any analysis of social class must necessarily deal with social stratification as well, these two terms are not synonymous. Theories of social class refer to the conditions affecting the existence of strata that have developed or should develop some "consciousness of kind," that is, some sense of existence as a group attribute of society. Stratification refers to the entire complex of hierarchical differentiation, whether group-related or not. Although this discussion is about social class, much of the analysis in it will involve stratification, since it is impossible to account for the way in which social classes are formed, change, and affect other aspects of society without referring to stratification systems as such.

I have distinguished two polar traditions of social thought that do not, of course, occur in pure form in real life. (A review of theoretical commonalities between Marxist and functionalist analyses can be found in chapter 1.) Marx, the foremost student of class and social change and the advocate, par excellence, of instability and revolution, was also aware of the functional aspects of social stratification. Many of his writings attempt to show how ideologies, values, and patterns of behavior—all at different class levels—serve to maintain the stability of the social order. In fact, Marxian analysis is replete with functional propositions.

The functionalists, on the other hand, are of course aware that change and conflict occur and that men not only accept but also reject the given stratification system. Thus (as is noted in more detail below) the most influential stimulator of functional thought in sociology, Emile Durkheim, sought to show the way in which strains in value emphases within the same system lead individuals and groups to reject the dominant value system and to deviate from expected forms of behavior. Where Marx saw alienation as inherent in social inequality, Durkheim suggested that anomie, or rulelessness, is endemic in all complex social systems.

To see the way these concerns with stability and change, with alienation, and with the formation of class sentiments have evolved in modern social thought, it is necessary to turn to an examination of the work of some of the key theorists, particularly Marx, Weber, and Durkheim.

The Marxist Theory of Class

Marxist sociology starts from the premise that the primary function of social organization is the satisfaction of basic human needs—food, clothing, and shelter. Hence, the productive system is the nucleus around which other elements of society are organized. Contemporary sociology has reversed this emphasis by stressing the distribution system, the stratification components of which are status and prestige. To Marx, however, distribution is a dependent function of production.

Stemming from the assumption of the primacy of production is the Marxist definition of class: any aggregate of persons who play the same part in the production mechanism. Marx, in *Capital*, outlined three main classes, differentiated according to relations to the means of production: (1) *capitalists*, or owners of the means of production; (2) *workers*, or all those who are employed by others; (3) *landowners*, who in Marx's theory seemingly differ from capitalists and are regarded as survivors of feudalism.[5] From Marx's various historical writings, it is clear that he had a more complex view than this of the hierarchical reality and that he realized, for instance, that there is differentiation within each of these basic categories. Thus, the small businessmen, or petty bourgeoisie, were perceived as a transitional class, a group that will be pressed by economic tendencies inherent in capitalism to bifurcate into those who descend to the working class and those who so improve their circumstances that they become significant capitalists.

Although Marx differentiated classes in objective terms, his primary interest was in understanding and facilitating the emergence of class consciousness among the depressed strata. He wished to see created among them a sense of identical class interests, as a basis for conflict with the dominant class. The fact that a group held a number of objective characteristics in common but did not have the means of reaching organized class consciousness meant for Marx that it could not play the role of a historically significant class. Thus, he noted in "The Eighteenth Brumaire of Louis Bonaparte" that the French peasants of that period possessed many attributes that implied a common class situation:

> The small-holding peasants form a vast mass, the members of which live in similar conditions, but without entering into manifold relations with one another. Their mode of production isolates them from one another, instead of bringing them into mutual intercourse. The isolation is increased by France's bad means of communication and by the poverty of the peasants. . . . In so far as millions of families live under economic conditions of existence that separate their mode of life, their interests and their culture from those of other classes, and put them in hostile opposition to the latter, they form a class. In so far as there is merely a local interconnection among these small-holding peasants, and the identity of their interests begets no community, no national bond and no political organization among them, they do not form a class.[6]

Nikolai Bukharin, one of the leading theoreticians of the Russian Communist party, who was more concerned with sociological theory and research than any other major Marxist figure, attempted to formalize the differences among the workers, the peasants, and the lumpenproletariat (unattached laborers), making the workers a class and the other two not classes. His analysis, based on the events of the early decades of the twentieth century, was elaborated beyond that of Marx.

TABLE 2.1
Bukharin's Analysis of Class Conditions

Class properties	Peasantry	Lumpen-proletariat	Proletariat
1. Economic exploitation	+	−	+
2. Political oppression	+	+	+
3. Poverty	+	+	+
4. Productivity	+	−	+
5. Freedom from private property	−	+	+
6. Condition of union in production, and common labor	−	−	+

Source: N. Bukharin, Historical Materialism (New York: Russell, 1965), p. 289.

The working class is exploited by a visible common oppressor, is brought together by conditions of work that encourage the spread of ideas and organization among them, and remains in a structured conflict situation with its employers over wages and working conditions. Consequently, over time it can become a conscious class.

Marx, however, did not expect there to be a high correlation between objective class position and subjective revolutionary class consciousness until the point at which the social system in question broke down: if there was to be total class consciousness in any given society, then by definition it would be in the midst of revolution. In normal times, structural factors press deprived strata to become conscious, but the inherent strength of the ruling class prevents class consciousness. The dominant class possesses social legitimacy, controls the media of communication, is supported by the various mechanisms of socialization and social control, such as the school and the church, and during its period of stability is able to "buy off" those inclined to lead or participate in opposition movements. The Marxist term that characterizes the ideology of the lower class in the period of the predominance of the other classes is "false consciousness."

Marx was not very concerned with analyzing the behavior of the capitalist upper class. Basically, he assumed that the powerful parts of such a class must be self-conscious and that the state as a vehicle of power necessarily serves the interests of the dominant class in the long run. But more important to Marx than the sociology of the privileged class was that of the workers; the important question for research and action concerned the factors that would bring about working-class consciousness.

The dilemma of the Marxist theory of class is also the dilemma of every other single-variable theory. We can locate a class member objectively, but this may tell us little about the subjective correlates (social outlook, attitudes, etc.) of class position. Marx never actually said that at any given point in history or for any individual there would necessarily have to be a relationship between class position and the attitudes of class members. He did believe, however, that common conditions of existence create the necessary base for the development of common class attitudes, but that at any point in time, sharp discrepancies may exist between class position and class attitudes or behavior. Marx attempted to deal with this problem by his theory of transitional stages in the development of class. The first stage, in which a class is a class "in itself" (the German *an sich*), occurs when the class members do not understand their class position, the controls over them, or their "true class interests." The proletariat, as long as they are simply fighting for higher wages without recognizing that this is part of a necessary class struggle between themselves and the bourgeoisie that will end in the victory of one or the other, are a class *an sich*. In ideal-type terms the opposite of the class in itself is the class "for itself" (*für sich*). The class *für sich* is a self-conscious class, a large proportion of whose members consciously identify with it and think in terms of the class's struggle with another class. As long as most persons in a lower class think in *an sich* terms, the behavior of class members will be characterized by intraclass competition in which individual members of the class strive to get ahead of other members. In such a period, class conflict will be weak. Only when *für sich* attitudes develop does the class struggle really emerge. Members of a lower class who do not yet identify with their class are, according to Marx, thinking in terms of values or concepts that are functional for the stability of the position of the dominant class. Any individual, therefore, though objectively a member of the lower class, may subjectively be identified with or may be acting in ways which correspond to the position of another class. At different periods varying portions of an underprivileged population may be either *an sich* or *für sich*. One of the purposes of Marxist analysis is the investigation of this discrepancy. In discussing the rise of the bourgeoisie, Marx suggested that the period during which the bourgeoisie was a class *an sich* was longer and required greater effort than the period during which it became self-conscious and took political class action to overthrow feudalism and monarchy.[7] Implicit in this discussion of the development of the bourgeois class is the idea that the emergence of self-consciousness among the workers will also take a long time. Marx in fact suggested "making a precise study of strikes, combinations and other forms of class activity" in order to find out how the proletariat organizes itself as a class.[8]

Alienation

A key element in the Marxist sociology of the exploited is the Hegelian concept of alienation. Men are distinguished from animals—are less animal and more human—insofar as they become increasingly self-conscious about and freely selective in their work and conditions of life. Insofar as men do not freely choose their work but, rather, do whatever tasks are set before them, simply in order to exist, they remain in a less than human state. If work (or leisure) is imposed on man, so far from being free, he is objectively exploited and alienated from the truly human, that is, autonomous, condition.[9]

Alienation, for Marx, is an objective, not a subjective, condition. It signifies lack of autonomy, of self-control. The fact that workers may say that they like their work or social conditions does not mean that they are free actors, even if they think they are. Thus, in a slave society the fact that some slaves may have believed that they preferred to be slaves, and even that they were better off as slaves than as freed men, did not change the fact that objectively they were slaves. Similarly, the fact that a wage worker likes his conditions of work does not affect his position of being alienated and economically exploited or his potential as a free human being. In this sense, class society is akin to slavery. Class society must produce alienated individuals who are distorted, partial people. Marx therefore sought to document the facts about alienation and to understand the conditions under which estrangement, resentment, and, ultimately, political class consciousness would arise. Both class and alienation, he thought, would be eliminated by ending the private ownership of the means of production, for as long as people are working for others, they do not have conscious control over their life space and therefore are not truly human. Fully human society would come about when the production system could produce abundance in an absolute sense, when the machines produced enough food, clothing, and shelter for all men, to have as much as they needed, so that they could then devote themselves not to fighting over the scarce fruits of production but to fostering the activities of the mind. In essence, he was arguing that all class societies were pre-human and that class must disappear.

The Weberian Approach to Stratification

While Marx placed almost exclusive emphasis on economic factors as determinants of social class, Weber suggested that economic interests should be seen as a special case of the larger category of "values," which included many things that are neither economic nor interests in the ordinary sense of the term. For Weber, the Marxist model, although a source of fruitful hypotheses, was too simple to handle the complexity of stratification. He therefore sought to differentiate among the various sources of hierarchical differentiation and potential cleavage. The two most important sets of hierarchies for Weber were class and status.[10]

Class

Weber reserved the concept of class for economically determined stratification. He defined a class as being composed of people who have life chances in common, as determined by their power to dispose of goods and skills for the sake of income. Property is a class asset, but it is not the only criterion of class. For Weber, the crucial aspect of a class situation is, ultimately, the market situation.

The existence of large groups of people who can be located in a common class situation need not produce communal or societal action—that is, conscious, interest-determined activity—although it should produce *similar* reactions in the sense that those in the same class situation should exhibit similar behavior and attitudes without having a sense of class consciousness. These similarities, such as patterns of voting behavior or of drinking habits, reflect the effect of variations in life chances among the classes.

Weber, like Marx, was concerned with the conditions under which class consciousness arises. For him, however, there was no single form of class consciousness. Rather, which groups develop a consciousness of common interest opposed to those of another group is a specific empirical question; different groups acquire historical significance at different times and in different places. The extent of consciousness of kind depends to a considerable degree on the general culture of a society, particularly the set of intellectual ideas current within it. Concepts or values that might foster or inhibit the emergence of class-conscious groups cannot be derived solely from knowledge about the objective economic structure of a society. The existence of different strata subjected to variations in life chances does not necessarily lead to class action. The causal relationship posited by Marx between the fact of group inferiority and other aspects of the structure that might be changed by action had to be demonstrated to people; consciousness of it need not develop spontaneously. The presence or absence of such consciousness is not, of course, a fortuitous matter. The extent to which ideas emerge pointing to a causal relationship between class position and other social conditions is linked to the transparency of the relationship—that is, to how obvious it is that one class will benefit by action directed against another.

An examination of the history of class struggles suggested to Weber that conflicts between creditors and debtors are perhaps the most visible form of conflict flowing from economic differentiation. The conflict between employers and workers is also highly visible under capitalism, but it is essentially a special case of the economic struggle between buyers and sellers, a form of interest tension normal within a capitalist market economy. It involves an act of creative imagination and perception to develop an ideology that the tension between employer and worker requires an attack on the entire system of private ownership through the common action of all workers against the capitalist class. Such an act is much more likely to come from the intellectuals, who thereby present the workers with an ideological formula, than from the workers themselves. In this respect, Weber came to conclusions similar to those drawn by Lenin, who also argued that workers by themselves could only reach the stage of economism, of trade union consciousness—that is, of conflict with their employers over wages and working conditions. For Lenin, as for Weber, the emergence of revolutionary class consciousness requires leadership, much of which would be drawn from other strata—in Lenin's case, the elite or vanguard party.[11] Weber explicitly formalized the conditions that facilitate the emergence of class consciousness in terms that incorporated the principal elements of the Marxist scheme almost intact, although he made the significant and important addition of common status:

> Organized activity of class groups is favored by the following circumstances: (a) the possibility of concentrating on opponents where the immediate conflict of interests is vital. Thus workers organize against management and not against security holders who are the ones who really draw income without working. . . . (b) The existence of a class status which is typically similar for large masses of people. (c) The technical possibility of being easily brought together. This is particularly true where large numbers work together in a small area, as in the modern factory. (d) Leadership directed to readily understandable goals. Such goals are very generally imposed or at least are interpreted by persons, such as intelligentsia, who do not belong to the class in question.[12]

Weber's condition (a) is essentially a rephrasing of Marx's antagonism factor, though Weber made a distinction, not made by Marx, concerning the direction of the antagonism—in this case, toward the visible overseer. Condition (b) was never explicitly discussed by Marx. Condition (c) is borrowed directly from Marx. As for condition (d), in Marx's works it appears as the role of the party, although Marx never faced up to the problems that arise when a worker's party has a middle-class leadership.

Status

The second major dimension of stratification, status, refers to the quality of perceived interaction. Status was defined by Weber as the positive or negative estimation of honor, or prestige, received by individuals or positions. Thus it involves the felt perceptions of people. Those in a similar status position tend to see themselves as located in a comparable position on the social hierarchy. Since status involves perception of how much one is valued by others, men value it more than economic gain.

Weber argued that since status is manifest, consciousness of kind is more likely to be linked to status differentiation than to class. In other words, those who are in a higher or lower status group are prone to support status-enhancing activities, whether or not these activities can be classed as political. Those groups with high status will be motivated to support values and institutions that seemingly serve to perpetuate their status. Weber regarded economic class as important primarily because it is perceived as a cause of status. Since it is usually easier to make or lose money than it is to gain or lose status, those in privileged status positions seek to dissociate status from class, that is, to urge that status reflects factors such as family origin, manners, education, and the like—attributes that are more difficult to attain or lose than economic wealth.

There is, of course, as Weber pointed out, a strong correlation between status and class positions. However, once a group has attained high status through given achievements, its members try to limit the chances that others will replace them. And this is often done by seeking to deny the original source of individual or family status. The economic and class orders are essentially universalistic and achievement-oriented. Those who get, are. He who secures more money is more important than he who has less. The status order, on the other hand, tends to be particularistic and ascriptive. It involves the assumption that high status reflects aspects of the system that are unachievable. Thus it operates to inhibit social mobility, up or down. Weber, in his writings on status, echoed the functional analysis of the role of style presented by Veblen.[13] For Weber, as for Veblen, the function of conspicuous consumption—that is, of emphasis on pragmatically useless styles of consumption that take many years to learn—was to prevent mobility and to institutionalize the privileges of those who had risen to the top in previous years or epochs. Status groups are therefore identifiable by specific styles of life. Even though the original source of status was economic achievement, a status system, once in existence, operates independently of the class system and even seeks to negate its values. This, as Weber and Veblen both suggested, explains the seemingly surprising phenomenon that even to an industrial capitalist society, money-making is considered vulgar by many in privileged positions, and the children of those who have made money are frequently to be found in noncommercial activities.

Class Relations and Status Relations

The distinction between class and status is also reflected in the different nature of the key set of interactions that characterizes each. Class relations are defined by interaction among unequals in a market situation; status is determined primarily by relations with equals, even though there are many status contacts among unequals. The sanctions, in the case of status, are greater when violating the norms for relations with equals than those for relations with unequals.

One value of differentiating between class and status is that while these two dimensions of stratification are correlated, there are many cases in which they are discrepant. Thus individuals or groups may be higher in status than in class, or vice versa. Weber argued that such discrepancies are important aids to understanding the dynamics of social change and of conflict; he detected an inherent strain between the norms of the market and those of status systems. Markets are the dynamic source of tension for modern industrial society. Success or failure in the market constantly upsets the relative position of groups and individuals: groups high in status and wealth often lose their relative economic position because of market innovations, failure to adjust to change, and the like, while others rise suddenly on the scale of wealth. Those who had status and its frequent concomitant, legitimate access to political authority, exert their influence and power against the *nouveaux riches*. For example, a common interpretation of the behavior of the French bourgeoisie during the Revolution of 1789 is that they had not pressed for economic rights and power because they already possessed all they needed. Rather, they had wanted to force the monarchy and aristocracy to accord them high status. Similarly, Weber's disciple Robert Michels suggested that the political radicalism of many quite wealthy European Jews before World War I was a consequence of their having been denied a status position commensurate with their class level in society.[14]

Social Structure and Political Conflict

An industrial society characterized by an elaborate, highly institutionalized status structure *combined* with the class tensions usually found in industrial societies is more likely to exhibit class-conscious politics than is one in which status lines are imprecise and not formally recognized. It has therefore been argued that Marxist, class-conscious parties have been stronger in societies, like the Wilhelmine Germany in which Weber lived most of his life, that maintain a very visible and fairly rigid status system derived from preindustrial society than in class societies, such as the United States, that lack a feudal tradition of estates. Moreover, insofar as the dynamics of a successful industrial society undermine the ascriptive status mechanisms inherited from the feudal precapitalist order, the amount of political conflict arising from class consciousness is reduced. Hence it would seem to follow from Weber's analysis that the growth of industrial capitalism, and the consequent imposition on the stratification system of capitalism's emphases on achievement and universalism, weaken rather than increase class-linked consciousness of kind.

This thesis of Weber's that stresses the consequences of structural changes on class relationships has been paralleled by T. H. Marshall's analysis of the relationship between citizenship and social class.[15] Citizenship, for Marshall, is a status that involves access to various rights and powers. In premodern times citizenship was limited to a small elite; social development in European states has consisted to a considerable extent in admitting new social strata—first the bourgeoisie and later the workers—to the status of citizen. The concept of the citizen that arose with the emergence of the bourgeoisie in the eighteenth century involved a claim to universalistic rights in the status order, as well as the political one. Marshall has suggested that class-conscious ideologies of the extreme sort are characteristic of new strata, such as the bourgeoisie or the working class, as they fight for the right to full social and political participation—that is, for citizenship. As long as they are denied citizenship, sizable segments of these classes endorse revolutionary ideologies. In turn, older strata and institutions seeking to preserve their ancient monopolies of power and status foster extreme conservative doctrines.

From this point of view, the history of political ideologies in democratic countries can be written in terms of the emergence of new social strata and their eventual integration into society and polity. In Europe, the struggle for such integration took the form of defining a place in the polity for the business strata and the working class alongside the preindustrial upper classes and the church. Unless class conflicts overlapped with continuing controversies concerning the place of religion, as they did in Latin Europe, or concerning the status of the traditional upper strata, as they did in Germany, intense ideological controversy declined soon after the new strata gained full citizenship rights.

Power, Status, and Bureaucracy

Power, which in the Marxist analysis derives from class position, is a much more complex phenomenon in the Weberian model. Weber defined power as the chance of a man or group to realize their will even against the opposition of others. Power may be a function of resources possessed in the economic, status, and political systems; both status and class are power resources. Since men want higher status, they tend to try to orient their behavior to that approved by those with the higher status which they value. Power resources can also be found in institutions that command the allegiance of people—religions, parties, trade unions, and the like. Anyone with followers or, like the military, with control of force, may have access to power. In large measure, the relative weight of different power resources is determined by the rules of the political game, whatever these may be in different societies. The structure of legal authority and its degree of legitimacy influence the way in which power is secured.

For Weber, the key source of power in modern society is *not* to be found in the ownership of the means of production. Rather, the increased complexity of modern industrial society leads to the development of vast bureaucracies that become increasingly interconnected and interdependent. The modern state, with its monopoly of arms and administration, becomes the dominant institution in bureaucratized society. Because of the increasing complexity of operating modern social institutions, even economic institutions are brought into a close, dependent relationship with the administrative and military bureaucracies of the state. Increasingly, therefore, as all social institutions, the key power resources become rigidly hierarchical large-scale bureaucracies.

Bureaucratization and Alienation

This concern with bureaucracy as the key hierarchical power-related structure of the stratification system of industrial society (whether the society is formally capitalist or socialist is irrelevant) led Weber to formulate a source of alienation very different from that of Marx. For Weber, it was not only the wage worker who becomes alienated through his lack of control over his human needs; the bureaucrat is even more subject to obsessive demands. Bureaucracy, in fact, has an inherent tendency to destroy men's autonomy. It is characterized by formalism and it involves, in Weber's terms: (1) subordination; (2) expertise (and hence a rigid division of labor); (3) obeying fixed rules.[16] Even members of small, nonbureaucratic structures have their freedom reduced if these structures are involved with bureaucracies. In this conclusion, Weber agreed with Marx. However, for Weber the key depersonalizing element is the expectation that the bureaucrat will give absolute loyalty to the organization. Loyalty within a bureaucracy is impersonal; no personal attachments are supposed to interfere with the functioning of the system. Thus the depersonalization of loyalty became the equivalent of what Marx called the alienation of man from his labor. Weber argued that, as a social mechanism, bureaucracy assumes absolute discipline and a high level of predictability. People in bureaucracies fulfill role requirements rather than their personal desires. Rational action in bureaucracies is not an end in itself but, rather, an aspect of the structure of social interaction. Individuals both judge others and interact on the basis of universalistic norms; personal motives are not considered. The bureaucratic structure functions for its own ends, not those of the people within it. In theory, all individuals in bureaucracies are expendable and only positions are important.

Preparation for a bureaucratic career involves increasing conformity. Bureaucracy requires that individuals become highly specialized. Success depends on the individual's ability to conform. As one enters a bureaucracy, he loses much of his freedom to change his life alternatives. He becomes highly specialized and therefore cannot move from one firm or type of job to another. Such specialization, such conformity to narrow role requirements—to the needs of the "machine"—means dehumanization, or alienation from true human choice.

The alienation inherent in bureaucracy is, for Weber, independent of the system of property relations. Socialism means more rather than less alienation, because it involves greater bureaucratization. There is little difference between capitalist and socialist societies in their class relations and their propensity to alienation. The source of alienation lies in bureaucracy, which is inherent in industrial society.

The growth of bureaucratization also has the effect of separating work roles from other activities, with socially destructive consequences. An individual within a bureaucracy has to conform to efficiency rules, production standards, and other impersonal goals that have no meaning in his life outside work, since they are the bureaucracy's goals, not his; he conforms to them while at work, but gets no guidance as to how to behave in other activities. Weber can be interpreted as having believed that the nonbureaucratic part of life was becoming increasingly normless while bureaucratic structures were becoming increasingly normative. As social institutions become more bureaucratized, individuals learn how to behave within bureaucracies but not outside of them.

In a sense, Weber raised Marx's ideas about the nature and consequences of stratification to a higher order of generalization. Marx's conclusions were based mainly on his analysis of social relations under capitalism; this analysis presupposed a social system in which the fruits of production were scarce and control over the means of production was inequitably distributed. Weber, by using more general analytical categories, sought to deal with issues that cut through all complex social systems. Thus he characterized every complex system according to the distribution of economic and honorific life chances in it. While Marx stressed that social stratification is a result of economic scarcity, Weber emphasized that honor and prestige are themselves scarce: economic goods could increase, and everyone could gain in an absolute sense, but, since prestige is determined by relative ranking, if one went up, another went down. The latter form of stratification involves a zero-sum game, and consequently occasions continual tensions in any society with unrestricted social mobility.

Alienation also is presented as a broader category in Weber's work than in that of Marx. Basically, alienation from self involves compulsive conformity to norms: the alienated individual is role-bound. Since such compulsive conformity is inherent in bureaucracy, which Weber saw as the dynamic element in modern society, he was much more pessimistic about the future of society than was Marx.

Much of contemporary writing by intellectuals and social scientists about alienation is derived more from Weber than from Marx. For instance, the ideas advanced by Erich Fromm, David Riesman, William F. Whyte, Robert K. Merton, Arnold Green, and C. Wright Mills concerning the "bureaucratic," "marketeer," or "other-directed" personality, the "organization man," and, in general, the individual who seeks to get ahead by selling his personality, are all related to the effects of bureaucracy on individuals. Weber is the intellectual father of these and all similar discussions. His ideas, therefore, constitute not only a contribution to sociological analysis but also a basic source for the moral criticism of society. They usually have not been perceived as such because Weber's empirical conclusion, that all complex societies will be both stratified and alienative, leads to no positive moral solution. This is because for Weber (as for C. Wright Mills), the only society that really makes individual autonomy possible is the nonbureaucratized society of small producers, and societies of this type are rapidly vanishing.

Functionalist Approaches

Although the ideas generated by Marx and Weber remain the most fruitful sources of theory on social stratification, much of contemporary sociology accepts the so-called functionalist approach to the subject. This approach is associated with the names of Emile Durkheim, Kingsley Davis, Talcott Parsons, and Robert K. Merton.

Durkheim and subsequent functionalists have assumed that since modern society has a complex and highly differentiated system of roles which must be performed, different men must be motivated to perform different roles.[17] They see man as a social animal whose needs are not primarily physical and satiable but, rather, culturally determined and potentially unlimited. However, if all individuals had the same set of unlimited desires, no complex social structure would be possible. Consequently, some social or moral force must shape and limit these potentially unlimited desires. Society prescribes varying goals for different individuals and groups, sets limits on these goals, and prescribes the means that may legitimately be used to attain them.

In analyzing the function of stratification, functionalists see it as the mechanism through which society encourages men to seek to achieve the diverse positions necessary in a complex social system. The vast variety of positions that must be filled differ in their requirements for skill, education, intelligence, commitment to work, willingness to exercise power resources against others, and the like. Functionalist theory posits that in an unstratified society—that is, one in which rewards are relatively equal for all tasks—those positions which require more work, postponement of gratification, greater anxiety, and the like will not be filled by the most able people. The stratification system is perceived, therefore, as a motivation system; it is society's mechanism for encouraging the most able people to perform the most demanding roles in order to have the society operate efficiently.

The theory also suggests that status—honorific prestige—is the most general and persistent form of stratification because what human beings as social animals most require to satisfy their ego needs is recognition from others. Beyond a certain point, economic rewards and power are valued, not for themselves, but because economic or power positions are symbolic indicators of high status. Hence, the functionalist school of stratification agrees with Weber that stratification, or differential hierarchical reward, is an inherent aspect of complex society and that status as a source of motivation is inherently a scarce resource.

The emphasis in functional analysis on the need for hierarchical differentiation does not, of course, explain how men evaluate different individuals in the stratification system. Parsons has pointed to three sets of characteristics which are used as a basis of ranking. These are *possessions,* or those attributes which people own; *qualities,* belonging to individuals and including traits that are ascribed, such as race, lineage, or sex, or that are attributed as permanent characteristics, such as a specific ability; and *performances,* or evaluations of the ways in which individuals have fulfilled their roles—in short, judgments about achievements. Societies, according to Parsons, vary considerably in the degree to which their central value systems emphasize possessions, qualities, or performances in locating people on the social hierarchy. Thus, ideally, a feudal social system stresses ascribed qualities, a capitalist society emphasizes possessions, and a pure communist system would assign prestige according to performance. Parsons has stated that no actual society has ever come close to any of these three "ideal-type" models; each society has included elements of all three. However, the variation in the core ideal values does inform the nature of the stratification system, patterns of mobility, and the like.[18]

If we assume, as most functionalists do, that the function of stratification is to act as a system of role allocation, then it follows that a key requisite for an operating social system is a relatively stable system of social rankings. That is, there must be consensus in a society about what sorts of activities and symbols are valued; without such consensus, the society could not operate. Given this assumption, an ongoing system of stratification requires a general set of ideological justifications. There must be various mechanisms which explain, justify, and propagate the system of inequality, and which cause men to accept as legitimate the fact of their own inequality. From an ideal-typical point of view, a system of stratification that is stable would set for various groups within societies goals that could be achieved by all within each group. Feudal societies, which theoretically separate the population from birth into distinct hierarchical strata which cannot be crossed, but within which men may succeed and gain social recognition for doing a good job, represent perhaps the extreme form of stratification as something that adjusts men to the needs of society. Theoretically, in a society in which individuals were socialized to accept attainable positions as the proper and necessary fulfillment of their role in life, men would feel "free" and satisfied. The sense of freedom, of being one's own master and of achieving what one thinks one wants to achieve, exists only where the means-ends relationship defined by society is stable—that is, where men do in fact get what they have been taught to want.

But it is extremely doubtful whether any such system of balanced means-ends relationships within a stratification system ever existed or could exist. The assumption that individuals seek to maximize the esteem in which they are held implies that those who are in low-valued positions are subject to punishment. To be valued negatively means to be told that one is no good, that one is bad. Consequently, it may be argued that there is an inherent tension between the need to maximize esteem and the requirements of a stratification system.

In actual stratification systems, this tension appears to be alleviated by various transvaluational mechanisms. That is, there seems in all societies to be a reverse stratification system, the most enduring form of which is usually found in religion. Inherent in many religions is the belief that wealth and power are associated with sin and evil, while virtue is associated with poverty. Christianity and Hinduism, for example, both posit that righteousness will somehow be rewarded in the hereafter, so that the virtuous poor will ultimately be able to look down upon the wicked rich. This mechanism, which holds out the hope of subsequent reward for adhering to the morality of the present, does not, of course, challenge the existing secular distribution of privilege. It does, however, reflect the inherent tension within stratified society, that there is both acceptance and rejection of the value system by the underprivileged.

Durkheim and Functionalist Theory

Durkheim assumed that preindustrial society had been reasonably stable in that it had prescribed different sets of goals for different strata. He assumed that the lowly in feudal society had not resented not being high and that feudalism had been so organized that a man could and did obtain a sense of self-respect within his own group. Industrial society, he thought, is quite different. Society no longer provides the individual with definitions of means and ends that allow him to attain the goals his society defines as worthwhile. A highly integrated normative order such as feudalism had provided everyone with the possibility of feeling that his life was meaningful and successful within a given castelike stratum. In modern society, however, wealth and power become ends in themselves, and most people, unable to attain high prestige, find their own lives in conflict with social norms. Such conflict of norms leads to anomie, the breakdown of normative order, which becomes a chronic condition in industrial society.[19]

Industrial society prescribes universalistic goals in monetary or bureaucratic terms. Since the norms of the market place and the bureaucracy prescribe common orientations and similar goals for all, it is inevitable that many men will experience life as failure. For Durkheim, the weakness of the stratification system of industrial society is that, basically, it encourages only one set of values, those involving individual success. This pressure on the individual to achieve results produces anomie—Durkheim's equivalent of alienation. The higher rate of suicide in industrial as compared with traditional society was, in part, explained by Durkheim in these terms. The individual no longer has the sense of being socially integrated that was possible in a *Gemeinschaft* society, that is, one with a strong set of closely related means and ends linked to the religious system. The individual does not have the means to achieve the universalistic goals set by modern society, and the society's normative order does not support him in his daily life, guide his activities, or give him a sense that his life is worthwhile. When the normative structure collapses, when individuals lose their sense of being involved in meaningful means-ends relationships, many break down, engage in obsessive behavior, and lose their ability to relate to achievable goals, and some commit suicide.

The key to understanding Durkheim's contribution to the discussion of alienation and stratification is his emphasis on a stable society as a prerequisite for an integrated personality. The absence of an established harmony of means and ends, far from producing freedom, produces, according to Durkheim, resentment and apathy—the war of each against all. Durkheim's theory therefore leads to the ironic conclusion that people should feel freest in a closed, integrated system in which they have little choice of occupation or opportunity for social mobility, while in an open, universalistic system they should feel coerced, dehumanized, estranged. In the latter case it follows that they will also experience a need to, in Erich Fromm's words, "escape from freedom." Society's emphasis on success thus becomes the principal source of alienation.

Durkheim's analysis of anomie ties into Weber's discussion of the alienative properties of bureaucracy for, as Fromm, Merton, Riesman, and others have pointed out, to succeed in a bureaucratic society, one must not simply conform to a work role—one must sell one's personality to one's superiors. This implies that the rules for success are often very imprecise and hence create confusion about means and ends.

Anomie, Social Change, and Rebellion

Durkheim's account of what Merton has called the "seeming contradictions between cultural goals and socially restricted access to these goals" is a key aspect of the theory of social change that is inherent in Durkheimian functionalism.[20] Since no complex society can achieve a complete balance between its emphases on ends and means, stratification systems always generate pressure on individuals and strata to deviate systematically from the cultural prescriptions of the society, and hence they foster social change. As Merton puts it:

> The distribution of statuses through competition must be so organized that positive incentives for adherence to status obligations are provided for *every position* within the distributive order. Otherwise, as will soon become plain, aberrant behavior ensues. It is, indeed, my central hypothesis that aberrant behavior may be regarded sociologically as a symptom of dissociation between culturally prescribed aspirations and socially structured avenues for realizing these aspirations.[21]

The outcome of the possible relations between approved goals and prescribed means has been analyzed in detail by Merton and by numerous other writers. These relations create a variety of strains fostering change. Thus innovation in the means of getting ahead occurs among those who feel strongly the culturally prescribed mandate to succeed but lack such culturally approved means to do so as access to capital, skills, education, and proper ascribed background characteristics. Innovation may have positive and negative consequences from the point of view of society. On the positive side is the effort to get ahead by "building a better mousetrap," that is, by providing services that did not exist before, such as credit buying, which was first diffused by Jewish businessmen. On the negative side are the forms of innovation that are regarded as illegitimate. As Bell has pointed out, organized crime has constituted a major avenue of mobility in American life.[22] Minority ethnic groups and those of recent immigrant stock have contributed disproportionately to the ranks of professional criminals.

While Merton has elaborated on the sources of social and individual tensions in this area, more pertinent here is his emphasis that such tensions may also produce rebellion. Rebellion by the lower strata, he has argued, may be viewed as an adaptive response called for when the existing social system is seen as an obstacle to the satisfaction of legitimate needs and wants. In means-ends terms, rebellion involves the establishment of a new set of goals which are attractive to those who feel themselves "outcasts" in the existing system. When rebellion is not a generalized response but is limited to relatively powerless groups, it can lead to the formation of subgroups alienated from the rest of the community but united among themselves. Of course, rebellion may also take a political form in an effort to overthrow the existing society and replace it with one that stresses other values.

Emphasis on these and allied sources of rebellion advances the study of alienation and prospective lower-class rebellion beyond the concern with objective social inferiority and economic exploitation. The study of values in this context helps to explain the phenomenon that many quite poverty-stricken strata in different countries do not rebel and are often even conservative conformists, while other, relatively affluent strata, whose position is improving objectively, may provide the mass base for widespread rebellion.[23] It is clearly possible, under the means-ends formula, for a very lowly group to accept its place and income because it has achieved as much as it has been socialized to aspire to. Conversely, a much more well-to-do group whose aspiration levels have been raised sharply as a result of rapid urbanization, greater education, access to international media, recent involvement in industry, and exposure to the blandishments of unions and leftist political parties may experience the phenomenon of unlimited "rising expectations" and hence feel dissatisfied and prove receptive to a new myth which locates "the source of large-scale frustrations in the social structure and . . . portray[s] an alternative structure" that would be more satisfying.[24]

Functionalist sociology stresses the way in which stratification fulfills certain basic needs of complex social systems and so becomes one of the principal stabilizing mechanisms of complex societies. Like the Marxist and Weberian forms of analysis, it points to ways in which the demands of a stratification system press men to act against their own interests, and alienate them from autonomous choice. However, the focus in functionalism on means–ends relationships reveals the conflict-generating potential of stratification systems, in which goals are inherently scarce resources. Hence, functional analysis, like the other two, locates sources of consensus and cleavage in the hierarchical structures of society.

Empirical Studies

A considerable amount of the research on stratification by American sociologists has stemmed directly from functional analysis. Perhaps the most extensive single set of studies is contained in the many volumes by W. Lloyd Warner and his associates reporting on the "social class" (i.e., status) system of a number of American communities.[25] Warner, an anthropologist by training and originally a follower of Durkheim, argued that any effort to deal in functional terms with the social system of a modern community must relate many of the institutional and behavioral patterns of the community to the needs of the classes within them rather than to the larger system as such. Using the method of reputational analysis (asking people in the community to rank others and seeing who associated with whom as status equals), Warner located five or six social classes ranging from "upper-upper" to "lower-lower." Each of them was found to possess a number of distinct class characteristics, such as intrafamily behavior, associational memberships, and attitudes on a variety of issues. On the whole, Warner saw class divisions as contributing to social stability rather than to conflict, because the strata are separated into relatively distinct elements that have a more or less balanced and integrated culture. He interpreted his data as indicating that those in lower positions tend to respect those above them in the status hierarchy and to follow their lead on many issues. While most sociologists would agree with Warner concerning the existence of the sort of status groupings that he described (Weber presented a picture of American status relations in much the same terms), many would disagree with him concerning the degree of consensus within the system as to where individuals are located and would tend to agree more with Merton that tensions and conflicts are inherent in any hierarchical order. It is interesting to note, however, that while the various community studies of the accorded status system do suggest considerable ambivalence about where various individuals or families rank, particularly if they are not close to the very top or bottom of the system, investigations concerning the prestige rankings of occupations indicate considerable consensus both within and among a variety of nations.[26] The prestige studies would seem to be in line with the assumption of functionalist theory that consensus in the desirability of different occupational roles is necessary in order to motivate the most competent individuals to seek those positions which are valued most.

Criticism of the Functionalist Approach

Functionalist theory has been sharply criticized by a number of sociologists who argue that while systems of widespread inequality characterize all existing complex societies, this fact does not demonstrate that inequality is a social requisite for a stable society, as many functionalists argue. Rather, these critics urge that systems of stratification persist and take the varying forms they do because the privileged strata have power and are able to impose their group interests on the society. The greater rewards in income and status received by various positions reflect greater power more than the need to motivate individuals to secure them. The value systems related to stratification therefore reflect the functional needs of the dominant strata, not those of the social system as such.[27] A Polish sociologist, Wlodzimierz Wesolowski, has suggested that functionalist sociologists, particularly Davis and Moore, who have written the most comprehensive contemporary statement of the functionalist position, are wrong when they emphasize the need for stratification as a system of motivation in the form of material advantage or prestige.[28] He has contended that there are alternative systems of social organization that can sharply reduce inequality in prestige and income while motivating people to seek higher education and fill responsible positions. Hence, class differences that derive from such forms of inequality may decline greatly. Wesolowski, however, agrees with the functionalists that complex social systems will continue to be organized on hierarchical lines, because systems of authority and command are necessary. Men will continue to be divided between those who occupy "positions of authority . . . who have the right (and duty) to give orders while the others have the duty to obey them." And he has noted that Friedrich Engels, Marx's closest intellectual collaborator, who "said that in a communist system the State as a weapon of class domination would wither away, nevertheless, declared that it would be impossible to think of any great modern industrial enterprise or of the organization of the future communist society without authority-or superiority-subordination relationships."[29]

Wesolowski agrees with the functionalists that stratification is inevitable because differentials in authority relationships, not variations in income or prestige, are necessary. As he puts it, "if there is any functional necessity for stratification, it is the necessity of stratification according to the criterion of authority and not according to the criterion of material advantage or prestige. Nor does the necessity of stratification derive from the need to induce people for the acquirement of qualifications, but from the very fact that humans live collectively."[30]

Wesolowski has presented in general terms a formulation very similar to that of the German sociologist Ralf Dahrendorf, who has tried to reformulate Marx's theoretical assumptions so as to deal more adequately with certain structural changes in Western society—especially those which have resulted in the divorce of ownership from management that is characteristic of the modern corporation.[31] Many have argued that this separation negates Marx, since it means the disappearance of the class of private capitalists as a powerful stratum. Dahrendorf, however, has suggested that the only significant difference this change makes is that it is now more meaningful to speak of the differential distribution of *authority* as the basis of class formation than it is to speak of the ownership of the means of production. It is differential access to authority positions and, therefore, to power and prestige that gives rise to contemporary class conflict, for those who are excluded from authority in "imperatively co-ordinated associations" (a term Dahrendorf borrowed from Weber) will be in conflict with those who have command over them. Articulation of manifest interest and organization of interest groups then become the dynamite for social-structural change.

Functionalism and Marxism

In urging that the universality of stratification, or hierarchical differentiation–though not, it should be noted, of social class–is linked to the functional requirements for a power hierarchy, Wesolowski has built an interesting theoretical bridge between Marxist and functionalist sociology. For his and Dahrendorf's lines of reasoning ultimately are not greatly different from the functionalist approach to power presented by Parsons. The latter, of course, does not emphasize the theme of power as self-interested, which is found in the Marxian tradition, or that of coercion, which was stressed by Weber. Rather, Parsons has suggested that power—in his terms, the ability to mobilize resources necessary for the operation of the system—should be viewed in value-neutral terms, as follows. Inherent in the structure of complex society, especially in the division of labor, is the existence of authority roles, holders of which are obligated to initiate acts that are socially necessary. Most of the things done by those at the summits of organizations or societies are necessary. If individuals and groups are to achieve their goals within the division of labor, it must include a complex system of interactions. The more complex the system, Parsons has argued, the more dependent individuals are on others for the attainment of their goals, that is, the less free or powerful they are. And power is basically control over the allocation of resources and roles so as to make a given system operative. Power, under any system of values, resides in having what people desire, because they will obey for the sake of getting what they want. Finally, unless the capacity to organize the behavior of those in a system existed, sharply differentiated societies could not operate.[32]

It should be noted that there is a coincidence of the Marxist and functionalist approaches to political power. Both approaches view it as a social utility— as the means, par excellence, through which societies attain their objectives, including the expansion of available resources. Elite theories of power, on the other hand, see it in ''zero-sum'' terms, that is, they assume a fixed amount of power, so that the gain of one group or individual necessarily involves the loss of others. Two reviews of C. Wright Mills's analysis of the American power elite—one by a functionalist, Parsons, and the other by the student of stratification who, among leading American sociologists, stands closest to Marxism, Robert S. Lynd—criticized Mills for having a zero-sum game approach to power and for identifying it with domination.[33] That is, both Lynd and Parsons agreed that power should be viewed, both sociologically and politically, in the light of its positive functions as an agency of the general community and that it is erroneous to view power, as Mills did, solely or even primarily in terms of powerholders seeking to enhance their own interests.

There is, of course, a link with stratification theory in Parsons's analysis of power, since he has assumed that what people value most are economic advantage and esteem. It follows from this that those who possess the qualities which place them at the upper levels of the economic and status hierarchies also have the most power. Money and influence, Parsons has noted, are exchangeable for power, since power is the ability to mobilize resources through controlling the action of others.

The Dimensions of Stratification

The foregoing discussion of the Marxist, Weberian, and functionalist approaches to social class analysis has distinguished a number of issues that continue to concern sociologists. Instead of moving toward one concept of social class, students of stratification have generally reacted to an awareness of the complexity of the subject by differentiating a large number of apparently relevant concepts, most of which are directly derivable from the three traditions discussed above. The differences in approach have, in large measure, reflected variations in the intellectual concerns of the scholars involved.

Contemporary students of stratification continue to be divided into two groups, those who urge that there is a single dimension underlying all stratification and those who believe that stratification may best be conceptualized as multidimensional. That is, they disagree as to whether economic class position, social status, power, income, and the like are related to one underlying factor in most societies, or whether they should be considered as distinct although related dimensions of the stratification system. To some degree this controversy may be perceived as a continuation on a more formal level of the differences between the approaches of Marx and Weber. However, some of those who uphold the single attribute position are far from being Marxists. They do not believe that position in the economic structure determines all other aspects of status; rather, they would argue that statistical analysis suggests the presence of a basic common factor. For analytic purposes, however, the controversy cannot be resolved by statistical manipulation, since some of those who favor a multidimensional approach would argue that even if it turns out that these various aspects of stratification do form part of a single latent attribute, there is enough variation among them to justify the need to analyze the cases in which individuals or groups are ranked higher on certain dimensions than on others.

If we assume, as most contemporary sociologists do, that stratification may most usefully be conceptualized in multidimensional terms, we are confronted with the variations in dimensions which various theorists emphasize. The dimensions they have suggested may be grouped into three categories: (1) *objective* status, or aspects of stratification that structure environments differently enough to evoke variations in behavior; (2) *accorded* status, or the prestige accorded to individuals and groups by others; (3) *subjective* status, or the personal sense of location within the social hierarchy felt by various individuals. These approaches in turn may be further broken down in terms of important variables, as follows.

Objective Class Concepts

Perhaps the most familiar component of objective status is power position within the economic structure. This is essentially Marx's criterion for class: persons are located according to their degree of control over the means of production. In the first analysis this serves to distinguish owners from employees. Owners, however, may vary in their degree of economic security and power, as large businessmen differ from small ones, and workers also may vary according to the bargaining power inherent in the relative scarcity of the skills they possess.

Another important concept in this area is extent of economic life chances. Weber perceived economic status not only in terms of ownership but also in terms of the probability of receiving a given economic return, or income. Thus an employee role, such as engineer or lawyer, which gave someone a higher probability than a small businessman's of earning high income, would place him in a higher class position. Essentially, this dimension refers to power in the market. Indeed, the simple difference in income received has been suggested as the best way to measure economic class.

Variation in the relative status of different occupations has also been seen as an important criterion for differentiating positions in the economic hierarchy. This approach has increasingly come to be used in studies of social mobility. Occupational prestige is, of course, a form of accorded status, except that what is being ranked are occupations, not individuals or groups.

Another aspect of stratification that is sometimes perceived as an objective one is power, which may be defined as the ability to affect the life chances of others, or conversely as the amount of freedom from control by others. Power may also be conceptualized as the set of probabilities that given role relationships will allow individuals to define their own will—that is, to impose their version of order even against the resistance of others. This dimension is extremely difficult to describe in operational terms: how, for instance, does one compare the different amounts and types of power possessed by labor leaders, Supreme Court justices, factory owners, and professors? It is also argued that power should not be regarded as an aspect of stratification in itself, as if it were comparable with economic class, but, rather, as the dynamic resultant of the forces brought into play in different types of social situations. Authority—legitimate power within a formal structure—is clearly hierarchical, but the rank order of authority usually applies only to a given authority structure within a society, not to the society itself.

Finally, a number of sociological studies have treated education as a major determinant of objective status and as a dimension of stratification. The differences in behavior and attitudes of those who are higher or lower in educational attainments have been demonstrated by empirical research. On the theoretical level, it is argued that education, like the various economic dimensions, affects the life chances of individuals–their degree of security, their status, and their ability to interact with others. People are given differential degrees of respect and influence according to their level of education.

Accorded Status

The dimension of accorded status is the one most sociologists tacitly or overtly refer to when they use the term "social class." This dimension involves the amount of status, honor, or deference that a given position commands in a society. Various methods are used to study accorded status, but in any case the location of individuals or groups in the status system depends on the opinion of the individuals who go to make up the system rather than the opinion of the sociologist who observes it. Accorded status, then, is a result of the felt perceptions of others, and a social class based on accorded status is composed of individuals who accept each other as equals and therefore as qualified for intimate association in friendship, marriage, and the like.

Since this concept depends on rankings by others, it is difficult to apply it to large-scale social systems, particularly nations, except at the level of the small uppermost social class. Individuals from different communities cannot rank each other unless they rely on criteria more objective than social acceptability. The social class consisting of individuals who have, roughly speaking, the same attributes will vary with size of community; for instance, the type of individual who may be in the highest social class of a small town will probably be in the middle class of a large city. It has, in fact, been argued that the larger the community, the more likely it is that accorded status will correspond to objective status. In other words, individuals who live in large communities are more prone to make status judgments about others on the basis of knowledge about their jobs, how much their homes are worth, how many years of education they have had, and the like.

Accorded status tends to become an ascribed characteristic, that is, one that can be inherited. "Background," which usually means family identification, is the way in which people define the source of accorded status. This implies that in addition to specific lineage, other visible ascribed characteristics, such as race, ethnicity, and religion, often constitute elements in status placement. In all societies that contain a variety of racial, ethnic, or religious groups, each such group is differentially ranked in honorific or status terms. Those groups which were present first and retain the highest economic and political positions tend to have the highest status. Thus in the United States, such traits as being white, Anglo-Saxon, and Protestant (preferably of the historically earliest American denominations, such as Episcopal, Congregational, or Quaker) convey high status on those possessing them. The status attributes of various socially visible groups are also determined by various typical characteristics of their members. Thus religious or ethnic groups which are poor on the average are of low status, and wealthy members of such groups tend to be discriminated against socially by comparably well-to-do members of more privileged groups (for instance, a well-to-do Baptist will have lower status in most American communities than a comparably affluent Episcopalian).

Status, it should be noted, is a power resource in much the same way as economic position or political authority. Since status involves being accepted by those in high positions, and since the desire for status is universal, men seek to accommodate their actions to those who can confer status on them.

Subjective Status

Unlike objective and accorded class concepts, which locate individuals in the stratification hierarchy according to the judgments of analysts or of the community, subjective status categories involve efforts to discover the way in which the individual himself perceives the stratification hierarchy. In sociology there are essentially two main traditions of dealing with subjective positions, one based on the methodological device of self-identification and the other on reference group theory.

Self-Identification. The technique of self-identification is used to determine the extent to which given individuals or portions of specific groups see themselves as members of a given class or other group that may be located in terms of stratification. Efforts to locate individuals have involved asking them to place themselves in one of a number of class categories furnished by the investigator in such questions as "Do you think of yourself as a member of the upper, middle, working, or lower class?"[34] The number of alternatives furnished respondents may, of course, be larger or smaller than this. Other investigators, instead of following this procedure, have sought to find out what categories people use to describe the social hierarchy.[35]

Reference Group Theory. The groups that individuals use as reference points by which to evaluate themselves or their activities are known in sociology as reference groups.[36] They can be, but need not be, groups to which an individual belongs. Thus a person may judge his degree of occupational achievement by comparing his attainments with those which preponderate among his fellow ethnic, racial, or religious group members, people he went to school with, neighbors, or those who are more privileged than he is and whose position he would like to attain.[37]

Reference group theory assumes that individuals rarely use the total social structure as a reference group but, rather, that they judge their own status by comparison with smaller, more closely visible groups. The extent of satisfaction or dissatisfaction with status is held to depend on one's reference groups.

Reference groups are often derivable from structural factors; thus neighborhoods, factories, employers, schoolmates, and the like often constitute relevant reference groups. On the other hand, relevant reference groups may be manipulated, as when organized groups that are competing for support seek to affect the reference groups of those whose support they want so as to increase their sense of satisfaction or dissatisfaction.[38] The formation of class consciousness may be seen as a process in which members of the lower social strata change their reference groups: while class consciousness is dormant or incipient, the lower-class individual relates himself to various small groups; with the full emergence of class consciousness, he relates himself to aspects of the larger social structure.

Objective and Subjective Orientations

The fact that social class may be conceptualized both objectively and subjectively does not mean that these are in any sense mutually exclusive ways of looking at the social hierarchy. Almost all analysts, regardless of which approach they choose to stress, are interested in examining the interrelations between their conception of class and other factors, which they view either as determinants or as consequences of class variations. Thus, as has been noted, Marx was intensely interested in the subjective reactions of people to their location in the class structure.

It is significant that Richard Centers, who is most identified with the social-psychological approach to class as involving self-definition, initiated his study of the subject as a way of finding out to what extent American workers were class-conscious in the Marxist sense. In fact, Centers' work is more directly inspired by Marx than is that of many sociologists, who are more wont to approach the subject in objective terms.

It should also be noted that there are close links between elements in Marx's thought and contemporary reference group theory. In seeking to suggest hypotheses that would explain the relationship between objective position and anticipated subjective reactions, Marx advanced a theory of relative deprivation. He suggested that although objective improvement in the economic position of the workers could take place under capitalism, this would not prevent the emergence of "true" class consciousness, since the position of the capitalists would improve more rapidly than that of the workers. As he put it, the "material position of the worker has improved, . . . but at the cost of his social position. The social gulf that divides him from the capitalist has widened."[39] In another work Marx illustrated this generalization with the story of a man who was very happy with a small house in which he lived until a wealthy man came along and built a mansion next door: then, wrote Marx, the house of the worker suddenly became a hut in his eyes.[40]

Similarly, although Marx never dealt with the distinction between class and status on a conceptual level, there are frequent references in his historical writings to distinctions among social strata in various countries. These distinctions actually reflect what would now be called variations among status groups. Perhaps the most interesting formulation related to this question may be found in a major Marxist classic by Engels. In discussing political life in nineteenth-century England, Engels pointed out in very clear terms that status may be an independent source of power, more important in a given situation than economic power:

> In England, the bourgeoisie never held undivided sway. Even the victory of 1832 left the landed aristocracy in almost exclusive possession of all the leading government offices. The meekness with which the wealthy middle class submitted to this remained inconceivable to me until the great Liberal manufacturer, Mr. W. E. Forster, in a public speech implored the young men of Bradford to learn French, as a means to get on in the world, and quoted from his own experience how sheepish he looked when, as a Cabinet Minister, he had to move in society where French was, at least, as necessary as English! The fact was, the English middle class of that time were, as a rule, quite uneducated upstarts, and could not help leaving to the aristocracy those superior government places where other qualifications were required than mere insular narrowness and insular conceit, seasoned by business sharpness. . . . The English bourgeoisie are, up to the present day [1892], so deeply penetrated by a sense of their social inferiority that they keep up, at their own expense and that of the nation, an ornamental caste of drones to represent the nation worthily at all state functions; and they consider themselves highly honored whenever one of themselves is found worthy of admission into this select and privileged body, manufactured, after all, by themselves.[41]

Clearly, what Engels was describing is a situation in which an old upper class, which had declined in economic power, continued to maintain its control over the governmental machinery because it remained the highest status group in the society. Those with less status but more economic resources conformed to the standards set up by the higher status group.

Stable and Unstable Status Systems

The relationships among the different dimensions of stratification vary in different types of societies and different periods; they are probably at their weakest during periods of rapid social change involving the rise of new occupational strata, shifts from rural to urban predominance, and changes in the status and authority of key institutions, such as religion and education. Of all the relatively stable types of society, the ones in which the various dimensions of stratification are most closely correlated are rural, caste, and feudal societies. The growth of industrial and urban society in Europe and America has resulted in a system of stratification characterized by wide discrepancies between class and objective status, and between both of these and the subjective attributes of status. Currently, as Western society moves into a "postindustrial" phase characterized by a considerable growth in the white-collar, technological, and service sectors of the economy and a relative decline in employment in manufacturing, the relationships among the dimensions have become more tenuous. Status, economic reward, and power are tied to educational achievement, position in some large-scale bureaucracy, access to political authority, and the like. In a predominantly bureaucratic society, property as such has become a less important source of status and social mobility. Complaints about alienation and dehumanization are found more commonly among students, intellectuals, and other sectors of the educated middle classes than among the working class. Most recently, sections of the radical Left have openly discussed the revolutionary role of university students and the petty bourgeoisie, and have seen the organized proletariat in Western society as a relatively conservative group, unavailable for radical politics.

These developments may reflect the fact that some of the most politically relevant discontent in the bureaucratic "affluent society" of the 1960s seems to be inherent in social tensions induced by *status inconsistencies*. However, the bulk of resentment against the stratification system is still rooted in objective deprivation and exploitation. The concept of status inconsistency introduced by Lenski, who derived it from Weber, refers to the situation of individuals or groups that are differentially located on various dimensions of stratification.[42] Persons in such a situation are exposed to conflicting sets of expectations: for instance, those who are high in educational attainments but are employed in relatively low-paid occupations tend to be more dissatisfied than those whose stratification attributes are totally consistent. As evidence in support of this assumption it is possible to cite research findings that among the relatively well to do, those with discrepant status attributes are more likely to favor change in the power structure and to have more liberal or leftist attitudes than those with status attributes that are mutually consistent.[43] Consequently, the increase in status discrepancy inherent in situations of rapid social change should result in an increase in overall discontent and, among those in the more ambiguous status positions (which now occurs largely in the well-educated middle strata), in greater receptivity to the myths justifying rebellion. In industrialized societies those who form the underprivileged strata but who have consistent status attributes remain politically on the left but show little interest in radical change. Because all social change generates status discrepancies, rebellious and extremist mass movements are more likely to be found during periods of rapid industrialization and economic growth, and in areas where immigration has caused sudden population growth, than in industrially mature urbanized areas.

Analysis of the consequences of status discrepancies has yielded seemingly contradictory results largely because some researchers treat all discrepancies as necessarily equal in their effects. For example, institutionalized discrepancies, such as those which result when a member of a minority group becomes rich but is still discriminated against, are equated with inconsistencies between education and occupation, or between occupation and income. Highly visible institutionalized discrepancies should result in more active expression of resentment and more efforts to bring about *social* change than do loosely structured personal inconsistencies. The latter are more likely to be reflected in efforts by the individual to change his personal situation through various forms of mobility, including change in occupation, residence, or organization. The consequences of status discrepancies should therefore be investigated within broad status categories rather than for total societies. For instance, discrepancies among the poor may have effects very different from those they have among the well-to-do. A manual worker with a claim, based on good education or family background, to higher status than his occupational position allows him is more likely to be politically conservative than workers whose status attributes are consistent. Among the well-to-do, however, status inconsistency will impair claims to high positions and will induce favorable attitudes toward liberal or egalitarian ideologies. The effects of status inconsistencies in societies with relatively rigid status lines are quite different from their effects in societies that have relatively fluid stratification systems. Clearly, the concept of status inconsistency, though potentially a useful tool in class analysis, presupposes some systematic treatment of how the relationship between the various dimensions of status varies from one type of stratification to another.

The Future of Social Class

To conclude on a note of irony, it may be observed that in a certain sense history has underwritten one of Marx's basic assumptions, which is that the cultural superstructure, including political behavior and status relationships, is a function of the underlying economic and technological structure. As Marx put it in the Preface to *Capital:* "The country that is more developed industrially only shows, to the less developed, the image of its own future."[44] The most economically developed society should also have the most advanced set of class and political relationships. Since the United States is the most advanced society economically, its class system, regarded as part of its cultural superstructure, should be more appropriate to a technologically advanced society than the class systems of the less developed economies of Europe. In addition, one might argue that the United States, since it lacks a feudal past, should evolve the institutions of a highly developed society in their purest form. Hence, an unpolitical Marxist sociology would expect the social class relationships of the United States to present an image of the future of other societies that are moving in the same general economic direction. Characteristic of such a social system is a decline in emphasis on social class, that is, a decline of distinct visible strata with a "felt consciousness of kind." The various dimensions of stratification are more likely to operate in a crisscrossing fashion, increasing the numbers who are relatively high on some components of status and low on others. Highly developed societies of this kind, whether variants of the communist or the capitalist model, are more likely to possess systems of social stratification—varied rankings—than social classes.

These comments suggest the need to view stratification in international as well as national terms.[45] The differences between the average per capita income of the poorest and wealthiest nations are on the order of 40 or 50 to 1, that is, much greater than the differences among social strata within the industrially advanced nations. These variations in national wealth constitute structural parameters that greatly affect the "class" relationships between nations. A Chinese communist has already advanced the thesis that the significant class struggle is between the predominantly rural nations, which are underdeveloped and very poor, and the urbanized, wealthy ones.[46] He has also argued that the wealth of the latter has to a considerable degree reduced the political expression of class tensions within them, but that this should be seen as a result of exploitation by the economically advanced countries of the underdeveloped ones. Whether this thesis is warranted by the facts of international trade relationships or not, it does seem true that any analysis of class structures and their political consequences must in the future consider the impact of variation in national incomes. Many in the elite of the poorer part of the world see themselves as the leaders of oppressed peoples; the radicalism of the intellectuals, university students, military officers, and the like in the less developed nations can be related to the social and economic inferiority of their countries, rather than to their position in the class structure. Such considerations take us far afield from the conventional Western sociological concerns with class relationships, but they clearly are relevant to any effort at specifying the sources of class behavior and ideologies. As sociology becomes more comparative in outlook and research, we may expect efforts to link class analysis of individual nations to the facts of international stratification.

Notes

1. Karl Marx, *Capital*, Vol. III (Moscow: Foreign Languages Publishing House, 1962), pp. 862–63.
2. David Ricardo, *Principles* (New York: E. P. Dutton, 1937).
3. Adam Smith, *The Wealth of Nations* (London: Methuen, 1930).
4. Daniel de Leon, *James Madison and Karl Marx* (New York: New York Labor News, 1932).
5. Marx, *Capital*, Vol. III.
6. Karl Marx, "The Eighteenth Brumaire of Louis Napoleon," in Marx, *Selected Works*, Vol. I (Moscow: Foreign Languages Publishing House, 1962), p. 334.
7. Karl Marx, *The Poverty of Philosophy* (New York: International Publishers, 1963), pp. 146–47.
8. *Ibid.*, p. 147.
9. Karl Marx, *Early Writings* (New York: McGraw-Hill, 1964), pp. 120–34.
10. Max Weber, *Essays in Sociology* H. H. Gerth and C. W. Mills (eds.) (New York: Oxford University Press, 1946), pp. 180–95.
11. V. I. Lenin, *What Is to Be Done?* (New York: International Publishers, 1929).
12. Max Weber, *The Theory of Social and Economic Organization* (London: Routledge & Kegan Paul, 1947), pp. 427–28.
13. Thorstein Veblen, *The Theory of the Leisure Class* (New York: Modern Library, 1934).
14. Robert Michels, *Political Parties* (New York: Free Press, 1966), pp. 247–48.
15. T. H. Marshall, *Class, Citizenship and Social Development* (Garden City: Doubleday-Anchor, 1965), pp. 71–134.
16. Weber, *Essays in Sociology*, pp. 196–98.
17. Emile Durkheim, *The Division of Labor* (Glencoe, Ill.: Free Press, 1947).
18. Talcott Parsons, "A Revised Analytical Approach to the Theory of Social Stratification," in R. Bendix and S. M. Lipset (eds.), *Class, Status and Power* (Glencoe, Ill.: Free Press, 1953), pp. 92–128.
19. Emile Durkheim, *Suicide* (Glencoe, Ill.: Free Press, 1951), pp. 246–57.
20. Robert K. Merton, *Social Theory and Social Structure* (Glencoe, Ill.: Free Press, 1957), p. 123.
21. *Ibid.*, p. 134.
22. Daniel Bell, *The End of Ideology* (Glencoe, Ill.: Free Press, 1960), pp. 115–36.
23. Durkheim, *Suicide*, p. 254.
24. Merton, *Social Theory and Social Structure*, p. 156.
25. W. L. Warner, J. O. Low, Paul S. Lunt, and Leo Srole, *Yankee City* (New Haven: Yale University Press, 1963).
26. Robert S. Hodge, Donald J. Treiman, and Peter H. Rossi, "A Comparative Study of Occupational Prestige," in R. Bendix and S. M. Lipset (eds.), *Class, Status, and Power: Social Stratification in Comparative Perspective* (New York: Free Press, 1966) rev. ed., pp. 309–21.
27. Melvin Tumin, "Some Principles of Stratification: A Critical Analysis," in Bendix and Lipset, *Class, Status and Power*, rev. ed., pp. 53–58; Walter Buckley, "Social Stratification and the Functional Theory of Social Differentiation," in S. M. Lipset and Neil Smelser (eds.), *Sociology: The Progress of a Decade* (Englewood Cliffs, N. J.: Prentice-Hall, 1961), pp. 478–84.
28. Wlodzimierz Wesolowski, "Some Notes on the Functional Theory of Stratification," in Bendix and Lipset, *Class, Status and Power*, rev. ed., pp. 64–69.

Kingsley Davis and Wilbert Moore, "Some Principles of Stratification," in Bendix and Lipset, *Class, Status and Power*, rev. ed., pp. 47–53.

29. Wesolowski, "Some Notes," p. 68.
30. Ibid., p. 69.
31. Ralf Dahrendorf, *Class and Class Conflict in Industrial Society* (Stanford: Stanford University Press, 1959). See also Gerhard Lenski, *Power and Privilege* (New York: McGraw-Hill, 1966).
32. Talcott Parsons, "On the Concept of Political Power," in Bendix and Lipset, *Class, Status and Power*, pp. 240–65.
33. C. Wright Mills, *The Power Elite* (New York: Oxford University Press, 1956). Talcott Parsons, "The Distribution of Power in American Society," *World Politics* 10 (1957): 123–43. Robert S. Lynd, "Power in the United States," *The Nation* 182 (12 May 1956): 408–11, and "Power in American Society as Resource and Problem," in Arthur Kornhauser (ed.), *Problems of Power in American Democracy* (Detroit: Wayne State University Press, 1957), pp. 1–45.
34. Richard Centers, *The Psychology of Social Class* (Princeton: Princeton University Press, 1949).
35. Jerome Manis and B. N. Meltzer, "Some Correlates of Class Consciousness among Textile Workers," *American Journal of Sociology* 69 (September 1963): 177–84.
36. Herbert H. Hyman, *The Psychology of Status*, Archives of Psychology, No. 269 (1942).
37. Merton, *Social Theory and Social Structure*, pp. 225–386.
38. S. M. Lipset and Martin Trow, "Reference Group Theory and Trade-Union Wage Policy," in Mirra Komarovsky (ed.), *Common Frontiers of the Social Sciences* (Glencoe, Ill.: Free Press, 1957), pp. 391–411.
39. Karl Marx, "Wage, Labor and Capital," in Marx, *Selected Works,* Vol. I, p. 273.
40. Karl Marx, "Value, Price and Profit," in ibid., pp. 268–69.
41. Friedrich Engels, *Socialism, Utopian and Scientific* (New York: International Publishers, 1938), pp. 25–26.
42. Gerhard Lenski, "Status Crystallization: A Non-Vertical Dimension of Social Status," in Lipset and Smelser, *Sociology*, pp. 485–94.
43. I. W. Goffman, "Status Consistency and Preference for Change in Power," *American Sociological Review* 22 (1957): 275–81.
44. Karl Marx, *Capital,* Vol. 1 (Moscow: Foreign Languages Publishing House, 1958), pp. 8–9.
45. Gustavo Lagos, *International Stratification and Underdeveloped Countries* (Chapel Hill: University of North Carolina Press, 1963); and Irving Louis Horowitz, *Three Worlds of Development: The Theory and Practice of International Stratification* (New York: Oxford University Press, 1966).
46. Lin Piao, "Long Live the Victory of the Peoples' War," *The Peking Review* 8 (3 September 1965): 9–39.

3

A Concept and Its History:
The End of Ideology

The proposition that advanced industrial or postindustrial society would be characterized by a "decline" in—or even the "end" of—ideology asserted by many writers during the 1950s and early 1960s came under sharp criticism in the late 1960s and early 1970s. Seemingly, the reemergence of left-wing politics in the form of assorted "New Lefts" and the growth of mass movements based on excluded elements (ethnic minorities, women, students) constitute *prima facie* evidence that the "end-of-ideology" writers were wrong. A whole host of left-wing intellectuals emphasized this "error" in order to discredit "pluralistic" political analysis. They argued that its basic inadequacy had been demonstrated by the fact that some of its more prominent spokesmen, particularly Raymond Aron, Daniel Bell, Edward Shils, and myself, mistakenly predicted "the end of ideology."[1] Typical of such attacks were comments made in a review in the *Times Literary Supplement* of a book dealing with ideologies:

> Not so very long ago Raymond Aron, Daniel Bell and Seymour Martin Lipset, among others, were confidently predicting the decline of ideological fervour in the Western industrialized countries. . . . The fact was, of course, that this itself was an ideology; a tacit one, no doubt, but one, nevertheless, that rationalized and supported the existing system. . . . In effect what the proponents of the idea of the decline of ideology were saying was that, in Mannheim's terms, utopia was dead. . . . This was wrong . . .; the past two decades have been characterized by a growth and proliferation of total ideologies.[2]

Kenneth Keniston, an American faculty supporter of the student activism of the 1960s, also criticized the writings of "Daniel Bell, Seymour Martin Lipset, and Edward Shils that the age of ideology was over" as patently wrong. He argued that their "historically parochial" liberal orientation prevented them "from anticipating, much less understanding, what was increasingly to happen among a growing minority of the young during the 1960s."[3]

A Russian scholar, L. N. Moskvichev, the deputy head of the Chair of Marxist-Leninist Philosophy of the Academy of Social Sciences of the Central Committee of the Communist Party of the Soviet Union, singled out the writings on the subject by Raymond Aron, Edward Shils, Daniel Bell, and Lipset. He noted that the theory of the end of ideology "is particularly popular among right-wing social democrats and modern revisionists and serves in some degree to substantiate their ideas of 'liberal' socialism, 'socialism with a human face' or various 'models' of socialist society."[4]

Although this chapter focuses on left-wing critics, it should be recognized that, as Moskvichov notes, "There are a number of authors who take a right-wing ideological stand for whom the theory is nothing more than irresponsible 'gobbledygook' which leads to the West being disarmed ideologically in the face of world communism."[5]

The implicit assumption in the leftist criticism is that an alternative and more accurate estimate was presented by radical thinkers, who anticipated a revival of revolutionary politics in the West. Generally, most of these polemicists make their point by ridiculing a variant of the "end of ideology" that was never stated by any of those attacked.[6] More significant, however, as a phenomenon to be studied by those interested in the sociology of knowledge—or the ethics of controversy, or indeed the selective ideological character of memory—is the way in which these critics conveniently ignore the varying ideological background of discussions of the decline of ideology and political conflict in the years preceding the rise of the New Left. It may be worthwhile recalling some of that history for the record.

The Origins of the Concept

As with many other "politically relevant" concepts, the famous phrase first appeared in a Marxist classic, Friedrich Engels' essay on Feuerbach. Engels argued that "there would be an *end to all ideology*" unless the material interests underlying all ideologies remained "of necessity unknown to these persons."[7] That is, insofar as true consciousness existed, as men became aware of their real interests, ideology—i.e., the elaboration of false consciousness—would disappear. As Lewis Feuer pointed out: "The obsolescence of ethical ideology is a corollary of historical materialism as applied to the superstructure of a socialist society."[8]

As noted in chapter 1, another fountainhead of ideas in political sociology, Max Weber, pointed to a secular decline in total ideologies as a consequence of the inherent shift over time within societies from an emphasis on *Wertrationalität*, or "substantive rationality," involving orientations toward ultimate values, to *Zweckrationalität*, or "functional rationality," referring to an emphasis on efficient means to attain goals.[9] Inherently a passionate commitment to absolute ends must break down. As William Delany has noted, "That continuous rationalization, demythicization and associated disillusionment are characteristic of Western religious institutions, capitalism, music, bureaucracy and political ideologies is, of course, the major theme in the life work of 'the sage of Heidelberg.'"[10]

With specific reference to contemporary politics, however, Weber, drawing on the work of the Russian scholar Moisei Ostrogorski, contended that a blurring of ideological differences is inherent in the situation of political parties operating under conditions of universal suffrage. In a letter to Robert Michels in 1906, discussing the German Social Democratic party, Weber predicted that, although the party still had "something like a *Weltanschauung*," the fact that it accepted the logic of a political democracy would lead to a decline in its ideological commitments in favor of a more pragmatic orientation.[11]

The first explicit formulation of the end- or decline-of-ideology thesis also came from Germany. Writing from his office in the Frankfurt Institute for Social Research in the late 1920s, Karl Mannheim, in the very book—*Ideology and Utopia*—that established the study of ideology as a major topic, discussed the conditions which were producing a "decline of ideology" and the "relinquishment of utopias," since total doctrines (*Weltanschauungen*) were being reduced to partial pragmatic ones.[12] The underlying logic of Mannheim's analysis reiterated the main points of Weber's assumptions concerning a shift from substantive to functional rationality as inherent in the development of bureaucratic industrial society. Mannheim also emphasized the way in which the logic of politics reduces ideological commitments, noting that, as a movement associated with utopian doctrines gains governmental or state power, "the more it gives up its original utopian impulses and with it its broad perspective."[13]

Following up on the implications, but not the politics, of Engels's assumption that ideology would decline with the resolution of the oppression of the masses, Mannheim suggested that such a change could occur without the triumph of socialism, since he anticipated that the impulses of the lower "strata whose aspirations are not yet fulfilled, and who are [therefore] striving towards communism and socialism" would decline as society is able "to reach a somewhat superior form of industrialism, which will be sufficiently elastic and which will give the lower strata a degree of relative well-being. . . . (From this point of view it makes no difference whether this superior form of social organization of industrialism, through the arrival at a position of power on the part of the lower strata, will eventuate in a capitalism which is sufficiently elastic to insure their relative well-being, or whether this capitalism will first be transformed into communism.)" Such developments in the political arena. Mannheim argued, were necessarily paralleled in various forms of intellectual life:

This process of the complete destruction of all spiritual elements, the utopian as well as the ideological, has its parallel in the most recent trends of modern life, and in their corresponding tendencies in the realm of art. Must we not regard the disappearance of humanitarianism from art, the emergence of a "matter of factness" (*Sachlichkeit*) in sexual life, art, and architecture, and the expression of the natural impulses in sports—must all these not be interpreted as symptomatic of the increasing regression of the ideological and utopian elements from the mentality of the strata which are coming to dominate the present situation? Must not the gradual reduction of politics to economics, towards which there is at least a discernible tendency, the conscious rejection of the past and of the notion of historical time, the conscious brushing aside of every "cultural ideal," be interpreted as a disappearance of every form of utopianism from the political arena as well?[14]

The tendencies Mannheim noted in 1929 seemed to become realities in the two decades following World War II, when the belief in diverse forms of charismatic *Wertrationalität* in the religious, economic, and political orders broke down, in part because the various ideologies and utopias proved to be failures or became routinized operational realities. Protestanism and Catholicism, fascism, capitalism, communism, and social democracy, all lost their power to inspire Western people to work hard, to live morally, or to change the world. The ideological legitimations of societies or political forces were expressed increasingly in secular *Zweckrationalität* terms, i.e., as efficiently operating social orders or representatives of interest groups.

Recent Formulations

These developments led a variety of political analysts to posit the decline of ideology, particularly as it affected the behavior of leftist or working-class movements after World War II. Thus Albert Camus, writing in the left-wing Paris daily *Combat*, in 1946, noted that socialists, by abandoning Marxism as "an absolute philosophy, limiting themselves to retaining its critical aspect . . ., will demonstrate that this era marks the end of ideologies."[15] Writing in 1949, the British sociologist (and socialist) T. H. Marshall advanced a general explanation for the rise and decline of total ideologies. He suggested that they initially emerged with the rise of new strata, such as the bourgeoisie or the working class, as they sought the rights of citizenship, that is, the right fully to participate socially and politically. As long as they were denied such rights, sizable segments of these strata endorsed revolutionary ideologies (or utopias). In turn, older strata and institutions, seeking to preserve their ancient monopolies of power and status, fostered conservative extremist doctrines. The source of the decline of such ideologies in democratic countries, from this point of view, lies in the eventual integration of these groups into society and polity.[16]

Another British scholar, Isaiah Berlin, in reviewing the development of political ideas in this century, came to similar conclusions in 1950, although from a different ideological and analytical perspective, that of a conservative political theorist. Berlin argued that the general acceptance in the postwar world of the "policy of diminishing strife and misery" through collectivist state action was resulting in an order whose "entire trend . . . is to reduce all issues to technical problems of lesser or greater complexity." "In Western Europe this tendency has taken the . . . form of a shift of emphasis away from disagreement about political principles (and from party struggles which sprang from genuine differences of moral and spiritual outlook) toward disagreements, ultimately technical, about methods. . . . Hence that noticeably growing lack of interest in long-term political issues—as opposed to current day-to-day economic or social problems."[17]

The first extensive scholarly analysis of the "end of political ideology" by an American was published in the spring of 1951 by a historian, H. Stuart Hughes. Although Hughes's analysis contained all the basic elements elaborated by subsequent commentators, his work has been studiously ignored by critics of the thesis. Perhaps this benevolent disregard is due to Hughes's record as a socialist supporter of left-wing causes (e.g., Henry Wallace's presidential campaign of 1948, SANE, TOCSIN, and other peace groups) and his running as a third-party leftist peace candidate for United States senator against Edward Kennedy in 1962, a record which tends to confound attempts to give the concept ideological links. Hughes's description, written in the first year of the 1950s, closely resembles others which appeared later in the decade:

> The process of ideological dissolution which began thirty years ago with the first successes of Italian Fascism and which the disillusionments following the Second World War notably accelerated now seems to have reached its logical conclusion.
>
> Quite predictably, the Left is hardest hit. The Left, vociferously ideological and doctrinaire, was more vulnerable to this sort of slow corrosion than the Right, which has learned skepticism and adaptability from its defeats of the last century. In fact, the end of the *mystique* of the Left is the clearest sign of what happened.
>
> Socialism as a political faith has very nearly abdicated. . . . Under present circumstances, a party that has chosen the course of participation in government can scarcely avoid the taint of conservatism, the negation of ideology currently associated with political power.
>
> By the same process of reclassification, the word "fascism" has lost most of its terrors. In conservative circles many people avoid the term entirely.
>
> Even the word "democracy" is losing its sacrosanct character. . . . Of the two major parts of the most generalized contemporary definition of democracy—

individual freedom and government by universal suffrage—it is only the former that has retained its power to inspire enthusiasm and sacrifice.

What has really gone glimmering is the promise of social equality. In the year 1950, the only sort of equality that most cultivated Europeans can see before them is a leveling up and down to a lower-middle-class standard of respectable grubbiness—the kind of daily living of which George Orwell gave so chilling a description in his *Nineteen Eighty-Four* and of which Britain under the Labour Government has provided a dignified foretaste. This is not the notion of equality which once inspired death on the barricades and the consecrated lives of revolutionaries. . . . The common man has lost his aura of sainthood. Those who a decade ago spoke of the century of the common man were perhaps simply in error by a hundred years: it was the century that was ending rather than the century that was opening before them.[18]

In 1955, the Frankfurt Institute was again to provide a "home" for another important expression of the thesis when Raymond Aron published his "Fin de l'âge idéologique?" in one of their volumes.[19] Although the leading spokespersons for "critical theory" did not agree with their "guests," Mannheim and Aron, they were to advance their own versions of the "end of ideology" in various works. As Martin Jay, the historian of the Frankfurt Institute, notes: "The Frankfurt School's version of the end-of-ideology grew out of their belief that liberal society was being replaced by an almost totally 'administered world' in which ideological justifications were no longer necessary."[20] Theodor Adorno, in an article published in 1951, concluded that "in the authentic sense of false consciousness there are no more ideologies."[21] In a collectively authored book, presented as the work of the Institute as a whole, which appeared in 1956, they called attention to the "weakening" of ideology from a high point reached "around the year 1910":

One can speak of ideology in a meaningful way only to the extent that something spiritual emerges from the social process as something independent, substantial, and with its own proper claims. . . . Today the characteristic of ideologies is much more the absence of this independence, rather than the delusion of their claims.

Nothing remains then of ideology but that which exists itself, the models of a behavior which submits to the overwhelming power of the existing conditions. . . . Ideology and reality are converging in this manner, because reality, due to the lack of any other convincing ideology, becomes its own ideology.[22]

More detailed efforts to explain the decline of ideology in Western society were advanced by two erstwhile members of the Frankfurt School who remained in the United States after the main body returned to Germany after the war: Otto Kirchheimer and Herbert Marcuse. Kirchheimer in three trenchant articles contended that partisan-based ideologies waned because the ideological "mass integration party, product of an age with harder class lines and more sharply protruding denominational structures, is transforming itself into a catch-all 'people's' party. . . . Under [the] present condition of spreading secular and mass consumer-goods orientation, with shifting and less obtrusive class lines, the former class-mass parties and denominational mass parties are both under pressure to become catch-all peoples' parties."[23]

In addition, according to Kirchheimer, "The modern welfare state can now provide solutions to problems of many social groups. This weakens the old clashes of immediate interests and converts them into mere conflicts of priority in the time sequence of satisfactions. . . . This situation allows . . . [party] policies to be determined by tactical requirements of the moment, relegating ideologically determined long-range goals to a remote corner."[24]

Herbert Marcuse's repeated emphases on the decline of ideology in modern society exposed him to criticism from the French Marxist sociologist Lucien Goldmann, who grouped "Aron, Marcuse, Bell, Riesman" as the sources of the "belief that Western society has been so stabilized that no serious opposition can be found within it."[25] Time and again in his writings and public lectures, Marcuse, as is noted in the preceding chapter, reiterated his belief that advanced industrial society, through its ability to sustain abundance and mass culture, no longer provides a basis for proletarian class-conscious politics.[26]

Marcuse's despair about the revolutionary potentiality of the working class is, of course, well known. Far less publicized is the fact that he was so pessimistic about the role of Blacks and students that he openly opposed the participation of the first in the political process and of the second in the governance of the university—because the system is able to seduce both into basically conforming to the status quo. At a symposium in 1965 at Rutgers University, Marcuse stated that Negroes have been brainwashed by American society and consequently follow middle-class norms in their political behavior: "When asked which situation he preferred—one in which the Negroes were deprived of their civil rights, including the power to vote, or one in which they freely exercised their civil rights to choose 'middle-class values,' Marcuse replied: 'Well, since I have already gone out on a limb, I might as well go all the way: I will prefer that they did not have the right to choose wrongly.'"[27]

Less than a month before the French "events" of May 1968, in an interview with *Le Monde*, Marcuse stated "everywhere and at all times, the overwhelming majority of students are conservative and even reactionary. So that student power, in the event of it being democratic, would be conservative or even reactionary."[28]

Reactions to the Student Revolt

By 1969, Marcuse, like many others, had learned that he was wrong. In his *Essay on Liberation*, he identified the American "ghetto population" and the student opposition as major disruptive forces. Yet, he still concluded that a liberating "revolution is not on the agenda" of the advanced Western industrial states; that the combination of the necessary "subjective factor" (political consciousness) and the "objective factor" ("the support and participation of the class which is at the base of production") only "coincide in large areas of the Third World."[29]

Similar ideas were advanced by Barrington Moore, Jr., the scholar who comes closer to being an exponent of Marxist analysis in American sociology than any other major figure in the field and who subsequently coauthored with Marcuse and Robert Wolff a radical tract for the late sixties, *A Critique of Pure Tolerance*. Writing in the fifties, Moore noted that

> as we reduce economic inequalities and privileges, we may also eliminate the sources of contrast and discontent that put drive into genuine political alternatives. . . . There is, I think, more than a dialectical flourish in the assertion that liberty requires the existence of an oppressed group in order to grow vigorously. . . . Once the ideal has been achieved, or is even close to realization, the driving force of discontent disappears, and a society settles down for a time to stolid acceptance of things as they are. Something of the sort seems to have happened in the United States.[30]

About the same time, T. B. Bottomore, who was to become the principal senior exponent of Marxism in British sociology and the successful candidate of the leftist forces for the presidency of the International Sociological Association in the mid-seventies, voiced comparable judgments with respect to the direction of change in Western society generally. Bottomore identified the decline in ideological conflict in the postwar world as reflecting a basic shift in class relations. As he put it in 1955, in *Classes in Modern Society:*

> Even though democratic governments still have a class character, this is no longer their most prominent feature, as it frequently was in the nineteenth century. . . . It should also be observed that in most modern democracies there is a large and growing area of social policy on which the main parties agree. The extent of this agreement on the interests of the community as a whole is a measure of the decline of sharp class antagonisms. It is a measure especially of the degree to which the privileged groups have surrendered their privileges and have abandoned the pursuit of purely selfish interests, and thus of the real diminution of class differences.[31]

Ten years later, in the second edition of this book, Bottomore, reacting to the reemergence of sharp ideological controversy among the Western intelligentsia, held up other proponents of the "end-of-ideology" thesis to scorn for their failure to have understood that the basic sources of radical appeal still continued under capitalism.[32] There is not the slightest suggestion in this revised edition that Bottomore himself had been an exponent of an extreme version of the thesis, one which, in its social optimism, went far beyond the analysis of such writers as Aron, Bell, Shils, and myself. He simply dropped his 1955 contention that ideological conflict had declined because

> property owners in the developed industrial democracies have ceased to be a ruling class in the sense of being able to maintain or improve their own situation in society or to resist the growing pressure for equality of condition. . . . The instruments of production can no longer be used without regard for the interests of the worker; they are hedged about with restrictions imposed by democratic governments. Property no longer automatically assures to its possessor a predominant share in the political affairs of his society. Power, in the contemporary democratic societies, is dispersed among numerous social groups, employers, trade unions, and voluntary associations of many kinds, each of which brings its influence to bear upon government policy.[33]

Possibly made aware of the discrepancy between the position taken in the two editions, Bottomore, in 1967, in discussing the "end of ideology" as "a phrase which rings strangely," nevertheless went on to note that "if what is meant is that the great nineteenth-century ideologies which divided societies internally have developed cracks and appear to be crumbling, and that they no longer exercise anything like their former sway over the minds of social critics, then the characterization may be accepted as plausible."[34]

Three years later, in 1970, Bottomore, in an essay in the then New Left-oriented *New York Review of Books*, once more reversed direction and severely criticized, as patently "discredited views," the "notorious doctrines proclaiming the 'end of ideology' and the achievement of 'stable democracy' in the Western industrial countries."[35] Again, there is no hint in this essay— which assumes that the exacerbation of political conflict in the late sixties constituted a self-evident refutation of the views under attack—that its author had advanced many of the arguments that he was now projecting onto the writings of others. Thus earlier, in a comparison of the Soviet Union with "the Western democracies," he suggested that the "unification of elites . . . characteristic of all the Communist countries" has resulted in "the formation of a new ruling class and the consolidation of its privileges and its power over the rest of the society," while the Western countries "differ . . . [in] that in them the power of one group is limited by the power of other independent groups, political parties, employers, trade unions, and a variety of other pressure groups. This is a very important difference, for the emergence of a single unified elite means the end of both freedom and equality."[36]

Bottomore included among the "notorious doctrines," linked to the "end of ideology," the concept of stable democracies, seemingly forgetting that he had once emphasized that "universal adult suffrage has made it possible, by peaceful means, to curb the power of property owners and to change the character of government. . . . Individual freedom in society can only be assured by political means, by institutions which must as a minimum exclude the single-party system and encourage dissent by the protection of minority groups."[37]

Bottomore, like other leftist critics of the "end-of-ideology school" of sociologists, in the flush of enthusiasm over the emergence of radical activism among students and sections of the intelligentsia in the late sixties, triumphantly argued in 1970 that the "source of this failing was its own unhistorical character, . . . that it encouraged a propensity to regard the fleeting present as an eternal order."[38] Curiously, in view of subsequent events in the 1970s, Bottomore presented as an example of this failing my 1967 estimate that the revived movement is likely to be "one of many unsuccessful attempts . . . to create a radical movement in an essentially unfertile environment," given the historical background that "in the United States, with its relatively stable social system and a fairly long tradition of political tranquillity, radical social movements of any kind have had difficulty in establishing themselves."[39] Bottomore might have better maintained his record as a prognosticator if he had held to his own pessimistic 1967 comment about student politics. He noted at the time that the possibility that the "new radicalism . . . [would last longer than previous short-lived waves] depends upon whether the new radicalism can find some basis in society less ephemeral than a student movement."[40]

By 1971, in an article evaluating the by then evident decline of the student movement, Bottomore wrote that it is "difficult to foresee the development of a broad radical movement" in the United States. He saw little hope for the radicalization of the working class "in conditions of growing prosperity and declining trade unionism."[41]

Participants in and faculty supporters of the student-activist wave of the sixties could only find words of total scorn for those like David Riesman and myself who called attention to the historical pattern of recurrent rises and rapid declines of student-based movements.[42] Yet, a few years later, such generalizations were to give sustenance to radicals depressed by the evident ebbing of protest. Bettina Aptheker, a Marxist leader of the Berkeley Revolt in 1964–65, took heart in 1973 from the fact that "all social movements go in waves. You cannot sustain a level of intensity for an indeterminate length of time . . .; if that analysis is right, the movement will recur."[43]

The assumption that basic structural trends in Western society had sharply reduced the factors making for intense ideological conflict was applied during the early sixties specifically to the prospects for student activism by a left-oriented scholar, Kenneth Keniston, who was to become the most significant sympathetic American student of the phenomenon during its high point in the last half of the decade. He first emphasized the "decline of Utopia" and "quiescence" among students. In commenting in the mid-seventies on the "view of the modern period as one of the 'decline of utopia' and the 'end of ideology,'" Joseph Gusfield was to emphasize the writings of Keniston as a major formulation of the approach.[44] Keniston's conviction that American youth was inherently "predominantly apolitical" led him in 1963 to put "political revival" in quotation marks in the title of an article discussing "signs of increasing political activity on a number of campuses," and to devote most of the essay to analyzing the enduring structural sources of "apathy."[45] He suggested that it "almost appears that affluence and education have a negative effect on political involvement, at least in America"—a conclusion he was to reverse a few years later.

Yet the same Kenneth Keniston was to single out for scorn the writings of Daniel Bell, Seymour Martin Lipset, and Edward Shils about the end of ideology. From the assumption that this group of "liberal" theorists "predicted precisely the opposite of what has actually happened," Keniston concluded that this "fact alone should impel us to question and redefine the basic assumptions from which liberalism began."[46] One may be forgiven an expression of astonishment in reading these words, coming as they do from a research specialist on the behavior of the young who insisted, even *after* the youth revolt of the sixties began, that it could not possibly reverse the basic forces making for apoliticism and apathy among students, and directed as they are against a group of scholars who explicitly anticipated in their writings on the end of ideology the reemergence of ideological or utopian politics based on a "rebellious younger generation." (Shils), "the young intellectual" (Bell), and "the intellectuals" (Lipset).[47]

My references to the work of a number of scholars who have been identified with Marxism, or whose scholarly writings include endorsement of various forms of left-wing activism as proponents of an extreme "end-of-conflict" variant of the "end-of-ideology" thesis, are not meant to suggest that their work gives the thesis a specific leftist ideological coloration. But, given the polemical context of the discussion, it is important to note that various political persuasions, each in its own way, lent support to the idea. These include, in addition to those discussed earlier, two prominent American sociologists, David Riesman and Talcott Parsons; Herbert Tingsten, long-time editor of Sweden's leading liberal newspaper, *Dagens Nyheter*; Gunnar Myrdal, the famous economist and Swedish socialist leader; Ralf Dahrendorf, probably the best known of contemporary German sociologists, writing in the mid-1950s while still an active socialist; Stein Rokkan, sometime president of the International Political Science Association; George Lichtheim, historian and theorist of socialism; Lewis Feuer, a current exponent of psychoanalytic approaches to social analysis; Michel Crozier and Alain Touraine, French sociologists of sharply different orientations; Mark Abrams, British pollster;

Robert Lane, Yale political behaviorist, former student leader, and current socialist activist; Judith Shklar, Harvard professor, writing from a viewpoint of political theory; and Thomas Molnar, a conservative political theorist, among the many who could be cited.[48]

The Kennedy Formulation

Although John F. Kennedy has been given credit by some as ending the political quiescence of the "silent '50s" in the United States by giving voice to a new ideological commitment to the country's egalitarian objectives, thus inspiring student political activism, Kennedy himself espoused a version of the "end-of-ideology" thesis in public discourse in statements the first drafts of which have been attributed to Arthur Schlesinger, Jr. Thus in May 1962 he proclaimed that ideological division over basic issues was over; that there was no further need for "the great sort of 'passionate movements' which have stirred this country so often in the past." A month later, in a commencement address at Yale, the young president concluded that "the central domestic problems of our time are more subtle and less simple. They do not relate to basic clashes of philosophy and ideology, but to ways and means of reaching common goals."[49]

The assumptions underlying these statements—that the basic economic problems of jobs, security, and inequality had largely been resolved—were presaged in the late fifties by two liberals who were to become the major intellectual spokesmen for the Kennedy era, Arthur Schlesinger, Jr., and John Kenneth Galbraith, both then Harvard professors. In 1957 the former wrote that "while there are things to be done in areas of economic direction and regulation, the major problems of economic structure seem to be solved; few liberals would seriously wish today to alter the mix in our present mixed economy. . . . Moreover, to a great degree, the present conservative Administration has nominally, at least, run away with the verbal objectives of the New Deal. . . . As Arthur Larson has suggested, we are all New Dealers now."[50]

Five years later Schlesinger elaborated these views on a global scale, noting that the rise of the welfare state or "mixed society" has "revealed classical capitalism and classical socialism as nineteenth-century doctrines. . . . It is evident now, for example, that the choice between private and public means . . . is not a matter of religious principle. . . . It is simply a practical question as to which means can best achieve the desired end. . . . Indeed, I would suggest that we might well banish the words 'capitalism' and 'socialism' from intellectual discourse."[51]

His academic colleague, subsequent co-member of the Kennedy administration, fellow enthusiast for the New Politics of the 1970s, and currently
self-proclaimed socialist, Galbraith, presented similar views, noting that

> as an economic and social concern, inequality has been declining in urgency.
> . . . Production has eliminated the more acute tensions associated with in-
> equality. And it has become evident to conservatives and liberals alike that
> increasing aggregate output is an alternative to redistribution or even to the
> reduction of inequality. The oldest and most agitated of social issues, if not
> resolved, is at least largely in abeyance, and the disputants have concentrated
> their attention, instead, on the goal of increasing productivity.

> The ancient preoccupations of economic life—with equality, security and pro-
> ductivity—have now narrowed down to a preoccupation with productivity and
> production. Production has become the solvent of the tensions once associated
> with inequality, and it has become the indispensable remedy for the discomforts,
> anxieties, and privations associated with economic insecurity.[52]

Anticipations of the New Politics

Much of the leftist criticism of the end-of-ideology theme has focused on
the writings of the so-called pluralist school of sociologists, Aron, Bell, Shils,
and myself, stressing the supposed disconfirmation of our hypothesis, given
the New Left revolt of the 1960s, which was based largely on students,
excluded minorities, and the intelligentsia. Each of us, however, had anticipated that political protest would continue and would be supported largely
by these strata. Thus, in his original article in *Encounter* in 1955, as noted
earlier, Edward Shils predicted that, unless Western society undertook "great
tasks" socially, "ideology," in the sense of extreme or revolutionary doctrines, would "creep in through the back door, or more particularly through
a rebellious younger generation."[53] Again, in an article published in 1958,
which represents his most extensive elaboration of the end-of-ideology thesis,
Shils emphasized the "tendency of intellectuals in modern Western countries,
and latterly in Asian and African countries, to incline toward ideological
politics . . . [since] most of the traditions of modern intellectuals seem
to dispose them toward an ideological outlook. It seems to be almost given
by their attachment to symbols which transcend everyday life and its
responsibilities."[54]

In the conclusion to his 1955 essay, "The End of the Ideological Age?,"
which also forms the end of his book on intellectuals, Raymond Aron explicitly
denied that with the decline of commitment to social reform and change:
"One does not cease to love God when one gives up converting the pagans
or the Jews and no longer reiterates: 'No salvation outside the church.' Will
one cease to desire a less unjust society and a less cruel lot for humanity as

a whole if one refuses to subscribe to a single class, a single technique of action, and a single ideological system?"[55]

A decade later, in returning to the theme in an essay whose title indicates its emphasis, "The End of Ideology and the Renaissance of Ideas," Aron reiterated that he was not anticipating an end to political outlooks or efforts to reform society but rather a decline in the appeal of total or integrated ideologies in the West. As he noted, "The breakdown of ideological syntheses does not lead to insipid pragmatism or lessen the values of intellectual controversy."[56] Aron explained his position in outlining the sources of the "anti-ideological" position of the moderate left:

> The moderate left is in fact, in the present circumstances, anti-ideological in a very precise and limited sense: in each particular situation it tries to reconcile in the best possible, or least unsatisfactory, way personal freedom, democratic legitimacy, economic progress, and the lessening of social inequalities. It is precisely because complete reconciliation [of all these objectives within one coherent ideology] is impossible except as a remote rational concept that the moderate left declares itself "anti-ideological" and stresses the diversity of political situations and the fragility of vast syntheses. It is because developed societies are at least partially succeeding in achieving such a reconciliation that they cannot or will not formulate an ideological synthesis.[57]

My own analysis of the decline of ideology, first published in 1960, was presented in the context of arguing *against* the theses of Barrington Moore and others on the *left* who stressed the impact of these changes in reducing class struggle. As I noted in my discussion there, described by Moskvichev as the one "in which the 'twilight of ideology' thesis received its fullest and most exhaustive analysis," I questioned "whether these intellectuals are not mistaking the decline of ideology in the domestic politics of Western society with the ending of the class conflict which has sustained domestic controversy. As the abundant evidence on the voting patterns in the United States and other countries indicates, the electorate as a whole does not see the end of the domestic class struggle envisioned by so many intellectuals. . . . The predictions of the end of class politics in the 'affluent society' ignore the relative character of any class system."

In specifying the factors underlying the decline of total ideologies in left-wing parties, I elaborated on the theme originally suggested by T. H. Marshall, discussed earlier, that because revolutionary mass politics in early industrial society was largely a phenomenon of the working-class struggle for citizenship, its ideological commitments eroded when "the workers . . . achieved industrial and political citizenship, [and] the conservatives . . . accepted the welfare state." But implicit in the assumption that "inclusion" reduces the need for total ideologies on the part of previously excluded groups is the recognition "that ethnic, racial, or religious groups, like American blacks or

Ulster Catholics, who are still deprived in citizenship terms, will continue to find uses for extreme tactics and occasionally ideologies.''

In discussing the decline of leftist sentiment among American intellectuals in the 1950s, in *Political Man*, I challenged the assumption that ''a permanent change in the [adversary] relationship of the American intellectual to his society is in process. In spite of the powerful conservatising forces, the inherent tendency to oppose the *status quo* will still remain. . . . Any *status quo* embodies rigidities and dogmatisms which it is the inalienable right of intellectuals to attack, whether from the standpoint of moving back to traditional values or forward toward the achievement of the equalitarian dream.''[58]

Similar conclusions about the continued concern of intellectuals, particularly young ones, for critical ideologies were reached by Daniel Bell in his analysis in *The End of Ideology*:

> The new generation of [intellectuals] . . . finds itself seeking new purposes within a framework of political society that has rejected, intellectually speaking, the old apocalyptic and chiliastic visions. In a search for a ''cause,'' there is a deep, desperate, almost pathetic anger. . . . In the U.S. . . . there is a restless search for a new intellectual radicalism. . . . The irony . . . for those who seek ''causes'' is that the workers, whose grievances were once the driving energy for social change, are more satisfied with the society than the intellectuals. The workers have not achieved utopia, but their expectations were less than those of the intellectuals, and the gains correspondingly larger.

> The young intellectual is unhappy because the ''middle way'' is for the middle-aged, not for him; it is without passion and is deadening. Ideology, which by its nature is an all-or-none affair . . . [is] temperamentally the thing he wants.[59]

Although the tone and ideological emphasis were quite different, C. Wright Mills, deeply steeped in the writings of Weber and Mannheim, arrived at almost identical conclusions to those of Bell and myself. Thus, in his famous ''Letter to the New Left'' (published in 1960), he stated: ''Generally it would seem that only at certain [earlier] stages of industrialisation, and in a political context of autocracy, etc., do wage-workers tend to become a class-for-themselves, etc.'' He described the belief of some radicals in the revolutionary role of the working class in ''advanced capitalist societies'' as running ''in the face of the really impressive historical evidence that now stands against this expectation . . . a legacy from Victorian Marxism that is now quite unrealistic.''[60] And Mills also suggested that the social group which is most likely, given its structural situation, to be a source of continuing anti-establishment struggle is the intellectuals: ''It is with this problem of agency [of change] in mind that I have been studying, for several years now, the cultural apparatus, the intellectuals—as a possible, immediate, radical agency of change . . . ; it turns out now, in the spring of 1960, that it may be a very relevant idea indeed.''[61]

Similar views were expressed by John Kenneth Galbraith in 1967, when he reiterated his views, first expressed a decade earlier, that the modern industrial system has confounded Marx's anticipations by its ability—a concomitant of economic affluence—to absorb class conflict and sharply reduce conflicts about "the goals of the society itself." Yet, like Mills, he noted the emergence of "an ill-defined discontent, especially among students and intellectuals, with the accepted and approved modalities of social thought."[62] Such discontent and potential for conflict with the dominant economic strata on the part of members of the "educational and scientific estate and the larger intellectual community" are, according to Galbraith, implicit in the sharply varying value orientations inherent in the structural position of the two major extragovernmental elites.

In emphasizing the role of intellectuals as a potential center for the revival of protest in the early sixties, Bell, Mills, and I were at variance with the assumptions of Marcuse and Bottomore. The latter, for example, argued as late as 1964 that "at the present time . . . it is probably the case that most intellectuals in the West European countries and in the U.S.A. belong to the right."[63]

Daniel Bell also discussed the ideological implications of the "end of chiliastic hopes, of millenarianism, of apocalyptic thinking"—what he means by ideology in his use of the famous phrase. And unlike a number of more pessimistic leftists, who espoused their own versions of the notion, Bell saw the "end of ideology" in politics as making realistic discussions of utopia possible for the first time: "The end of ideology is not—should not—be the end of utopia as well. If anything, one can begin anew the discussion of utopia only by being aware of the trap of ideology."[64]

More recently, in his analyses of the emergence of postindustrial society which have concerned him during the past decade. Bell has also stressed the special propensity of intellectuals to foster antinomian ideological attitudes— attitudes which, repeatedly appearing among the culture creators, reflect their desire to reduce or abolish restraints in order "to attain some form of ecstasy." Such attitudes are in sharp opposition to the orientation of the workaday world, "the economy, technology, and occupational system . . . [which] is rooted in functional rationality and efficiency . . . shaped by the principle of calculation, the rationalization of work and of time, and a linear sense of progress."[65] In various writings since the late '50s, I have also emphasized the extent to which the "adversary culture" of the intellectuals, their continued opposition to the basic values and institutions of the owners and controllers of industry and politics in capitalist and postcapitalist societies, is inherent in the nature of their work, with its emphasis on creativity, originality and "breakthroughs."[66]

As noted in chapter 1, Max Weber presciently anticipated these views, noting the desire of many intellectuals to find some form of ecstasy in a period characterized "by rationalization . . . and, above all, by the 'disenchantment of the world.' " Faced with "disenchantment," with the absence of charismatic total ideologies, some will shift their value emphasis "into the transcendental realm of mystic life or into the brotherliness of direct and personal human relations." They may try "intellectually to construe new religions without a new and genuine prophecy," which can only result in "miserable monstrosities. And academic prophecy, finally, will create only fanatical sects but never a genuine community." For Weber, the most ethical reaction for the intellectual "who cannot bear the fate of the times" is to return to traditional religion. "In my eyes, such religious return stands higher than the academic prophecy, which does not realize that in the lecture-rooms of the university no other virtue holds but plain intellectual integrity."[67]

A few years later, Karl Mannheim, in the same essay in which he anticipated the decline of ideology and utopia, noted the difficulty for intellectuals of living in "congruence with the realities of . . . a world, utterly without any transcendent element, either in the form of a utopia or an ideology." He foretold the rise of an emphasis on " 'genuineness' and 'frankness' in place of the old ideals."[68] And, like Weber before him, Mannheim predicted that it would be the "intellectuals . . . even more than now in increasing proportions recruited from all social strata rather than merely from the more privileged ones," who, unable to accommodate to a situation without ideological conflict, will seek "to reach out beyond that tensionless situation."[69]

Returning to the theme in the late thirties, Mannheim almost seems to be describing the New Left intelligentsia of the 1960s when he notes that the intellectual critics of advanced liberal democratic society "refuse to utter even the slightest solutions for the future":

> It is regarded as a higher sort of wisdom to say nothing specific, to despise the use of reason in attempting to mould the future, and to require no more than blind faith. One enjoys then the double advantage of having to use reason only in criticizing one's opponents and, at the same time, of being able to mobilize without restraint and to one's own profit all the negative emotions of hatred and resentment which—according to Simmel's principle of the "negative character of collective behaviour"—can unify a large number of people more easily than any positive programme.[70]

It is interesting to note that, in commenting on the writings of Daniel Bell and myself dealing with the "end of ideology," James C. Davies suggests that the malaise that basically underlies our writings is a "sense of the inadequacy of capitalist and socialist systems . . . [to] provide adequate criteria or adequate means for developing individuals and cultures beyond the level of material abundance.''[71]

The Ideology of the End of Ideology

One specific criticism of the concept of the ''end of ideology'' has been made by some radicals who, admitting a congruence of empirical judgment with their own evaluation of the erosion of ideological controversy among the major-party protagonists in the Western democracies, still argue that those who have proclaimed the ''end of ideology'' have failed to recognize that the concept is a conservative ideological one and that it contributes to the undermining of efforts at radical change. Thus, Stephen Rousseas and James Farganis have commented that ''there can be little doubt that . . . [Bell's] arguments and that of Lipset on the decline, if not the end, of ideology as an operative force in the Western world are based largely on fact,'' but they go on to argue that ''C. Wright Mills would agree that the end of ideology makes a fetish of empiricism and entails an ideology of its own—an ideology of political complacency for the justification of things as they are.''[72] But, obviously, such an argument only repeats a component part of the analysis they are criticizing. In 1963 I attempted a comprehensive discussion of the sources and consequences of the ''decline of ideology'':

> Not only do class conflicts over issues related to division of the total economic pie, influence over various institutions, symbolic status, and opportunity, continue in the absence of *Weltanschauungen,* but . . . the decline of such total ideologies does *not* mean the end of ideology. Clearly, commitment to the politics of pragmatism, to the rules of the game of collective bargaining, to gradual change whether in the direction favoured by the left or the right, to opposition both to an all-powerful central state and to *laissez-faire* constitutes the component parts of an ideology. The ''agreement on fundamentals,'' the political consensus of Western society, now increasingly has come up to include a position on matters which once sharply separated the Left from the Right. And this ideological agreement, which might best be described as ''conservative socialism,'' has become *the* ideology of the major parties in the developed states of Europe and America.[73]

In making these contentions, I was only reiterating the argument stated by H. Stuart Hughes in the conclusion to ''The End of Political Ideology,'' when he noted that ''the creeds of 'progress'—liberalism, democracy, socialism—have made their peace with what remains of traditional conservatism. . . . Is it surprising, then, that the new conservatism of 1950 . . . should have fused all ideologies in an unresolved concord in which the one clear note is the name of freedom?''[74]

In all fairness, it should be noted that a Communist critic, L. N. Mosk-vichev, does recognize that the main body of writings about "the end of ideology in industrially developed states of the West does not imply the demise of all ideology or the absence of any political or ideological differences. The phrase 'end of ideology,' according to its authors and supporters, means only that, first, the so-called universal ideologies no longer serve to guide mass political actions and this applies above all to Marxism-Leninism; secondly, in the advanced capitalist states, acute ideological and political conflicts gradually die down."[75]

It should be clear from the references to some of Aron's, Shils', Bell's, and my own writings that, in the same works in which we discussed the "end" or "decline" of ideology, neither we nor most of the others who wrote on the subject ever meant the end of systems of integrated political concepts, of utopian thinking, of class conflict, and their correlates in political positions espoused by the representatives of different classes or other political interest groups. Rather, what we were referring to was a judgment that the passionate attachments of an integrated revolutionary set of doctrines to the anti-system struggles of working-class movements—and the consequent coherent counterrevolutionary doctrines of some of their opponents—were declining; that they were, to repeat C. Wright Mills's term, "a legacy from Victorian Marxism." They would not reemerge in advanced industrial or "postindustrial societies," although they would continue to exist in the less-developed nations, whose social structures and processes of change resemble those of Europe during the Industrial Revolution. Ideology is not the common-sense term, meaning *any* kind of political thinking, that some of our radical critics seem to think it is. One radical sociologist, Franz Schurmann, has even argued that, from a Marxist point of view, the concept of a revolutionary ideology is meaningless. "Ideology is a tricky word. For Marx, ideology was false consciousness." And Schurmann goes on to ask (in terms reminiscent of Bell's earlier discussion of the consequences of postindustrial society for political thinking): "In this 'end of ideology,' are there the seeds of a new moral-political order?"[76]

(Parenthetically, it may be noted that the Soviet scholar L. N. Moskvichov challenges interpretations of Marx such as Schurmann's. He cites a number of passages from Marx and Engels which refer to ideology as "comprising political and legal views, philosophy and religion, by no means applying any negative connotation to the term. . . . Marx and Engels emphasized the class essence of ideology in society divided into antagonistic classes." He goes on to note that Lenin wrote of the need to "carry on propaganda for the proletarian ideology—the theory of scientific socialism."')[77]

Curiously, the strongest tribute to the concerns of the "academic sociologists" who write from the "pluralist" perspective has come from the pen of another radical sociologist, Alvin Gouldner, who in 1970 noted that a group of scholars, whom he identifies with the approach of Talcott Parsons, have "focused attention on some of the new sources and sites of social change in the modern social world":

> For example, and to be provocatively invidious about it, it was not the Marxists but Talcott Parsons and other functionalists who early spotted the importance of the emerging "youth culture," and at least lifted it out as an object for attention. It was the academic sociologists, not the Marxists, in the United States who helped many to get their first concrete picture of how Blacks and other subjugated groups live, and who contributed to such practical political developments as the Supreme Court's desegregation decision. It is the ethnography of conventional academic sociologists that has also given us the best picture of the emerging psychedelic and drug cultures, which are hardening the separation and conflict of generations.[78]

In large part the polemical controversies concerning the validity of the analyses of the end of ideology have revolved around different meanings of the term "ideology." The critics have been able to demonstrate to their own satisfaction that ideologies continue to exist—that, with the decline in the cold war, intellectuals, the intelligentsia, and educated young people have intensified their commitment to anti-establishment outlooks. In his article on "Ideology" written for the *International Encyclopedia of the Social Sciences* (1968), Edward Shils has effectively pointed out that he and other exponents of the end-of-ideology thesis never implied that "ideals, ethical standards, general or comprehensive social views and policies, were no longer either relevant or possible in human society." And, as he stresses in his recent book,

> It is obvious that no society can exist without a cognitive, moral, and expressive culture. Standards of truth, beauty, goodness are inherent in the structure of human action. The culture which is generated from cognitive, moral, and expressive needs and which is transmitted and sustained by tradition is part of the very constitution of society. Thus every society, having a culture, will have a complex set of orientations toward man, society, and the universe in which ethical and metaphysical propositions, aesthetic judgments, and scientific knowledge will be present. These will form the outlooks and suboutlooks of the society. Thus there can never be an "end" of outlooks or suboutlooks. The contention arose from the failure to distinguish these and ideology in the sense here understood.

> Moreover, the exponents of the "end of ideology" did not assert or imply that the human race had reached a condition or a stage of development in and after which ideologies could no longer occur. The potentiality for ideology seems to be a permanent part of the human constitution. In conditions of crisis when hitherto prevailing elites fail and are discredited, when the central institutions and culture with which they associate themselves seem unable to find the right

course of action, ideological propensities are heightened. The need for a direct contact with the sources of powers of creativity and legitimacy and for a comprehensive organization of life permeated by those powers is an intermittent and occasional need in most human beings and an overwhelming and continued need in a few. The confluence of the aroused need in the former with the presence of the latter generates and intensifies ideological orientations. As long as human societies are afflicted by crises, and as long as man has a need to be in direct contact with the sacred, ideological elements in the tradition contained in the modern Western outlook are almost a guarantee of the persistent potentiality.[79]

Empirical Analyses

Much of the debate concerning the concept of the end of ideology has obviously involved ideological differences. Yet the idea in its modern format was advanced by a number of sociologists and historians as an empirical hypothesis about the consequences of social development on the character of class-related partisan controversy. For the most part, the radical critics have ignored the issue of the validity of the hypothesis; they usually have taken its falseness as *prima facie*, as self-evident—given the fact that political passions and radical protest movements continue to exist. But while some have engaged in polemics, a few others have indeed attempted to evaluate the validity of the proposition. A considerable literature, some of it quantitative in methodology, has sought to compare the intensity of ideological cleavages among different societies or to examine the changes within nations over time. Three political scientists (Rejai, Mason, and Beller, not previously involved in the controversy) examined these disparate studies and concluded that the hypothesis holds up: "The end-of-ideology hypothesis, then, has occasioned a large body of scholarly output over the past decade. In general terms, this hypothesis seeks to establish a negative correlation between the degree of economic development and the intensity of ideological politics within a given country. The hypothesis has held up quite well in empirical investigations in a number of advanced industrial societies."[80]

Another political scientist, John Clayton Thomas, systematically coded the position of fifty-four political parties in twelve industrialized nations on ten dimensions for seven five-year periods from the 1870s to the 1960s. He reports "significant patterns of convergence (i.e., declining average deviations) from the 1910s to the 1960s and from the 1930s to the 1960s."[81] Nonleftist parties, i.e., conservative, liberal and Christian Democratic ones, "moved steadily, and sometimes dramatically, leftward between the 1890s and 1960s."[82] Similarly, "an examination of the average amount of advocacy of change by British Commonwealth labour, Socialist/social democratic, and Communist parties . . . [revealed] consistent and sizeable decreases in their radicalism on almost all of the issues. In many cases the degree of deradicalization is comparable to the high degree of depolarization the non-labor parties experienced."[83]

More recently, Thomas has updated his analysis to include the 1971–76 period. He finds that for nine out of ten industrialized nations (the single exception is the United States), the average difference in party positions on socio-economic issues has declined from the 1960s to the 1970s. As he notes, "partisan issue differences declined between the 1960s and 1970s in all party systems (other than that of the United States), regardless of whether the comparison is restricted to the two major party blocs or extended to all parties with a five percent share of the vote."[84] The American exception is puzzling, particularly since overall ideological differences seem smaller in America than in countries with socialist and conservative parties. Thomas suggests that the American exception, the sharper variation in policy positions, may reflect the "weakness of American parties in implementing their policy positions." That is, precisely because American parties have less structure and discipline than those in Europe and Japan, they may place a greater emphasis in campaign statements on differences between them than in countries where party organizations may be held accountable for policy.[85]

While Thomas' work in general provides the most comprehensive test and apparent verification of the basic assumptions in the end-of-ideology literature, it is important to note one major modification. He finds that the nonleftist parties have changed their policy positions more dramatically than have the labor-oriented ones, although most end-of-ideology writers have emphasized the shift by leftist parties and have underplayed those by other groups. Thomas suggests that the reason for the displaced emphases may have been the fact that the status quo in industrialized society has shifted to the left, i.e., to the welfare-planning society. Hence, "a party's position could change, but the change would not be perceived if the status quo changed in the same direction. This explanation could account for inattention to the massive depolarization of non-labour parties. Second, a party's position might not change, but change would nonetheless be perceived if the status quo changed. This would account for the exaggeration of the degree of labour party depolarization."[86]

The differences in evaluation of the thesis—between those who have carefully sought to test it, and that of the polemical critics—led Rejai and his colleagues to look for an explanation of how people could reach such disparate conclusions. They found it in the fact that most of the critics demonstrate an "apparent willingness to disregard the empirical significance of the hypothesis in question and to rely, instead, on semantic justification." The critics are able to challenge it "by adopting definitions of ideology that have serious deficiencies . . . that are so vague, so general, and so broad as to minimize their relevance for empirical investigation."[87]

At the moment, the political-party systems, institutionalized to accommodate the conflicts of modern society and ideologically moderated, as Bottomore noted, by the workings of democratic electoral systems, still remain dominant. As a quantitative study of electoral patterns in "Western party systems since 1915" by the Strathclyde political scientists, Richard Rose and Derek Urwin, indicates, there has been little change in the relative strength of the political parties, whose behavior has corresponded to Weber's anticipations: "Whatever index of change is used—a measure of trends or of several measures of fluctuations—the picture is the same: the electoral strength of most parties in Western nations since the War has changed very little from election to election, from decade to decade, or within the lifespan of a generation. . . . In short, the first priority of social scientists concerned with the development of parties and party systems since 1945 is to explain the absence of change in a far from static period in political history."[88]

Conclusion

Writing in 1981 in the *New York Review of Books,* one of the chief spokespersons of the New Politics, John Kenneth Galbraith, reiterated his previously voiced conclusion that there has been "agreement on a broad range of ideas and policies . . . in the industrial countries since World War II." As he noted: "There has been a broad consensus in the United States extending to most Republicans and most Democrats. Similarly as between Christian Democrats and Social Democrats in Germany and Austria, the Labour and Tory parties in Britain, Liberals and Progressive Conservatives in Canada. Policies in France, Italy, Switzerland and Scandinavia have generally conformed" to this pattern.[89]

And in line with Thomas's empirical findings that the consensus has involved more of an adjustment by those on the right to the policies advocated by the left than the reverse, Galbraith identified the agreement among the major political parties as involving an acceptance of a "broad macroeconomic, public-service and social-welfare commitment," planning, welfare and regulatory policies forming a "consensus . . . of greatest importance for those of lowest income." As a result, in his judgment, the most severe challenges to the consensus have come not from the left, but from conservatives, most recently reflected in the attacks on the planning-welfare state voiced by Margaret Thatcher in Britain and Ronald Reagan in the United States. But Galbraith denied that their electoral victories represented "a genuine shift of opinion" and argued that in office they will not be able fundamentally to change the policies underlying the consensus. Although a socialist, he offered a fairly moderate set of political objectives for those of his persuasion, which if successful will hardly upset the pattern: "Thus the task. The consensus must, of course, be defended at its positions of present strength. But here there will be great support from circumstance. The real task is to repair, renew, and redesign it at its points of present failure."[90]

To reiterate, the revival of total ideologies among a segment of intellectuals and students in various Western countries in the late 1960s does not, in and of itself, challenge the theses advanced by those who wrote of the decline of ideology among mass-based social movements in Western countries. As noted earlier, these writings often *explicitly* exempted intellectuals and students from the generalization.

Efforts to find a mass base, beyond an affluent minority of the intelligentsia, on the part of New Left groups which reject the established Social Democratic, Communist, and Democratic parties, all oriented to the electoral system, have failed dramatically in areas as diverse as France, Germany, Italy, Northern Europe, and the United States. The vast majority of American New Leftists, including some of their most prominent spokespersons, have joined the Democratic Party in the United States, finding sufficient ideological sustenance in the liberal and populist positions that have been identified with George McGovern and Edward Kennedy.

The empirical content subsumed in the concept of the "end of ideology" has commended itself to scholars of sharply different political persuasions. Nevertheless, some of those who have enunciated it have been selectively singled out as supposedly having denied that the sharp type of ideological controversy which emerged in the 1960s could ever occur. This attack illustrates the extent to which ideological evaluations of underlying motives have been confused with validity. Richard Simpson, in noting the increase in such forms of criticism in sociology, has warned: "A central idea . . . is that when we pin an ideological tag on a theory . . . we say something about the validity of the theory. This notion is alarming, for it would turn sociology into substandard moral philosophy with the resonating of sentiments replacing reason and observation as the basis for constructing and judging theories."[91]

Notes

1. The relevant writings of this group include: Raymond Aron, "Fin de l'âge idéologique?" in Theodor W. Adorno and Walter Dirks (eds.), *Sociologica* (Frankfurt: Europäisch Verlagsanstalt, 1955), pp. 219–33, in English in Aron, *The Opium of the Intellectuals,* trans. Terence Kilmartin (New York: W. W. Norton, 1962), pp. 305–24; "Nations and Ideologies," *Encounter* 4 (January 1955): 23–33; "The End of Ideology and the Renaissance of Ideas," in *The Industrial Society* (New York: Praeger, 1967), pp. 92–183. Daniel Bell, *Marxism-Leninism: A*

Doctrine on the Defensive: The "End of Ideology" in the Soviet Union (New York: Columbia University Research Institute on Communist Affairs, 1955); *The End of Ideology*, rev. ed. (New York: Collier, 1962); Bell and Henry D. Aiken, "Ideology—A Debate," *Commentary* 37 (October 1964): 69–76; "Ideology and Soviet Politics," *Slavic Review* 24 (December 1965): 591–603; *The Coming of Post-Industrial Society* (New York: Basic Books, 1973). S. M. Lipset, "The State of Democratic Politics," *Canadian Forum* 35 (November 1955): 170–71; "Socialism—Left and Right—East and West," *Confluence* 7 (Summer 1958): 173–92; "The End of Ideology?" in the first, 1960 edition of *Political Man*, pp. 403–17; "The Changing Class Structure and Contemporary European Politics," *Daedalus* 93 (Winter 1964): 271–303, reprinted in revised form in Lipset, *Revolution and Counterrevolution*, rev. ed. (Garden City, N.Y.: Doubleday-Anchor, 1970), pp. 267–304; "Some Further Comments on 'The End of Ideology,' " *American Political Science Review* 60 (1966): 17–19. Edward Shils, "The End of Ideology?" *Encounter* 5 (November 1955): 52–58; "Ideology and Civility: On the Politics of the Intellectuals," *Sewanee Review* 66 (July–September 1958): 450–80; "The Concept and Function of Ideology," in the *International Encyclopedia of the Social Sciences*, David L. Sills, 17 vols. (New York: Macmillan and Free Press, 1968), 7:66–76. The latter two articles are reprinted in slightly revised form in Shils, *The Intellectuals and the Powers and Other Essays* (Chicago: University of Chicago Press, 1972).

2. "We're All Totalitarians," *Times Literary Supplement* (London), 5 May 1972, p. 507.

3. Kenneth Keniston, "Revolution or Counterrevolution?" in R. J. Lifton and E. Olson (eds.), *Explorations in Psycho-history: The Wellfleet Papers* (New York: Simon & Schuster, 1974), pp. 293–94.

4. L. N. Moskvichev, *The End of Ideology Theory: Illusions and Reality* (Moscow: Progress Publishers, 1974), pp. 8, 11–12.

5. Ibid., pp. 181–82.

6. Criticisms of the "end-of-ideology" school include: Henry D. Aiken, "The Revolt against Ideology," *Commentary* 37 (April 1964): 29–39; Norman Birnbaum, "The Sociological Study of Ideology (1940–1960)," *Current Sociology* 9 (1960), esp. pp. 115–17; William Connolly, *Political Science and Ideology* (New York: Atherton Press, 1967), esp. pp. 51–53; R. Alan Haber, "The End of Ideology as Ideology," *Our Generation* (November 1966): 51–68; Nigel Harris, *Beliefs in Society: The Problem of Ideology* (London: C. A. Watts, 1968), pp. 10–12; Joseph LaPalombara, "Decline of Ideology: A Dissent and an Interpretation," *American Political Science Review* 60 (March 1966): 5–16; Ralph Miliband, "Mills and Politics," in I. L. Horowitz (ed.), *The New Sociology* (New York: Oxford University Press, 1964), pp. 86–87; Stephen W. Rousseas and James Farganis, "American Politics and the End of Ideology," in Horowitz (ed.), *The New Sociology*, pp. 268–89; Dusky Lee Smith, "The Sunshine Boys: Toward a Sociology of Happiness," in Larry T. Reynolds and Janice M. Reynolds (eds.), *The Sociology of Sociology* (New York: David McKay, 1970), pp. 371–87; C. H. Anderson, *Toward a New Sociology* (Homewood, Ill.: Dorsey Press, 1971), p. 38; Giuseppe Di Palma, *The Study of Conflict in Western Society: A Critique of the End of Ideology* (Morristown, N.J.: General Learning Press, 1973); Dennis H. Wrong, "Reflections on the End of Ideology," *Dissent* 7 (Summer 1960): 286–91; Michael Harrington, "The Anti-Ideology Ideologues," in C. I. Waxman (ed.), *The End of Ideology Debate* (New York: Funk & Wagnalls, 1968), pp. 342–51;

Donald Clark Hodges, "The End of 'The End of Ideology,' " *American Journal of Economics and Sociology* 26 (April 1967): 135–46; Peter Clecak, *Radical Paradoxes* (New York: Harper & Row, 1974), pp. 238–39.

7. Friedrich Engels, "Ludwig Feuerbach and the End of Classical German Philosophy" (1886), in K. Marx and F. Engels, *On Religion* (Moscow: Foreign Languages Publishing House, 1957), p. 263.

8. Lewis Feuer, "Ethical Theories and Historical Materialism," *Science and Society* 6 (Summer 1942): 269.

9. See *From Max Weber: Essays in Sociology*, edited by H. H. Gerth and C. Wright Mills (New York: Oxford University Press, 1946), pp. 155–56. For basic conceptualization, see Max Weber, *Economy and Society*, trans. Ephraim Fischoff et al. (Totowa, N. J.: Bedminster, 1968), pp. 24–26, and *The Theory of Social and Economic Organization*, trans. A. M. Henderson and Talcott Parsons (New York: Oxford University Press, 1947), pp. 115–18.

10. William Delany, "The Role of Ideology: A Summation," in Waxman (ed.), *The End of Ideology Debate*, p. 304.

11. As discussed and cited in Guenther Roth, *The Social Democrats in Imperial Germany* (Totowa, N. J.: Bedminster, 1963), p. 252.

12. Karl Mannheim, *Ideology and Utopia*, trans. Louis Wirth and Edward Shils (1929) (New York: Harcourt, Brace, 1949), pp. 222–36.

13. Ibid., p. 235.

14. Ibid., p. 230.

15. As quoted in Roy Pierce, "Anti-Ideological Thought in France," in M. Rejai, ed., *Decline of Ideology?* (Chicago: Aldine/Atherton, 1971), p. 287. See also Albert Camus, *Resistance, Rebellion, and Death* (London: Hamish Hamilton, 1969), pp. 197–98.

16. This thesis is presented by T. H. Marshall in his now-classic essay, "Citizenship and Social Class," in his *Citizenship and Social Class and Other Essays* (Cambridge: Cambridge University Press, 1950), pp. 1–85, reprinted in his *Class, Citizenship, and Social Development* (Garden City, N.Y.: Doubleday, 1964), pp. 65–122.

17. Isaiah Berlin, "Political Ideas in the Twentieth Century," *Foreign Affairs* 28 (April 1950): 376–77.

18. H. Stuart Hughes, "The End of Political Ideology," *Measure* 2 (Spring 1951): 150, 151, 154–55.

19. Aron, "Fin de l'âge idéologique?" in Adorno and Dirks (eds.), *Sociologica*.

20. Martin Jay, "The Frankfurt School's Critique of Karl Mannheim and the Sociology of Knowledge," *Telos* 20 (Summer 1974), p. 84.

21. Theodor W. Adorno, *Prismen* (Berlin: Suhrkamp, 1955), p. 30.

22. Frankfurt Institute for Social Research, *Aspects of Sociology* (Boston: Beacon, 1972), pp. 199, 202–3.

23. Otto Kirchheimer, "The Transformation of the Western Party Systems," in Joseph LaPalombara and Myron Weiner (eds.), *Political Parties and Political Development* (Princeton, N. J.: Princeton University Press, 1966), pp. 184, 190.

24. Otto Kirchheimer, "Germany: The Vanishing Opposition," in Robert Dahl (ed.), *Political Oppositions in Western Democracies* (New Haven: Yale University Press, 1966), p. 247. See also Otto Kirchheimer, "The Waning of Opposition in Parliamentary Regimes," *Social Research* 24 (Summer 1957): 128–56. In a note to his article in the Dahl volume, Kirchheimer remarks that these points

have been discussed by a number of others, including Herbert Tingsten, Manfred Friedrich, Karl Bracher, and Lipset. See his "Germany," p. 247.

25. Lucien Goldmann, "Understanding Marcuse," *Partisan Review* 38 (1971): 258.
26. Herbert Marcuse, *One-Dimensional Man* (Boston: Beacon, 1964), pp. xii–xiii.
27. Leo Rosten, *A Trumpet for Reason* (Garden City, N. Y.: Doubleday, 1970), pp. 64–65.
28. This interview, published in *Le Monde* for 11 April 1968, is cited in "Upsurge of the Youth Movement in Capitalist Countries," *World Marxist Review* 11 (July 1968): 8.
29. Herbert Marcuse, *An Essay on Liberation* (Boston: Beacon, 1969), p. 56.
30. Barrington Moore, Jr., *Political Power and Social Theory* (Cambridge, Mass.: Harvard University Press, 1958), p. 183.
31. T. B. Bottomore, *Classes in Modern Society* (London: Ampersand, 1955), pp. 52–53.
32. T. B. Bottomore, *Classes in Modern Society*, 2d rev. ed. (New York: Pantheon Books, 1966), pp. 95–96.
33. Bottomore, *Classes in Modern Society*, 1st ed., p. 52.
34. T. B. Bottomore, *Critics of Society: Radical Thought in North America* (London: Allen & Unwin, 1967), p. 19.
35. T. B. Bottomore, "Conservative Man," *New York Review of Books*, 8 October 1970, p. 20.
36. Bottomore, *Classes in Modern Society*, 1st ed., pp. 46–48.
37. Ibid., pp. 53–55.
38. Bottomore, "Conservative Man," p. 21.
39. Quoted, ibid., p. 22. The quote is from S. M. Lipset and Philip Altbach, "Student Politics and Higher Education in the United States," in S. M. Lipset (ed.), *Student Politics* (New York: Basic Books, 1967), p. 244.
40. Bottomore, *Critics of Society*, p. 133.
41. T. B. Bottomore, "The Prospect for Radicalism," in Bernard Landis and Edward S. Tauber (eds.), *In the Name of Life: Essays in Honor of Erich Fromm* (New York: Rinehart & Winston, 1971), p. 319.
42. S. M. Lipset, *Rebellion in the University* (Chicago: University of Chicago Press, 1976), p. 195.
43. Quoted in Beverly Stephen, "Veterans of the Student Revolution," San Francisco *Chronicle*, 31 October 1973.
44. Joseph R. Gusfield, *Utopian Myths and Movements in Modern Societies* (Morristown, N. J.: General Learning Press, 1973), p. 1.
45. See, especially, his book, *The Uncommitted* (New York: Harcourt, Brace, 1965), and his articles, "Alienation and the Decline of Utopia," *American Scholar* 29 (Spring 1960): 1–10, and "American Students and the 'Political Revival,' " *American Scholar* 32 (Winter 1963): 40–64. Both articles are included in his collection of essays, *Youth and Dissent* (New York: Harcourt, Brace, Jovanovich, 1971), in which Keniston allows his readers to share his changes in evaluation as the years progressed.
46. Kenneth Keniston, "Revolution or Counterrevolution?," pp. 293–94.
47. See discussion and citations, pp. 93–96.
48. For representative literature presenting different variants of the thesis, not cited elsewhere in this article, see Herbert Tingsten, "Stability and Vitality in Swedish Democracy," *Political Quarterly* 26 (April–June 1955): 140–51; Lewis Feuer, *Psychoanalysis and Ethics* (Springfield, Ill.: Charles C. Thomas, 1955), pp. 126–

30; Stein Rokkan, *Sammenlignende Poliiskisosilogi* (Bergen: Chr. Michelsens Instittutt, 1958); Ralf Dahrendorf, *Class and Class Conflict in Industrial Society* (Stanford: Stanford University Press, 1959), esp. pp. 241–318; Gunnar Myrdal, *Beyond the Welfare State* (New Haven: Yale University Press, 1960); George Lichtheim, *The New Europe* (New York: Praeger, 1963), esp. pp. 175–215; Robert E. Lane, "The Politics of Consensus in an Age of Affluence," *American Political Science Review* 59 (1965): 874–95; Robert E. Lane, "The Decline of Politics and Ideology in a Knowledgeable Society," *American Sociological Review* 31 (1966): 649–62; Robert Tucker, "The Deradicalization of Marxist Movements," *American Political Science Review* 61 (1967): 343–58; Mark Abrams, "Social Trends and Electoral Behavior," *British Journal of Sociology* 13 (1962): 228–41; Manfred Friedrich, *Opposition ohne Alternative* (Cologne: Verlag Wissenschaft und Politik, 1962); Judith Shklar, *After Utopia: The Decline of Political Faith* (Princeton: Princeton University Press, 1957); Talcott Parsons, "An Approach to the Sociology of Knowledge," *Transactions of the Fourth World Congress of Sociology* (Louvain: International Sociological Association, 1959), 4:25–49; Thomas Molnar, *The Decline of the Intellectual* (Cleveland: Meridian, 1961), esp. pp. 199–222; Stephen R. Graubard (ed.), *A New Europe?* (Boston: Houghton Mifflin, 1964), esp. essays by Ernst B. Haas, Karl Dietrich Bracher, Ralf Dahrendorf, S. M. Lipset, Alain Touraine, Eric Weil, and Michel Crozier; David Riesman, "Introduction" to Stimson Bullitt, *To Be a Politician* (New York: Doubleday, 1959), esp. p. 20.

49. Quoted in Rousseas and Farganis, "American Politics and the End of Ideology," p. 284.

50. Arthur Schlesinger, Jr., "Where Does the Liberal Go from Here?" *New York Times Magazine*, 4 August 1957, pp. 7, 36.

51. Arthur Schlesinger, Jr., "Epilogue: The One against the Many," in A. M. Schlesinger, Jr., and Morton White (eds.), *Paths of American Thought* (Boston: Houghton Mifflin, 1963), p. 536.

52. John Kenneth Galbraith, *The Affluent Society* (Boston: Houghton Mifflin, 1958), pp. 97, 119.

53. Shils, "The End of Ideology?," p. 57.

54. Shils, *The Intellectuals and the Powers*, p. 55.

55. Aron, *The Opium of the Intellectuals*, p. 323.

56. Aron, *The Industrial Society*, p. 169.

57. Ibid., p. 161.

58. Lipset, *Political Man*, p. 444; Lipset, *Revolution and Counterrevolution*, pp. 268–70; Lipset, *Political Man*, p. 371. See also Talcott Parsons, *Politics and Social Structure* (New York: Free Press, 1969), pp. 252, 257–59, 261, 277.

59. Bell, *The End of Ideology*, p. 404.

60. C. Wright Mills, *Power, Politics, and People* (New York: Ballantine, 1963), p. 256.

61. Ibid., pp. 256–57.

62. John Kenneth Galbraith, *The New Industrial State* (New York: Signet, 1968), pp. 330–31.

63. T. B. Bottomore, *Elites and Society* (London: Watts, 1964), p. 70.

64. Bell, *The End of Ideology*, p. 405.

65. Bell, *The Coming of Post-Industrial Society*, pp. 477–78.

66. S. M. Lipset and Richard Dobson, "The Intellectual as Critic and Rebel: With Special Reference to the United States and the Soviet Union," *Daedalus* 101

(Summer 1972): 137–98; S. M. Lipset, "Academia and Politics in America," in T. J. Nossiter et al. (eds.), *Imagination and Precision in the Social Sciences* (London: Faber, 1972), pp. 211–89; E. C. Ladd, Jr. and S. M. Lipset, *The Divided Academy: Professors and Politics* (New York: Norton, 1976), esp. pp. 125–48; S. M. Lipset and Asoke Basu, "Intellectual Types and Political Roles," in Lewis Coser (ed.), *The Idea of Social Structure* (New York: Harcourt, Brace, 1975), pp. 433–70.

67. *From Max Weber: Essays in Sociology*, p. 155.
68. Mannheim, *Ideology and Utopia*, pp. 230–31.
69. Ibid., pp. 232–33.
70. Karl Mannheim, *Man and Society in an Age of Reconstruction*, trans. Edward Shils (New York: Harcourt, Brace, 1950), p. 110.
71. James C. Davies, *Ideology: Its Causes and a Partial Cure* (Morristown, N. J.: General Learning Press, 1974), p. 3.
72. Rousseas and Farganis, "American Politics and the End of Ideology," p. 274.
73. Lipset, *Revolution and Counterrevolution*, p. 303.
74. Hughes, "The End of Political Ideology," p. 158.
75. Moskvichev, *The End of Ideology Theory*, p. 28.
76. Franz Schurmann, "System, Contradictions, and Revolutions in America," in Roderick Ayn and Norman Miller (eds.), *The New American Revolution* (New York: Free Press, 1971), p. 61.
77. Moskvichev, *The End of Ideology Theory*, pp. 62–66.
78. Alvin W. Gouldner, "Toward a Radical Reconstruction of Sociology," *Social Policy* 1 (May–June 1970): 21.
79. Shils, *The Intellectuals and the Powers*, pp. 40–41.
80. M. Rejai, W. L. Mason, and D. C. Beller, "Empirical Relevance of the Hypothesis of Decline," in Rejai (ed.), *Decline of Ideology*, pp. 274–75. See also Paul R. Abramson, "Social Class and Political Change in Western Europe," *Comparative Political Studies* 4 (July 1971), esp. pp. 146–47, and David R. Schweitzer, *Status Frustration and Conservatism in Comparative Perspective: The Swiss Case* (Beverly Hills, Calif.: Sage, 1974), pp. 17–21.
81. John Clayton Thomas, *The Decline of Ideology in Western Political Parties: A Study of Changing Policy Orientations* (Beverly Hills, Calif.: Sage, 1974), p. 13.
82. Ibid., p. 26.
83. Ibid., p. 44.
84. John Clayton Thomas, "The Changing Nature of Partisan Divisions in the West: Trends in Domestic Policy Orientations in Ten Party Systems," *European Journal of Political Research* 7 (December 1979): 403–5.
85. Ibid., p. 406.
86. Thomas, *The Decline of Ideology*, pp. 45–46.
87. Rejai, Mason, and Beller, "Empirical Relevance of the Hypothesis of Decline," in Rejai (ed.), *Decline of Ideology*, p. 275.
88. Richard Rose and Derek W. Urwin, "Persistence and Change in Western Party Systems since 1945," *Political Studies* 18 (September 1970): 295.
89. John Kenneth Galbraith, "The Conservative Onslaught," *New York Review of Books* 27 (22 January 1981): 30.
90. Ibid., p. 36.
91. Richard Simpson, "Systems and Humanism in Social Science," *Science* 173 (May 1971): 664.

PART II

CONFLICT AND POLITICS

4

Cleavage Structures, Party Systems, and Voter Alignments

With Stein Rokkam

Initial Formulations

Questions for Comparative Analysis

This chapter deals with a series of central questions in the comparative sociology of politics.

The first set of questions concerns *the genesis of the system of contrasts and cleavages* within the national community. Which conflicts came first and which later? Which ones proved temporary and secondary? Which proved obdurate and pervasive? Which cut across each other and produced overlaps between allies and enemies, and which reinforced each other and tended to polarize the national citizenry?

A second group of questions focuses on *the conditions for the development of a stable system of cleavage and oppositions* in national political life: Why did some early conflicts establish party oppositions and others not? Which of the many conflicting interests and outlooks in the national community produced direct opposition between competing parties, and which of them could be aggregated *within* the broad party fronts? Which conditions favored extensive aggregations of oppositional groups, and which offered greater incentive to fragmented articulation of single interests or narrowly defined causes? To what extent were these developments affected by changes in the legal and the administrative conditions of political activity, through the extension of the rights of participation, through the introduction of secret voting and the development of strict controls of electoral corruption, and through the retention of plurality decisions or the introduction of some variety of Proportional Representation?

A third and final set of questions bears on *the behavior of the mass of rank-and-file citizens* within the resultant party systems: How quickly were the parties able to recruit support among the new masses of enfranchized citizens, and what were the core characteristics of the groups of voters mobilized by each party? Which conditions helped and which conditions hindered the mobilization efforts of each party within the different groups of the mass citizenry? How quickly did the changes in economic, social, and cultural conditions brought about through economic growth or stagnation translate themselves into changes in the strengths and the strategies of the parties? How did political success affect the rates of mobilization and the inflow of new support to each party? Did the parties tend to recruit new clienteles and change their followings as they established their viability as useful channels of influence in the decision-making processes?

All these issues have an important *historical* dimension. They all in one way or another confront us with tasks of *developmental comparison:* to understand the current alignments of voters behind each of the parties, we have to map variations in the *sequences of alternatives* set for the active and the passive citizens within each system since the emergence of competitive politics. Parties do not simply present themselves *de novo* to the citizen at each election; they each have a history and so have the constellations of alternatives they present to the electorate. In single-nation studies we need not always take this history into account in analyzing current alignments: we assume that the parties are equally visible "givens" to all citizens within the nation. But as soon as we move into comparative analysis we have to add an historical dimension. We simply cannot make sense of variations in current alignments without detailed data on differences in the sequences of party formation and in the character of the alternatives presented to the electorates before and after the extension of the suffrage.[1] We have to carry out our comparative analyses in several steps: we first have to consider the initial developments toward competitive politics and the institutionalization of mass elections, we next must disentangle the constellation of cleavages and oppositions which produced the national system of mass organizations for electoral action, and then, and only then, can we make headway toward some understanding of the forces producing the current alignments of voters behind the historically given alternatives. In our Western democracies the voters are only rarely called upon to express their stands on single issues. They are typically faced with choices among historically given "packages" of programs, commitments, outlooks, and, sometimes, *Weltanschauungen*, and their current behavior cannot be understood without some knowledge of the sequences of events and the combinations of forces that produced these "packages." Our task is to develop realistic models to explain the formation of different systems of such "packages" under different conditions of national politics and socioeconomic development and to fit information on these variations in the character of the alternatives into our schemes for the analysis of current electoral behavior. We hope to throw light on the origins and the "freezing" of different types of *party systems,* and we seek to assemble materials for comparative analyses of the *current alignments of voters* behind the historically given "packages" in the different systems.

In this statement we limit ourselves to a few salient points of comparison. A full comparative treatment of the party systems and the voter alignments of the West, not to speak of the competitive systems in other regions of the world, must await the completion of a number of detailed sociological analyses of national political developments.[2] We shall first discuss a typology of possible cleavage bases within national political communities; we shall then move on to a consideration of the actual party systems in Western polities, and we shall finally point to differences between party systems in the voters' characteristic alignments behind the alternatives among which they are asked to choose. In this final section we shall give attention not only to alignments by such obvious sociocultural criteria as *region, class,* and *religious denomination,* but also to alignments by strictly political criteria of membership in "we" versus "they" groups. We shall consider the possibility that the *parties themselves* might establish themselves as significant poles of attraction and produce their own alignments independently of the geographical, the social, and the cultural underpinnings of the movements.

(Parenthetically, to observe the "freezing" of different types of party systems and voter alignments does not eliminate the possibility that these alignments cannot be "thawed." In chapter 4, "Radicalism or Reformism: The Sources of Working-class Politics," written in 1982, fifteen years after this one, I note that as a result of an unprecedented era of economic growth and prosperity following the Second World War many postfeudal elements "have declined greatly or have disappeared in the industrialized countries." Moreover, the development of new cleavages clustering around postmaterialist values "have changed the divisions between the left and the right and have affected their bases of support. These new issues are linked to an increase in middle-class political radicalism and working-class social conservatism." This observation is developed and documented in chapter 5, "The Industrial Proletariat and the Intelligentsia in Comparative Perspective." The understanding of contemporary politics must, however, as Stein Rokkan and I insisted, begin with the genesis of the current party systems and voter alignments.)

The Political Party: Agent of Conflict and Instrument of Integration

"Party" has throughout the history of Western government stood for division, conflict, opposition within a body politic.[3] "Party" is etymologically derived from "part" and since it first appeared in political discourse in the late Middle Ages has always retained this reference to one set of elements in competition or in controversy with another set of elements within some unified whole.[4]

It will be objected that since the twentieth century has given us an abundance of monolithic parties, totalitarian parties, and "one-party systems" these suggest another sense of the term, a divergent usage. This represents an old ambiguity in the use of the term. In his *Wirtschaft und Gesellschaft* Max Weber discussed the use of the term "party" in descriptions of medieval Italian city politics and asserted that the Florentine Guelfs "ceased to be a party" in the sociological sense once they had been incorporated as part of the governing bureaucracy of the city.[5] Weber explicitly refused to accept any equivalence between "party" as used in descriptions of competitive voluntary politics and "party" as used of monolithic systems. The distinction is of obvious analytical importance, but there is still a latent unity of usage. The totalitarian party does not function through *freie Werbung*—through free competition in the political market—but it is still a *part* of a much larger whole and it is still in *opposition* to other forces within that whole. The typical totalitarian party is composed of the active, mobilizing part of the national system: it does not compete with other parties for offices and favors, but it still seeks to mobilize the populace *against* something—against conspiratorial counterforces within the national community or against the threatening pressures from foreign enemies. Totalitarian elections may not make much sense from a Western perspective, but they nevertheless serve important legitimizing functions: they are "rituals of confirmation" in a continuous campaign against the "hidden" opposition, the illegitimate opponents of the established regime.

Whatever the structure of the polity, parties have served as essential agencies of mobilization and as such have helped to integrate local communities into the nation or the broader federation. This was true of the earliest competitive party systems, and it is eminently true of the single-party nations of the postcolonial era. In his insightful analysis of the formation of the American party system, William Chambers has assembled a wide range of indications of the integrative role of the first national parties, the Federalists and the Democratic-Republicans: they were the first genuinely national organizations; they represented the first successful efforts to pull Americans out of their local community and their state and to give them roles in the national polity.[6] Analyses of parties in the new nations of the twentieth century arrive at similar conclusions. Ruth Schachter has shown how the African single-party organizations have been used by the political leaders to "awaken a wider national sense of community" and to create ties of communication and cooperation across territorial and ethnic populations.[7]

In competitive party systems this process of integration can be analyzed at two levels: on the one hand, each party establishes a network of cross-local communication channels and in that way helps to strengthen national identities; on the other, its very competiveness helps to set the national system of government *above* any particular set of officeholders. This cuts both ways: the citizens are encouraged to distinguish between their loyalty to the total political system and their attitudes to the sets of competing politicians, and the contenders for power will, at least if they have some chance of gaining office, have some interest in maintaining this attachment of all citizens to the polity and its rules of alternation. In a monolithic polity citizens are not encouraged to distinguish between the system and current officeholders. The citizenry tends to identify the polity with the policies of particular leaders, and the power-holders habitually exploit the established national loyalties to rally support for themselves. In such societies any attack on the political leaders or on the dominant party tends to turn into an attack on the political system itself. Quarrels over particular policies or particular incumbencies immediately raise fundamental issues of system survival. In a competitive party system opponents of the current governing team may well be accused of weakening the state or betraying the traditions of the nation, but the continued existence of the political system is not in jeopardy. A competitive party system protects the nation against the discontents of its citizens: grievances and attacks are deflected from the overall system and directed toward the current set of powerholders.[8]

Sociologists such as E. A. Ross[9] and Georg Simmel[10] have analyzed the integrative role of institutionalized conflicts within political systems. The establishment of regular channels for the expression of conflicting interests has helped to stabilize the structure of a great number of nation-states. The effective equalization of the status of different denominations has helped to take much of the brunt off the earlier conflicts over religious issues. The extension of the suffrage and the enforcement of the freedom of political expression also helped to strengthen the legitimacy of the nation-state. The opening up of channels for the expression of manifest or latent conflicts between the established and the underprivileged classes may have brought many systems out of equilibrium in the earlier phase but tended to strengthen the body politic over time.

This conflict-integration dialectic is of central concern in current research on the comparative sociology of political parties. In this essay the emphasis is on *conflicts and their translation into party systems*. This does not mean that we neglect the integrative functions of parties. We have simply chosen to start out from the latent or manifest strains and cleavages and deal with trends toward compromise and reconciliation against the background of the initial conflicts. Our concern is with parties as *alliances in conflicts over policies and value commitments within the larger body politic*. For the sociologist, parties exert a double fascination. They help to crystallize and make explicit the conflicting interests, the latent strains and contrasts in the existing social structure, and they force subjects and citizens to ally themselves across structural cleavage lines and to set up priorities among their commitments to established or prospective roles in the system. Parties have an *expressive* function; they develop a rhetoric for the translation of contrasts in the social and the cultural structure into demands and pressures for action or inaction. But they also have *instrumental* and *representative* functions: they force the spokesmen for the many contrasting interests and outlooks to strike bargains, to stagger demands, and to aggregate pressures. Small parties may content themselves with expressive functions, but no party can hope to gain decisive influence on the affairs of a community without some willingness to cut across existing cleavages to establish common fronts with potential enemies and opponents. This was true at the early stage of embryonic party formations around cliques and clubs of *notables* and legislators, but the need for such broad alliances became even more pronounced with the extension of the rights of participation to new strata of the citizenry.

No one has given us a more concise literary analysis of this process of aggregation during the early phase of mass mobilization than H. G. Wells in *The New Machiavelli*:

> Multitudinousness had always been the Liberal characteristic. Liberalism never has been nor even can be anything but a diversified crowd. Essentially it is the party of criticism, the "Anti" party. It is a system of hostilities and objections that somehow achieves at times an elusive common soul. It is a gathering together of all the smaller interests which find themselves at a disadvantage against the big established classes, the leasehold tenant as against the landowner, the retail tradesman as against the merchant and the money-lender, the Non-conformist as against the Churchman, the smaller employer as against the demoralising hospitable publican, the man without introductions and broad connections against the man who has these things. . . . It has no more essential reason for loving the Collectivist state than the Conservatives; the smaller dealer is doomed to absorption in that just as much as the large one; but it resorts to the state against its antagonists as in the middle ages common men pitted themselves against the barons by siding with the king. The Liberal Party is the party against "class privilege" because it represents no class advantages, but it is also the party that is on the whole most set against Collective control because it represents no established responsibility. It is constructive only as far as its antagonism to the great owner is more powerful than its jealousy of the state. It organizes only because organization is forced upon it by the organization of its adversaries. It lapses in and out of alliance with Labour as it sways between hostility to wealth and hostility to public expenditure.[11]

Similar, if less vivid, descriptions could be given of most of the parties aspiring to majority positions in the West: they are conglomerates of groups differing on wide ranges of issues, but still united in their greater hostility to their competitors in the other camps. Conflicts and controversies can arise out of a great variety of relationships in the social structure, but only a few of these tend to polarize the politics of any given system. There is a *hierarchy of cleavage bases* in each system and these orders of political primacy not only vary among polities, but also tend to undergo changes over time. Such differences and changes in the political weight of sociocultural cleavages set fundamental problems for comparative research: When is region, language, or ethnicity most likely to prove polarizing? When will class take primacy and when will denominational commitments and religious identities prove equally important cleavage bases? Which sets of circumstances are most likely to favor accommodations of such oppositions *within* parties and in which circumstances are they more apt to constitute issues *between* the parties? Which types of alliances tend to maximize the strain on the polity and which ones help to integrate it? Questions such as these will be on the agenda of comparative political sociology for years to come. There is no dearth of hypotheses, but so far very little in the way of systematic analysis across several systems. It has often been suggested that systems will come under much heavier strain if the main lines of cleavage are over morals and the nature of human destiny than if they concern such mundane and negotiable matters as the prices of commodities, the rights of debtors and creditors, wages and profits, and the ownership of property. However, this does not take us very far; what we want to know is when the one type of cleavage will prove more salient than the other, what kind of alliances they have produced and what consequences these constellations of forces have had for consensus-building within the nation-state. We do not pretend to find clear-cut answers, but we have tried to move the analysis one step further. We shall start out with a review of a variety of *logically possible* sources of strains and oppositions in social structures and shall then proceed to an inventory of the *empirically extant examples of political expressions of each set of conflicts*. We have not tried to present a comprehensive scheme of analysis in this context but would like to point to one possible line of approach.

Dimensions of Cleavage: A Possible Model

The much-debated fourfold schema devised by Talcott Parsons for the classification of the functions of a social system offers a convenient point of departure for an inventory of potential cleavage bases.

The four-function scheme was originally developed in *Working Papers in the Theory of Action*[12] and was derived from a cross-classification of four basic dilemmas of orientation in the roles taken by actors in social systems:

Categorization of situational objects	Attitudes to objects	Corresponding functions for the system
I. Universalism *vs.* Particularism	III. Specificity *vs.* Diffuseness	Adaptation Integration
II. Performance *vs.* Quality	IV. Affectivity *vs.* Neutrality	Goal attainment Latency: pattern maintenance and tension release

This abstract schema came to serve as a basic paradigm in a series of successive attempts[13] to map the flows and the media of interchange among the actors and the collectivities within social systems or within total territorial societies. The paradigm posited four "functional subsystems" of every society and six lines of interchange between each pair:

FIGURE 4.1
The Parsonian Paradigm of Societal Interchanges

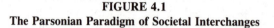

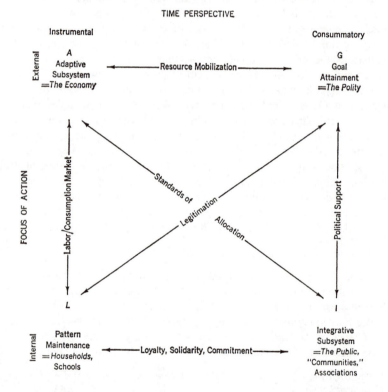

Three of these sets of interchanges are of crucial concern to the political sociologist:

He wants to know how the solidary collectivities, the latent communalities of interests and prospects, and the manifest associations and movements within a given territorial society limit the alternatives and influence the decisions of governmental leaders and their executive agencies—these are all processes of interchange between the *I* and *G* subsystems.[14]

He wants to know how ready or how reluctant individual subjects and households in the society are to be mobilized for action by the different associations and movements and how they make up their minds in cases of competition and conflict between different mobilizing agencies—these are all questions about interchanges between the *L* and *I* subsystems.

He is concerned finally to find out about regularities in the behavior of individual subjects and households in their direct interchanges (*L* to *G*, *G* to *L*) with the territorial agencies of government, be it as observers of legal regulations, as taxpayers and conscripted manpower, or as voters in institutionalized elections and consultations.

However, our task in this chapter is narrower. We do not intend to deal with *all* the interchanges between *I* and *G*, between *I* and *L*, or between *L* and *G*. We are only concerned with the *I–G* interchanges insofar as they press forward the development of *systems of competing parties*. We are only interested in the *I–L* interchanges insofar as they help to establish *distinct links of membership, identification, and readiness for mobilization* between given parties and given categories of subjects and households. And we are not interested in *all* the *L–G* interchanges, but only in the ones that find expression in *elections* and in arrangements for *formal representation*.

In terms of the Parsonian paradigm our tasks are in fact fourfold:

1. We first have to examine the *internal structure* of the *I* quadrant in a range of territorial societies: What cleavages had manifested themselves in the national community in the early phases of consolidation, and what cleavages emerged in the subsequent phases of centralization and economic growth? Questions of this type will be dealt with in the next section.
2. Our next job is to compare *sequences of I–G interchanges* to trace regularities in the processes of *party formation*. How did the inherited cleavages find political expression, and how did the territorial organization of the nation-state, the division of powers between governors and representatives, and the broadening of the rights of participation and consultation affect the development of alliances and oppositions among political tendencies and movements and eventually produce a distinctive party system? Questions along these lines will occupy us in the two succeeding sections.
3. Our third job is to study the consequences of these developments for the *I–L interchanges*. Which identities, which solidarities, which communalities of experience and fate could be reinforced and made use of by the emerging parties and which ones had to be softened or ignored? Where in the social structure did the parties find it easiest to mobilize stable support, and where did they meet the most impenetrable barriers of suspicion and rejection? We shall touch on these questions in the final section but cannot go into the details on particular national party systems.
4. And our final task is to bring all these diverse data to bear on the analysis of the *L–G interchanges* in the operation of *elections and the recruitment of representatives*. How far do electoral distributions reflect structural

cleavages in the given society; how is electoral behavior affected by the narrowing of alternatives brought about by the party system; and how far are the efforts of indoctrination and mobilization hampered through the development of a politically neutral electoral machinery, the formalizing and the standardization of procedures, and the introduction of secret voting?[15]

Underlying this interpretation of the Parsonian scheme is a simple three-phase model of the process of nation-building:

In the first phase the thrusts of penetration and standardization from the national center increase territorial resistances and raise issues of cultural identity. Robert E. Lee's "am I a Virginian or an American?" is a typical expression of the G–L strains generated through the processes of nation-building.

In the second phase these local oppositions to centralization produce a *variety of alliances* across the communities of the nation: the commonalities of family fates in the L quadrangle generate associations and organizations in the I quadrangle. In some cases these alliances will pit one part of the national territory against another. This is typically the case in countries where a number of counterestablishment loyalties converge: ethnicity, religion, and class in Ireland under the raj, language and class in Belgium, Finland, Spain, and Canada. In other cases the alliances will tend to spread throughout the nation and pit opponents against each other in all localities.

In the third phase the alliances in the I quadrangle will enter the G quadrangle and gain some measure of control, not only over the use of central national resources (G–A interchanges) but also over the channeling of the flows of legitimation from L to G. This may find expression in franchise reforms, in changes in the procedures of registration and polling, in new rules of electoral aggregation, and in extensions of the domains of legislative intervention.

This model can be developed in several directions. We have chosen to focus initial attention on the possible differentiations within the I quadrangle—the locus for the formation of parties and party constellations in mass democracies.

Dimensions of Cleavage And Alliance

Two Dimensions of Cleavage: The Territorial-Cultural and the Functional

Talcott Parsons has so far given surprisingly little attention to the possibilities of internal differentiation within the I quadrant. Among his collaborators, Smelser has devoted much ingenuity to the development of an abstract schema for the explanation of collective reactions and movements,[16] but this elaborate level-by-level procedure of analysis bears essentially on the emergence of single manifestations and offers no direct clues to the classification and comparison of *systems* of social movements and political parties within historically given societies. We cannot hope to fill this lacuna in the theoretical literature but feel tempted to suggest one line of conceptual development from the basic A–G–I–L paradigm. Our suggestion is that the crucial cleavages and their political expressions can be ordered within the two-dimensional space generated by the two diagonals of the double dichotomy:

FIGURE 4.2
A Possible Interpretation of the Internal Structure of the I Quadrant

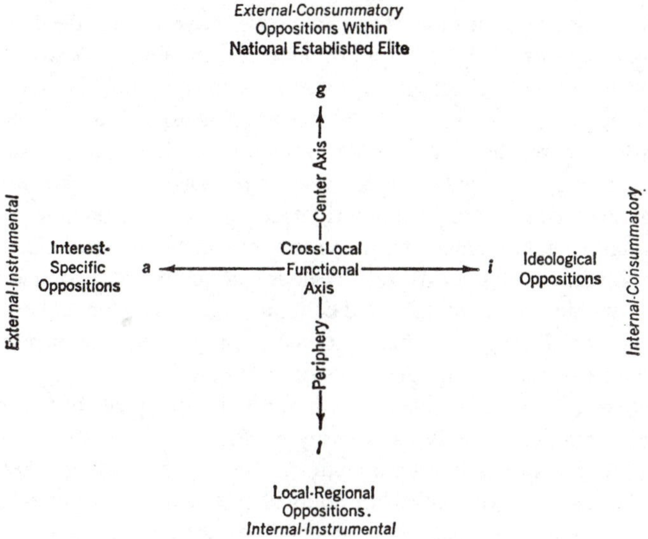

External-Consummatory
Oppositions Within
National Established Elite

g

Center Axis

| Interest-Specific Oppositions | a ← Cross-Local Functional Axis → i | Ideological Oppositions |

External-Instrumental

Internal-Consummatory

Periphery

l

Local-Regional
Oppositions.
Internal-Instrumental

In this model the Parsonian dichotomies have been transformed into continuous coordinates: the l–g line represents a *territorial* dimension of the national cleavage structure and the a–i line a *functional* dimension.[17]

At the l end of the territorial axis we would find strictly local oppositions to encroachments of the aspiring or the dominant national elites and their bureaucracies: the typical reactions of peripheral regions, linguistic minorities, and culturally threatened populations to the pressures of the centralizing, standardizing, and "rationalizing" machinery of the nation-state. At the g end of the axis we would find conflicts not between territorial units *within* the system but over the control, the organization, the goals, and the policy options of the system *as a whole*. These might be nothing more than direct struggles among competing elites for central power, but they might also reflect deeper differences in conceptions of nationhood, over domestic priorities and over external strategies.

Conflicts along the $a-i$ axis *cut across* the territorial units of the nation. They produce alliances of similarly situated or similarly oriented subjects and households over wide ranges of localities and tend to undermine the inherited solidarity of the established territorial communities. At the a end of this dimension we would find the typical conflict over short-term or long-term allocations of resources, products, and benefits in the economy: conflicts between producers and buyers, between workers and employers, between borrowers and lenders, between tenants and owners, between contributors and beneficiaries. At this end the alignments are specific and the conflicts tend to be solved through rational bargaining and the establishment of universalistic rules of allocation. The farther we move toward the i end of the axis, the more diffuse the criteria of alignment, the more intensive the identification with the "we" group, and the more uncompromising the rejection of the "they" group. At the i end of the dimension we find the typical "friend-foe" oppositions of tight-knit religious or ideological movements to the surrounding community. The conflict is no longer over specific gains or losses but over conceptions of moral right and over the interpretation of history and human destiny; membership is no longer a matter of multiple affiliation in many directions, but a diffuse "24-hour" commitment incompatible with other ties within the community; and communication is no longer kept flowing freely over the cleavage lines but restricted and regulated to protect the movement against impurities and the seeds of compromise.

Historically documented cleavages rarely fall at the poles of the two axes: a concrete conflict is rarely exclusively territorial or exclusively functional but will feed on strains in both directions. The model essentially serves as a *grid* in the comparative analysis of political systems: the task is to locate the alliances behind given parties at given times within this two-dimensional space. The axes are not easily quantifiable, and they may not satisfy any criteria of strict scalability; nevertheless, they seem heuristically useful in attempts such as ours at linking up empirical variations in political structures with current conceptualizations in sociological theory.

A few concrete illustrations of party developments may help to clarify the distinctions in our model.

In Britain, the first nation-state to recognize the legitimacy of party oppositions, the initial conflicts were essentially of the types we have located at the l end of the vertical axis. The heads of independent landed families in the counties opposed the powers and the decisions of the government and the administration in London. The opposition between the "Country party" of knights and squires and the "Court and Treasury party" of the Whig magnates and the "placemen" was primarily territorial. The animosities of the Tories were not necessarily directed against the predominance of London in the affairs of the nation, but they were certainly aroused by the high-handed manipulations of the influential officeholders in the administration and their powerful allies in the boroughs. The conflict was not over general policies but over patronage and places. The gentry did not get their share of the *quid pro quo* exchanges of local influence against governmental offices and never established a clear-cut common front against the central power-holders. "Toryism about 1750 was primarily the opposition of the local rulers to central authority and vanished wherever members of that class entered the orbit of Government."[18]

Such particularistic, kin-centered, "ins-outs" oppositions are common in the early phases of nation-building: the electoral clienteles are small, undifferentiated, and easily controlled, and the stakes to be gained or lost in public life tend to be personal and concrete rather than collective and general.

Purely territorial oppositions rarely survive extensions of the suffrage. Much will depend, of course, on the timing of the crucial steps in the building of the nation: territorial unification, the establishment of legitimate government and the monopolization of the agencies of violence, the takeoff toward industrialization and economic growth, the development of popular education, and the entry of the lower classes into organized politics. Early democratization will not necessarily generate clear-cut divisions on functional lines. The initial result of a widening of the suffrage will often be an accentuation of the contrasts between the countryside and the urban centers and between the orthodox-fundamentalist beliefs of the peasantry and the small-town citizens and the secularism fostered in the larger cities and the metropolis. In the United States, the cleavages were typically cultural and religious. The struggles between the Jeffersonians and the Federalists, the Jacksonians and the Whigs, the Democrats and the Republicans centered on contrasting conceptions of public morality and pitted Puritans and other Protestants against Deists, Freemasons, and immigrant Catholics and Jews.[19] The accelerating influx of lower-class immigrants into the metropolitan areas and the centers of industry accentuated the contrasts between the rural and the urban cultural environments and between the backward and the advanced states of the Union. Such cumulations of territorial and cultural cleavages in the early phases of democratization can be documented for country after country. In Norway, all freehold and most leasehold peasants were given the vote as early as in 1814, but took several decades to mobilize in opposition to the King's officials and the dominance of the cities in the national economy.

The crucial cleavages brought out into the open in the seventies were essentially territorial and cultural: the provinces were pitted against the capital; the increasingly estate-conscious peasants defended their traditions and their culture against the standards forced on them by the bureaucracy and the urban bourgeoisie. Interestingly, the extension of the suffrage to the landless laborers in the countryside and the propertyless workers in the cities did not bring about an immediate polarization of the polity on class lines. Issues of language, religion, and morality kept up the territorial oppositions in the system and cut across issues between the poorer and the better-off strata of the population. There were significant variations, however, between localities and between religions: the initial "politics of cultural defense" survived the extension of the suffrage in the egalitarian communities of the South and the West, but lost to straight class politics in the economically backward, hierarchically organized communities of the North.[20] The developments in the South and West of Norway find interesting parallels in the "Celtic fringe" of Britain. In these areas, particularly in Wales, opposition to the territorial, cultural, and economic dominance of the English offered a basis for communitywide support for the Liberals and retarded the development of straight class politics, even in the coalfields.[21] The sudden upsurge of Socialist strength in the northern periphery of Norway parallels the spectacular victory of the Finnish working-class party at the first election under universal suffrage: the fishermen and the crofters of the Norwegian North backed a distinct lower-class party as soon as they got the vote, and so did the Finnish rural proletariat.[22] In terms of our abstract model the politics of the western peripheries of Norway and Britain has its focus at the lower end of the l–g axis, whereas the politics of the backward districts of Finland and the Norwegian North represent alliance formations closer to g and at varying points of the a–i axis. In the one case the decisive criterion of alignment is *commitment to the locality and its dominant culture:* you vote with your community and its leaders irrespective of your economic position. In the other the criterion is *commitment to a class and its collective interests:* you vote with others in the same position as yourself whatever their localities, and you are willing to do so even if this brings you into opposition with members of your community. We rarely find one criterion of alignment completely dominant. There will be deviants from straight territorial voting just as often as from straight class voting. But we often find marked differences between regions in the *weight* of the one or the other criterion of alignment. Here ecological analyses of electoral records and census data for the early phases of mobilization may help us to map such variations in greater detail and to pin-point factors strengthening the dominance of territorial politics and factors accelerating the process of class polarization.[23]

The Two Revolutions: The National and the Industrial

Territorial oppositions set limits to the process of nation-building; pushed to their extreme they lead to war, secession, possibly even population transfers. Functional oppositions can only develop after some initial consolidation of the national territory. They emerge with increasing interaction and communication across the localities and the regions, and they spread through a process of "social mobilization."[24] The growing nation-state developed a wide range of agencies of unification and standardization and gradually penetrated the bastions of "primordial" local culture.[25] So did the organizations of the Church, sometimes in close cooperation with the secular administrators, often in opposition to and competition with the officers of the state. And so did the many autonomous agencies of economic development and growth, the networks of traders and merchants, of bankers and financiers, of artisans and industrial entrepreneurs.

The early growth of the national bureaucracy tended to produce essentially territorial oppositions, but the subsequent widening of the scope of governmental activities and the acceleration of cross-local interactions gradually made for much more complex systems of alignments, some of them *between* localities, and others *across* and *within* localities.

The early waves of countermobilization often threatened the territorial unity of the nation, the federation, or the empire. The mobilization of the peasantry in Norway and in Sweden made it gradually impossible to keep up the union; the mobilization of the subject peoples of the Hapsburg territories broke up the empire; the mobilization of the Irish Catholics led to civil war and secession. The current strains of nation-building in the new states of Africa and Asia reflect similar conflicts between dominant and subject cultures; the postwar histories of the Congo, India, Indonesia, Malaysia, Nigeria, and the Sudan can all be written in such terms. In some cases the early waves of mobilization may not have brought the territorial system to the brink of disruption but left an intractable heritage of territorial-cultural conflict: the Catalan-Basque-Castilian oppositions in Spain, the conflict between Flemings and Walloons in Belgium, and the English-French cleavages in Canada. The conditions for the softening or hardening of such cleavage lines in fully mobilized polities have been poorly studied. The multiple ethnic-religious cleavages of Switzerland and the language conflicts in Finland and Norway have proved much more manageable than the conflict between *Nederlands*-speakers and *francophones* in Belgium and between Quebec and the English-speaking provinces of Canada.

To account for such variations we clearly cannot proceed cleavage by cleavage but must analyze *constellations* of conflict lines within each polity. To account for the variations in such constellations we have found it illuminating to distinguish *four critical lines of cleavage*, as suggested in Figure 4.3.

FIGURE 4.3
Suggested Locations of Four Critical Cleavages in the *a–g–i–l* Paradigm

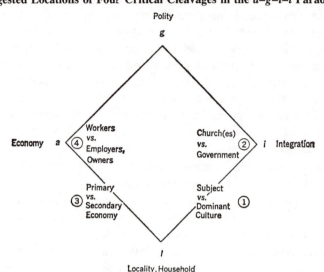

Two of these cleavages are direct products of what we might call the *National* Revolution: the conflict between *the central nation-building culture* and the increasing resistance of the ethnically, linguistically, or religiously distinct *subject populations* in the provinces and the peripheries (1 in Figure 4.3); the conflict between the centralizing, standardizing, and mobilizing *Nation-State* and the historically established corporate privileges of the *Church* (2).

Two of them are products of the *Industrial* Revolution: the conflict between the *landed interests* and the rising class of *industrial entrepreneurs* (3); the conflict between *owners and employers* on the one side and *tenants, laborers, and workers* on the other (4).

Much of the history of Europe since the beginning of the nineteenth century can be described in terms of the interaction between these two processes of revolutionary change: the one triggered in France and the other originating in Britain. Both had consequences for the cleavage structure of each nation, but the French Revolution produced the deepest and the bitterest oppositions. The decisive battle came to stand between *the aspirations of the mobilizing nation-state and the corporate claims of the churches*. This was far more than a matter of economics. It is true that the status of church properties and the financing of religious activities were the subjects of violent controversy, but the fundamental issue was one of morals, of the control of community norms. This found reflection in fights over such matters as the solemnization of marriage and the granting of divorces, the organization of charities and the handling of deviants, the functions of medical versus religious officers, and the arrangements for funerals. However, the fundamental issue between Church and State focused on the *control of education*.

The Church, whether Roman Catholic, Lutheran, or Reformed, had for centuries claimed the right to represent man's "spiritual estate" and to control the education of children in the right faith. In the Lutheran countries, steps were taken as early as in the seventeenth century to enforce elementary education in the vernacular for all children. The established national churches simply became agents of the state and had no reason to oppose such measures. In the religiously mixed countries and in purely Catholic ones, however, the ideas of the French Revolution proved highly divisive. The development of compulsory education under centralized secular control for all children of the nation came into direct conflict with the established rights of the religious *pouvoirs intermédiaires* and triggered waves of mass mobilization into nationwide parties of protest. To the radicals and liberals inspired by the French Revolution, the introduction of compulsory education was only one among several measures in a systematic effort to create direct links of influence and control between the nation-state and the individual citizen, but their attempt to penetrate directly to the children without consulting the parents and their spiritual authorities aroused widespread opposition and bitter fights.[26]

The parties of religious defense generated through this process grew into broad mass movements after the introduction of manhood suffrage and were able to claim the loyalties of remarkably high proportions of the churchgoers in the working class. These proportions increased even more, of course, as the franchise was extended to women on a par with men. Through a process very similar to the one to be described for the Socialist parties, these church movements tended to isolate their supporters from outside influence through the development of a wide variety of parallel organizations and agencies: they not only built up schools and youth movements of their own, but also developed confessionally distinct trade unions, sports clubs, leisure associations, publishing houses, magazines, newspapers, in one or two cases even radio and television stations.[27]

Perhaps the best example of institutionalized segmentation is found in the Netherlands; in fact, the Dutch word *Verzuiling* has recently become a standard term for tendencies to develop vertical networks (*zuilen,* columns or pillars) of associations and institutions to ensure maximum loyalty to each church and to protect the supporters from cross-cutting communications and pressures. Dutch society has for close to a century been divided into three distinct subcultures: the national-liberal-secular, frequently referred to as the *algemene*, the "general" sector; the orthodox Protestant column; and the Roman Catholic column.[28]

The orthodox Protestant column developed through a series of violent conflicts over doctrinal issues within the established National Church. The

Nederlands Hervormde Kerk came under heavy pressure in the decades after the French Revolution and the Napoleonic upheavals. With the spread of secularism and rationalism, the fundamentalists were increasingly pushed into a minority position, both within the Church and in the field of education. Originally, the orthodox protests against these developments restricted themselves to intellectual evangelical movements within the Establishment and to an isolationist walkout of pietistic lower-class elements in the separation (*Afscheiding*) of 1843. But from the 1860s onward, the movement achieved massive momentum under the organizational inspiration of Abraham Kuyper. This fundamentalist clergyman organized an Anti-School-Law League in 1872 and in 1879 succeeded in bringing together a variety of orthodox groups in a party explicitly directed against the ideas of the French Revolution, the Anti-Revolutionary party. This vigorous mass movement soon split up, however, over issues of doctrine and of cultural identification. Kuyper led his followers out of the Mother Church in 1886 and defended the rights of the *Kerkvolk*, the committed Calvinist Christians, to establish their own cultural community, free of any ties to the state and the nation. The very extremism of this anti-establishment posture produced several countermovements within the *Hervormde Kerk*. Important groups of orthodox Calvinists did *not* want to leave the Mother Church but wanted to reform it from within; they wanted a broad *Volkskerk* rather than an isolated *Kerkvolk*. The conflict between these two conceptions of the Christian community led to the breakup of the Anti-Revolutionary party in 1894 and the gradual formation of a second Calvinist party, the Christian Historical Union, formally consolidated in 1908. These two parties became the core organizations of the two wings of the orthodox Protestant front in Dutch society: the Anti-Revolutionaries deriving their essential strength from *Gereformeerden*, whether in separate dissenter churches or in *Hervormde* congregations controlled by clergymen of the same persuasion; the Christian Historicals deriving practically all their support from other orthodox segments *within* the Mother Church.

The Roman Catholic minority had at first found it to their advantage to work with the Liberal majority, but from the sixties onward took steps to form distinct political and social organizations. This was a slow process, however; the first federation of Catholic voters' associations was not formed until 1904 and a formally organized national party was not established until the twenties.[29]

Both the Protestant and the Catholic movements eventually developed large networks of associations and institutions for their members and were able to establish remarkably stable bases of support even within the working class. A nationwide survey carried out in 1956[30] tells a great deal about the importance of religious commitments for political choice in the Dutch system:

TABLE 4.1
**Denomination, Church Attendance, and Party Choice in the Netherlands:
Survey Evidence for 1956**

Denomination: Attendance:	NONE	HERVORMD		GEREFORMEERD		ROMAN CATH.	
		Yes	No	Yes	No	Yes	No
Party							
KPN (Communist)	7%	—	—	—	—	—	—
PvdA (Socialist)	75	22%	51%	2%	27%	3%	30%
VVD (Liberals)	11	7	18	—	—	—	9
Christian Historical	—	45	19	3	—	—	—
Anti-Revolutionary	—	17	6	90	63	—	6
Calvinist Extremist	—	5	3	1	5	—	—
KVP (Catholic)	1	—	—	—	—	94	52
Other	6	4	3	4	5	2	3
N = 100%	(218)	(134)	(236)	(101)	(22)	(329)	(33)

The segmentation is most complete within the active and intransigent minority movements: the *Gereformeerden,* the religiously active *Hervormden*, and the Catholics.

The passive members of the traditional National Church and the *onkerkelijken* tend to be aligned by class rather than by religious commitment: this was for long the only segment in which there was effective crosscutting of influences in the Dutch electorate.

In terms of our paradigm the orthodox Protestants and the Catholics form political fronts near the *i* pole of the cross-local axis. If all *three* of the subcultures had developed such strong barriers against each other, the system might conceivably have exploded, much in the way the Austrian polity did in 1934. The lower level of *Verzuiling* in the "national" sector and the greater possibilities of compromises and accommodation in a triangular system of oppositions may go far to explain the successful operation of corporate pluralism in the Dutch polity.

Analysts of the Dutch data on the three subcultures have tried to establish a variety of indicators of *changes over time* in the degree of insulation of each of the vertical segments: they use the term *Ontzuiling* for reductions in the distinctiveness of each segment and *Verzuiling* for increases.[31] In our paradigm these correspond to movements along the *a–i* axis: the more *ontzuild* a given opposition, the more crisscrossing of multiple memberships in the system and, in general, the less intolerance and distrust of citizens on the "other" side; the more *verzuild* the opposition, the fewer the cross-pressures and the rarer the memberships across the cleavages. In a highly *ontzuild* system there is *low membership crystallization;* most of the participants tend to be tied to organizations and environments exposing them to *divergent* political pressures. By contrast in a highly *verzuild* system there is *high* membership crystallization; most of the participants tend to be exposed to messages and persuasive efforts in the *same* general direction in *all* their "24-hour-7-day" environments.[32]

This dimension cuts across the whole range of functional cleavages in our paradigm, whether economic, social, or religious. The symmetric representation of the four basic cleavage lines in Figure 4.3 refers to *average tendencies* only and does not exclude wide variations in location along the *a–i* axis. Conflicts over the civic integration of recalcitrant regional cultures (1) or religious organizations (2) need not always lead to *Verzuiling*. An analysis of the contrasts between Switzerland and the Netherlands would tell us a great deal about differences in the conditions for the development of pluralist insulation. Conflicts between primary producers and the urban-industrial interests have *normally* tended towards the *a* pole of the axis, but there are many examples of highly ideologized peasant oppositions to officials and burghers. Conflicts between workers and employers have always contained elements of economic bargaining, but there have also often been strong elements of cultural opposition and ideological insulation. Working-class parties in opposition and without power have tended to be more *verzuild*, more wrapped up in their own distinct mythology, more insulated against the rest of the society. By contrast the victorious Labor parties have tended to become *ontzuild*, domesticated, more open to influence from all segments within the national society.

Similar variations will occur at a wide range of points on the *territorial* axis of our schema. In our initial discussion of the *l* pole we gave examples of *cultural* and *religious* resistances to the domination of the central national elite, but such oppositions are not always *purely* territorial. The movements may be completely dominant in their provincial strongholds but may also find allies in the central areas and thus contribute to the development of *cross-local* and *cross-regional* fronts.

The opposition of the Old Left in Norway was essentially of this character. It was from the outset a movement of territorial protest against the dominance of the central elite of officials and patricians but gradually broadened into a mass movement of cultural opposition to the dominant urban strata. As the suffrage was extended and the mobilization efforts proceeded it was also able to entrench itself in the central cities and even gain control in some of them.[33] This very broadening of the movement made the Old Left increasingly vulnerable to fragmentation. One wing moved toward the *a* pole and set itself up as an Agrarian party (3 in Figure 4.3); another wing moved toward the *i* pole and after a long history of strains within the mother party established itself as the Christian People's Party (1 in Figure 4.3). The Scandinavian countries have seen the formation of several such moralist-evangelist parties opposed to the tolerant pragmatism of the Established Lutheran Church.[34] They differ from the Christian parties on the Continent: they have not opposed national education as such and have not built up extensive networks of functional organizations around their followers; they have been primarily concerned to defend the traditions of orthodox evangelism against the onslaught of urban secularism and to use the legislative and the executive machinery of the state to protect the young against the evils of modern life. In their rejection of the lukewarm latitudinarianism of the national Mother Church they resemble the nonconformists in Great Britain and the Anti-Revolutionaries in the Netherlands, but the contexts of their efforts have been very different. In the British case the religious activists could work *within* the Liberal Party (later, of course, also within Labour) and found it possible to advance their views without establishing a party of their own. In the Dutch case, the orthodox dissidents not only set up their own party but built up a strong column of vertical organizations around it.

The National Revolution forced ever-widening circles of the territorial population to choose sides in conflicts over *values* and *cultural identities*. The Industrial Revolution also triggered a variety of cultural countermovements, but in the longer run tended to cut across the value communities within the nation and to force the enfranchised citizenry to choose sides in terms of their *economic interests*, their shares in the increased wealth generated through the spread of the new technologies and the widening markets.

In our *a–g–i–l* paradigm we have distinguished two types of such interest cleavages: cleavages between rural and urban interests (3) and cleavages between worker and employer interests (4).

The spectacular growth of world trade and industrial production generated increasing strains between the primary producers in the countryside and the merchants and the entrepreneurs in the towns and the cities. On the continent, the conflicting interests of the rural and the urban areas had been recognized since the Middle Ages in the separate representation of the estates: the nobility and, in exceptional cases, the freehold peasants spoke for the land, and the burghers spoke for the cities. The Industrial Revolution deepened these conflicts and in country after country produced distinct rural-urban alignments in the national legislatures. Often the old divisions between estates were simply carried over into the unified parliaments and found expression in oppositions between Conservative-Agrarian and Liberal-Radical parties. The conflicts between rural and urban interests had been much less marked in Great Britain than on the continent. The House of Commons was not an assembly of the burgher estate but a body of legislators representing the constituent localities of the realm, the counties and the boroughs.[35] Yet even there the Industrial Revolution produced deep and bitter cleavages between the landed interests and the urban; in England, if not in Wales and Scotland, the opposition between Conservatives and Liberals fed largely on these strains until the 1880s.[36]

There was a hard core of economic conflict in these oppositions, but what made them so deep and bitter was the struggle for the maintenance of acquired status and the recognition of achievement. In England, the landed elite ruled the country, and the rising class of industrial entrepreneurs, many of them religiously at odds with the established church, for decades aligned themselves in opposition both to defend their economic interests and to assert their claims to status. It would be a misunderstanding, says the historian George Kitson Clark,[37] to think of agriculture "as an industry organized like any other industry—primarily for the purposes of efficient production. *It was . . . rather organized to ensure the survival intact of a caste*. The proprietors of the great estates were not just very rich men whose capital happened to be invested in land, they were rather the life tenants of very considerable positions which it was their duty to leave intact to their successors. In a way it was the estate that mattered and not the holder of the estate." The conflict between Conservatives and Liberals reflected an opposition between two value orientations: the recognition of status through *ascription and kin connections* versus the claims for status through *achievement and enterprise*.

These are typical strains in all transitional societies; they tend to be most intensive in the early phases of industrialization and to soften as the rising elite establishes itself in the community. In England, this process of reconciliation proceeded quite rapidly. In a society open to extensive mobility and intermarriage, urban and industrial wealth could gradually be translated into full recognition within the traditional hierarchy of the landed families. More and more mergers took place between the agricultural and the business interests, and this consolidation of the national elite soon changed the character of the Conservative-Liberal conflict. As James Cornford has shown through his detailed ecological studies, the movement of the business owners into the countryside and the suburbs divorced them from their workers and brought them into close relations with the landed gentry. The result was a softening of the rural-urban conflict in the system and a rapidly increasing class polarization of the widened electorate.[38]

A similar *rapprochement* took place between the east Elbian agricultural interests and the western business bourgeoisie in Germany, but there, significantly, the bulk of the Liberals sided with the Conservatives and did not try to rally the working-class electorate on their side in the way the British party did during the period up to World War I. The result was a deepening of the chasm between burghers and workers and a variety of desperate attempts to bridge it through appeals to national and military values.[39]

In other countries of the European continent the rural-urban cleavage continued to assert itself in national politics far into the twentieth century, but the political expressions of the cleavage varied widely. Much depended on the concentrations of wealth and political control in the cities and on the ownership structure in the rural economy. In the Low Countries, France, Italy, and Spain, rural-urban cleavages rarely found direct expression in the development of party oppositions. Other cleavages, particularly between the state and the churches and between owners and tenants, had greater impact on the alignments of the electorates. By contrast, in the five Nordic countries the cities had traditionally dominated national political life, and the struggle for democracy and parliamentary rule was triggered off through a broad process of mobilization within the peasantry.[40] This was essentially an expression of protest against the central elite of officials and patricians (a cleavage on the l–g axis in our model), but there were also elements of economic opposition in the movement: the peasants felt exploited in their dealings with city folk and wanted to shift the tax burdens to the expanding urban economies. These economic cleavages became more and more pronounced as the primary-producing communities entered into the national money and market economy. The result was the formation of a broad front of interest organizations and cooperatives and the development of distinctive Agrarian parties. Even after the rise of the working-class parties to national dominance, these Agrarian parties did not find it possible to establish common fronts with the Conservative defenders of the business community. The cultural contrasts between the countryside and the cities were still strong, and the strict market controls favored by the Agrarians could not easily be reconciled with the philosophy of free competition espoused by many Conservatives.

The current conflicts over the prices of primary products between developed and underdeveloped countries can be seen as projections of these cleavages at the level of world economy. The Chinese Communists have for a long time seen the struggles of the emerging nations of Asia and Africa in these terms: as a fight of the peasantry against the city interests. As Lin Piao put it in a policy statement: "The countryside, and the countryside alone, can offer the revolutionary bases from which the Revolution can go forward to final victory. . . . In a sense, the contemporary world revolution also presents the picture of the encirclement of the cities by the rural areas."[41]

The conflict between landed and urban interests was centered in the *commodity* market. The peasants wanted to sell their wares at the best possible prices and to buy what they needed from the industrial and urban producers at low cost. Such conflicts did not invariably prove party-forming. They could be dealt with within broad party fronts or could be channeled through interest organizations into narrower arenas of functional representation and bargaining. Distinctly agrarian parties have only emerged where strong cultural oppositions have deepened and embittered the strictly economic conflicts.

Conflicts in the *labor* market proved much more uniformly divisive. Working-class parties emerged in every country of Europe in the wake of the early waves of industrialization. The rising masses of wage earners, whether in large-scale farming, in forestry, or in industry, resented their conditions of work and the insecurity of their contracts, and many of them felt socially and culturally alienated from the owners and the employers. The result was the formation of a variety of labor unions and the development of nationwide Socialist parties. The success of such movements depended on a variety of factors: the strength of the paternalist traditions of ascriptive recognition of the worker status, the size of the work unit and the local ties of the workers, the level of prosperity and the stability of employment in the given industry, and the chances of improvements and promotion through loyal devotion or through education and achievement.

A crucial factor in the development of distinct working-class movements was the *openness* of the given society: Was the worker status a lifetime predicament or were there openings for advancement? How easy was it to get an education qualifying for a change in status? What prospects were there for striking out on one's own, for establishing independent work units? The contrasts between American and European developments must clearly be analyzed in these terms; the American workers were not only given the vote much earlier than their comrades in Europe; but they also found their way into the national system much more easily because of the greater stress on equality and achievement, because of the many openings to better education, and, last but not least, because the established workers could advance to better positions as new waves of immigrants took over the lower-status jobs.[42] A similar process is currently under way in the advanced countries of Western Europe. The immigrant proletariats from the Mediterranean countries and from the West Indies allow the children of the established national working class to move into the middle class, and these new waves of mobility tend to drain off traditional sources of resentment.

In nineteenth and early twentieth century Europe the status barriers were markedly higher. The traditions from the estate-divided society kept the workers in their place, and the narrowness of the educational channels of mobility also made it difficult for sons and daughters to rise above their fathers. There were, however, important variations among the countries of Europe in the attitudes of the established and the rising elites to the claims of the workers, and these differences clearly affected the development of the unions and the Socialist parties. In Britain and the Scandinavian countries the attitudes of the elites tended to be open and pragmatic. As in all other countries there was active resistance to the claims of the workers, but little or no direct repression. These are today the countries with the largest and the most domesticated Labor parties in Europe. In Germany and Austria, France, Italy, and Spain the cleavages went much deeper. A number of attempts were made to repress the unions and the Socialists, and the working-class organizations consequently tended to isolate themselves from the national culture and to develop *soziale Ghettoparteien*,[43] strongly ideological movements seeking to isolate their members and their supporters from influences from the encompassing social environments. In terms of our paradigm, these parties were just as close to the *i* pole as their opponents in the religious camp. This "anti-system" orientation of large sections of the European working class was brought to a climax in the aftermath of the Russian Revolution. The Communist movement did not just speak for an alienated stratum of the territorial community but came to be seen as an external conspiracy against the nation. These developments brought a number of European countries to the point of civil war in the twenties and the thirties. The greater the numbers of citizens caught in such direct "friend-foe" oppositions to each other the greater the danger of total disruption of the body politic.

Developments since World War II have pointed toward a reduction of such pitched oppositions and some softening of ideological tensions: a movement from the *i* toward the *a* pole in our paradigm.[44] A variety of factors contributed to this development: the experience of national cooperation during the war, the improvements in the standard of living in the fifties, the rapid growth of a "new middle class" bridging the gaps between the traditional working class and the bourgeoisie. But the most important factor was possibly the *entrenchment of the working-class parties in local and national governmental structures* and their consequent "domestication" within the established system. The developments in Austria offer a particularly revealing example. The extreme opposition between Socialists and Catholics had ended in civil war in 1934, but after the experience of National Socialist domination, war, and occupation, the two parties settled down to share government responsibilities under a *Proporz* system, a settlement still based on mutual distrust between the two camps but at least one that recognized the necessity for coexistence.[45] Comparisons of the positions taken by the two leading Communist parties in Western Europe, the Italian and the French, also point to the importance of entrenchments in the national system of government. The French party has been much less involved in the running of local communities and has remained much more isolated within the national system, while the Italian party has responded much more dynamically to the exigencies of community decision-making.[46] Erik Allardt has implicitly demonstrated the importance of similar factors in a comparison of levels of class polarization in the Nordic countries. He points out that while the percentage of working-class voters siding with the Left (Communists and Social Democrats) is roughly the same in Finland as in Norway and Sweden, the percentage of middle-class leftists used to be much lower in Finland than in the two other countries. This difference appears to be related to a contrast in the chances of upward mobility from the working class: very low in Finland, markedly higher in the other countries.[47] The continued isolation of the Finnish working-class parties may reflect a lower level of participation in responsible decision-making in the local communities and in the nation. This has not yet been investigated in detail, but studies of working-class mobility and political changes carried out in Norway[48] suggest that the principal channels of advancement were in the public sector and that the decisive wave of "bourgeoisification" came in the wake of the accession of the Labor party to a position of dominance in the system. In Finland the protracted period of underground communism until 1944 and the deep split in the working-class movement during the next decades tended to keep the two parties from decisive influence on the public sector and maintained the old barriers against mobility; in the other Scandinavian countries the victories of the Social Democrat Labor parties had opened up new channels of mobility and helped to break down the isolation of the working class.

Cleavages in Fully Mobilized Polities

The four critical cleavages described in terms of our paradigm were all movements of protest against the *established* national elite and its cultural standards and were parts of a broad wave of emancipation and mobilization. Quite different types of protest alignments have tended to occur in *fully mobilized nation states*. In these the focus of protest has no longer been the traditional central culture but the rising networks of new elites, such as the leaders of the new large bureaucracies of industry and government, those who control the various sectors of the communications industry, the heads of mass organizations, the leaders in some countries of once weak or low-status minority ethnic or religious groups, and the like. Protest against these new elites and the institutions which foster them has often taken "anti-system" form, though the ideology has varied from country to country: Fascism in Italy, National Socialism in Germany, Poujadism in France, "radical rightism" in the United States. In our paradigm such protest movements would cut across the territorial axis very near the g pole; the conflict is no longer between constituent territorial units of the nation, but between different conceptions of the constitution and the organization of the national polity. These have all been *nationalist* movements: they not only accept, they venerate the historically given nation and its culture, but they reject the system of decision-making and control developed through the process of democratic mobilization and bargaining. Their aim is not just to gain recognition for a particular set of interests within a pluralist system of give and take but to *replace* this system by more authoritarian procedures of allocation.

In one way or another they all express deeply felt convictions about the destiny and the mission of the nation, some quite inchoate, others highly systematized; and they all endeavor to develop networks of organizations to keep their supporters loyal to the cause. They aim at *Verzuiling* but want only one column in the nation.

In our *a–g–i–l* schema, therefore, a fully *verzuild* nationalist movement would have to be placed at the *g–i* intersection outside what we might call the "competitive politics" diamond:

FIGURE 4.4

Suggested Locations of Four "Extremes" in the *a–g–i–l* Schema

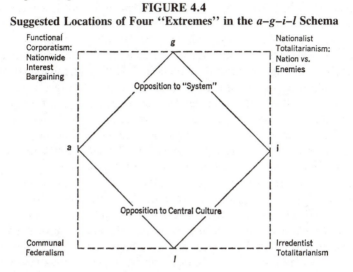

In its early varieties such nationalist movements essentially reflected the reactions of the lower-class strata of the dominant culture against the rising tides of mobilization within subject populations. In Hapsburg Austria the rise of the intransigent Pan-Germans was decisively accelerated through the alliance between the university *Burschenschaften* and Schönerer's nationalist workers' associations; these essentially recruited support among German-speaking craftsmen and workers threatened by the invasion of the Czechs into the new centers of industry.[49] The xenophobia of the Austrian working class proved contagious. There are clear historical links between the early working-class nationalism of the eighties and nineties and the National Socialist movement after the defeat in 1918.[50] Hitler inherited his hatred of the Slavs and the Jews from the Austrian working-class nationalists. In our terminology, the National Socialist movement was an alliance at the *g* end of the territorial-cultural axis, the counterpart within the *dominant* national culture to an *l* opposition within some subject population at the periphery.

A variety of attempts have been made to determine the conditions for the emergence of such conflicts at the *g* pole of the political system. Contrasts in the continuity and regularity of nation-building have certainly counted. Austria, Germany, France, Italy, Spain, and the United States have all gone through extremely painful crises of nation-building and have still to contend with legacies of conflicts over national integration. Ralf Dahrendorf has recently interpreted the rise of National Socialism as the final breakthrough toward political modernization in Germany. It broke down the local pockets of insulation and established "*die traditionsfreie Gleichheit der Ausgangsstellung aller Menschen*," an achievement-oriented society unfettered by diffuse status barriers.[51] The statistical histories of a number of "anti-system" movements of this type suggest that they made their greatest electoral gains through appeals to the "kleiner Mann," the isolated "unit citizen" threatened by the rise of strong and complex corporations within a pluralist body politic. The "small man" came out not only against the great financial interests, the corporations, and the entrenched bureaucracies but also against the power of the churches, the trade unions, and the cooperatives. Studies of the crucial German elections of 1930, 1932, and 1933 show beyond doubt that the decisive thrust of mass support for the National Socialists came from owners of small and medium-sized farms, from artisans, shopkeepers, and other independents in the lower rungs of the middle class, most of them Protestants, all of them in more or less direct opposition to the giant cartels and the financial networks, to the unions, and to the forbidding column of Catholic organizations around the *Zentrum*.[52] Similar alignments have been documented for Italy, Norway, France, and the United States. There are obvious contextual variations, but the findings suggest important invariances in the conditions for the growth of such "anti-system" movements.[53]

We have come to the end of a cursory review of the typical cleavages generated in Western polities during the early phases of national consolidation and the later phases of suffrage extension and organizational growth. We have proceeded by way of exemplification rather than rigorous developmental comparison. Our purpose has not been to give an exhaustive account of differences and similarities country by country but to explore the potentialities of a scheme of classification developed from central concepts in current sociological theory. We hope to go further in this direction in other contexts; here we have simply wanted to initiate discussion of these possibilities and to point to new ways of analyzing the historical experience of these very different countries.

Whatever the shortcomings of the empirical applications, we feel confident that the Parsonian *A–G–I–L* schema can generate a set of analytical tools of great value in developmental comparisons of political systems. We have no doubt departed on several points from the standard interpretations of the Parsonian model and perhaps done violence to it in transforming it into a two-dimensional system of coordinates. To us this is of minor importance. We have simply used the original schema as a springboard for an attempt to bring some order into the comparative analysis of party-political developments. We might no doubt have come up with a very similar paradigm without recourse to the Parsonian core model, but we see great intellectual advantages in the unification of conceptualizations across several sectors of social life. The very fact that the same abstract schema has inspired analytical developments in such disparate fields as the family, the professions, religion, and politics seem to us to promise definite payoffs in the future.

Our use of the Parsonian categories is novel in two respects. First of all we have used them to bring some order into the comparative analysis of *conflicts, cleavages, and oppositions*. We think we have shown that they do not just serve to describe the functional requirements of viable social systems and the conditions of consensus and integration, but can be equally fruitful in analyses of sources of disequilibrium and disruption. Second, we have used the categories for purposes of *distinctly developmental* analysis. We have shown how the basic scheme of double dichotomies can be transformed into a model of step-by-step shifts in cleavage dimensions, from l to i, from i to a, and from i or a toward g.

We are aware that some of these innovations may prove to be purely terminological. We hope to show in our further development of these lines of analysis that they open up possibilities of direct gains in the intellectual control of the vast masses of information about party developments across the countries of the world.

The Transformation of Cleavage Structures into Party Systems

Conditions for the Channeling of Opposition

Thus far, we have focused on the emergence of *one cleavage at a time* and only incidentally concerned ourselves with the growth of *cleavage systems* and their translations into *constellations of political parties*. In terms of our schema we have limited ourselves to the analysis of the *internal differentiations* of the I quadrant and only by implication touched on *interchanges* between I and G, I and L, and L and G. But cleavages do not translate themselves into party oppositions as a matter of course: there are considerations of organizational and electoral strategy; there is the weighing of payoffs of alliances against losses through split-offs; and there is the successive narrowing of the "mobilization market" through the time sequences of organizational efforts. Here we enter into an area of crucial concern in current theorizing and research, and area of great fascination crying out for detailed cooperative research. Very much needs to be done in reanalyzing the evidence for each national party system and even more in exploring the possibilities of fitting such findings into a wider framework of developmental theory. We cannot hope to deal exhaustively with such possibilities of comparison here and shall limit ourselves to a discussion of a few characteristic developments and suggest a rough typology.

How does a sociocultural conflict get translated into an opposition between parties? To approach an understanding of the variations in such processes of translation we have to sift out a great deal of information about the *conditions for the expression of protest and the representation of interests* in each society.

First, we must know about the *traditions of decision-making* in the polity: the prevalence of conciliar versus autocratic procedures of central government, the rules established for the handling of grievances and protests, the measures taken to control or to protect political associations, the freedom of communication, and the organization of demonstrations.[54]

Second, we must know about the *channels for the expression and mobilization of protest*: Was there a system of representation and if so how accessible were the representatives, who had a right to choose them, and how were they chosen? Was the conflict primarily expressed through direct demonstrations, through strikes, sabotage, or open violence, or could it be channeled through regular elections and through pressures on legitimately established representatives?

Third, we need information about *the opportunities, the payoffs, and the costs of alliances* in the system: How ready or reluctant were the old movements to broaden their bases of support and how easy or difficult was it for new movements to gain representation on their own?

Fourth and finally, we must know about *the possibilities, the implications, and the limitations of majority rule* in the system: What alliances would be most likely to bring about majority control of the organs of representation and how much influence could such majorities in fact exert on the basic structuring of the institutions and the allocations within the system?

The Four Thresholds

These series of questions suggest a *sequence of thresholds* in the path of any movement pressing forward new sets of demands within a political system.

First, the threshold of *legitimation*: Are all protests rejected as conspiratorial, or is there some recognition of the right of petition, criticism, and opposition?

Second, the threshold of *incorporation*: Are all or most of the supporters of the movement denied status as participants in the choice of representatives or are they given political citizenship rights on a par with their opponents?

Third, the threshold of *representation*: Must the new movement join larger and older movements to ensure access to representative organs or can it gain representation on its own?

Fourth, the threshold of *majority power*: Are there built-in checks and counterforces against numerical majority rule in the system or will a victory at the polls give a party or an alliance power to bring about major structural changes in the national system?

This gives us a crude four-variable typology of conditions for the development of party systems.

Level of Each Threshold				Resulting Party System
Legiti-mation	Incorpo-ration	Represen-tation	Majority power	
High	H	H	H	Autocratic or oligarchic regimes, *Verfemung* of all parties:[55] protests and grievances either channeled through the field administration or through estate representation.
Medium	H	H	H	Embryonic internal party system: cliques of representatives, clubs of *notables*. Examples: Britain before 1832, Sweden during the quarrels between "Hats" and "Caps."[56]
M	M	H	H or M	Internal party systems generating rudimentary outside support through registration associations predominant in Western Europe during period between the breakdown of monarchic absolutism and the introduction of parliamentary rule under manhood suffrage.
Low	M	H	H	Initial phase in development of external party system: lower-class movements free to develop, but suffrage still limited and/or unequal. Example: Sweden before 1909.
L	M	H	M	Same but with parliamentary rule: Belgium before 1899; Norway, 1884–1900.
M	L	H	H	Isolation of lower-class or religious minority parties from the national system: restrictive measures against political organizations but full manhood suffrage. Examples: the Wilhelmine *Reich* during the period of the *Sozialistengesetze*, 1878–1890; France during the Second Empire and early decades of the Third Republic.
L	L	H	H	Competitive party system under universal and equal manhood suffrage but with high payoffs for alliances

Level of Each Threshold				*Resulting Party System*
Legiti- mation	Incorpo- ration	Represen- tation	Majority power	
				and with a clear separation of legislative and executive powers. The best example would be the United States if it were not for past restrictions on Communist Party activities and the low *de facto* enfranchisement of Blacks in the South. France under the Fifth Republic may be a better example.
L	L	H	M	Same but with parliamentary rule. Examples: France under later decades of the Third Republic and most of the Fourth; Great Britain since 1918.
L	L	M	M	Same but with medium threshold PR (Proportional Representation): little need for alliances to achieve representation but safeguards introduced against fragmentation through explicit or implicit electoral minima. Examples: the Nordic countries, Belgium, the Netherlands, and Switzerland since 1918–20.
L	L	L	L	Same but with maximal PR and fewer restraints against majority power: the fragmented, centrifugal parliament and the plebiscitarian presidency of the Weimar Republic.

Empirically, changes in one such threshold sooner or later generated pressures to change one or more others, but there were many variations in the sequences of change. There is no "scalable" dimension of political development from a condition of four "high" thresholds to one of four "low" thresholds.

Clear-cut progressions toward lower thresholds are generally observed at the early stages of change: the recognition of freedoms of association, the extension of the suffrage. Much greater variations in the paths of development can be observed at the later stages. In fact there is no single terminal stage in the series of changes but several alternative ones:

LLHH—high-threshold majoritarian representation and separation of
        powers.

LLHM—high-threshold majoritarian parliamentarism.
LLMM—medium-threshold PR parliamentarism.
LLLL—low-threshold PR and plebiscitarian majority rule.

The early comparative literature on the growth of parties and party systems focused on the consequences of the lowering of the two first thresholds: the emergence of parliamentary opposition and a free press, and the extension of the franchise. Tocqueville and Ostrogorski, Weber and Michels, all in their various ways, sought to gain insight into that central institution of the modern polity, the competitive mass party.[57] The later literature, particularly since the 1920s, changed its focus to the third and the fourth thresholds: the consequences of the electoral system and the structure of the decision-making arena for the formation and the functioning of party systems. The fierce debates over the pros and cons of electoral systems stimulated a great variety of efforts at comparative analysis, but the heavy emotional commitments on the one or the other side often led to questionable interpretations of the data and to overhasty generalizations from meager evidence. Few of the writers could content themselves with comparisons of sequences of change in different countries. They wanted to influence the future course of events, and they tended to be highly optimistic about the possibilities of bringing about changes in established party systems through electoral engineering. What they tended to forget was that parties once established develop their own internal structure and build up long-term commitments among core supporters. The electoral arrangements may prevent or delay the formation of a party, but once it has been established and entrenched, it will prove difficult to change its character simply through variations in the conditions of electoral aggregation. In fact, in most cases it makes little sense to treat electoral systems as independent variables and party systems as dependent. The party strategists will generally have decisive influence on electoral legislation and opt for the systems of aggregation most likely to consolidate their position, whether through increases in their representation, through the strengthening of the preferred alliances, or through safeguards against splinter movements. In abstract theoretical terms it may well make sense to hypothesize that simple majority systems will produce two-party oppositions within the culturally more homogeneous areas of a polity and only generate further parties through territorial cleavages, but the only convincing evidence for such a generalization comes from countries with a continuous history of simple majority aggregations from the beginnings of democratic mass politics. There is little hard evidence and much uncertainty about the effects of *later changes* in election laws on the national party system: one simple reason is that the parties already entrenched in the polity will exert a great deal of influence on the extent and the direction of any such changes and at least prove reluctant to see themselves voted out of existence.

Any attempt at systematic analysis of variations in the conditions and the strategies of party competition must start out from such differentiations of developmental phases. We cannot, in this context, proceed to detailed country-by-country comparisons but have to limit ourselves to a review of evidence for two distinct sequences of change: the rise of *lower-class* movements and parties and the decline of *régime censitaire* parties.

The Rules of the Electoral Game

The early electoral systems all set a high threshold for rising parties. It was everywhere very difficult for working-class movements to gain representation on their own, but there were significant variations in the openness of the systems to pressures from the new strata. The second ballot systems so well known from the Wilhelmine *Reich* and from the Third and the Fifth French Republics set the highest possible barrier, absolute majority, but at the same time made possible a variety of local alliances among the opponents of the Socialists: the system kept the new entrants underrepresented, yet did not force the old parties to merge or to ally themselves nationally. The blatant injustices of the electoral system added further to the alienation of the working classes from the national institutions and generated what Giovanni Sartori has described as systems of "centrifugal pluralism":[58] one major movement *outside* the established political arena and several opposed parties *within* it.

Simple majority systems of the British-American type also set high barriers against rising movements of new entrants into the political arena; however, the initial level is not standardized at 50 percent of the votes cast in each constituency but *varies from the outset with the strategies adopted by the established parties*. If they join together in defence of their common interests, the threshold is high; if each competes on its own, it is low. In the early phases of working-class mobilization, these systems have encouraged alliances of the "Lib-Lab" type. The new entrants into the electorate have seen their only chances of representation as lying in joint candidatures with the more reformist of the established parties. In later phases distinctly Socialist parties were able to gain representation on their own in areas of high industrial concentration and high class segregation, but this did not invariably bring about counteralliances of the older parties. In Britain, the decisive lower-class breakthrough came in the elections of 1918 and 1922. Before World War I the Labour Party had presented its own candidates in a few constituencies only and had not won more than 42 out of 670 seats; in 1918 they suddenly brought forth candidates in 388 constituencies and won 63 of them, and then in 1922 advanced to 411 constituencies and 142 seats. The simple-majority system did not force an immediate restructuring of the party system, however.

The Liberals continued to fight on their own and did not give way to the Conservatives until the emergency election of 1931. The inveterate hostilities between the two established parties helped to keep the average threshold for the newcomers tolerably low, but the very ease of this process of incorporation produced a split within the ranks of Labour. The currency crisis forced the leaders to choose between their loyalty to the historical nation and their solidarity with the finally mobilized working class.

Not all the simple-majority polities developed such strong and distinct working-class parties, however. Canada and the United States stayed at what we might call the "Lib-Lab" stage. Analysts of these two "deviant" nations have given prominence to factors such as early enfranchisement, high mobility, entrenched federalism, and marked regional, ethnic, and religious diversity.[59] There are important differences between the two cases, however, and these tell us a great deal about the importance of the *fourth* of our thresholds: the safeguards against direct majority power. In his comparison of the Canadian and the American party systems, Leon D. Epstein has argued with admirable cogency that the crucial differences reflect contrasts in the constitutionally set procedures of central decision-making: in Canada cabinet responsibility to a parliamentary majority, in the United States separate powers acquired through two distinct channels of representation.[60] The parliamentary system lowers the power threshold for numerical majorities, but the government depends for its existence on disciplined voting within the party or the parties supporting it in the legislature. The separation-of-powers system makes it more difficult to translate numerical victories into distinct changes of policy but also allows for much more flexible alliances within each of the parties. The Canadian party tends to be united in its legislative behavior and to maintain strict control over the recruitment of candidates. The American party tends to be a loose federation with a minimum of internal structure and is forced by the system of primaries to leave decisions on recruitment to a wider electoral market. As a result the Canadian system has tended to encourage regional and cultural protest parties, while the American parties have proved remarkably open to factional or local demands from a variety of movements and interests. The straight two-party system prevalent in the United States cannot be taken as a normal outcome of simple majority elections. American parties differ markedly in structure and in character from other parties produced under this system of elections and can best be explained through an analysis of the constitutionally established separation of the two arenas of decision-making, the Congress and the presidential Executive.

This brings us to a crucial point in our discussion of the translation of cleavage structure into party systems: *the costs and the payoffs of mergers, alliances, and coalitions.* The height of the representation threshold and the rules of central decision-making may increase or decrease the net returns of joint action, but the intensity of inherited hostilities and the openness of communications across the cleavage lines will decide whether mergers or alliances are actually workable. There must be some minimum of trust among the leaders, and there must be some justification for expecting that the channels to the decision-makers will be kept open whoever wins the election. The British electoral system can only be understood against the background of the long-established traditions of territorial representation; the M.P. represents *all* his constituents, not just those who voted him in. But this system makes heavy demands on the loyalty of the constituents: in two-party contests up to 49 percent of them may have to abide by the decisions of a representative they did not want; in three-cornered fights, as much as 66 percent.

Such demands are bound to produce strains in ethnically, culturally, or religiously divided communities: the deeper the cleavages the less the likelihood of loyal acceptance of decisions by representatives of the other side. It was no accident that the earliest moves toward Proportional Representation came in the ethnically most heterogeneous of the European countries, Denmark (to accommodate Schleswig-Holstein), as early as 1855, the Swiss cantons from 1891 onward, Belgium from 1899, Moravia from 1905, and Finland from 1906.[61] The great historian of electoral systems, Karl Braunias, distinguishes two phases in the spread of PR: the "minority protection" phase before World War I and the "anti-socialist" phase in the years immediately after the armistice.[62] In linguistically and religiously divided societies majority elections could clearly threaten the continued existence of the political system. The introduction of some element of minority representation came to be seen as an essential step in a strategy of territorial consolidation.

As the pressures mounted for extensions of the suffrage, demands for proportionality were also heard in the culturally more homogeneous nation-states. In most cases the victory of the new principle of representation came about through a convergence of pressures from below and from above. The rising working class wanted to lower the threshold of representation to gain access to the legislatures, and the most threatened of the old established parties demanded PR to protect their positions against the new waves of mobilized voters under universal suffrage. In Belgium the introduction of graduated manhood suffrage in 1893 brought about an increasing polarization between Labor and Catholics and threatened the continued existence of the Liberals; the introduction of PR restored some equilibrium to the system.[63] The history of the struggles over electoral procedures in Sweden and in Norway tells us a great deal about the consequences of the lowering of one threshold for the bargaining over the level of the next. In Sweden, the Liberals and the Social Democrats fought a long fight for universal and equal suffrage and at first also advocated PR to ensure easier access to the legislature. The remarkable success of their mobilization efforts made them change their strategy, however. From 1904 onward they advocated majority elections in single-member constituencies. This aroused fears among the farmers and the urban Conservatives, and to protect their interests they made the introduction of PR a condition for their acceptance of manhood suffrage. As a result the two barriers fell together: it became easier to enter the electorate and easier to gain representation.[64] In Norway there was a much longer lag between the waves of mobilization. The franchise was much wider from the outset, and the first wave of peasant mobilization brought down the old regime as early as in 1884. As a result the suffrage was extended well before the final mobilization of the rural proletariat and the industrial workers under the impact of rapid economic change. The victorious radical-agrarian "Left" felt no need to lower the threshold of representation and in fact helped to increase it through the introduction of a two-ballot system of the French type in 1906. There is little doubt that this contributed heavily to the radicalization and the alienation of the Norwegian Labor Party. By 1915 it had gained 32 percent of all the votes cast but was given barely 15 percent of the seats. The Left did not give in until 1921. The decisive motive was clearly not just a sense of equalitarian justice but the fear of rapid decline with further advances of the Labor Party across the majority threshold.

In all these cases high thresholds might have been kept up if the parties of the property-owning classes had been able to make common cause against the rising working-class movements. But the inheritance of hostility and distrust was too strong. The Belgian Liberals could not face the possibility of a merger with the Catholics, and the cleavages between the rural and the urban interests went too deep in the Nordic countries to make it possible to build up any joint antisocialist front. By contrast, the higher level of industrialization and the progressive merger of rural and urban interests in Britain made it possible to withstand the demand for a change in the system of representation. Labour was seriously underrepresented only during a brief initial period, and the Conservatives were able to establish broad enough alliances in the counties and the suburbs to keep their votes well above the critical point.

A Model for the Generation of the European Party System

Four Decisive Dimensions of Opposition

This review of the conditions for the translation of sociocultural cleavages into political oppositions suggests three conclusions.

First, the constitutive contrasts in the national system of party constellations generally tended to manifest themselves *before* any lowering of the threshold of representation. The decisive sequences of party formation took place at the early stage of competitive politics, in some cases well before the extension of the franchise, in other cases on the very eve of the rush to mobilize the finally enfranchised masses.

Second, the high thresholds of representation during the phase of mass politicization set severe tests for the rising political organizations. The surviving formations tended to be firmly entrenched in the inherited social structure and could not easily be dislodged through changes in the rules of the electoral game.

Third, the decisive moves to lower the threshold of representation reflected divisions among the established *régime censitaire* parties rather than pressures from the new mass movements. The introduction of PR added a few additional splinters but essentially served to ensure the separate survival of parties unable to come together in common defense against the rising contenders for majority power.

What happened at the decisive party-forming phase in each national society? Which of the many contrasts and conflicts were translated into party oppositions, and how were these oppositions built into the stable systems?

This is not the place to enter into detailed comparisons of developmental sequences nation by nation. Our task is to suggest a framework for the explanation of variations in cleavage bases and party constellations.

In the abstract schema set out in Figure 4.3 we distinguished four decisive dimensions of oppositions in Western politics: two of them were products of what we called the *National* Revolution (1 and 2); and two of them were generated through the *Industrial* Revolution (3 and 4).

In their basic characteristics the party systems that emerged in the Western European polities during the early phase of competition and mobilization can be interpreted as products of *sequential interactions between these two fundamental processes of change*.

Differences in the timing and character of the *National* Revolution set the stage for striking divergencies in the European party system. In the Protestant countries the conflicts between the claims of the State and the Church had been temporarily settled by royal *fiats* at the time of the Reformation, and the processes of centralization and standardization triggered off after 1789 did not immediately bring about a conflict between the two. The temporal and the spiritual establishments were at one in the defense of the central nation-building culture but came increasingly under attack by the leaders and ideologists of countermovements in the provinces, in the peripheries and within the underprivileged strata of peasants, craftsmen and workers. The other countries of Western Europe were all split to the core in the wake of the secularizing French Revolution and without exception developed strong parties for the defense of the Church, either explicitly as in Germany, the Low Countries, Switzerland, Austria, Italy, and Spain or implicitly as in the case of the Right in France.[65]

Differences in the timing and character of the *Industrial* Revolution also made for contrasts among the national party systems in Europe.

Conflicts in the *commodity* market tended to produce highly divergent party alliances in Europe. In some countries the majority of the market farmers found it possible to join with the owner interests in the secondary sector of the economy; in others the two remained in opposition to each other and developed parties of their own. Conflicts in the *labor* market, by contrast, proved much more uniformly divisive: all countries of Western Europe developed lower-class mass parties at some point or other before World War I. These were rarely unified into one single working-class party. In Latin Europe the lower-class movements were sharply divided among revolutionary anarchist, anarchosyndicalist and Marxist factions on the one hand and revisionist socialists on the other. The Russian Revolution of 1917 split the working-class organizations throughout Europe. Today we find in practically all countries of the West divisions between Communists, left Socialist splinters, and revisionist Social Democrat parties.

Our task, however, is not just to account for the emergence of single parties but to analyze the processes of alliance formation that led to the development of stable *systems* of political organizations in country after country. To approach some understanding of these alliance formations, we have to study the *interactions* between the two revolutionary processes of change in each polity: How far had the National Revolution proceeded at the point of the industrial ''takeoff'' and how did the two processes of mobilization, the cultural and the economic, affect each other, positively by producing common fronts or negatively by maintaining divisions?

The decisive contrasts among the Western party systems clearly reflect differences in the *national histories of conflict and compromise across the first three of the four cleavage lines* distinguished in our analytical schema: the ''center-periphery,'' the state-church, and the land-industry cleavages generated national developments in *divergent* directions, while the owner-worker cleavage tended to bring the party systems *closer to each other* in their basic structure. The crucial differences among the party systems emerged in the early phases of competitive politics, before the final phase of mass mobilization. They reflected basic contrasts in the conditions and sequences of nation-building and in the structure of the economy at the point of take-off toward sustained growth. This, to be sure, does not mean that the systems vary exclusively on the Right and at the center, but are much more alike on the Left of the political spectrum. There are working-class movements throughout the West, but they differ conspicuously in size, in cohesion, in ideological orientation, and in the extent of their integration into, or alienation from, the historically given national policy. Our point is simply that the factors generating these differences on the Left are *secondary*. The decisive contrasts among the systems had emerged before the entry of the working-class parties into the political arena, and the character of these mass parties was heavily influenced by the constellations of ideologies, movements, and organizations they had to confront in that arena.

A Model in Three Steps

To understand the differences among the Western party systems we have to start out from an analysis of the *situation of the active nation-building elite on the eve of the breakthrough to democratization and mass mobilization*: What had they achieved and where had they met most resistance? What were their resources, who were their nearest allies, and where could they hope to find further support? Who were their enemies, what were their resources, and where could they recruit allies and rally reinforcement?

Any attempt at comparative analysis across so many divergent national histories is fraught with grave risks. It is easy to get lost in the wealth of fascinating detail, and it is equally easy to succumb to facile generalities and irresponsible abstractions. Scholarly prudence prompts us to proceed case by case, but intellectual impatience urges us to go beyond the analysis of concrete contrasts and try out alternative schemes of systematization across the known cases.

To clarify the logic of our approach to the comparative analysis of party systems, we have developed a *model of alternative alliances and oppositions*. We have posited several sets of actors, have set up a series of rules of alliance and opposition among these, and have tested the resultant typology of potential party systems against a range of empirically known cases.

Our model bears on relationships of alliance, neutrality or opposition among seven sets of actors. To underscore the abstract character of our exercise we shall refer to each set by a shorthand symbol:

N—a central core of cooperating "nation-builders" controlling major elements of the machinery of the "state";

C—an ecclesiastical body established within the national territory and given a large measure of control over education;

R—the supranationally established ecclesiastical body organized under the Roman Curia and the Pope;

D—a dissident, nonconformist body of religious activists opposed to C and R;

L—a cooperating body of established landowners controlling a substantial share of the total primary production of the national territory;

U—a cooperating body of urban commercial and industrial entrepreneurs controlling the advancing secondary sectors of the national economy;

P—a movement of resistance in the subject periphery against central national control.

The model sets these *restrictions on alliance formation*:

1. N and D and N and P will invariably be opposed, never in any joint alliance;
2. N must decide on alliances on two fronts: the *religious* and the *economic*;
3. on the religious front, N is faced with three options:
   —alliance with C,
   —a secular posture S,
   —alliance with R;
4. on the economic front, N is restricted to two alliance options:
   —with L,
   —with U;
5. N's alliances determine P's choice of alliances but with these restrictions: (a) if N is allied to C, the model allows two contingent outcomes: (aa) if C is dominant, the only P option on the religious front is D, (bb) if R still constitutes a strong minority, P will be split in two alliance-groups: the response to N–C–L will be P_1–S–U and P_2–R, the response to N–C–U will be P_1–D–L and P_2–R–L; (b) if N chooses S or R, the only possible P alliances are P–S–U and P–R–L or simply P–U and P–L; P–R–U and P–S–L do not occur.

These various elements and restrictions combine to produce an eightfold typology of basic political oppositions:

TYPE	N'S COMMITMENTS		P'S RESPONSE		CLOSEST EMPIRICAL EXAMPLES		
	Religious front	Economic front		Country	"N" party (parties)	"P" parties	
	Option	Conditions					
I	C	C dominant	L	P–D–U	Britain	CONS. vs.	LIB:	Celtic fringe / Dissenters / Industry
II	C	C dominant	U	P–D–L	Scandinavia	CONS. vs.	"LEFT"	AGRARIANS / CHRISTIANS / RADICALS
III	C	R strong minority	L	$\dfrac{P_1\text{–S–U}}{P_2\text{–R}}$	Prussia/ Reich	CONS. vs.		BAVARIANS / LIB. / ZENTRUM
IV	C	R strong minority	U	$\dfrac{P_1\text{–D–L}}{P_2\text{–R–L}}$	Netherlands	LIB. vs.		Calvinists: CHU, AR / Catholics: KVP
V	S		L	$\dfrac{P_1\text{–U}}{P_2\text{–R}}$	Spain	LIB. vs.		Catalan LLIGA / Carlists

VI	S	U	P–R–L	France Italy	LIB./RAD. vs.	CONS.–CATH.–CHR.
VII	R	L	P–S–U	Austria	CHR. vs. LIB.	{ Pan-Germans Industry
VIII	R	U	P–L	Belgium	CHR./LIB. vs.	Flemish separatists

This typological exercise may appear excessively abstract and unnecessarily mechanical. To us the gains in analytical perspective outweigh the loss in historical immediacy: the model not only offers a grid for the mapping of parallels and contrasts among national developments, it also represents an attempt to establish an explanatory paradigm of the simplest possible structure to account for a wide range of empirical variations. The literature on democratic politics is replete with examples of isolated discussions of parallels and contrasts among national party systems: ours, we believe, is the first attempt to develop a general typology of such variations from a unified set of postulates and hypotheses.

Our model seeks to reduce the bewildering variety of empirical party systems *to a set of ordered consequences of decisions and developments at three crucial junctures in the history of each nation*:

first, during the *Reformation*—the struggle for the control of the ecclesiastical organizations within the national territory;

second, in the wake of the "*Democratic Revolution*" after 1789—the conflict over the control of the vast machineries of mass education to be built up by the mobilizing nation-states;

finally, during the early phases of the *Industrial Revolution*—the opposition between landed interests and the claims of the rising commercial and industrial leadership in cities and towns.

Our eight types of alliance-opposition structure are in fact the simple combinatorial products of three successive dichotomies:

FIRST DICHOTOMY: THE REFORMATION

I–IV	V–VIII
State Controls National Church	State Allied to Roman Catholic Church

SECOND DICHOTOMY: THE "DEMOCRATIC REVOLUTION"

I–II	III–IV	V–VI	VII–VIII
National Church Dominant	Strong Roman Minority	Secularizing Revolution	State Allied to Roman Church

THIRD DICHOTOMY: THE INDUSTRIAL REVOLUTION

Commitment to		Commitment to		Commitment to		Commitment to	
Landed	Urban	Landed	Urban	Landed	Urban	Landed	Urban
Interests		Interests		Interests		Interests	

Type:	I	II	III	IV	V	VI	VII	VIII

The model spells out the consequences of the fateful division of Europe brought about through Reformation and the Counter-Reformation. The outcomes of the early struggles between State and Church determined the structure of national politics in the era of democratization and mass mobilization three hundred years later. In Southern and Central Europe the Counter-Reformation had consolidated the position of the Church and tied its fate to the privileged bodies of the *ancien régime*. The result was a polarization of politics between a national-radical-secular movement and a Catholic-traditionalist one. In Northwest Europe, in Britain, and in Scandinavia, the settlement of the sixteenth century gave a very different structure to the cleavages of the nineteenth. The established churches did not stand in opposition to the nation-builders in the way the Roman Catholic Church did on the continent, and the Left movements opposed to the religious establishment found most of their support among newly enfranchised dissenters, nonconformists, and fundamentalists in the peripheries and within the rising urban strata. In Southern and Central Europe the bourgeois opposition to the *ancien régime* tended to be indifferent if not hostile to the teachings of the Church: the cultural integration of the nation came first and the Church had to find whatever place it could within the new political order. In Northwest Europe the opposition to the *ancien régime* was far from indifferent to religious values. The broad Left coalitions against the established powers recruited decisive support among orthodox Protestants in a variety of sectarian movements outside and inside the national churches.

The distinction between these two types of Left alliances against the inherited political structure is fundamental for an understanding of European political developments in the age of mass elections. It is of particular importance in the analysis of the religiously most divided of the European polities: types III and IV in our 2 × 2 × 2 schema. The religious frontiers of Europe went straight through the territories of the Low Countries, the old German *Reich*, and Switzerland; in each of these the clash between the nation-builders and the strong Roman Catholic minorities produced lasting divisions of the bodies politic and determined the structure of their party systems. The Dutch system came closest to a direct merger of the Southern-Central type (VI-VIII) and the Northwestern: on the one hand a nation-building party of increasingly secularized Liberals, on the other hand a Protestant Left recruited from orthodox milieus of the same type as those behind the old opposition parties in England and Scandinavia.

The difference between England and the Netherlands is indeed instructive. Both countries had their strong peripheral concentrations of Catholics opposed to central authority: the English in Ireland, the Dutch in the south. In Ireland, the cumulation of ethnic, social, and religious conflicts could not be resolved within the old system; the result was a history of intermittent violence and finally territorial separation. In the Netherlands the secession of the Belgians still left a sizable Catholic minority, but the inherited tradition of corporate pluralism helped to ease them into the system. The Catholics established their own broad column of associations and a strong political party and gradually found acceptance within a markedly segmented but still cohesive national polity.

A comparison of the Dutch and the Swiss cases would add further depth to this analysis of the conditions for the differentiation of parties within national systems. Both countries come close to our type IV: Protestant national leadership, strong Catholic minorities, predominance of the cities in the national economy. In setting the assumptions of our model we predicted a split in the peripheral opposition to the nation-builders: one orthodox Protestant opposition (P–D–L) and one Roman Catholic (P–R–L). This clearly fits the Dutch case but not so well the Swiss. How is this to be accounted for? Contrasts of this type open up fascinating possibilities of comparative historical analysis; all we can do here is to suggest a simple hypothesis. Our model not only simplifies complex historical developments through its strict selection of conditioning variables, it also reduces empirical continuities to crude dichotomies. The difference between the Dutch and the Swiss cases can possibly be accounted for through further differentiation in the center-periphery axis. The drive for national centralization was stronger in the Netherlands and had been slowed down in Switzerland through the experiences of the war between the Protestant cantons and the Catholic *Sonderbund*. In the Netherlands the Liberal drive for centralization produced resistance both among the Protestants and the Catholics. In Switzerland the Radicals had few difficulties on the Protestant side and needed support in their opposition to the Catholics. The result was a party system of essentially the same structure as in the typical Southern-Central cases.[66]

Further differentiations of the "N–P" axis in our model will also make it easier to fit the extraordinary case of France into this system of controlled dimension-by-dimension comparisons.

In our model we have placed France with Italy as an example of an alliance-opposition system of type VI: Catholic dominance through the Counter-Reformation, secularization and religious conflict during the next phase of nation-building in the nineteenth century, clear predominance of the cities in national politics. But this is an analytical juxtaposition of polities with diametrically opposed histories of development and consolidation—France one of the oldest and most centralized nation-states in Europe, Italy a territory unified long after the French revolutions had paved the way for the "participant nation," the integrated political structure committing the entire territorial population to the same historical destiny. To us this is not a weakness in our model, however. The party systems of the countries *are* curiously similar, and any scheme of comparative analysis must somehow or other bring this out. The point is that our distinction between "nation-builder" alliances and "periphery" alliances must take on very different meanings in the two contexts. In France the distinction between "center" and "periphery" was far more than a matter of geography; it reflected long-standing historical commitments for or against the Revolution. As is spelled out in detail in Siegfried's classic *Tableau*, the *Droite* had its strongholds in the districts which had most stubbornly resisted the revolutionary drive for centralization and equalization,[67] but it was far more than a movement of peripheral protest—it was a broad alliance of alienated elite groups, of frustrated nation-builders who felt that their rightful powers had been usurped by men without faith and roots. In Italy there was no basis for such a broad alliance against the secular nation-builders, since the established local elites offered little resistance to the lures of *trasformismo*, and the Church kept its faithful followers out of national politics for nearly two generations.

These contrasts during the initial phases of mass mobilization had far-reaching consequences for each party system. With the broadening of the electorates and the strengthening of the working-class parties, the Church felt impelled to defend its position through its own resources. In France, the result was an attempt to divorce the defense of the Catholic schools from the defense of the established rural hierarchy. This trend had first found expression through the establishment of Christian trade unions and in 1944 finally led to the formation of the MRP. The burden of historic commitments was too strong, however; the young party was unable to establish itself as a broad mass party defending the principles of Christian democracy. By contrast, in Italy, history had left the Church with only insignificant rivals to the right of the working class parties. The result was the formation of a broad alliance of a variety of interests and movements, frequently at logger-heads with each other, but united in their defense of the rights of the central institution of the fragmented *ancien régime*, the Roman Catholic Church. In both cases there was a clear-cut tendency toward religious polarization, but differences in the histories of nation-building made for differences in the resultant systems of party alliances and oppositions.

We could go into further detail on every one of the eight types distinguished in our model, but this would take us too far into single-country histories. We are less concerned with the specifics of the degrees of fit in each national case than with the overall structure of the model. There is clearly nothing final about any such scheme; it simply sets a series of themes for detailed comparisons and suggests ways of organizing the results within a manageable conceptual framework. The model is a tool and its utility can be tested only through continuous development: through the addition of further variables to account for observed differences as well as through refinements in the definition and grading of the variables already included.

Two developments from the model require immediate detailed consideration: (1) What variables have to be added to account for the formation of *distinctly territorial* parties? (2) What criteria should count in differentiating between N–L and N–U alliances, and what conditional variables can be entered into the model to account for the emergence of *explicitly agrarian parties*?

Developments and Deviations: Parties for Territorial Defense

Nation-building invariably generates territorial resistances and cultural strains. There will be competition between potential centers of political control; there may be conflict between the capital and the areas of growth in the provinces; and there will be unavoidable tension between the culturally and economically advanced areas and the backward periphery.[68] Some of these territorial-cultural conflicts were solved through secession or boundary changes, but others were intensified through unification movements. To take one obvious example, the dismemberment of the Hapsburg Empire certainly settled a great number of hopelessly entangled conflicts, but it also led to the political unification of such culturally and economically heterogeneous entities as Italy, Yugoslavia, and Czechoslovakia. Territorial-cultural conflicts do not just find political expression in secessionist and irredentist movements, however; they feed into the overall cleavage structure in the national community and help to condition the development not only of each nationwide party organization but even more of the entire system of party oppositions and alignments.

The contrast between the British and the Scandinavian party systems stands out with great clarity in our step-by-step accounting scheme. The countries of Northwest Europe had all opted for national religious solutions at the time of the Reformation, but they nevertheless developed markedly different party systems during the early phases of democratization and mobilization. This contrast in political development clearly did not reflect a difference in the salience of *any single* line of cleavage but a difference in the *joint* operation of two sets of cleavages: the opposition between the central nation-building culture and the traditions of the periphery, and the opposition between the primary and the secondary sectors of the economy. In Britain the central culture was upheld and reinforced by a vast network of *landed* families, in the Nordic countries by an essentially *urban* elite of officials and patricians. In Britain the two cleavage lines *cut across* each other; in Scandinavia they *reinforced* each other. The British structure encouraged a gradual merger of urban and rural interests, while the Scandinavian made for division and opposition.[69] The British Conservative Party was able to establish a joint front of landed and industrial owner interests, while the Scandinavian Right remained essentially urban and proved unable to establish any durable alliance with the Agrarians and the peripheral Left.

Similar processes of interaction can be observed at work in the development of the continental party system. Conflicts between mobilizing elites and peripheral cultures have in some cases been reinforced, in some cases dampened, by conflicts between the State and the Church and by oppositions between urban and rural interests. Belgium offers a striking example of cleavage reinforcement. The "Union of Oppositions" of the early years of nation-building broke up over the schools issue, but this was only the first step in a gradual deepening of cleavages. The continuing processes of economic, social, and cultural mobilization brought the country closer to a polarization between French-speaking, secular and industrial Wallonia and *Nederlands*-speaking, Catholic and agricultural Flanders.[70] This polarizing cleavage structure contrasts dramatically with the crisscrossing of religious and linguistic oppositions in Switzerland. Of the five French-speaking cantons three are Protestant and two Catholic, and of the nineteen Alemannic cantons or half-cantons ten are Protestant and nine Catholic. "This creates loyalties and affinities which counterbalance the linguistic inter-relationships."[71]

Conditions for the emergence and consolidation of territorial counter-cultures have varied significantly within Europe. Organized resistance against the centralizing apparatus of the mobilizing nation-state appears to have been most likely to develop in three sets of situations:

- heavy concentration of the counter-culture within one clear-cut territory;
- few ties of communication, alliance, and bargaining experience toward the national center and more toward external centers of cultural or economic influence;
- minimal economic dependence on the political metropolis.

Federalist, autonomist, and separatist movements and parties are most likely to occur through a cumulation of such conditions. A comparison of Spain and Italy tells us a great deal about such processes of cleavage cumulation. Both countries have for centuries been heavily dominated by the Catholic Church. Both were caught in a violent conflict between secular power and ecclesiastical privileges in the wake of the National Revolution, and both have remained highly heterogeneous in their ethnic structure, in cultural traditions, and in historical commitments. Yet they differed markedly in the character of the party systems they developed in the phase of initial mass mobilization. Spanish politics was dominated by territorial oppositions; Italy developed a national party system, fragmented but with irredentist-separatist parties only in such extreme cases as the South Tyrol and the Val d'Aosta.

In Spain, the opposition of the Pyrennean periphery to the centralizing Castilian regime first found expression in the mobilization of the Carlist peasantry in defense of the Church and their local liberties against the liberals and the Freemasons in the army and government bureaucracy during the second half of the nineteenth century. Around 1900, the Catalan industrial bourgeoisie and significant parts of the Basque middle classes and peasantry turned to regionalist and separatist parties to fight the parasitic central administration identified with the economically backward center of the nation. In the Basque areas, strong religious loyalties contributed to increase the hostility toward an anticlerical central government. In Catalonia, separatist sentiments could not repress cleavages along class lines. The conflicts between businessmen and workers, landowners and tenant-farmers divided the regionalist forces into a Right (the *Lliga*) and a Left (the *Esquerra*).[72]

In Italy, the thrust of national mobilization came from the economically advanced North. The impoverished provinces to the South and on the islands resisted the new administrators as alien usurpers but did not develop parties of regional resistance: the prefects ruled through varying mixtures of *combinazione* and force and proved as efficient instruments of centralization in the backward areas of Italy as the *caciques* in the regions of Spain controlled from Madrid.[73] There was an obvious element of territorial protest in the papal repudiation of the new nation-state, but it took several decades before this conflict found expression in the formation of a distinctly Catholic party. The loyal Catholics did not just oppose the Piedmontese administration as a threat to the established privileges of the Church; Rome fought the Liberal nation-builders as the conquerors of the Papal territories. But these resentments were not channeled into national politics. The intransigent policy of *non expedit* kept the Catholics out of the give and take of electoral bargaining and discouraged the eager advocates of a mass party for the defense of the Church. This policy of isolation divided the communities throughout the Italian territory. When the Pope finally gave in on the eve of the introduction of mass suffrage, these cross-local cleavages produced a nationwide system of oppositions among Liberals, Catholics, and Socialists. There were marked regional variations in the strength of each camp. Dogan's work on regional variations in the stratification of the Italian vote tells us a great deal about the factors at work.[74] But in contrast to the development in Spain, the territorial conflict within Italy found no direct expression in the party system. This was not a sign of national integration, however; the country was torn by irreconcilable conflicts among ideologically distinct camps, but the conflict cut across the communities and the regions. There were still unsettled and unsettling territorial problems, but these were at the frontiers. The irredentist claims against France and the Hapsburgs generated a nationalist-imperialist ideology and prepared the ground for the rise of Fascism.[75]

Such comparisons can be multiplied throughout Europe. In the multi-centered German Reich the contrasts between East and West, North and South generated a variety of territorial tensions. The conflict between the Hamburg Liberals and the East Elbian Conservatives went far beyond the tariff issue—it reflected an important cultural opposition. The Bavarian particularists again and again set up parties of their own and have to this day found it difficult to fit into a nationwide system of party oppositions.[76] By contrast, in hydrocephalic France conflicts between the capital and the provincial "desert"[77] had been endemic since the sixteenth century but did *not* generate distinct regional parties. Paris was without serious competitors for political, economic, and cultural power—there was no basis for durable alliances against the center. "Paris was not only comparable to New York and Washington, as was London, but also to Chicago in transport, Detroit and Cincinnati in manufacturing, and Boston in letters and education."[78]

Developments and Deviations: Parties for Agrarian Defense

We distinguished in our initial paradigm (Figure 4.3) between two "typical" cleavages at the *l* end of the territorial-cultural axis: on the *i* side the opposition of ethnic-linguistic minorities against the upholders of the dominant culture (1), on the *a* side the opposition of the peasantry against economic exploitation by the financial, commercial, and industrial interests in the cities. Our discussion of the "party formation" model brought out a few hypotheses about the transformation of cleavages of type 1 into distinct parties for territorial defense. We shall now proceed to a parallel discussion for cleavages of type 3 in Figure 4.3.

Our model predicts that agrarian interests are most likely to find direct political expression in systems of close alliance between nation-builders and the urban economic leadership—the four N–U cases in our eightfold typology. But in three of the four cases the opposition of the peasantry to the dominance of the cities tended to be closely linked to a rejection of the moral and religious standards of the nation-builders. This produced D–L alliances in Scandinavia (type II) and the Netherlands (type IV) and R–L alliances in the secularizing southern countries (type VI). In the fourth N–U case (type VIII) there was no basis for explicit mergers of agrarian with religious opposition movements: the Belgian Roman Catholics were strong both in the urban "establishment" and among the farmers but, as it happened, were themselves torn between the *l* and the *g* poles over issues of ethnic-linguistic identity between Flemings and Walloons.

In only one of these four cases did distinctly agrarian parties emerge as stable elements of the national systems of electoral constellations—in the five countries of the North. A peasant party also established itself in the Protestant cantons of Switzerland. In the other countries of the West there may have been peasant lists at a few elections, but the interests of agriculture were generally aggregated into broader party fronts: the Conservative parties in Britain, in Prussia, and in France, the Christian parties elsewhere.

Why these differences? This raises a number of difficult questions about the economics of nation-building. In our three-step model we brutally reduced the options of the central elite to a choice between an alliance with the *landed* interests and with the *urban-financial-commercial-industrial* interests. This, of course, was never a matter of either/or but of continuing adjustment to changes in the overall equilibrium of forces in each territory. Our dichotomy does not help the description of any single case but simply serves to bring out contrasts among systems in the *relative* openness to alliances in the one direction or the other at the decisive stages of partisan mobilization.

To understand the conditions for alliance options in the one direction or the other it is essential to go into details of the *organization of rural society* at the time of the extensions of the suffrage. What counted more than anything else was the *concentration of resources for the control of the process of mobilization*, and in the countryside the *size of the units of production* and the *hierarchies of dependence* expressed in the tenure systems counted more than any other factors: the greater the concentration of economic power and social prestige the easier it was to control the rural votes and the greater the political payoffs of alliances with landowners. It was no accident that Conservative leaders such as Bismarck and Disraeli took a lead in the extension of the suffrage; they counted on the loyalty and obedience of the dependent tenants and the agricultural workers.[79] To measure the political potentialities of the land-owning classes it would be essential to assemble comparative statistics on the proportions of the arable land and the agricultural manpower under the control of the large estate owners in each country. Unfortunately there are many lacunae in the historical statistics and comparisons are fraught with many hazards. The data at hand suggest the countries we identified as typical "N–L cases" (types I, III, V, and VII in our eightfold model) all tended to be dominated by large estates, at least in their central territories. This was the case in most of England and Scotland, in Prussia east of the Elbe, in the *Reconquista* provinces of Spain, and in lowland Austria.[80] There were, to be sure, large estates in many of the countries we have identified as "N–U cases" (types II, IV, VI, and VIII), but such alliances as there were between urban and rural elites still left large groups of self-owning peasants free to join counter-alliances on their own. In Belgium and the Netherlands the holdings tended to be small and closely tied in with the urban economy. In France and Italy there were always marked regional variations in the size of holdings and the systems of land tenure, and the peasantry was deeply divided over cultural, religious, and economic issues. There were large estates in Jutland, in southern Sweden, and in southwestern Finland, and the owners of these helped to consolidate the conservative establishments in the early phases of competitive politics, but the broad masses of the Nordic peasantry could not be brought into any such alliances with the established urban elites. The traditions of independent peasant representation were strong and there was widespread rejection of the cultural influences from the encroaching cities. In Denmark, Norway, and Sweden the decisive "Left" fronts against the old regime were coalitions of urban radicals and increasingly estate-conscious peasants, but these coalitions broke up as soon as the new parties entered government. In Denmark the urban Radicals left the agrarian *Venstre*; in Norway and Sweden the old "Left" was split in several directions on moralist-religious as well as on economic lines. Distinctly agrarian parties also emerged in the two still "colonial" countries of the North, Finland and Iceland. In these predominantly primary-producing countries the struggle for external independence dominated political life in the decades after the introduction of universal suffrage, and there was not the same need for broad opposition fronts against the establishments *within* each nation.

Typically, agrarian parties appear to have emerged in countries or provinces:

1. where the cities and the industrial centers were still numerically weak at the time of the decisive extensions of the suffrage;
2. where the bulk of the agricultural populations were active in family-size farming and either owned their farms themselves or were legally protected lease-holders largely independent of socially superior landowners;
3. where there were important cultural barriers between the countryside and the cities and much resistence to the incorporation of farm production in the capitalist economy of the cities; and
4. where the Catholic Church was without significant influence.

These criteria fit not only the Nordic countries but also the Protestant cantons of Switzerland and even some areas of German Austria. A *Bauern-, Gewerbe- und Bürgerpartei* emerged in Berne, Zurich, and other heavily Alemannic-Protestant cantons after the introduction of PR in Switzerland in 1919. This was essentially a splinter from the old Radical-Liberal Party and recruited most of its support in the countryside. In the Catholic cantons the peasants remained loyal to their old party even after PR. Similarly in the Austrian First Republic the Nationalist *Lager* was split in a middle-class *Grossdeutsche Volkspartei* and a *Landbund* recruited among the anticlerical peasants in Carinthia and Styria. The Christian Social Party recruited the bulk of its support among the Catholic peasantry but was able to keep the rural-urban tension within bounds through elaborate organizational differentiations within the party.

*The Fourth Step: Variations in the Strength and Structure of the
Working-Class Movements*

Our three-step model stops short at a point before the decisive thrust toward universal suffrage. It pinpoints sources of variations in the systems of division within the "independent" strata of the European national electorates, among the owners of property and the holders of professional or educational privileges qualifying them for the vote during the *régime censitaire*.

But this is hardly more than half the story. The extension of the suffrage to the lower classes changed the character of each national political system, generated new cleavages, and brought about a restructuring of the old alignments.

Why did we not bring these important developments into our model of European party systems? Clearly not because the three first cleavage lines were more important than the fourth in the explanation of *any one national party system*. On the contrary, in sheer statistical terms the fourth cleavage line will in at least half of the cases under consideration explain much more of the variance in the distributions of full-suffrage votes than any one of the others.[81] We focused on the first three cleavage lines because these were the ones that appeared to account for most of the variance *among systems*: the interactions of the "center-periphery," state-church, and land-industry cleavages tended to produce much more marked, and apparently much more stubborn, differences among the national party systems than any of the cleavages brought about through the rise of the working-class movements.

We could of course have gone on to present a four-step model immediately (in fact, we did in an earlier draft), but this proved very cumbersome and produced a variety of uncomfortable redundancies. Clearly what had to be explained was not the emergence of a distinctive working-class movement at some point or other before or after the extension of the suffrage but the *strength and solidarity* of any such movement, its capacity to mobilize the underprivileged classes for action and its ability to maintain unity in the face of the many forces making for division and fragmentation. All the European polities developed some sort of working-class movement at some point between the first extensions of the suffrage and the various "postdemocratic" attempts at the repression of partisan pluralism. To predict the *presence* of such movements was simple; to predict which ones would be strong and which ones weak, which ones unified and which ones split down the middle, required much more knowledge of national conditions and developments and a much more elaborate model of the historical interaction process. Our three-step model does not go this far for *any* party; it predicts the presence of such-and-such parties in polities characterized by such-and-such cleavages, but it does not give any formula for accounting for the strength or the cohesion of any one party. This *could* be built into the model through the introduction of various population parameters (percent speaking each language or dialect, percent committed to each of the churches or dissenting bodies, ratios of concentrations of wealth and dependent labor in industry versus landed estates), and possibly of some indicators of the cleavage "distance" (differences in the chances of interaction across the cleavage line, whether physically determined or normatively regulated), but any attempt in this direction would take us much too far in this all-too-long essay. At this point we limit ourselves to an elementary discussion of the between-system variations which would have to be explained through such an extension of our model. We shall suggest a "fourth step" and point to a possible scheme for the explanation of differences in the formation of national party systems under the impact of universal suffrage.

Our initial scheme of analysis posited four decisive dimensions of cleavage in Western polities. Our model for the generation of party systems pinpointed three crucial junctures in national history corresponding to the first three of these dimensions:

Cleavage	*Critical juncture*	*Issues*
Center-Periphery	Reformation–Counter-Reformation: 16th-17th centuries	National vs. supranational religion National language vs. Latin
State-Church	National Revolution: 1789 and after	Secular vs. religious control of mass education
Land-Industry	Industrial Revolution: 19th century	Tariff levels for agricultural products; control vs. freedom for industrial enterprise

It is tempting to add to this a fourth dimension and a fourth juncture:

Cleavage	*Critical juncture*	*Issues*
Owner-Worker	The Russian Revolution: 1917 and after	Integration into national polity vs. commitment to international revolutionary movement

There is an intriguing cyclical movement in this scheme. The process gets under way with the breakdown of one supranational order and the establishment of strong territorial bureaucracies legitimizing themselves through the standardizing of nationally distinct religions and languages, and it ends with a conflict over national versus international loyalties within the last of the strata to be formally integrated into the nation-state, the rural and the industrial workers.

The conditions for the development of distinctive working-class parties varied markedly from country to country within Europe. These differences emerged well before World War I. The Russian Revolution did not generate new cleavages but simply accentuated long-established lines of division within the working-class elite.

Our three-step model does not produce clear-cut predictions of these developments. True enough, the most unified and the most "domesticable" working-class movements emerged in the Protestant-dominated countries with the smoothest histories of nation-building: Britain, Denmark, and Sweden (types I and II in our model). Equally true, the Catholic-dominated countries with difficult or very recent histories of nation-building also produced deeply divided, largely alienated working-class movements—France, Italy, Spain (types V and VI). But other variables clearly have to be brought into account for variations in the intermediary zone between the Protestant Northwest and the Latin South (types III and IV, VII and VIII). Both the Austrian and the German working-class movements developed their distinctive counter-cultures against the dominant national elites. The Austrian Socialist *Lager*, heavily concentrated as it was in Vienna, was able to maintain its unity in the face of the clerical-conservatives and the pan-German nationalists after the dissolution of the Hapsburg Empire.[82] By contrast, the German working-class movement was deeply divided after the defeat in 1918. Sharply contrasted conceptions of the rules of the political game stood opposed to each other and were to prove fatal in the fight against the wave of mass nationalism of the early thirties.[83] In Switzerland and the Netherlands (both type IV in our scheme), the Russian and the German revolutions produced a few disturbances, but the leftward split-offs from the main working class by parties were of little significance. The marked cultural and religious cleavages reduced the potentials for the Socialist parties, but the traditions of pluralism were gradually to help their entry into national politics.

Of all the intermediary countries Belgium (type VIII in our model) presents perhaps the most interesting case. By our overall rule, the Belgian working class should be deeply divided: a thoroughly Catholic country with a particularly difficult history of nation-building across two distinct language communities. In this case the smallness and the international dependence of the nation may well have created restraints on the internal forces of division and fragmentation. Val Lorwin has pointed to such factors in his analysis of Belgian-French contrasts:

> The reconciliation of the Belgian working class to the political and social order, divided though the workers are by language and religion and the Flemish-Walloon question, makes a vivid contrast with the experience of France. The differences did not arise from the material fruits of economic growth, for both long were rather low-wage countries, and Belgian wages were the lower. In

some ways the two countries had similar economic development. But Belgium's industrialization began earlier; it was more dependent on international commerce, both for markets and for its transit trade; it had a faster growing population; and it became much more urbanized than France. The small new nation, "the cockpit of Europe," could not permit itself social and political conflict to the breaking point. Perhaps France could not either, but it was harder for the bigger nation to realize it.[84]

The contrast between France, Italy, and Spain on the one hand and Austria and Belgium on the other suggests a possible generalization: the working-class movement tended to be much more divided in the countries where the "nation-builders" and the Church were openly or latently opposed to each other during the crucial phases of educational development and mass mobilization (our "S" cases, types V and VI) than in the countries where the Church had, at least initially, sided with the nation-builders against some common enemy outside (our "R" cases, an alliance against Protestant Prussia and the dependent Hapsburg peoples in the case of Austria; against the Calvinist Dutch in the case of Belgium). This fits the Irish case as well. The Catholic Church was no less hostile to the English than the secular nationalists, and the union of the two forces not only reduced the possibilities of a polarization of Irish politics on class lines but made the likelihood of a Communist splinter of any importance very small indeed.

It is tempting to apply a similar generalization to the Protestant North: the greater the internal division during the struggle for nationhood, the greater the impact of the Russian Revolution on the divisions within the working class. We have already pointed to the profound split within the German working class. The German Reich was a late-comer among European nations, and none of the territorial and religious conflicts within the nation was anywhere near settlement by the time the working-class parties entered the political arena. Among the northern countries the two oldest nations, Denmark and Sweden, were least affected by the Communist-Socialist division. The three countries emerging from colonial status were much more directly affected: Norway (domestically independent from 1814, a sovereign state from 1905) for only a brief period in the early 1920s; Finland (independent in 1917); and Iceland (domestically independent in 1916 and a sovereign state from 1944) for a much longer period. These differences among the northern countries have been frequently commented on in the literature of comparative politics. The radicalization of the Norwegian Labor Party has been interpreted within several alternative models, one emphasizing the alliance options of the party leaders, another the grass-roots reactions to sudden industrialization in the peripheral countryside, and a third the openness of the party structure and the possibilities of quick feedback from the mobilized voters. There is no doubt that the early mobilization of the peasantry and the quick victory over the old regime of the officials had left the emerging Norwegian working-class party much more isolated, much less important as a coalition partner, than its Danish and Swedish counterparts.[85] There is also a great deal of evidence to support the old Bull hypothesis of the radicalizing effects of sudden industrialization, but more recent research suggests that this was only one element in a broad process of political change. The Labor Party recruited many more of its voters in the established cities and in the forestry and the fisheries districts, but the openness of the party structure allowed the radicals to establish themselves very quickly and to take over the majority wing of the party during the crucial years just after the Russian Revolution.[86] This very openness to rank-and-file influences made the alliance with Moscow very short-lived; the Communists split off in 1924 and the old majority party "joined the nation" step by step until it took power in 1935.[87]

Only two of the Scandinavian countries retained strong Communist parties after World War II—Finland and Iceland. Superficially these countries have two features in common: prolonged struggles for cultural and political independence, and late industrialization. In fact the two countries went through very different processes of political change from the initial phase of nationalist mobilization to the final formation of the full-suffrage party system. One obvious source of variation was the distance from Russia. The sudden upsurge of the Socialist Party in Finland in 1906 (the party gained 37 percent of the votes cast at the first election under universal suffrage) was part of a general wave of mobilization against the Tsarist regime. The Russian Revolution of 1917 split Finland down the middle; the working-class voters were torn between their loyalty to their national culture and its social hierarchy and their solidarity with their class and its revolutionary defenders.[88] The victory of the "Whites" and the subsequent suppression of the Communist Party (1919–21, 1923–25, 1930–44) left deep scars; the upsurge of the leftist SKDL after the Soviet victory in 1945 reflected deep-seated resentments not only against the "lords" and the employers of labor but generally against the upholders of the central national culture. The split in the Icelandic labor movement was much less dramatic; in the oldest and smallest of the European democracies there was little basis for mass conflicts, and the oppositions between communist sympathizers and socialists appeared to reflect essentially personal antagonisms among groups of activists.[89]

Implications for Comparative Political Sociology

We have pushed our attempt at a systematization of the comparative history of partisan oppositions in European polities up to some point in the 1920s, to the freezing of the major party alternatives in the wake of the extension of the suffrage and the mobilization of major sections of the new reservoirs of potential supporters. Why stop there? Why not pursue this exercise in comparative cleavage analysis right up to the present? The reason is deceptively simple: *the contemporary party systems reflected, with few but significant exceptions, the cleavage structures of the 1920s*. This is a crucial characteristic of Western competitive politics in the age of "high mass consumption": *the party alternatives, and in remarkably many cases the party organizations, are older than the majorities of the national electorates*. To most of the citizens of the West the currently active parties have been part of the political landscape since their childhood or at least since they were first faced with the choice between alternative "packages" on election day.

This continuity is often taken as a matter of course; in fact it poses an intriguing set of problems for comparative sociological research. An amazing number of the parties which had established themselves by the end of World War I survived not only the onslaughts of Fascism and National Socialism but also another world war and a series of profound changes in the social and cultural structure of the polities they were part of. How was this possible? How were these parties able to survive so many changes in the political, social, and economic conditions of their operation? How could they keep such large bodies of citizens identifying with them over such long periods of time, and how could they renew their core clienteles from generation to generation?

There is no straightforward answer to any of these questions. We know much less about the internal management and the organizational functioning of political parties than we do about their sociocultural base and their history of participation in public decision-making.[90]

To get closer to an answer we would clearly have to start out from a comparative analysis of the "old" and the "new" parties: the early mass parties formed during the final phase of suffrage extension, and the later attempts to launch new parties during the first decades of universal suffrage. It is difficult to see any significant exceptions to the rule that the parties which were able to establish mass organizations and entrench themselves in the local government structures *before* the final drive toward maximal mobilization have proved the most viable. The narrowing of the "support market" brought about through the growth of mass parties during this final thrust toward full-suffrage democracy clearly left very few openings for new movements. Where the challenge of the emerging working-class parties had been met by concerted efforts of countermobilization through nationwide mass organizations on the liberal and the conservative fronts, the leeway for new party formations was particularly small; this was the case whether the threshold of representation was low, as in Scandinavia, or quite high, as in Britain.[91] Correspondingly the "postdemocratic" party systems proved markedly more fragile and open to newcomers in the countries where the privileged strata had relied on their local power resources rather than on nationwide mass organizations in their efforts at mobilization.

France was one of the first countries to bring a maximal electorate into the political arena, but the mobilization efforts of the established strata tended to be local and personal. A mass organization corresponding to the Conservative Party in Britain was never developed. There was very little ''narrowing of the support market'' to the right of the PCF and the SFIO and consequently a great deal of leeway for innovation in the party system even in the later phases of democratization.

There was similar asymmetry in Germany: strong mass organizations on the left but marked fragmentation on the right. The contrast between Germany and Britain has been rubbed in at several points in our analysis of cleavage structures. The contrast with Austria is equally revealing; there the three-*Lager* constellation established itself very early in the mobilization process, and the party system changed astoundingly little from the Empire to the First Republic, and from the First to the Second. The consolidation of the conservative support around the mass organizations of the Catholic Church clearly soaked up a great deal of the mobilization potential for new parties. In Wilhelmine and Weimar Germany the only genuine mass organization to the right of the Social Democrats was the Catholic *Zentrum*; this still left a great deal of leeway for ''post-democratic'' party formations on the Protestant right. Ironically, it was the defeat of the National Socialist regime and the loss of the Protestant East which opened up an opportunity for some stabilization of the German party system. With the establishment of the regionally divided CDU/CSU the Germans were for the first time able to approximate a broad conservative party of the British type. It was not able to establish as solid a membership organization but proved, at least until the debacle of 1966, amazingly effective in aggregating interests across a wide range of strata and sectors of the federal community.

Two other countries of the West have experienced spectacular changes in their party systems since the introduction of universal suffrage and deserve some comment in this context—Italy and Spain. The Italian case comes close to the German: both went through a painful process of belated unification; both were deeply divided within their privileged strata between ''nation-builders'' (Prussians, Piedmontese) and Catholics; both had been slow to recognize the rights of working-class organizations. The essential difference lay in the *timing* of party developments. In the Reich a differentiated party structure had been allowed to develop during the initial mobilization phase and had been given another fifteen years of functioning during the Weimar Republic. In Italy, by contrast, the State-Church split was so profound that a structurally responsive party system did not see the light before 1919— three years before the March on Rome. There had simply been no time for the "freezing" of any party system before the postdemocratic revolution, and there was very little in the way of a traditional party system to fall back on after the defeat of the Fascist regime in 1944. True, the Socialists and the *Popolari* had had their brief spell of experience of electoral mobilization, and this certainly counted when the PCI and the DC established themselves in the wake of the war. But the other political forces had never been organized for concerted electoral politics and left a great deal of leeway for irregularities in the mobilization market. The Spanish case has a great deal in common with the French: early unification but deep resentments against central power in some of the provinces and early universalization of the suffrage but weak and divided party organizations. The Spanish system of sham parliamentarism and *caciquismo* had not produced electoral mass parties of any importance by the time the double threat of secessionist mobilization and working-class militancy triggered off nationalist counterrevolutions, first under Primo de Rivera in 1923, then with the Civil War in 1936. The entire history of Spanish electoral mass politics is contained in the five years of the Republic from 1931 to 1936; this is not much to go on and it is significant that a lucid and realistic analyst like Juan Linz did not base his projections about the possible structuring of a future Spanish party system on the experiences of those five years but on a projection from Italian voting alignments.[92]

These four spectacular cases of disruptions in the development of national party systems do not in themselves invalidate our initial formulation. The most important of the party alternatives got set for each national citizenry during the phases of mobilization just before or just after the final extension of the suffrage and have remained roughly the same through decades of subsequent changes in the structural conditions of partisan choice. Even in the three cases of France, Germany, and Italy the continuities in the alternatives are as striking as the disruptions in their organizational expressions. On this score the French case is in many ways the most intriguing. There was no period of internally generated disruption of electoral politics (the Pétain-Laval phase would clearly not have occurred if the Germans had not won in 1940), but there have been a number of violent oscillations between plebiscitarian and representative models of democracy and marked organizational fragmentation both at the level of interest articulation and at the level of parties. In spite of these frequent upheavals no analyst of French politics is in much doubt about the underlying continuities of sentiment and identification on the right no less than on the left of the political spectrum. The voter does not just react to immediate issues but is caught in an historically given constellation of diffuse options for the system as a whole.

This "historicity" of the party alternatives is of crucial importance not only in the study of differences and similarities *across* nations but also *within* nations. The party alternatives vary in "age" and dominance not only from one overall system to another but equally from one locality to another within the same polity. To gain any detailed understanding of the processes of mobilization and alignment within any single nation we clearly need information not just about turnout and the division of votes but about the *timing of the formation of local party organizations*. This process of local entrenchment can be pinpointed in several ways: through organizational records, through membership registers, and through information about the lists presented at local elections. Representation in localities will in most countries of the West open up much more direct access to power resources than representation at the national level. The local officeholders tend to form the backbone of the party organization and are able to attract nuclei of active supporters through the distribution of whatever rewards their positions may command. To the parties of the underprivileged, access to the local machineries of government has tended to be of crucial importance for the development and maintenance of their organizational networks. They may have survived on their trade union strength, but the additional resource potentials inherent in local offices have meant much more to them than to the parties deriving their essential strength from the networks of economic power-holders or from the organizations of the Church.

The study of these processes of local entrenchment is still in its infancy in most countries, and serious comparative studies have so far never been attempted.[93] This is one of the great lacunae in empirical political sociology. There is an unfortunate asymmetry in our knowledge and our efforts at systematization: we know very little of the processes through which political alternatives *get set* for different local electorates, but we have a great deal of information about the circumstances in which one alternative or the other *gets chosen*. This, obviously, reflects differences in the access to data. It is a time-consuming and frustrating job to assemble data locality by locality on the formation, development, and, possibly, stagnation or disappearance, of party organizations. It is vastly easier to find out about choices among the alternatives once they are set; the machineries of electoral bookkeeping have for decade after decade heaped up data about mass choices and so have, at least since World War II, the mushrooming organizations of pollsters and surveyors. What is needed now are systematic efforts to bring together information about the timing of local party entrenchments to pin down their consequences for voter alignments.[94] With the development of ecological data archives[95] in historical depth such analyses are bound to multiply. What is needed now is an international effort to maximize the coordination of such efforts.

With the development of such archives the *time dimension* is bound to gain prominence in the comparative study of mass politics. The early school of French electoral geographers were deeply conscious of the importance of local entrenchments and their perpetuation through time. Statistical ecologists such as Tingsten were less concerned with diachronic stability than with rates of change, particularly through the mobilization of the latest entrants into the national electorates, the workers and women. The introduction of the sample survey as a technique of data gathering and analysis shortened the time perspective and brought about a concentration on synchronic variations; the panel technique focused attention on short-term fluctuations, and even the questions about past voting and family political traditions did not help to make surveys an adequate tool of developmental research. We have seen, however, an important reversal in this trend. There is not only a marked increase in scholarly interest in historical *time series data* for elections and other mass data[96] but also a greater concentration of work on *organizational developments and the freezing of political alternatives*. These are essential prerequisites for the growth of a truly comparative sociology of Western mass politics. To understand the current alignments of voters in our different countries it is not enough to analyze the contemporary issues and the contemporary sociocultural structure; it is even more important to go back to the initial formation of party alternatives and to analyze the interaction between the historically established foci of identification and the subsequent changes in the structural conditions of choice.

This joining of diachronic and synchronic analysis strategies is of particular importance for an understanding of the mass politics of the organizationally saturated "high mass consumption" societies of the sixties. Decades of structural change and economic growth made the old, established alternatives increasingly irrelevant, but the high level of organizational mobilization of most sectors of the community left very little leeway for a decisive breakthrough of new party alternatives. It is not an accident that situations of this type generated a great deal of frustration, alienation, and protestation within the organizationally least committed sections of the community, the *young* and, quite particularly, the *students*. The "revolt of the young" found many varieties of expression in the sixties: new types of criminality and new styles of living but also new types of politics. The rejection of the old alternatives, of the politics of party representation, perhaps found its most spectacular expression in the civil rights struggle and the student protest movement in the United States,[97] but the disaffection of the young from the established parties, particularly the parties in power, has been a widespread phenomenon even in Europe. The widespread disagreements with the national powers-that-be over foreign and military policy constitute only one among several sources of such disillusionment; the distance between levels of aspiration and levels of achievement in the welfare state has clearly also been of importance.

The probability that such resentments will coalesce into movements broad enough to form viable new parties is on the whole low, but the processes of socialization and recruitment within the old ones will clearly be affected.

Much, of course, depends on local concentrations and the height of the thresholds of representation. In the low-threshold Scandinavian system the waves of disaffection have already disrupted the equilibrium of the old parties: there have been important splinter movements on the Socialist Left, and these have sapped some of the strategic strength of the old Social Democratic parties. This happened first in Denmark: the split-up of the Communist party led to the development of a remarkably vigorous national-Titoist party on the Socialist Left and brought about serious losses for the Social Democrats. Much the same sort of development has taken place in Norway since 1961. A splinter movement within the governing Labor Party suddenly broke through and gained two seats in 1961; for the first time since the war Labor was brought into a minority position. This was the beginning of a series of crises. By 1965 the Left splinter had grown to 6 percent of the votes cast and the Labor Party was finally out of power. Results for Sweden show similar developments there; the CP has switched to a "national" line close to the Danish model and has gained ground.

There is a crucial consideration in any comparative analysis of such changes in party strength: Which parties have been in power, which ones have been in opposition? In the fifties many observers feared the development of permanent majority parties. It was argued that the parties in government had all the advantages and could mobilize so many strategic resources on their side that the opposition might be left powerless forever more. It is heartening to see how quickly these observers had to change their minds. In the sixties the mounting "revolutions of rising expectations" clearly tended to place governing parties at a terrifying disadvantage: they had to take the responsibility for predicaments they could no longer control; they became the targets of continuous waves of demands, grievances, criticisms, and no longer commanded the resources needed to meet them. The troubles of the Labor parties in Scandinavia and in Great Britain can be understood only in this light. The welfare state, the spread of the "car and TV" culture, the educational explosion—all these developments have placed the leftists under increasing strains and made it very difficult for the old working-class parties to retain the loyalties of the younger generation. Even the Swedish Social Democrats, the most intelligent and the most farsighted of the Labor parties in Europe, seem finally to have reached the end of their era. They met the demands for an extension of the welfare state with innovative skill through the development of the supplementary pensions scheme after 1956, but they could not live on that forever. Their recent troubles center on the "*queuing society*": queues in front of the vocational schools and the universities, queues for housing, queues for health services. Swedish workers enjoy perhaps the highest standard of living in the world, but this does not help the Swedish Social Democratic government. The working-class youngsters see others get more education, better housing, better services than they do, and they develop signs of frustration and alienation. It is significant that in all three Scandinavian countries the Social Democratic losses have been most marked in the cities and quite small in the rural periphery; the leftist parties run into the greatest difficulties in the areas where the "revolution of rising expectations" has run the furthest.

It is still too early to say what kinds of politics this will engender. There will clearly be greater fluctuations than before. This may increase the chances of government by regular alternation, but it may also trigger off new varieties of coalition-mongering: politicians are naturally tempted to "spread the blame," to escape electoral retaliation through the sharing of responsibilities with competing parties. Developments in Denmark suggest a trend toward open negotiations across all established party barriers. Norway is experiencing a four-party coalition of the non-Socialist front; there are strains among the four but it seems to work because each party finds it easy to blame its failure to perform on electoral promises on the need for unity within the government. The events in the German *Bundesrepublik* show similar processes at work in quite a different political setting: an increasing disenchantment with the top political leadership and with the established system of decision-making, whatever the party coloring of the current incumbents.

To understand these developments and to gauge the probabilities of the possible projections into the future it will be essential to build up, monograph by monograph, analysis by analysis, a comparative sociology of competitive mass politics.

Notes

1. Single-nation analysts sometimes reveal extraordinarily little awareness of this historical dimension of political research. In their final theoretical chapter of *Voting* (Chicago: University of Chicago Press, 1954), Bernard Berelson and his colleagues ask themselves why "democracies have survived *through the centuries*" (p. 311, our italics). What is problematic about this loose formulation is not the error of historical fact (only the United States had had competitive politics and near-universal suffrage, although for white males only, for more than a hundred years, and most Western polities did not reach the stage of full-suffrage democracy before the end of World War I) but the assumption that mass democracy had had such a long history that events at the early stages of political mobilization no longer had any impact on current electoral alignments. In fact in most of the Western polities the decisive party-forming developments took place in the decades immediately before and after the extension of the suffrage, and even in the 1950s these very events were still alive in the personal memories of large proportions of the electorates.
2. For a review of current efforts to establish "statistical histories of national political developments" see S. Rokkan, "Electoral Mobilization, Party Competition and National Integration," a chapter in J. LaPalombara and Myron Weiner (eds.),

Political Parties and Political Development (Princeton: Princeton University Press, 1966), pp. 241–65.

3. For a highly illuminating analysis of the place of the theory of parties in the history of political thought see Erwin Faul, "Verfemung, Duldung und Anerkennung des Parteiwesens in der Geschichte des politischen Denkens," *Pol. Viertelj.schr.* 5 (1) (March 1964): 60–80.

4. For a general discussion of current usages of the term "party" in the context of a comparative analysis of pluralistic vs. monolithic political systems, see Giovanni Sartori, *Parties and Party Systems* (New York: Harper & Row, 1967).

5. "Wenn eine Partei eine geschlossene, durch die Verbandsordnung dem Verwaltungsstab eingegliederte Vergesellschaftung wird—wie z.B. die 'parte Guelfa' . . .—, *so ist sie keine Partei mehr sondern ein Teilverband des politischen Verbandes*" (our italics), *Wirtschaft und Gesellschaft*, 4th ed. (Tübingen: Mohr, 1956), Vol. I, p. 168; see the attempted translation in *The Theory of Social and Economic Organization* (New York: Free Press, 1947), pp. 409–10.

6. W. Chambers, *Parties in a New Nation* (New York: Oxford University Press, 1963), p. 80.

7. Ruth Schachter, "Single-Party Systems in West Africa," *American Political Science Review* 55 (1961): 301.

8. For a general analysis of this process see S. M. Lipset, M. Trow and J. S. Coleman, *Union Democracy* (New York: Free Press, 1956), pp. 268–9.

9. E. A. Ross, *The Principles of Sociology* (New York: Century, 1920), pp. 164–65. ("Society is sewn together by its inner conflicts.")

10. G. Simmel, *Soziologie* (Berlin: Duncker & Humblot, 1923 and 1958), chap. 4; see the translation in *Conflict* and *The Web of Group Affiliations* (New York: Free Press, 1964).

11. First published in London, The Bodley Head, 1911; quoted from Penguin ed., 1946, p. 238.

12. T. Parsons, R. F. Bales, and E. A. Shils, *Working Papers in the Theory of Action* (New York: Free Press, 1953), chaps. 3 and 5.

13. The first extensive development of the schema is found in T. Parsons and N. J. Smelser, *Economy and Society* (London: Routledge, 1956). A simplified restatement is found in T. Parsons, "General Theory in Sociology," in R. K. Merton et al. (eds.), *Sociology Today* (New York: Basic Books, 1959), pp. 39–78. Extensive revisions in the schema were adumbrated in T. Parsons, "Pattern Variables Revisited," *Am. Sociol. Rev.* 25 (1960): 467–83, and have been presented in further detail in "On the Concept of Political Power," *Pro. Amer. Philos. Soc.* 107 (1963): 232–62. For an attempt to use the Parsonian schema in political analysis see William Mitchell, *The Polity* (New York: Free Press, 1962); see also his *Sociological Analysis and Politics: The Theories of Talcott Parsons* (Englewood Cliffs, N.J.: Prentice-Hall, 1967).

14. Parsons has specified the "inputs" and "outputs" of the I–G interchange in these terms:

	Generalized Support ←	
	Effective Leadership →	
G: POLITY	Advocacy of Policies ←	PUBLIC: I
	Binding Decisions →	

See "Voting and the Equilibrium of the American Political System," in E. Burdick and A. Brodbeck (eds.), *American Voting Behavior* (New York: Free Press, 1959), pp. 80–120.

15. Talcott Parsons, in a private communication, has pointed out a number of difficulties in these formulations. We have singled out the dominant functional attributes of a series of concrete political acts without considering their many secondary functions. Clearly a vote can be treated as an act of support of a particular movement (*L–I*) or a particular set of leaders (*I–G*) as well as a counter in the direct interactions between households and constituted territorial authorities (*L–G*). Our point is that in the study of electoral mass politics in the competitive systems of the West a crucial distinction has to made between the vote as formal act of legitimation (the elected representative is legitimated through the votes cast, *even* by those of his opponents) and the vote as an expression of party loyalty. The standardization of electoral procedures and the formalization of the act of preference underscored this distinction between legitimation (*L–G*) and support (*L–I*). For further discussion of these developments see S. Rokkan, "Mass Suffrage, Secret Voting and Political Participation," *Arch. Eur. Sociol.* 2 (1961): 132–52, and T. Parsons, "Evolutionary Universals in Society," *Amer. Sociol. Rev.* 29 (June 1964): 339–57, particularly the discussion of Rokkan's article, pp. 354–56.

16. Neil J. Smelser, *Theory of Collective Behaviour*, (London: Routledge, 1962).

17. In conformity with Parsonian conventions we use *lower-case* symbols for the parts of *sub*systems and *capitals* for the parts of *total* systems.

18. Sir Lewis Namier, *England in the Age of the American Revolution* (London: Macmillan, 1930), quoted from 2d ed. (1961), p. 183.

19. For detailed discussion of the linkage between religious cleavages and political alliances in the United States see Seymour Martin Lipset, *The First New Nation* (New York: Basic Books, 1963), chap. 4, and "Religion and Politics in the American Past and Present" in R. Lee and M. Martin, *Religion and Social Conflict* (New York: Oxford University Press, 1964), pp. 69–126.

20. For details see S. Rokkan and H. Valen, "Regional Contrasts in Norwegian Politics" in E. Allardt and Y. Littunen (eds.), *Cleavages, Ideologies and Party Systems* (Helsinki: Westermarck Society, 1964), pp. 162–238; S. Rokkan, "Geography, Religion, and Social Class: Crosscutting Cleavages in Norwegian Politics," in S. M. Lipset and S. Rokkan (eds.), *Party Systems and Voter Alignments* (New York: Free Press, 1967), pp. 367–444.

21. See Kenneth O. Morgan, *Wales in British Politics 1868–1922* (Cardiff: University of Wales Press, 1963), pp. 245–55. For a detailed ecological analysis of vote distributions in Wales 1861–1951 see K. R. Cox, *Regional Anomalies in the Voting Behavior of the Population of England and Wales: 1921–1951*, Ph.D. diss., University of Illinois, 1966. Cox explains the strength of the Liberals in Wales in much the same terms as Rokkan and Valen explain the strength of the Left "counterculture" in the south and west of Norway: the predominance of small farms, the egalitarian class structure, linguistic opposition, and religious nonconformity.

22. For Norway see the writings of S. Rokkan already cited. For Finland see Pirkko Rommi, "Finland" in *Problemer i nordisk historie-forskning*. II. Framveksten av de politiske partier i de nordiske land på 1800–tallet (Bergen: Universitetsforlaget, 1964), pp. 103–30; E. Allardt, "Patterns of Class Conflict and Working Class Consciousness in Finnish Politics," in E. Allardt and Y. Littunen (eds.),

Cleavages, Ideologies and Party Systems, pp. 97–131; E. Allardt and P. Pesonen, "Cleavages in Finnish Politics," in Lipset and Rokkan (eds.), *Party Systems and Voter Alignments*, pp. 325–66.

23. See S. Rokkan, "Electoral Mobilization."

24. For a definition of this concept and a specification of possible indicators see Karl Deutsch, "Social Mobilization and Political Development," *Am. Pol. Sci. Rev.* 55 (1961): 493–514.

25. The contrast between "primordial attachment" to the "givens" of social existence (contiguity, kinship, local languages, and religious customs—all at our *l* pole) and "national identification" (our *g* pole) has been described with great acumen by Clifford Geertz in "The Integrative Revolution," in C. Geertz (ed.), *Old Societies and New States* (New York: Free Press, 1963), pp. 105–57; see Edward Shils, "Primordial, Personal, Sacred and Civil Ties," *Brit. J. Sociol.* 7 (1957): 130–45.

26. For an analysis of steps in the extension of citizenship rights and duties to all accountable adults see S. Rokkan, "Mass Suffrage, Secret Voting and Political Participation," and the chapter by R. Bendix and S. Rokkan, "The Extension of Citizenship to the Lower Classes," in R. Bendix, *Nation-Building and Citizenship* (New York: Wiley, 1964), pp. 74–104. For a review of the politics of educational developments see R. Ulich, *The Education of Nations* (Cambridge: Harvard University Press, 1961).

27. This, of course, was not a peculiarity of Catholic-Calvinist countries; it can be observed in a number of polities with geographically dispersed if locally segregated ethnic minorities. For an insightful discussion of a similar development in Russia, see C. E. Woodhouse and H. J. Tobias, "Primordial Ties and Political Process in Pre-Revolutionary Russia: The Case of the Jewish Bund," *Comp. Stud. Soc. Hist.* 8 (1966): 331–60.

28. For detailed statistics see J. P. Kruijt, *Verzuiling* (Zaandijk: Heijnis, 1959) and J. P. Kruijt and W. Goddijn, "Verzuiling en ontzuiling als sociologisch proces" in A. J. den Hollander et al. (eds.), *Drift en Koers* (Assen: Van Gorcum 1962), pp. 227–63. For an attempt at a broader interpretation of *Verzuiling* and its consequences for the theory of democracy, see Arend Lijphart, *The Politics of Accommodation: Pluralism and Democracy in the Netherlands* (Berkeley: University of California Press, 1968). For comparative interpretations of data on religious segmentation see David O. Moberg, "Religion and Society in the Netherlands and in America," *Am. Quart.* 13 (1961): 172–78, and G. Lenski, *The Religious Factor*, rev. ed. (Garden City: Doubleday Anchor, 1963), pp. 359–66; see also J. Mathes (ed.), *Religiöser Pluralismus und Gesellschaftsstruktur* (Cologne: Westdeutscher Verlag, 1965).

29. For general accounts of the development of party oppositions and segmented politics in the Netherlands, see H. Daalder, "Parties and Politics in the Netherlands," *Pol. Studies* 3 (1955): 1–16 and his chapter in R. A. Dahl (ed.), *Political Oppositions in Western Democracies* (New Haven: Yale University Press, 1966). Detailed party chronologies and "pedigrees" are given in H. Daalder, "Nederland: het politieke stelsel" in L. van der Land (ed.), *Repertorium van de Sociale Wetenschappen*, I (Amsterdam: Elsevier, 1958), pp. 213–38.

30. Cited in S. M. Lipset, *Political Man*, p. 258; for further breakdowns from a sample of a suburb of Amsterdam see L. van der Land, et al., *Kiezer en verkiezing* (Amsterdam: Nederlandse Kring voor Wetenschap der Politiek, 1963), mimeo.

For analyses of a nationwide survey from 1964 see Lijphart, *The Politics of Accommodation*, chap. 2.

31. Kruijt and Goddijn, "Verzuiling."

32. The concept of "membership crystallization" has been formulated by analogy with the concept of *status* crystallization developed by Gerhard Lenski in "Social Participation and Status Crystallization," *Amer. Sociol. Rev.* 21 (1956): 458–64; see Erik Allardt, "Community Activity, Leisure Use and Social Structure," and Ulf Himmelstrand, "A Theoretical and Empirical Approach to Depoliticization and Political Involvement," both in S. Rokkan (ed.), *Approaches to the Study of Political Participation* (Bergen: Chr. Michelsen Institute, 1962), pp. 67–110.

33. For an analysis of this process see Ulf Torgersen, "The Structure of Urban Parties in Norway During the First Period of Extended Suffrage 1884–1898," in E. Allardt and Y. Littunen (eds.), *Cleavages*, pp. 377–99.

34. The Swedish Liberals split into two parties over alcohol policies in 1923 but these merged again in 1934. A new party, the Christian Democrat Union, was set up by Free Church leaders in 1964, but failed in the election that year.

35. For a comparative analysis of differences in the organization of estate assemblies, see especially Otto Hintze, "Typologie der ständischen Verfassung des Abendlandes," *Hist. Zs.* 141 (1930): 229–48; F. Hartung and R. Mousnier, "Quelques problèmes concernant la monarchie absolue," *Relazioni X Congr. Int. Sci. Storiche*, IV (Florence, 1955); and R. R. Palmer, *The Age of Democratic Revolution: The Challenge* (Princeton: Princeton University Press, 1959), chap. 2.

36. The critical issue between the two sectors of the economy concerned foreign trade: Should domestic agriculture be protected against the cheaper grain produced overseas or should the manufacturing industry be supported through the supply of cheaper food for their workers? For a comparative review of the politics of the grain tariffs see Alexander Gerschenkron, *Bread and Democracy in Germany* (Berkeley: University of California Press, 1943).

37. *The Making of Victorian England* (London: Methuen, 1962), p. 218, our italics. For a broader treatment see F. M. L. Thompson, *English Landed Society in the Nineteenth Century* (London: Routledge, 1963).

38. James Cornford, "The Transformation of Conservatism in the Late 19th Century," *Victorian Studies* 7 (1963): 35–66.

39. On the unsuccessful attempts of the Progressive Liberals to broaden their working-class base, see especially Thomas Niperdey, *Die Organisation der deutschen Parteien vor 1918* (Düsseldorf: Droste, 1963), pp. 187–92, and W. Link "Das Nationalverein für das liberale Deutschland," *Pol. Vierteliahreschr.* 5 (1964): 422–44. On the "plebiscitarian nationalism" of Friedrich Naumann and Max Weber, see Theodor Heuss, *Friedrich Naumann* (Stuttgart: Deutsche Verlagsanstalt, 1957), W. Mommsen, *Max Weber und die deutsche Politik 1890–1920* (Tübingen: Mohr, 1959), and the discussions at the Weber centenary conference at Heidelberg reported in O. Stammer (ed.), *Max Weber und die Soziologie heute* (Tübingen: Mohr, 1965).

40. For a detailed presentation of the background of these developments see Bryn J. Hovde, *The Scandinavian Countries 1720–1865* (Ithaca: Cornell University Press, 1948), particularly chaps. 8, 9, and 13.

41. Lin Piao, "Long Live the Victory of the People's War," *Peking Review* 8 (3 September 1965): 24.

42. See Lipset, *The First New Nation*, chaps. 5, 6, and 7.

43. This is the phrase used by Ernest Fraenkel, "Parlament und öffentliche Meinung," in *Zur Geschichte und Problematik der Demokratie: Festgabe für H. Herzfeld* (Berlin: Duncker & Humblot, 1958), p. 178. For further details on German developments, see the recent study by Günther Roth, *The Social Democrats in Imperial Germany* (Totowa: Bedminster Press, 1963), chaps. 7–10.

44. One of the first political analysts to call attention to these developments was Herbert Tingsten, then editor-in-chief of the leading Swedish newspaper *Dagens Nyheter*, see his autobiography, *Mitt Liv: Tidningen* (Stockholm: Norstedts, 1963), pp. 224–31. For further details see S. M. Lipset, " The Changing Class Structure and Contemporary European Politics," *Daedalus* 93 (1964): 271–303.

45. On Austrian politics since 1945 see A. Vodopivec, *Wer regiert in Österreich?* (Vienna: Verlag für Geschichte und Politik, 1961), and the chapter by F. C. Engelmann on Austria in R. A. Dahl (ed.), *Political Oppositions in Western Democracies*, pp. 260–83.

46. See Walter Laqueur and Leopold Labedz (eds.), *Polycentrism: The New Factor in International Communism* (New York: Praeger, 1962); L. Labedz (ed.), *Revisionism* (New York: Praeger, 1962), and S. M. Lipset, "The Changing Class Structure."

47. Erik Allardt, "Patterns of Class Conflict and Working Class Consciousness in Finnish Politics" in E. Allardt and Y. Littunen (eds.), *Cleavages, Ideologies, and Party Systems*. pp. 93–131.

48. See S. Rokkan, "Geography, Religion," and the study by Egil Fivelsdal of unionization and politics among white-collar workers in Norway, *Funksjonærenes syn på faglige og politiske spørsmål* (Oslo: Universitetsforlaget, 1964).

49. See Andrew G. Whiteside, *Austrian National Socialism before 1918* (The Hague: Nijhoff, 1962), and his article on Austria in T. Rogger and E. Weber (eds.), *The European Right* (London: Weidenfeld, 1965), pp. 328–63.

50. For a detailed analysis of the Austrian "invention" of mass anti-Semitism see Peter Pulzer, *The Rise of Political Anti-Semitism in Germany and Austria* (New York: Wiley, 1964).

51. R. Dahrendorf, *Gesellschaft und Demokratie in Deutschland* (Munich: Piper, 1965), esp. chap. 26.

52. On the electoral support for the NSDAP, see especially Sten S. Nilson, "Wahlsoziologische Probleme des Nationalsozialismus" *Zs. Ges Staatswiss* 110 (1954): 229–311; K. D. Bracher, *Die Auflösung der Weimarer Republik* (3d ed.; Villingen: Ring-Verlag, 1960), chap. 6; and Alfred Milatz, "Das Ende der Parteien im Spiegel der Wahlen 1930 bis 1933," in E. Matthias and R. Morsey (eds.), *Das Ende der Parteien 1933* (Düsseldorf: Droste, 1960), pp. 741–93. A summary of evidence from electoral analyses is given in S. M. Lipset, *Political Man*, pp. 140–51. The best analysis of the rural strength of the NSDAP is still Rudolf Herberle's *From Democracy to Nazism* (Baton Rouge: Louisiana State University Press, 1945). The fuller German manuscript from 1932 has been published as *Landbevölkerung und Nationalsozialismus* (Stuttgart: Deutsche Verlagsanstalt, 1963).

53. Such similarities in social bases and in attitudes to national authority obviously do not necessarily imply similarities in organizational tactics and in actual behavior toward opponents. There is no implication that all such movements would conform to the Fascist or the National Socialist *ethos* if victorious. For a discussion of the evidence for Italy, France, and the United States see S. M. Lipset, *Political Man*,

chap. 5, as well as "Radical Rightists of Three Decades—Coughlinites, McCarthyites and Birchers," in Daniel Bell (ed.), *The Radical Right* (New York: Doubleday, 1963), and "Beyond the Backlash," *Encounter* 23 (November 1964): 11–24. For Norway, see Nilson, "Wahlsoziologische." For an interesting analysis of the Social Credit movement in Canada in similar terms see Donald Smiley, "Canada's Poujadists: a New Look at Social Credit," *The Canadian Forum* 42 (September 1962): 121–23. The Socreds are anti-metropolitan and anti-institutional and they advocate pure plebiscitarian politics against organized group interests and established elites.

54. In a review of Western European developments Hans Daalder has argued this point with great force. It is impossible to understand the development, structure, and operation of party systems without a study of the extent of elite competition *before* the industrial and the democratic revolutions. He singles out Britain, the Low Countries, Switzerland, and Sweden as the countries with the strongest traditions of conciliar pluralism and points to the consequences of these preconditions for the development of integrated party systems. See H. Daalder, "Parties, Elites and Political Developments in Western Europe," in J. LaPalombara and M. Weiner (eds.), *Political Parties and Political Developments*. For a fuller discussion of contrasts in the character of the nation-building process, see S. P. Huntington, "Political Modernization: America vs. Europe," *World Politics* 18 (1966): 378–414.

55. This is Faul's term for the initial phase in the growth of parties, "Verfemung," pp. 62–69.

56. See especially Gunnar Olsson, *Hattar och mössor: Studier over partiväsendet i Sverige 1751–1762* (Gothenburg: Akademi-förlaget, 1963).

57. For a review of this literature see S. M. Lipset, "Introduction: Ostrogorski and the Analytical Approach to the Comparative Study of Political Parties," in M. I. Ostrogorski, *Democracy and the Organization of Political Parties*, abridged ed. (New York: Doubleday, 1964), pp. ix–lxv.

58. "European Political Parties: The Case of Polarized Pluralism" in J. LaPalombara and M. Weiner (eds.), *Political Parties and Political Development*.

59. For reviews of similarities and differences among two English-speaking democracies, see R. R. Alford, "Class Voting in the Anglo-American Political Systems," and A. D. Robinson, "Class Voting in New Zealand: A Comment on Alford's Comparison of Class Voting in the Anglo-American Political Systems," in Lipset and Rokkan (eds.), *Party Systems and Voter Alignments*, pp. 67–93, 95–114; L. Lipson, "Party Systems in the United Kingdom and the Older Commonwealth," *Pol. Studies* 7 (1959): 12–31; S. M. Lipset, *The First New Nation*, chaps. 5, 6, and 7; and R. Alford, *Party and Society: The Anglo-American Democracies* (Chicago: Rand McNally, 1963), esp. chap. 12.

60. Leon D. Epstein, "A Comparative Study of Canadian Parties," *Amer. Pol. Sci. Rev.* 63 (March 1964): 46–59.

61. The basic reference work on the history of PR in Europe is still Karl Braunias, *Das parlamentarische Wahlrecht* (Berlin: de Gruyter, 1932) I–II. Polemical works such as F. A. Hermens, *Democracy or Anarchy?* (Notre Dame: University of Notre Dame Press, 1941); E. Lakeman and J. D. Lambert, *Voting in Democracies* (London: Faber, 1955); and H. Unkelbach, *Grundlagen der Wahlsystematik* (Göttingen: Vandenhoeck u. Rupprecht, 1956) offer a great wealth of information but do not contribute much to the understanding of the *sociocultural conditions* for

the success of the one or the other procedure of electoral aggregation. See S. Rokkan, "Electoral Systems," article in *International Encyclopedia of the Social Sciences*.

62. Braunias, *Das parlamentarische,* II, pp. 201–4.
63. See J. Gilissen, *Le régime représentatif en Belgique depuis 1790* (Brussels: Renaissance du Livre, 1958), pp. 126–30.
64. The rise of the nationwide movement for universal suffrage and the parallel mobilization of support for the Liberals and the Social Democrats has been described in great detail by S. Carlsson, *Lantmannapolitiken och industrialismen* (Lund: Gleerup, 1952), and T. Vallinder, *I kamp för demokratien* (Stockholm: Natur o. kultur, 1962). For a convenient account of the bargaining over suffrage extension and PR see Douglas V. Verney, *Parliamentary Reform in Sweden 1866–1921* (Oxford: Clarendon, 1957), chap. 7.
65. On the ties between the Church and the Right in France, see René Rémond, *La droite en France de 1815 à nos jours* (Paris: Aubier, 1954), pp. 239–45.
66. Types VI to VII in our typology, the deviant type V is discussed in detail below.
67. For an illuminating analysis of the sociocultural characteristics of the classic region of counterrevolutionary resistance, see Charles Tilly, *The Vendée* (London: Arnold, 1965).
68. For an interesting approach to the analysis of the political consequences of "monocephality" vs. "polycephality" see Juan Linz and A. de Miguel, "Within-Nation Differences and Comparisons: The Eight Spains," in R. L. Merritt and S. Rokkan (eds.), *Comparing Nations* (New Haven: Yale University Press, 1966), pp. 267–319.
69. This point has been developed in further detail in S. Rokkan, "Electoral Mobilization, Party Competition and National Integration."
70. For an analysis of the three decisive cleavage lines in Belgian politics, the language conflict, the church-school issue, and the owner-worker opposition, see Val Lorwin's chapter on Belgium in R. A. Dahl (ed.), *Political Oppositions in Western Democracies*. It is interesting to note that the same factors disrupted Belgian Fascism during the 1930s and made it impossible to build a single major nationalist-Fascist party; see Jean Stengers, "Belgium," in Rogger and Weber (eds.), *The European Right*, pp. 128–67.
71. Herbert Luethy, "Has Switzerland a Future? The Dilemma of a Small Nation," *Encounter* 19 (December 1962): 25.
72. For sociological analyses of the system of cleavages in Spanish society after 1815 see Gerald Brenan, *The Spanish Labyrinth* (London: Cambridge University Press, 1943; 2d ed., 1950; paperback, 1960); Carlos A. Rama, *La crise espagnole au XXe siècle* (Paris: Fischbacher, 1962); Juan Linz, "Spain: an Authoritarian Regime" in E. Allardt and Y. Littunen (eds.), *Cleavages, Ideologies and Party Systems*, pp. 290–341. See also the analysis of the elections of 1931, 1933, and 1936 in J. Becarud, *La Deuxième République Espagnole* (Paris: Centre d'Etude des Relations Internationales, 1962), mimeo.
73. On the function of the *cacique* as the controller of rural support in the initial phase of mass mobilization, see Brenan, *The Spanish Labyrinth*, pp. 5–8; Raymond Carr, *Spain, 1908–1939* (Oxford: Clarendon, 1966), pp. 366–79; and the classic analyses in Joaquín Costa (ed.), *Oligarquía y caciquismo como el forma actual de gobierno en España* (Madrid: Hernández, 1902).
74. See Mattei Dogan, "La stratificazione sociale dei suffragi," in A. Spreafico and J. LaPalombara (eds.), *Elezioni e comportamento politico in Italia* (Milan: Ed.

di Comunita, 1963) pp. 407–74, and M. Dogan, "Political Cleavage and Social Stratification in France and Italy," in Lipset and Rokkan (eds.), *Party Systems and Voter Alignments*, pp. 129–95.

75. See R. A. Webster *The Cross and the Fasces* (Stanford: Stanford University Press, 1960).
76. On the origin of particularist movements in Germany see especially W. Conze (ed.), *Staat und Gesellschaft im deutschen Vormärz 1815–1848* (Stuttgart: Klett, 1962).
77. The vivid expression coined by Jean-François Gravier in *Paris et le désert français*, 2d ed. (Paris: Flammarion, 1958).
78. Charles P. Kindleberger, *Economic Growth in France and Britain 1851–1950* (Cambridge: Harvard University Press, 1964), p. 255.
79. For details see S. Rokkan, "Mass Suffrage, Secret Voting, and Political Participation."
80. For a detailed evaluation of the comparative statistics of agricultural holdings see F. Dovring, *Land and Labour in Europe 1900–1950*, 2d ed. (The Hague: Nijhoff, 1960), chap. 3 and appendices. The standard source on nineteenth-century statistics of landholdings in Britain is J. Bateman, *The Great Landowners of Great Britain and Ireland* (London, 1883); see F. M. L. Thompson, *English Landed Society*, chap. 5. On *latifundia* and *minimifundia* in Spain see Brenan, *The Spanish Labyrinth*, chap. 6.
81. Advances in the techniques of electoral analysis make it possible to test such statements about the weight of the different cleavage dimensions in conditioning the alignments of voters. For data from *sample surveys* the development of *"tree analysis"* procedures opens up interesting possibilities of comparison. A "tree analysis" of data for the *Bundesrepublik* for 1957, 1961, and 1965 gives interesting evidence of the interaction of two major cleavage dimensions in that setting:

Owner-worker cleavage: status of head of household	Church-state commitment of respondent	Percent voting SPD in total electrate		
		1957	1961	1965
Worker, unionized	None	56	61	64
Worker, not unionized	None	37	41	43
Worker, middle-class aspirations	—	18	28	28
Worker, unionized	Committed Catholic	14	24	33
Worker, not unionized	Committed Catholic	15	10	15
Middle class, of working-class origins	—	27	24	41
Salaried, civil servants, unionized	—	25	39	52
Middle class	Committed Catholic	6	5	9

Source: K. Liepelt, "Wählerbewegungen in der Bundesrepublik," Paper, Arbeitstagung 21, July 1966, Institut für angewandte Sozialforschung, Bad Godesberg.

For periods before the advent of the sample survey similar analyses can be produced through ecological regression analysis. So far very few statistically sophisticated analyses have been carried out for European electoral time series before the 1950s: an exception is K. Cox, *Regional Anomalies in the Voting Behavior of the Population of England and Wales*; this includes a factor analysis of the rural vote in Wales from 1861 to 1921. For an illuminating example of a possible procedure, see the analysis of the French rural cantons by Mattei Dogan, "Les contextes politiques en France," Paper, Symposium on Quantitative Ecological Analysis, Evian, September 1966. His Tables 11 and 13 give these correlation coefficients for the electoral strengths of the two left parties in 1956.

	PCF				SFIO			
	Rural France	West	Center	North	Rural France	West	Center	North
Percent industrial workers:								
—direct correlation	.28	.26	.16	.55	.33	.19	.05	.03
—partial correlation	.25	.12	.08	.39	.01	.09	.03	.19
Percent attending mass								
—direct correlation	−.60	−.62	−.48	−.67	−.21	−.39	−.10	.30
—partial correlation	−.59	−.59	−.47	−.58	−.21	−.36	−.09	.35
Multiple correlation	.64	.62	.49	.73	.21	.40	.10	.35

Within rural France the traditions of anticlericalism clearly count heavier than class in the generation of votes for the Left. If the Parisian suburbs and the other urban areas had been included in the analysis they would obviously have weighed much heavier in the equation; see Dogan's chapter in Lipset and Rokkan (eds.), *Party Systems and Voter Alignment*, pp. 129–95. To test the implications of our model, analyses along the lines suggested by Cox and Dogan ought to be carried out for the elections just before and just after the extensions of the suffrage in a number of different countries; see the contrasted maps for 1849 and 1936 in Georges Dupeux, *Le Front Populaire et les élections de 1936* (Paris: Colin, 1959), pp. 169–70 and discussion pp. 157–71.

82. For an insightful analysis of the conditions for the development of these three *Lager* see A. Wandruszka, "Österreichs politische Struktur" in H. Benedikt (ed.), *Geschichte der Republik Österreich* (Vienna: Verl. für Geschichte und Politik, 1952), pp. 298–485, 618–21.

83. See K. Bracher, *Die Auflösung der Weimarer Republik*, 3d ed. (Villingen: Ring, 1960), chaps. 3–4, and E. Matthias and R. Morsey (eds.), *Das Ende der Parteien 1933* (Düsseldorf: Droste, 1960), pp. 154–58, 655–739.

84. Val R. Lorwin, "Working Class Politics and Economic Development in Western Europe," *Amer. Hist. Rev.* 63 (1958): 338–51.

85. This was a major point in the classic article by the elder Edvard Bull in "Die Entwicklung der Arbeiterbewegung in den drei skandinavischen Ländern," *Arch. f. Geschichte des Sozialismus* 10 (1922): 329–61.

86. This has been brought out in an important paper by Ulf Torgersen, *Landsmøtet i norsk partistruktur 1884–1940* (Oslo: Institute for Social Research, 1966), mimeo, pp. 39–46, 73–98.

87. For an account of the period from 1924 to 1935 see I. Roset, *Det Norske Arbeiderparti og Hornsruds regjeringsdannelse i 1928* (Oslo: Universitetsförlaget, 1964), and the summary in S. Rokkan, "Norway: Numerical Democracy and Corporate Pluralism" in R. A. Dahl (ed.), *Political Oppositions in Western Democracies* (New Haven: Yale University Press, 1966), pp. 81–84.

88. See especially John H. Hodgson, *Communism in Finland* (Princeton: Princeton University Press, 1966).

89. On Icelandic parties see Mary S. Olmsted, "Communism in Iceland," *Foreign Affairs* 36 (1958): 340–47, and Donald E. Nuechterlein, *Iceland: Reluctant Ally* (Ithaca: Cornell University Press, 1961), chap. 1.

90. A book such as Samuel J. Eldersveld's *Political Parties: a Behavioral Analysis* (Chicago: Rand McNally, 1964), suggests important themes for research, but its utility for comparative analysis is severely limited by its overconcentration on perhaps the most atypical of all existing party organizations, the American.

91. To substantiate such generalization it will clearly be necessary to proceed to a comparative census of "ephemeral" parties in Europe. Hans Daalder has made a useful beginning through his inventory of small parties in the Netherlands since 1918, the country with the longest record of minimal-threshold PR; see "De kleine politieke partijen—een voorlopige poging tot inventarisatie," *Acta politica* 1 (1965–66): 172–96.

92. J. Linz, "The Party System of Spain: Past and Future," in Lipset and Rokkan, (eds.), *Party Systems and Voter Alignments*, pp. 197–282.

93. This is a major theme in the Norwegian program of electoral research; see especially S. Rokkan and H. Valen, "The Mobilization of the Periphery," in S. Rokkan (ed.), *Approaches to the Study of Political Participation*, pp. 111–58, and T. Hjellum, *Partiene i lokalpolitikken* (Oslo: Gyldendal, 1967). The possibilities of comparative research on the "politicization" of local government are discussed in S. Rokkan, "Electoral Mobilization, Party Competition and National Integration," in J. LaPalombara and M. Weiner, pp. 241–65.

94. For a general statement of the need for such controls for the character of the local party alternatives see S. Rokkan, "The Comparative Study of Political Participation" in A. Ranney (ed.), *Essays on the Behavioral Study of Politics* (Urbana: University of Illinois Press, 1962), pp. 45–90.

95. On the development of this type of data files for computer processing see S. Rokkan (ed.), *Data Archives for the Social Sciences* (Paris: Mouton, 1966), and the report by Mattei Dogan and S. Rokkan on the Symposium on Quantitative Ecological Analysis held at Evian, France, in September, 1966.

96. In the United States the central figures in this movement were V. O. Key and Lee Benson. It is interesting to note, however, that their work has been vigorously followed up by such experts on survey analysis as Angus Campbell and his colleagues Philip Converse, Warren Miller, and Donald Stokes; see *Elections and the Political Order* (New York: Wiley, 1966), chaps. 1–3, and 9.

97. For a detailed effort to integrate the findings of various studies of American student activism see S. M. Lipset and Philip Altbach, "Student Politics and Higher Education in the United States," *Comparative Education Rev.* 10 (1966): 320–49. This article appears also in revised and expanded form in S. M. Lipset (ed.), *Students and Politics* (New York: Basic Books, 1967). Another comprehensive discussion of the relevant literature may be found in Jeanne Block, Norma Haan, and M. Brewster Smith, "Activism and Apathy in Contemporary Adolescents," in James F. Adams (ed.), *Contributions to the Understanding of Adolescence* (Boston: Allyn & Bacon, 1968).

5

The Industrial Proletariat and the Intelligentsia in Comparative Perspective

Much of the recent discussion of the politics of advanced industrial or postindustrial societies has focused on the emergence of an oppositionist intelligentsia, one based on the well-educated strata, which resembles in its behavior that of the intelligentsia of the Czarist Empire or the less developed nations. This group seemingly has become the most dynamic agent of change, taking over the role assigned by Marxism for the proletariat. Writing in 1960, C. Wright Mills sharply criticized those who continue to regard the working class as a continuing agency of radical change. He minced no words in pointing to "the really impressive historical evidence that now stands against this expectation," "a legacy from Victorian Marxism that is now quite unrealistic." He proposed that those on the left direct their attention to "the cultural apparatus, the intellectuals—as a possible, immediate, radical agency of change."[1]

The loss of faith in the working class of technologically advanced society created by their relative political passivity, ironically, has been countered by the behavior of workers in Eastern Europe, from the revolt in the German Democratic Republic in 1953 to the Polish strikes of the 1980s. To what extent do Marxian beliefs about the relationship between economic and political developments and the proletariat's struggle to achieve socialism hold up in the late twentieth century? To evaluate the usefulness of Marxian analysis, it is necessary to distinguish between Marx as a chiliastic revolutionary, convinced of the outcome of the class struggle under capitalism, and Marx the sociologist, whose propositions and analytic methodology still furnish important insights, even though events have sharply challenged his political expectations.

To do this involves looking at class politics in relation to industrialization, assuming that the stratification system and the class struggle are deeply affected by the technological period at hand, whether it be preindustrial, industrial, or, as many countries are today, postindustrial. This chapter first deals with Marxist assumptions about the relationship of economic development to the politics of industrial nations. It then turns to a discussion of the effects of "postindustrial" technology on political conflict. These sections are followed by an examination of some consequences of inequality in socialist nations.

Historical Materialism and the Class Struggle

Marx's concept of historical materialism is central to his theory of social change. It assumes that the economic and technological forces are primary, or the base, and that politics and values are functionally derivative, or the superstructure. Given this postulate, he believed that the socialist movement, and ultimately the proletarian revolution, would develop with the growth of capitalist industrialization. The common experience of economic exploitation would lead the workers to class consciousness and to the realization that they must join together to overthrow capitalism. The prediction that socialism was inevitable rested on the further belief that the workers would become the large majority of industrial society, and that once this majority became class-conscious it would necessarily triumph. Of course the argument was buttressed by Marx's economics which held that capitalism, as an economic system, would break down once it had brought society to a high level of industrialization.

Following this logic, as noted in chapter 2, Marx believed that the most developed society should have the most advanced set of class and political relationships.[2] This meant that socialism as a movement and ultimately as a social system would emerge most strongly and triumph first in the most developed capitalist country, which, from the late nineteenth century on, has been the United States.

Many Marxists, therefore, repeatedly looked to America as the country that would show others the way to socialism, in spite of the glaring weakness of socialist parties in the United States. As Howard Quint points out, they "found the United States, of all the countries in the world, most ripe for socialism, not only in the light of Marxian law of economic development, but also by the express opinion of Friedrick Engels."[3] Karl Kautsky, considered the leading Marxist theoretician in the German Social Democratic Party, announced in 1902 that "America shows us our future, in so far as one country can reveal it at all to another."[4] He elaborated this view in 1910, anticipating the "sharpening of class conflict . . . more strongly" there than anywhere else.[5] The British Marxist H. M. Hyndman noted in 1904 that "just as North America is to-day the most advanced country, economically and socially, so it will be the first in which Socialism will find open and legal expression."[6]

Werner Sombart emphasized this point in his classic book on American socialism written in 1906:

> If . . . modern socialism follows as a necessary reaction to capitalism, the country with the most advanced capitalist development, namely the United States, would at the same time be the one providing the classic case of Socialism, and its working class would be supporters of the most radical of Socialist movements.[7]

Maxim Gorki, who supported the Bolsheviks from 1903 on, wrote in 1906 of his conviction that "socialism would be realized in the United States before any other country in the world."[8] August Bebel, the political leader of the German Social Democrats, in an interview in the American socialist paper, *Appeal to Reason*, stated unequivocally in 1907, "You Americans will be the first to usher in a Socialist Republic." His belief, at a time when his party was already a mass movement with many elected members of the Reichstag, and the American Socialist Party had secured less than 2 percent of the vote, was based on the fact that the United States was "far ahead of Germany in industrial development." He reiterated this opinion in a second interview in 1912, when the discrepancy between the strength of the two movements was even greater, saying that America would "be the first nation to declare a Cooperative Commonwealth."[9] The French socialist Paul Lefargue, who was also Marx's son-in-law, paraphrased Marx on the flyleaf of his book on America by asserting that "the most industrially advanced country shows to those who follow it on the industrial ladder the image of their own future."[10]

American Marxists, though perhaps more aware of the problems facing their movement than were their European comrades, also recognized that the assumptions of historical materialism required that the United States should be in the lead.[11] Thus, at the 1904 Amsterdam Congress of the Socialist International, which was attended by representatives of much stronger European parties, the leader of the Socialist Labor Party, Daniel De Leon, regarded by Lenin as the one creative American Marxist theorist, reported that "taking into consideration only certain cardinal principles, the conclusion cannot be escaped that America is the theatre where the crest of capitalism would first be shorn by the falchion of socialism."[12] Shortly thereafter, De Leon proclaimed to the 1906 convention of the Industrial Workers of the World (IWW): "If my reading of history is correct, the prophecy of Marx will be fulfilled and America will ring the downfall of capitalism the world over."[13]

The desire to see their theoretical anticipations confirmed led Marxists to draw enthusiastic, but inevitably exaggerated, conclusions that the American workers were finally awakening and that a mass socialist movement was on its way. Yet, these expectations came to naught. Max Beer, whose fifty-year career in international socialism included participation in the Austrian, German and British parties, described the anxiety and embarrassment created by the weakness of socialism in America before World War I:

> The attitude of American Labour appeared to stand out as a living contradiction of the Marxian theory that the concentration of capitalist production, and attendant proletarization of the masses, was necessarily bound to lead to class struggles and to the formation of an independent Labour movement with Socialist aims and ends . . . Was the generalization faulty, or were there forces in operation that neutralized it?[14]

The problem, summed up by Beer, is still present, although since 1917 and the Russian Revolution there has been little discussion of the implications for Marxist theory of the weakness of socialism in the United States. In effect, latter-day Marxists have simply chosen to ignore the clear implications of historical materialism. One exception was Leon Trotsky, who, in an essay on Marxism written for an American audience in 1939, explicitly faced up to the issue. He quoted Marx's statement that the most developed country "only shows to the less developed the image of its own future" and then wrote: "Under no circumstances can this thought be taken literally."[15] (As we have seen, Marxists did take it literally before 1917.)

If we consider the logic implicit in an apolitical sociological Marxism and return to the proposition that the most advanced country shows to the less developed ones the image of their own future, then it should follow that the social, political and ideological relationships which actually have emerged in the United States should show to other countries how they will develop. American politics, far from being backward and behind the politics of Europe, actually must be regarded as more advanced. Other countries should begin to resemble the United States as they become industrialized and affluent, rather than America take on the forms of less industrialized and poorer countries.

This is not the place to go into an analysis of "Why no socialism in the United States," a topic I elaborate on later in this volume and in other essays.[16] It is worth noting, however, that the evidence and arguments presented by a large number of scholars suggest that socialist class politics, as it developed in Europe, was less an outgrowth of capitalist social relations than of preindustrial, feudal society, which explicitly structured relationships according to fixed, almost hereditary, social classes. Hence, the emerging working class reacted to the political world in such terms. Walter Dean Burnham has aptly summarized this overall thesis: "No feudalism, no socialism: with these four words one can summarize the basic sociocultural realities that underlie American electoral politics in the industrial era."[17]

The severe social strains of early rapid industrialization in societies that took class for granted brought about working-class political action. And as Lenin, Kautsky, and others[18] have commented, many of the European working-class parties came into being in the struggle for democracy, a factor absent in the American case, where the workers benefited from the "free gift of the ballot."[19]

As the industrial nations thrived economically, the rigid preindustrial social class lines gradually broke down in most of Europe. This development weakened the correlation between class position and party allegiance.[20] The socialist parties moved away from Marxism to become more "catch-all" in order to appeal across class lines, especially to the burgeoning new middle class. This phenomenon has been documented for many European socialist and social democratic parties.[21]

In fact, it is possible to argue that the assumptions of an apolitical historical Marxism have been borne out; the more explicit forms of class consciousness that existed in Europe have been declining, and class is less important as a source of political struggle in advanced industrial society than it once was. Figure 5.1 shows the trend in class voting for Sweden, Germany, Great Britain and the United States from 1952 to 1980. The Alford Index used here is the difference between the proportions of the manual workers and the nonmanual workers who vote for the left party.[22] Therefore, the higher the number, the greater is the correlation between class and party preference. As Figure 5.1 documents, there has been a discernible decline in class voting across a number of advanced industrial countries.

Writing in the mid-1960s, the German-American Marxist Herbert Marcuse emphasized that the historical record indicated that affluent capitalism had eliminated all but the slightest possibility for radical protest from the working class. He commented that,

> in the capitalist world, there are still the basic classes [capitalists and workers]. . . . [But] an overriding interest in the preservation and improvement of the institutional *status quo* unites the former antagonists in the most advanced areas of contemporary society.[23]

French Marxists Lucien Goldmann and Henri Lefebvre criticized Marcuse, arguing that his interpretation was not "correct as far as it applies to the European countries; but . . . it is possible that his analysis might very well be true of America." According to Serge Mallet, Marcuse replied with the classic Marxist historical materialist position, "that, since the United States is economically more advanced than the European countries, it cannot be long before the phenomena . . . spread to western Europe."[24]

Of course, one may point to the fact that parties which call themselves Marxist hold power in many countries, and there are still mass "Marxist"

FIGURE 5.1
The Trend in Class Voting in Four Western Democracies, 1948–80

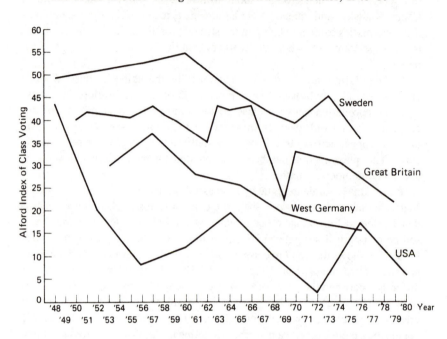

Sources: British Data, 1950–1970: J.W. Books and J.B. Reynolds, "A Note on Class Voting in Great Britain and the United States," *Comparative Political Studies* 8 (1975): 360–75; British Data 1974, 1979: calculated from S.E. Finer, *The Changing British Party System, 1945–1979* (Washington D.C.: American Enterprise Institute, 1980); Swedish Data: J.D. Stephens, Social Class, Contextual Effects and Party Preference: Theoretical Approaches and Some Evidence From the Swedish Case," (unpublished paper, 1980): German Data: K. Hildebrandt and R.I. Dalton, "The New Politics: Political Change or Sunshine Politics?," in M. Kaase and K. von Beyme (eds.), *Elections and Parties: Socio-political Change and Participation in the West German Election of 1976* (Beverly Hills: Sage, 1978), pp. 69–96; American Data, 1948–1972; P.R. Abramson, "Class Voting in the 1976 Election," *Journal of Politics* 40 (1974): 1066–72; American Data, 1976–1980: calculated from results of CBS *New York Times* Election Day Exit Polls.

(communist) parties in some Western industrialized countries. But as we know, communist revolutions have succeeded in preindustrial, agrarian societies—in Czarist Russia, in China, in Vietnam. The large communist parties of Europe took root primarily in what were then the more economically backward nations of Southern Europe, especially France and Italy. Marxism clearly failed or declined greatly in the more industrialized nations of Northern Europe.

No crueler joke has been played in history, and no theory has been more confounded, than that of Marxism, as it became the banner for movements in predominantly rural societies. As Marcuse stressed in 1969, "revolution is not on the agenda" of the advanced Western industrial states, while the combination of the necessary "subjective factor" (political consciousness) and the "objective factor" ("the support and participation of the class which is at the base of production") only "coincide in large areas of the Third World."[25] Marx's fundamental premise has been totally refuted by history. Regimes identified as socialist or communist have come to power on the shoulders of the peasants of poor, underdeveloped economies. Socialist revolutions have occurred, but they have not been Marx's revolutions.

It should be noted, of course, that Marx (and others) was right in assuming that occupational position would be a major determinant of political orientation and class organization in industrial society. In all democratic nations, including the United States, there has been a correlation between socioeconomic status and political beliefs and voting.[26] The less privileged have supported parties that have stood for greater equality and protection against the strains of a free enterprise economy through government intervention. Trade unions have gained strength in all industrialized nations. The state has become more powerful and has used its power to redistribute wealth and income. But such politics are not Marxist politics. The presence of parties and unions representing the less privileged in democratic politics has served to stabilize these societies, to help win the allegiance of the proletariat to their national systems. To paraphrase Disraeli, workers have been "angels in marble," prospective supporters rather than the "gravediggers of capitalism."[27]

Postindustrial Society

The changes in the class and political relations of developed societies may be analyzed within the framework of an apolitical Marxism, that is, the assumption that the level of technology will determine their forms. Some contemporary analysts have suggested that these systems are passing into a new stage, which, for want of a better name, they call postindustrial.[28]

These societies are postindustrial because the trends analyzed by Marx— increasing involvement of the labor force in the industrial productive apparatus, the growth of factories, large farms, etc.—have ended. Tertiary service occupations rather than production jobs are growing rapidly. The proportion and, in some countries, the absolute number of manual workers is declining. The occupations that are expanding are white-collar, technical, professional, scientific and service oriented. The class structure now resembles a diamond bulging at the middle much more than a pyramid. High levels of education are needed for such societies and the number of students has increased many times. Education, science and intellectual activities have become more important.

Western scholars such as Daniel Bell, Zbigniew Brzezinski, John Kenneth Galbraith and Alain Touraine, and Eastern scholars such as Radovan Richta and his associates in the Czechoslovak Academy of Sciences, and Soviet analysts such as P. N. Fedoseev and V. Kosolapov, have stressed the extent to which theoretical and scientific knowledge have become the principal source of social and economic change, altering social structure, values and *mores*, developments that have given considerable prestige and power to the scientific technological elites.[29] Soviet scholars and political leaders speak of the Scientific-Technological Revolution, a concept closely akin to that of the postindustrial society.[30] In the words of the Russian sociologist Fedoseev, it "is a sweeping qualitative transformation of productive forces as a result of science being made the principal factor in the development of social production."[31] Richta *et al.* noted in 1968 that

> science is emerging as the leading variable in the national economy. . . . There are signs of a new type of growth, with a new dynamic stemming from continual structural changes in the productive forces, with the amount of means of production and manpower becoming less important than their changing quality and degree of utilization.[32]

They pointed to "a relative decline in the amount of labor absorbed by industry and associated activities" and the prospect that the tertiary sector will encompass 40–60 percent of the national labor force in industrial countries in the coming decades, as is already the case in the United States.[33] Touraine, though still a supporter of left-wing causes in France, suggests that the basis of power in the West has changed as a result of the trends. "If property was the criterion of membership in the former dominant class, the new dominant class is defined by knowledge and a certain level of education."[34]

Much of the analysis of postindustrial society may be seen as congruent with, or derivative from, the Marxist orientation of historical materialism, which is based on the methodological premise that the principal determining factor in social development is change in the technological structure, that the cultural and political superstructures vary with level of technology.[35] This is not surprising, since a number of the key figures in this approach are socialists or neo-Marxists, such as Daniel Bell, John Kenneth Galbraith, Alain Touraine and Radovan Richta. The emerging strata of postindustrialism—whose roots are in the university, the scientific and intellectual worlds, and who are heavily represented in the public sectors and in the professions—have developed their own distinctive values. According to Ronald Inglehart, these "postmaterialist" values (labeled "postbourgeois" in his original formulation) are related to "self-actualization" needs (aesthetic, intellectual, belonging and esteem).

These values manifest themselves in a desire for a less impersonal, cleaner, more cultured society, a freer personal life, and democratization of political work and community life. Such concerns run counter to those that dominate among the traditional classes of industrial society, which are more preoccupied with satisfying material needs, namely, sustenance and safety. For people with these objectives, the most salient concerns are a high standard of living, a stable economy, economic growth, an enduring family life, fighting crime and maintaining order.[36]

Another student of changes in values, Scott Flanagan, has reconceptualized and broadened the distinctions. He suggests that advanced technology has led to change from traditional consciousness to libertarian consciousness, shifting "along four dimensions: frugality versus self-indulgence, pietism versus secularism, conformity versus independence and devotion to authority versus self-assertiveness."[37] Inglehart has also noted that these value changes are related to the general climate of affluence and absence of major wars. The generations that came of age during the post–World War II era hold vastly different values from the previous cohorts, who were reared in economic scarcity and experienced severe economic depressions and international conflicts. While there is a generational effect, postbourgeois values are clearly much more common among better-educated and wealthier individuals.[38]

These formulations are important, although some of their assumptions about the decline of materialistic concerns may be questioned. Alan Marsh, in an analysis of British data, finds that the postmaterialists are not personally antimaterialistic. His research shows no differences between the materialists and the postbourgeois on concerns about "not having enough money, or financial debt, or needing extra income." What differentiates the two groups for Marsh is simply their political ideologies, not their attitudes toward materialism. "Postbourgeois groups," notes Marsh, "are distinguished from Acquisitives by their relative youth, wealth, and education *and by their concern for ideology.*"[39]

The Politics of Postindustrialism

Regardless of what we call this change in orientations, it has profoundly affected the political arena. As Inglehart has stated:

> The political implications of these hypotheses are significant. First, they imply that rising prosperity would not bring an end to political conflict, as the "End of Ideology" thesis seemed to promise—even though this thesis was partially correct, in that rising prosperity apparently did bring a decline in traditional forms of social class conflict. What this thesis failed to anticipate, however, was that new grounds for conflict are likely to emerge, as new goals come to the fore.[40]

The basic political division of industrial society was materialist, a struggle over the distribution of the wealth and income that exists side by side with the continuing religious, ethnic and regional conflicts surviving from the preindustrial world.[41] But postindustrial politics is increasingly concerned with noneconomic or social issues—a clean environment, a better culture, equal status for women and minorities, the quality of education, international relations, greater democratization, and a more permissive morality, particularly as affecting familial and sexual issues.

These concerns have produced new bases for political cleavage which vary from those of industrial society and have given rise to a variety of "single-issue" protest movements. Since the existing political parties have found it difficult to link positions on the new issues to their traditional socioeconomic bases of support, party loyalties and even rates of voting participation have declined in many countries. In effect, cross-pressures deriving from differential commitments to economic and social values have reduced the salience of loyalty to parties, previously tied largely to the structural sources of cleavage in industrial society.

The reform elements concerned with postmaterialist or social issues largely derive their strength not from the workers and the less privileged, the social base of the Left in industrial society, but from segments of the well-educated, and affluent, students, academics, journalists, professionals and civil servants. The New Left, the New Politics, the Green parties, receive their support from such strata. Most workers, on the other hand, remain concerned with material questions. Less educated, less cosmopolitan, less affluent, less secure, they are also more traditional, more conservative in their social views.

There are now two Lefts, the materialist and the postmaterialist, which are rooted in different classes. A conflict of interest has emerged between them with respect to the consequences of policies that affect economic growth. The materialist Left wants an ever-growing pie so the less privileged can have more, while the postmaterialists are more interested in the quality of life. As political scientist Willard Johnson argues, the postmaterialist Left

> is guilty of debating the issues in terms of values that, for all their humaneness, ignore the concerns of the poor. . . . No doubt their concerns feed on a genuine consideration for the quality of life, but they seem to me mistaken about the contribution material goods can make to it.[42]

Or, as the late Anthony Crosland, Cabinet member in various British Labour governments, contended, those who seek to limit growth to protect the environment are "kindly and dedicated people. But they are affluent, and fundamentally, though of course not consciously, they want to kick the ladder down behind them."[43]

Both Lefts are often in the same party, democratic, social democratic, even communist, as in Italy, but they have different views and interests. One commentator sees a parallel between these two Lefts and the conflict between Marx and the utopian socialists; that is, they both favor equality but dispute over the role of economic development in attaining it.[44] The New Politics intelligentsia does not like trade unions which, like business, it considers materialistic rather than public-interested. Some workers move Right as a result, over to more conservative groupings which espouse growth, a competitive mobile society, and retain beliefs in traditional social values. The Left, however, picks up support from the growing ranks of the intelligentsia. Thus, as mentioned earlier, the correlations between class and party voting have been reduced.

In line with the classic logic of historical materialism, as the most developed nation the United States should be among the first to exhibit the characteristic politics of postindustrialism. The record would seem to sustain the assumption. As the French political analyst Jean-François Revel pointed out in 1971,

> one of the most striking features of the past decade is that the only new revolutionary stirrings in the world have had their origin in the United States. . . . I mean the complex of new oppositional phenomena designated by the term "dissent."[45]

A critical intelligentsia, based on the new middle class, emerged as early as the 1950s, with the formation of the "reform" movement within the Democratic Party, and constituted the beginning of what was subsequently labeled the New Politics. "The appearance of significant numbers of college-educated, socially mobile, issue-oriented voters in urban and suburban reform clubs was noted by political observers in New York, California, Wisconsin, Missouri and elsewhere."[46]

The 1960s witnessed the full-flowering of the New Politics in the form of opposition to the Vietnam War, struggles for civil rights, women's and gays' liberation, and environmentalism, as well as the emergence of new lifestyles. Jeane Kirkpatrick emphasizes the way

> the involvement of basic cultural symbols in the political arena has become a regular feature of our politics. As *avant garde* culture spread through rising college enrollments, the electronic media, and mass-circulation magazines, anti-bourgeois attitudes . . . became the bases of the anti-establishment politics of the 1960s. . . . It is now clear that the assault on the traditional culture was mounted by young and not-so-young representatives of the relatively privileged classes, while the basic institutions of the society were defended by less-prosperous, less-educated, lower-status citizens.[47]

The conflict between the New Politics Left and the traditional working-class-based Left has occurred largely within the Democratic Party. Its defeats in the presidential elections of 1968 and 1972 can be attributed in part to the split between the Old Left and New Left. As noted in Figure 5.1, class voting in the United States fell in 1952 and 1956, rose in 1960 and 1964, declined to an almost negligible level in 1968 and 1972, increased in 1976 and fell off again in 1980. Since 1952, the Democrats have won every election in which class voting has increased. In 1952 and 1956, the defeated Democratic candidate for president was Adlai Stevenson, who has often been called the initiator of the New Politics phenomenon in America. He consciously sought to avoid the New Deal economic and class conflict issues and emphasized cultural and social concerns.

Class voting moved up somewhat in 1960, largely reflecting John F. Kennedy's special appeal to less-privileged Catholic ethnic voters. It rose dramatically in 1964, when Senator Goldwater, the Republican nominee, advocated repeal of many of the welfare state and pro-trade union policies, while Lyndon Johnson was emphasizing New Deal reform measures. In 1968 Hubert Humphrey, a New Dealer, was the Democratic candidate for the presidency, but he lost votes to the left and the right because of the saliency of noneconomic issues. Many blue-collar voters supported George Wallace, reacting against Humphrey's stand on civil rights, while the New Politics Left, who had voted for Eugene McCarthy or Bobby Kennedy in the primaries, refused to back Humphrey because of his lack of commitment to ending the war in Vietnam, and his links to the old politics.

These factors continued to affect electoral behavior in the ensuing decade. In 1972 the New Politics Left won the Democratic Party nomination for its candidate George McGovern, but was defeated soundly in the general election. McGovern was the first Democratic presidential nominee since the 1920s not to receive the support of the labor movement, as blue-collar voters deserted the Democrats to vote for Richard Nixon, who campaigned for traditional values and law and order. The split between the two lefts in the Democratic Party can be seen in the epithet the Humphrey trade union-based wing of the party circulated, depicting McGovern as the candidate of "amnesty, abortion and acid." Four years later, however, the Democrats were able to win back the White House, when both major parties nominated candidates who were identified as social conservatives. Thus, many workers who had voted previously for Nixon or Wallace returned to the Democratic line to support Jimmy Carter.

The Democratic nomination contest in 1980 was, in some part, a fight between Jimmy Carter, viewed as socially conservative, and a New Politics challenger, Edward Kennedy, who also sought to appeal to workers and minorities on economic issues. The opinion surveys reported a strong relationship between socioeconomic status and candidate preference, with the less privileged and the older voters supporting the incumbent and the more affluent, better-educated and younger people backing his opponent. The post-materialist elements found both major party nominees, Reagan and Carter, objectionable. As of mid-summer 1980, they were supporting an independent alternative, John Anderson, whose campaign stressed social liberalism. In a full-page advertisement in the *New York Times* of 27 June 1980 (p. 22E), the Anderson campaign organization called for support because of their candidate's record on five issues: protecting the environment, civil rights, the Equal Rights Amendment, federal funds for abortions for the poor and reduction of excessive government regulations. The opinion polls reported that Anderson's strength (around 22 percent in July) consisted largely of college graduates, professionals, Jews and self-identified liberals.[48] Survey data also indicated that Anderson's followers were much more socially liberal than Carter's supporters. The trade unions, on the other hand, were strongly opposed to Anderson, and endorsed the Democratic nominee, whose strength came disproportionately from the older, less-educated, poorer and working-class sections of the population.

In the 1980 elections themselves, class factors once again became less important as Anderson's support dropped off rapidly, following a pattern typical of third party candidates in the United States. Differences in party orientation toward social issues were more important than in 1976. The Republicans explicitly rejected many of the social programs of the New Politics, the Equal Rights Amendment, government financing of abortions for poor people, and measures such as busing designed to foster racial integration. Ronald Reagan linked his campaign to the efforts of highly moralistic evangelical religious groups opposing politicans who favored the new social permissiveness.

Although Jimmy Carter tried to avoid being identified with the social policies advocated by the New Politics wing of his party, he could not openly repudiate them and hope to retain their support. Hence, social issues played a somewhat greater role in the outcome of the 1980 election than they had four years earlier.

The 1984 Democratic presidential primaries involving former Vice-President Mondale, Colorado Senator Hart, and Reverend Jackson led to renewed fissures between establishment Democrats, represented by the AFL-CIO, and the New Politics wing of the party represented by George McGovern's 1972 presidential campaign manager, Gary Hart. Mondale, throughout the campaign, emphasized his traditional Democratic roots in the New Deal-Hubert Humphrey mold. He sought and gained the early endorsement of the AFL-CIO and was endorsed by a majority of federal and state office-holders within the party. Gary Hart, on the other hand, emphasized his lack of ties to organized labor and special interest groups, and appealed for votes on the basis of "new ideas" and a "new generation of leadership." Jesse Jackson's campaign challenged the Democratic Party, particularly in the South, to end alleged discriminatory practices such as run-off elections and to amend its delegate allocation rules which tend to favor, Jackson argued, well-organized, well-financed candidates.

The political faultlines clearly manifested the division between the Old and New Politics wings of the party. Throughout most of the primaries, but especially in the industrial smokestack states, Mondale's supporters were union members, strong Democrats, older voters, and the poor, while Hart voters were younger, more affluent, better educated professionals who tend to distrust the party establishment, and weak Democrats and Independents. At least 70 percent of Jackson's support came from black voters, many of them voting in their first election.

As Revel has stressed, the new American style of activism, single-issue movements and radical cultural politics spread during the 1960s to other parts of the developed world, which were entering the stage of postindustrialism. Campus-based protest occurred in all the European countries. Sizable left-wing tendencies rooted in the new middle-class groups challenged the moderate union-based leadership of the socialist parties. But these developments were

> imitations of the American prototype, or extensions of it, and subsequent to it. European dissenters, who represent the only force which has been able to rouse both the Left and the Right, the East and the West, from their academic torpor, are the disciples of the American movements.[49]

In Sweden, the Social Democrats, who actively pursue progrowth measures as the best way to achieve a better, more equitable world, have been weakened by the nuclear power debate. In the late 1970s, while a number of intellectuals and the youth within the party were antinuclear, the trade unions adamantly favored building more nuclear power plants.[50] This division seriously hampered the party's election efforts, thus contributing to its first defeat in forty-four years. The principal victor in terms of electoral gains was the Centre Party, the most active antigrowth, antinuclear party. A number of analysts, both journalists and scholars, attributed the defeat to the Social Democrats' support of nuclear power.[51] Hans Zetterberg has summarized the problem that nuclear power posed for the Social Democrats:

> Swedish voters had difficulty fitting the atom power issue into their habitual political patterns of thought. Young leftists considered that the Centre Party atom power policy lay to the left of the Social Democrats. The usual left-right line-up between the parties broke down on the atom power issue: Centre took a left view and the Social Democrats a more rightist one.[52]

The Social Democrats remained divided during the nuclear power referendum campaign in March 1980. A number of leading party intellectuals openly supported the most antinuclear alternative on the ballot, siding with the Centre Party. This division within the Left has affected support for the labor movement. A general strike called by the labor federation (LO), in May 1980, was supported by only 25 percent of those polled in a national survey, although the Social Democratic and Communist vote is normally close to 50 percent. Political observers reported that reactions to the strike were affected by the pronuclear role of the labor movement in the referendum debate. At the height of the strike a leading left-wing intellectual and environmentalist published an article in the country's major newspaper criticizing the union movement for its crass materialism, for engaging in "nothing more than a bid for a still higher living standard in a country already boasting one of the world's highest."[53]

In France, the difference between the two Lefts was in many ways responsible for the collapse of the *Union de la Gauche* and its *Programme Commun* in the 1970s. Initially conflicts over postmaterialist issues made the forming of a coalition among leftist parties difficult. The socialist and the CFDT unions, both of which gained many supporters among the new middle class, were extremely critical of the communists and the Common Program. The main points of disagreement surrounded the role of the state and nationalization in furthering the interests of the working class, with the CFDT taking the position that the communists were "much too state-oriented, the *Programme Commun* presupposes that a decisive social and political change will result merely from the nationalization of the leading companies by the state." They also differed about growth.

> The *Programme Commun*, states the CFDT, is based upon the same logic as the type of economic growth proposed by the capitalist theorists: the exclusive criteria of a high level of production and profit. Now since 1970, the CFDT has come out in favour of a "new type of growth" which is more qualitative than quantitative.[54]

While the socialists and communists maintained an uneasy alliance until the election in 1978, these differences proved fatal to the Union of the Left. Jean-Louis Moynot, a secretary of the communist-dominated CGT union, explained the electoral failure of the communists as flowing from "the stubbornness and intransigency of the Communists and the CGT concerning the minimum wage, nationalizations, or even concerning their lack of interest in such issues as women's rights, ecology, the nuclear threat and education."[55] A French communist historian, Jean Ellenstein, also argued in 1978 that his party had lost support because of its failure to emphasize the social issues. He noted that prospective supporters have not always been at ease with the "proletarian" style adopted by the Communist Party in its electoral campaign. . . . They are increasingly concerned with qualitative problems, even if some quantitative problems continue to exist.[56]

The election of France's first majority socialist government in May 1981 was due, in part, to an uneasy electoral truce with the weak, Moscow-leaning Communist Party. Mitterand's campaign and government, the latter including four communist ministers until 1984, promised to nationalize banks and major businesses, raise the minimum wage, provide jobs for the unemployed, and enlarge the scope of the welfare state. Three years later, with unemployment at 8 percent, a flat rate of growth in GNP, a foreign debt of 53 billion dollars, much of it accumulated in their first year of office, Mitterrand changed course. The government's new steel plan envisions the loss of 25 percent of the jobs in that industry. The government can no longer subsidize inefficiency. The socialists also plan to cut government expenditures in order to fulfill a campaign promise to reduce taxes by 1985. This reversal of economic policy has led to divisions between the more middle-class based socialists and the major trade unions, particularly the communist-dominated CGT, and to the departure of the communists from the government.

A study of German electoral behavior points to similar phenomena in that country. During the Weimar Republic and in West Germany in the 1950s, traditional class divisions determined the support for left and right parties, while "the issues which divided the groups were primarily economy and security related." Starting in the 1960s, the new middle class, civil servants and salaried people, developed "a liberal position on New Politics [social] issues," while the old middle class, the self-employed, remained conservative on "the New as well as the Old [materialistic] Politics." The workers, however, began to "move in the opposite direction from the new middle-class, from a Left stance in the conflicts of the Old Politics, to a more conservative position on the New Politics issues." An electoral manifestation of the New Politics is the Green Party, which is opposed to "nuclear energy, nuclear weapons, pollution, big corporations, advertising, inequalities of wealth, conventional politics and exploitation in the Third World." Around 60 percent of the party's members are under 35 years of age, between 35 and 40 percent are women, and many hold jobs which "depend only indirectly on economic growth, such as the law and teaching." As Davy points out, the trade unions and workers have not supported the Green Party because "unionists see nuclear power stations, roads and new industries as providers of jobs and engines of growth, not as threats to the environment." Recently, however, the Greens were able to increase their share of the vote in Baden-Württemberg from 5.3 to 8 percent due to the acid rain which is killing the Black Forest located within that state. This upturn in voting for the Greens at the state level would seemingly support Hildebrandt's and Dalton's prediction that "as postmaterialist concerns and values become more predominant in politics and more salient to growing portions of the German electorate, the traditional bourgeois/proletariat cleavage should continue to decline in importance and clarity."[57]

Comparable processes have been at work in Japan, which has moved more rapidly than other countries from a preindustrial to an industrial to a postindustrial society. Many Japanese, although experiencing the advantages of rapid growth, have become increasingly disturbed by its social costs. As of 1971,

> seven times as many people in Japan regarded environmental pollution as the top-priority task for the nation as those who considered further economic growth the most important national business. The number of consumer protests . . . rose twenty-seven fold between 1962 and 1970, and protest and petitions about pollution doubled during a recent three-year period.[58]

The *benefits* of successful industrialization, as Taketsugu Tsurutani points out, are selective and class-related, while "the *costs* of industrialism . . . tend to be egalitarian, catholic, indiscriminate, hence cross-stratal in nature."[59]

> Indeed, petrochemical smog, for instance, does not know the difference between upper-middle class children and working-class children . . . the rich and the not-so-rich alike love fish in Japan, but fish, in all too many cases, are poisoned by chemical waste that industrial plants so callously disposed of into all convenient bodies of water.[60]

Scott Flanagan, analyzing Japanese electoral opinion data, concludes that

> the increasing importance of value issues appears, in part, to be responsible for the weakening association between occupational class and voting behavior. Since economic and value cleavages are cross-cutting, a third dimension that measures the relative salience of value issues was necessary to predict voting choices more accurately. I have shown that those voters who are cross-pressured by their value preferences and occupational class will tend to vote in line with their value preferences if they place greater stress on nonmaterial priorities and value issues, and with their occupational class if they attach greater importance to material priorities and economic issues.[61]

Curiously, the prototypical country with respect to the breakdown in class-linked politics has been Denmark. There "the relative number of workers voting for the Social Democrats declined from 80% in 1957 to 39% in 1973 . . . and the Conservatives who were supported by 39% of all employers in

1957 were down to 9% in . . . 1973.''[62] Support for the two small New Left socialist parties ''nowadays is not . . . characterized by close communications with the working class. Voters for these parties are younger; they are better educated than the average voter; quite a few of them are still in the process of educating themselves for academic or semi-academic positions.''[63] As Mogens Pedersen emphasizes:

> In a comparative perspective it can be argued that this development, the basic feature of which is the decomposition of the traditional class-based party system, does not differ from the development in other European systems, at least not with regard to the character and direction of the change. Everywhere social class tends to lose in importance.[64]

What do these trends portend for working-class influence and power? The answer, in part, hinges on whether postmaterialistic politics is a short-run or a long-term phenomenon. If prosperity is the most important variable in the emergence of these new values, then we can expect them to decline if the economy becomes seriously troubled. Yet evidence from West Germany suggests that even with the economic decline of the 1970s, the New Politics has a firm foundation.[65] As Max Kaase and Samuel Barnes argue, postmaterialism

> displays too much of a structural component, and therefore permanence, to be considered just a fad of the young. . . . Future politics will be increasingly Postmaterialist politics. [That] . . . does not imply that material values are not relevant; they will continue to be so. The point is that Postmaterialist values become *relatively* more important, and here is where we see potential sources of strain for postindustrial societies.[66]

If postmaterialist politics is a structural phenomenon related to the shifting occupational structure, support for the New Politics should increase since there is a growing number of jobs outside the industrial sector, whose holders will presumably be more disposed to oppose growth.

But beyond the staying power of the New Left, it is important to note that the classic political division of industrial society still predominates in affecting partisan support. The electorate of the left comes largely from the working class and the more deprived, while the conservative parties are based on the more affluent strata. Organized labor has gained a new source of influence through an increasing involvement in the economic planning process in a number of advanced industrial societies.[67] Many elites in these countries currently see economic growth as their *raison d'être* and need organized labor to sustain it.[68] In any case, the working class will continue to maintain socioeconomic leverage through what Finer calls their ''power to disrupt.''[69]

It is far from certain, however, that the two Lefts will oppose each other at the ballot box. Touraine believes that the new middle strata which he describes as a "new working class" will support radical politics. He sees them as increasingly alienated, reduced in status and subject to capitalist controls, much like the proletariat. As a result they will cooperate with the manual working class.[70] Inglehart has also noted:

> There can be acute strains between an older Left that emphasizes the economic gains for the working class, and a newer Left that is more concerned with life-style changes, with qualitative rather than quantitative gains. But both factions share a common concern with social change in an egalitarian direction, and precisely because the goal of equality appeals to different groups for different reasons, it may serve as a bond that holds the Left together.[71]

Flanagan estimates that over the long run, the influences which press new middle-class elements to move to the left on social issues should be stronger than those which dispose working-class traditionalists to switch to the right.[72]

Michael Harrington, President of the Democratic Socialists in the United States, has suggested the possibility of a coalition between the two Lefts. He hopes that a middle ground can be found: "not either cancerous growth or no growth, but . . . planned growth on a human scale."[73] Certainly, not all environmental efforts are zero-sum games. Concern about pollution and toxic waste disposal, as evidenced in the Love Canal tragedy in New York, is an example of an issue that cuts across the two Lefts. Indeed, some leaders in each group, realizing that they need each other for political strength, try to endorse policies of concern to the other. Environmentalists for Full Employment publicly backed both the full employment and labor law reform bills,[74] and efforts at consumer protection have brought the unions and the New Politics together in the United States.[75] Yet there remain more divisive areas than mediating ones; fundamental differences exist on such issues as foreign policy, nuclear energy, social and moral concerns, as well as the profound distrust the different types of people in the two Lefts feel toward each other. In essence the future depends on the degree of flexibility and compromise shown by ideologically different groups who have the pursuit of greater equality as common ground.

Inequality under Socialism

If the Marxist theory of proletarian revolution has been confounded and disconfirmed by the pattern of politics in different countries, it should be noted that a related aspect and prediction of historical materialism has been verified in events and processes which have occurred in the countries which call themselves socialist or communist. As we have seen, Marx assumed that socialism as a system, a relatively egalitarian society, could only be established in highly developed industrial nations. His premise for this was the belief that inequality, intense stratification, was a result of scarcity. Marx argued that in systems that did not produce enough economic goods for all to live well, inequality and class exploitation must exist, that the dominant position-holders in such societies would necessarily take a disproportionate share of the goods for themselves. The basic condition for equality, according to Marx, is abundance, having enough goods so that, if shared, all can live very well. The historically progressive task of capitalism was not only to create the working class, which would eventually overthrow it, but also to produce the advanced technology and affluence necessary for socialism. Hence, socialism is impossible until economic abundance exists.

Marx, of course, wrote polemically against those who believed that socialism could occur prior to abundance. He described such socialists as "utopians."[76] His brand of socialism was "scientific" because it was premised on historical materialism, on relating social forms or systems to appropriate material conditions. Now what would happen if socialists tried to create socialism under "utopian" conditions, if they overthrew capitalism before it had exhausted its historical mission to create an advanced affluent industrial system? His answer in *The German Ideology* was clear. In order to build socialism it is necessary to have

> a great increase in productive power, a high degree of its development. . . . This development of productive forces . . . is absolutely necessary as a practical premise: for the reason that without it only *want* is made general, and with *want* the struggle for necessities and all the old filthy business [the German word was *Scheisse*] would necessarily be reproduced.[77]

Trotsky discussed this passage in *The Revolution Betrayed*, in his effort to explain why Stalinism occurred and resulted in a system of intense inequality.[78]

In other words, efforts to create an egalitarian society under conditions of economic scarcity must fail, must result in a new system of exploitation, of class domination. As Rosa Luxemburg described the contradiction, "elementary conceptions of socialist politics and an insight into their historically necessary prerequisites force us to understand that under such fatal conditions even the most gigantic idealism and the most storm-tested revolutionary energy are incapable of realizing democracy and socialism but only distorted attempts at either."[79] This is, of course, what has happened in the less-developed countries which have become communist. They cannot be workers' states, for they are class-ridden societies. As one pair of scholars from Eastern Europe has stated it, there is merely the emergence of "the next class."[80]

Karl Wittfogel has taken this analysis one step further by drawing on another category in Marx's writings, the concepts of Asiatic society and Oriental despotism.[81] Wittfogel notes that Marx described a societal system, which had existed in certain Asian states in which large irrigation works were a prime condition for agriculture. In these societies, the state rather than private property was the key source of class rule. The state became powerful and maintained control because only a strong state could establish and allocate water resources. The ruling class was the group which controlled the state. Such systems were highly centralized, despotic and sharply stratified. Using Marxist categories, Wittfogel argues that communist societies should be seen as forms of Oriental despotism; their characteristics, class and political relations, resemble those described by Marx as inherent in Asiatic systems.

Wittfogel points to indications that Lenin, who knew his Marx, was consciously worried that the Soviet Union was becoming an Oriental despotism, that he had helped to create a new exploitative regime. He quotes a speech Lenin delivered on 20 April 1921 at the 10th Party Congress, in which he said: "Socialism is better than capitalism, but capitalism is better than medievalism, small production, and a bureaucracy connected with the dispersed character of the small producers." Lenin then observed that the roots of bureaucracy in the Soviet Union were "the fragmented and dispersed character of the small producer, his poverty, the lack of culture." To understand Lenin's implications, Wittfogel notes that "the initiated will recall Marx's and Engels' view that self-sufficient, dispersed and isolated communities form the solid and natural foundation of Oriental despotism." And Wittfogel concludes, "in Aesopian language he was obviously expressing his fear that an Asiatic restoration was taking place and that a new type of Oriental despotism was in the making."[82]

At the same 1921 party congress, Lenin advocated independent trade unions, which would have the right to strike, to protect the workers against the bureaucracy which dominated industry and the state. This suggests his concern over the potential of the new communist bureaucracy to exploit the Russian people. In a passage that the compilers of the latest official Moscow edition of his party congress speeches have seen fit to edit out, Lenin stated:

> Ours is a workers' government with a bureaucratic twist. Our present government is such that the proletariat, organized to the last man, must protect itself against it. And we must use the workers' organizations for the protection of the workers against their government.[83]

Lenin, of course, cannot be exempted from responsibility for the creation of the oppressive Soviet state. He was warned by Trotsky in 1903 that his highly centralized party structure would lead to a "pseudo-Jacobin dictatorship over the masses," which would end with the use of the "guillotine" to eliminate dissidents. Trotsky prophesied that the Leninist seizure of power would result in a situation in which the "organization of the Party takes the place of the Party itself; the Central Committee takes the place of the organization; and finally the dictator takes the place of the Central Committee."[84] The martyred leader of the abortive German communist revolution, Rosa Luxemburg, anticipated in 1918 that the curtailment of the rights of opposition in the Soviet Union would result in a totally repressive society, "in which only the bureaucracy remains as the active element."[85] As she noted, "without a free and untrammelled press, without the unlimited right of association and assembly, the rule of the broad masses of the people is unthinkable."[86]

In taking these positions Trotsky and Luxemburg were closer than Lenin to the classic Marxist orientation. Thus, Friedrich Engels had explicitly written, "if anything has been established for certain, it is this, that our party and the working class can achieve rule only under the form of the democratic republic. This is even the *specific form* for the dictatorship of the proletariat."[87] On the same page of the edition of the Marx-Engels *Correspondence* from which the Engels statement is taken, the Russian editors inserted a comment by Lenin from his book, *State and Revolution*, in which he reported that Engels had said "the democratic republic is the *nearest approach* to the dictatorship of the proletariat." The Stalinist editors noted that this formulation constituted a "revision of Marxist views about democracy." It is clear that Lenin changed Engels's formulation, possibly to deny that the specific form of a state dominated by the workers should be a democratic republic.

Thus, we see that Marx's theory of historical materialism relied on advanced industrial systems to generate the conditions under which the working class would come to power and a free, egalitarian, socialist society could flourish. Capitalism led to a highly efficient, very productive industrial society. The workers in the most industrialized countries have not turned to revolutionary socialism, however, but rather to labor party and trade union action to improve their life situation. "Marxists," on the other hand, have taken power in preindustrialized, poverty-stricken societies and, as Marx anticipated, have revived "the old filthy business," whether one wants to call their nations Oriental despotisms or not.

The "New Class" in Socialist Society

The communist countries are also experiencing the strains flowing from inequality and the rapid growth of scientific and technological professions. As already demonstrated in a number of East European countries, as well as the Soviet Union itself, considerable discontent and protest exists among the well-educated strata.[88] Workers have engaged in strikes and in protest movements, sometimes in alliance with segments of the intelligentsia and student population, although there is a considerable gap in the concerns of the different strata. At the moment, however, most are in the stage of industrialization. Hence, their workers face experiences comparable to those in the West some time ago, but they lack the protection of workers' parties and unions. As a number of socialist intellectuals have recognized, they require the erection of class defense organizations to protect them against the socialist bureaucrats or the new ruling class.

At the turn of the century, a Polish revolutionary and former Marxist, Jan Machajski, "produced what might be called a Marxist interpretation of Marxism."[89] He argued that the triumph of socialists would bring about a society controlled by the educated classes who would exploit the underprivileged strata. And, Machajski suggested, concepts of participatory democracy, of control of the machinery of complex industrial society by the masses, were utopian and would only serve to conceal the fact that socialism would be severely stratified with respect to power and privilege.[90]

Some years later, in 1911, the German sociologist Robert Michels, while still a member of the Social Democratic Party, published his classic work, *Political Parties*, which elaborated on the structural determinants of "oligarchy" in all political parties and types of societies. He concluded that a socialist revolution would necessarily result in a

> dictatorship in the hands of those leaders who have been sufficiently astute and sufficiently powerful to grasp the sceptre of dominion in the name of socialism. . . . The socialist might conquer, but not socialism, which would perish in the moment of its adherents' triumph.[91]

More recently, while discussing the objectives of the postmaterialist protestors of contemporary society, Alan Marsh revived Machajski's theme that the populist slogans of radical elites are expression of their feeling that they, rather than older dominant groups, should be in power. He argues that postmaterialist "radicalism" is a response to the "power-frustration experienced by many young middle-class Europeans who are excluded from the exercise of such power and from positions of high social respect." By speaking out "against their class interests they . . . also acquire a reputation for altruism," but he suggests, congruent with Machajski's analysis of the objectives of the radical mandarins of the Czarist Empire, what they are seeking is power and status for themselves.[92]

These analyses, of course, parallel the interpretation which Marxists and others have given of the role of the democratic and egalitarian ideologies of the American and French Revolutions in legitimating bourgeois class rule. Given the impossibility of abolishing the structural causes of class domination, Machajski argued that the only honest position for anyone interested in improving the position of the masses is to help them resist those in power through organizations independent of the state and dominant class. Michels also emphasized the need to help "the masses, so that they might be enabled, within the limits of what is possible, to counteract the oligarchic tendencies." He

called for support of oppositionist movements "as contributing to the enfee-
blement of oligarchic tendencies," as long as the groups do not take power:

> Democracy is a treasure which no one will discover by deliberate search. But
> in continuing our search, in laboring indefatigably to discover the undiscov-
> erable, we will perform a work which will have fertile results in a democratic
> sense.[93]

It should be noted that a few of the contemporary postmaterialists implicitly
take a position close to that advocated by Machajski and Michels. Organizations such as the civic initiative groups in West Germany or Acorn in the
United States seek to work with underprivileged people outside of the electoral
process so that, regardless of which political party holds office, they can
continue to press for increased rights and representation.

The analyses of Machajski and Michels implied that Marx was a political
"utopian" in the sense in which he, himself, used the word. They believed
that the structure of large-scale society makes a nonexploitative egalitarian
system impossible, that it requires a domineering class which uses its power
to enhance its privileges. But at the same time, they agreed with his method
of analysis. Michels explicitly accepted the Marxist materialist conception of
history. As he emphasized, his own approach as elaborated in *Political Parties*

> completes that conception and reinforces it. There is no essential contradiction
> between the doctrine that history is the record of continued class struggles and
> the doctrine that class struggles invariably culminate in the creation of new
> oligarchies which undergo fusion with the old. The existence of a political class
> does not conflict with the essential content of Marxism, considered not as an
> economic dogma, but as a philosophy of history.[94]

Although contemporary Marxists have chosen to ignore Machajski and
Michels, it is worth noting that a leading theoretician of the Russian Communist Party, Nicolai Bukharin, in his book *Historical Materialism*, published
in 1925, discussed Michels's ideas and acknowledged both their intellectual
importance and the possibility that Michels might turn out to be correct.
Bukharin agreed that in "the *transition period* from capitalism to socialism,
i.e., the period of the proletarian dictatorship . . . there will inevitably be a
tendency to 'degeneration,' i.e., the excretion of a leading stratum in the
form of a class-germ." But he countered Michels with the argument:

> This tendency will be retarded by two opposing tendencies; first, by the growth
> of the productive forces; second, by the abolition of the educational monopoly.
> The increasing reproduction of technologists and of organizers in general, out
> of the working class, will undermine the possible new class alignment. The
> outcome of the struggle will depend on which tendencies turn out to be stronger.[95]

A myriad of scholarly analyses demonstrate which tendency has won out.[96] In the words of Tito's former second-in-command, Milovan Djilas, "the Communist revolution, conducted in the name of doing away with classes, has resulted in the most complete authority of any single new class. Everything else is a sham and illusion."[97]

In the final year of his life, Leon Trotsky faced up to the possibility that Marxism might be a utopian doctrine, that the working class of advanced industrial societies, the countries which had the prerequisites for building socialism, were incapable of taking or holding power. If the revolution did not occur in the Western developed world, then, as his biographer and follower Isaac Deutscher summed up Trotsky's views,

> the Marxist view of capitalist society and socialism must be admitted to have been wrong, for Marxism had proclaimed that socialism would either be the work of the proletariat or it would not be at all. Was Marxism then just another "ideology" or another form of the false consciousness that causes oppressed classes and their parties to believe that they struggle for their own purposes when in truth they are only promoting the interests of a new, or even of an old, ruling class? Viewed from this angle, the defeat of the pristine Bolshevism would indeed appear to be of the same order as the defeat of the Jacobins— the result of a collision between Utopia and a new social order—and Stalin's victory would present itself as a triumph of reality over illusion.[98]

Or in Trotsky's words, if the "proletariat should actually prove incapable of fulfilling the mission placed on it by the course of develᴧpment, nothing else would remain except only to recognize that the socialist programme based on the internal contradictions of capitalist society, ended as a Utopia."[99]

Trotsky did not put off the test of the Marxist hypothesis to the far-off future. Rather, recognizing that the record of left-wing failures in industrial societies argued for the negative, he stated unequivocally that World War II, which had just begun, presented the "decisive test." As Deutscher notes, "He defined the terms of the test with painful precision . . . a matter of the next few years."[100] If World War II did "not lead to proletarian revolution in the West, then the place of decaying capitalism would indeed be taken not by socialism but by a new bureaucratic and totalitarian system of exploitation," based on state power.[101]

Trotsky, unfortunately, was not allowed by Stalin to live long enough to react to the continued failure of Marxism in developed societies and the expansion of communist bureaucratic rule in less developed nations. He retained his faith in Marxism and the revolution through to his assassination in August 1940. His movement has continued to the present, seemingly unconcerned with the fact that the date for Trotsky's final test has long passed. Isaac Deutscher, in words reminiscent of Trotsky's own reaction to the implications of American developments for Marx's theory, describes Trotsky's specification of a decisive test of the Marxist hypothesis as "one of those overemphatic and hyperbolic statements . . . which taken literally leads to endless confusion."[102]

But it should be noted that Trotsky left specific advice to revolutionaries as to what they should do if Marxism turned out to be Utopian. His recommendation was the same as those proposed by Machajski and Michels: support the masses against the oppressors. "It is self-evident that a new 'minimum' programme would be required for the defense of the slaves of the totalitarian bureaucratic society."[103]

In the contemporary world to think of "proletarian class struggle" is to focus on the position of the workers in Eastern Europe. The "revolution" has come and gone, and they are now beginning, in political circumstances almost inconceivable in Marx's day, to find ways in which to develop yet again class-consciousness and class organization under the alien conditions of state socialism. Ironically, as the Polish strikes demonstrate, the usefulness of Marx's sociological insights concerning the way the social situation of the industrial proletariat enables them to organize more effectively against their oppressors than does that of any other class, has been demonstrated by events in the communist world.

Notes

1. C. Wright Mills, *Power, Politics and People: The Collected Essays of C. Wright Mills* (Baltimore: Johns Hopkins University Press, 1970), p. 256.
2. K. Marx, *Capital*, Vol. 1 (Moscow: Foreign Languages Publishing House, 1958), pp. 8–9.
3. Howard Quint, *The Forging of American Socialism: Origins of the Modern Movement* (Indianapolis: Bobbs-Merrill, 1953), p. 380.
4. R.L. Moore, *European Socialists and the American Promised Land* (New York: Oxford University Press, 1970), p. 58.
5. Ibid., p. 102.
6. Ibid., p. 77.
7. Werner Sombart, *Why Is There No Socialism in the United States?* (White Plains: International Arts & Sciences Press, 1976), p. 15.
8. J.E. Good, *Strangers in a Strange Land: Five Russian Radicals Visit the United States* (Ph.D. diss., American University, 1979), p. 231.
9. Moore, *European Socialists*, pp. 78–79.
10. Ibid., p. 91.
11. Quint, *The Forging of American Socialism*, pp. 380–81.
12. D. De Leon, *Flashlights of the Amsterdam Conference* (New York: New York Labor News, 1904), p. 133.
13. J.D. Young, "Daniel De Leon and Anglo-American Socialism," *Labour History* 17 (1976): p. 344.
14. M. Beer, *Fifty Years of International Socialism* (London: Allen & Unwin, 1935), pp. 109–110.

15. L. Trotsky, *The Living Thoughts of Karl Marx* (New York: Longmans, Green, 1939), pp. 38–39.
16. Discussion of this topic can be found in "Radicalism or Reformism: The Sources of Working-Class Politics," in this volume, and S. M. Lipset, "Why No Socialism in the United States?" in S. Bialer and S. Sluzar (eds.), *Sources of Contemporary Radicalism*, Vol. 1 (Boulder, Colo.: Westview, 1977), pp. 31–149.
17. W.D. Burnham, "The United States: The Politics of Heterogeneity," in R. Rose (ed.), *Electoral Behavior* (New York: Free Press, 1974), p. 718.
18. V.I. Lenin, *On Britain* (Moscow: Foreign Languages Publishing House, n.d.), p. 51; Moore, *European Socialists*, p. 110; Lipset, "Why No Socialism in the United States?," pp. 58–59.
19. J.R. Commons, "American Labour History: Introduction," in J.R. Commons et al., *History of Labor in the United States* (New York: Macmillan, 1926), p. 5; S. Perlman, *A Theory of the Labor Movement* (New York: Macmillan, 1928), pp. 167–68.
20. P.R. Abramson, "Social Class and Political Change in Western Europe: A Cross-national Longitudinal Analysis," *Comparative Political Studies* 4 (1971): 131–55; D. Butler and D. Stokes, *Political Change in Britain*, 2d. ed. (New York: St. Martin's, 1976); K. Hildebrandt and R.I. Dalton, "The New Politics: Political Change or Sunshine Politics?," in M. Kaase and K. von Beyme (eds.), *Elections and Parties: Socio-political Change and Participation in the West German Federal Election of 1976* (Beverly Hills: Sage, 1978), pp. 69–96.
21. O. Kirchheimer, "The Transformation of the Western European Party Systems," in J. La Palombara and M. Weiner (eds.), *Political Parties and Political Development* (Princeton: Princeton University Press, 1966), pp. 177–200; K. von Beyme, "The Changing Relations between Trade Unions and the Social Democratic Party in West Germany," *Government and Opposition* 13 (1978): 399–416; L. Minkin, "The Party Connection: Divergence and Convergence in the British Labour Movement," *Government and Opposition* 13 (1978): 458–85; F.E. Myers, "Social Class and Political Change in Advanced Industrial Societies," *Comparative Politics* 2 (1970): 389–412; M.D. Hancock, *Sweden: The Politics of Post-Industrial Change* (Hinsdale: Dryden, 1972).
22. R. Alford, *Party and Society: The Anglo-American Democracies* (Chicago: Rand McNally, 1963).
23. H. Marcuse, *One-Dimensional Man* (Boston: Beacon, 1964), pp. xii–xiii.
24. S. Mallet, *Essays on the New Working Class* (St. Louis: Telos, 1975), p. 48.
25. H. Marcuse, *An Essay on Liberation* (Boston: Beacon, 1969), p. 56.
26. S.M. Lipset, *Political Man* (Baltimore: Johns Hopkins University Press, 1981), p. 234.
27. R. McKenzie and A. Silver, *Angels in Marble: Working Class Conservatives in Urban England* (London: Heinemann, 1968), p. ii; W. Korpi, *The Working Class in Welfare Capitalism: Work, Unions and Politics in Sweden* (London: Routledge & Kegan Paul, 1978), pp. 1–2.
28. D. Bell, *The Coming of Post-Industrial Society* (New York: Basic Books, 1973); A. Touraine, *The Post-Industrial Society: Tomorrow's Social History: Classes, Conflict, and Culture in the the Programmed Society* (New York: Random House, 1971); J. Gershuny, *After Industrial Society? The Emerging Self-Service Economy* (London: Macmillan, 1978).

29. J.K. Galbraith, *The Affluent Society* (Boston: Houghton Mifflin, 1958); J.K. Galbraith, *The New Industrial State*, 3d. ed. (Boston: Houghton Mifflin, 1978); Bell, *The Coming of Post-Industrial Society*; Z. Brzezinski, *Between Two Ages: America's Role in the Technetronic Era* (New York: Viking, 1970); Touraine, *The Post-Industrial Society*; Gershuny, *After Industrial Society?*; R. Richta et al., *Civilization at the Crossroads* (White Plains: International Arts & Sciences Press, 1969); A.W. Gouldner, *The Future of Intellectuals and the Rise of the New Class* (New York: Seabury, 1979); B. Bruce-Briggs, "An Introduction to the Idea of the New Class," in B. Bruce-Briggs (ed.), *The New Class?* (New Brunswick, N.J.: Transaction, 1979), pp. 1–18.

30. V. Ferkiss, "Daniel Bell's Concept of Post-Industrial Society: Theory, Myth, and Ideology," *Political Science Reviewer* 9 (1979): 97–99.

31. P.N. Fedoseev, "The Social Significance of the Scientific and Technological Revolution," *International Social Science Journal* 27 (1975): 152; Ferkiss, "Daniel Bell's Concept of Post-Industrial Society," p. 97.

32. Richta, *Civilization at the Crossroads*, p. 39.

33. Ibid., pp. 120–24. D.R. Cameron, *Postindustrial Change and Secular Realignment* (Ph.D. diss., University of Michigan, 1976), pp. 17–47; T. La Porte and C.J. Abrams, "Alternative Patterns of Postindustrialism: the California Experience," in L.N. Lindberg (ed.), *Politics and the Future of Industrial Society* (New York: McKay, 1976), pp. 28–36; Gershuny, *After Industrial Society?*, pp. 92–136; Gouldner, *The Future of Intellectuals*, p. 15; S. Pollard, "The Rise of the Service Industries and White Collar Employment," in B. Gustafsson (ed.), *Post-Industrial Society* (New York: St. Martin's, 1979), pp. 17–47.

34. Touraine, *The Post-Industrial Society*, p. 51; Gouldner, *The Future of Intellectuals*, p. 83.

35. Ferkiss, "Daniel Bell's Concept of Post-Industrial Society," pp. 66–68.

36. R. Inglehart, "The Silent Revolution in Europe: Intergenerational Change in Post-Industrial Societies," *American Political Science Review* 65 (1971): 991–1017; R. Inglehart, *The Silent Revolution: Changing Values and Political Styles among Western Publics* (Princeton: Princeton University Press, 1977); R. Inglehart, "Value Priorities and Socioeconomic Change," in S.H. Barnes and M. Kaase (eds.), *Political Action: Mass Participation in Five Western Democracies* (Beverly Hills: Sage, 1979), pp. 305–43.

37. S.C. Flanagan, "Value Cleavages, Economic Cleavages, and the Japanese Voter," *American Journal of Political Science* 24 (1980): 274.

38. Inglehart, "The Silent Revolution in Europe"; Inglehart, "Value Priorities and Socioeconomic Change."

39. A. Marsh, "The Silent Revolution, Value Priorities, and the Quality of Life in Britain," *American Political Science Review* 69 (1975): 28.

40. Inglehart, "Value Priorities and Socioeconomic Change," pp. 210–11.

41. S.M. Lipset and S. Rokkan, "Cleavage Structures, Party Systems, and Voter Alignments," chapter 4 in this volume.

42. W.R. Johnson, "Should the Poor Buy No Growth?" *Daedalus* 102 (1973): 174.

43. A. Crosland, *Socialism Now* (London: Jonathan Cape, 1974), pp. 77–78.

44. N.S.J. Watts, "Post-material Values and Political Change: Hypotheses for Comparative Research," (paper presented for the 2d Annual Meeting of the International Society for Political Psychology in Washington D.C., 1979).

45. J. Revel, *Without Marx or Jesus* (Garden City: Doubleday, 1971), p. 6.

46. J.J. Kirkpatrick, "Politics and the New Class," in B. Bruce-Briggs (ed.), *The New Class* (New Brunswick, N.J.: Transaction, 1979), p. 43.
47. Ibid., pp. 44–45.
48. E.C. Ladd and G.D. Ferree, "John Anderson: Candidate of the New Class?" *Public Opinion* 3 (June/July 1980): 11–15.
49. Revel, *Without Marx or Jesus*, pp. 6–7.
50. H. Zetterberg, "The Swedish Election of 1976," (paper presented for the 9th World Congress of Sociology in Uppsala, Sweden, 1978), p. 35.
51. D. Abrahamson, "Governments Fall as Consensus Gives Way to Debate," *The Bulletin of the Atomic Scientists* 35 (1979): 30–31; Korpi, *The Working Class in Welfare Capitalism*, pp. 90, 271, 306, 330–31.
52. Zetterberg, "The Swedish Election of 1976," p. 36.
53. D. Noble, "Sweden Struggles to End Crippling Strike," *The Guardian* (London), 9 May 1980, p. 1.
54. G. Lavau, "The Changing Relations between Trade Unions and Working-Class Parties in France," *Government and Opposition* 13 (1978): 453.
55. Ibid., p. 451.
56. "Editorial," *Government and Opposition* 13 (1978): 264.
57. R. Davy, "West Germany's 'Green' Party," *Journal of the Institute for Socioeconomic Studies* 7 (1982): 34–36; James S. Markham, "In a 'Dying' Forest, the German Soul Withers Too," *New York Times* 25 May 1984, p. 8; Hildebrandt and Dalton, "The New Politics," pp. 87–89.
58. T. Tsurutani, "Japan as a Postindustrial Society," in L. Lindberg (ed.), *Politics and the Future of Industrial Society* (New York: McKay, 1976), p. 105.
59. T. Tsurutani, *Political Change in Japan: Response to Postindustrial Challenge* (New York: McKay, 1977), p. 48.
60. Ibid., p. 50.
61. Flanagan, "Value Cleavages," pp. 201–2.
62. M.N. Pedersen, "Denmark: the Breakdown of a Working Multiparty System," (unpublished paper, Odense University, Odense, Denmark, 1979), pp. 43–44.
63. Ibid., p. 49.
64. Ibid., p. 44.
65. Hildebrandt and Dalton, "The New Politics."
66. M. Kaase and S.H. Barnes, "In Conclusion: The Future of Political Protest in Western Democracies," in S.H. Barnes and M. Kaase (eds.), *Political Action*, pp. 524–25.
67. P. Schmitter, "Still the Century of Corporatism?," *The Review of Politics* 36 (1974): 85–131; D. Coombs, "Trade Unions and Political Parties in Britain, France, Italy, and West Germany," *Government and Opposition* 13 (1978): 485–95.
68. R.D. Putnam, "Elite Transformation in Advanced Industrial Societies: An Empirical Assessment of the Theory of Technocracy," *Comparative Political Studies* 10 (1977): 383–413.
69. J. Hayward, "Trade Unions and Their Politico-Economic Environments: A Preliminary Framework," *West European Politics* 3 (1980): 1–10.
70. Touraine, *The Post-Industrial Society*.
71. Inglehart, *The Silent Revolution*, p. 366.
72. Flanagan, "Value Cleavages," pp. 202–3.
73. M. Harrington, *Decade of Decision: The Crisis of the American System* (New York: Simon & Schuster, 1980), p. 325.

74. Harrington, *Decade of Decision*, p. 309; D. Vogel, "The New Class: Conservatism's Chimerical Villain," *Working Papers for a New Society* 5 (1978): 68–71.

75. Vogel, "The New Class," p. 70.

76. K. Marx, *Selected Works*, Vol, I (New York; International Publishers, 1933), pp. 237–40.

77. K. Marx, *The German Ideology* (New York: International Publishers, 1947), pp. 24–25.

78. L. Trotsky, *The Revolution Betrayed: What Is the Soviet Union and Where Is It Going?* (Garden City: Doubleday, Doran, 1937), pp. 56–64.

79. R. Luxemburg, *The Russian Revolution* (Ann Arbor: University of Michigan Press, 1961), p. 28.

80. G. Konrad and I. Szelenyi, *The Intellectuals on the Road to Class Power* (New York: Harcourt, Brace & Jovanovich, 1979).

81. K. Wittfogel, *Oriental Despotism* (New Haven: Yale University Press, 1957).

82. Ibid., pp. 399–400.

83. M. Gordon, *Workers Before and After Lenin* (New York: Dutton, 1941), pp. 88–89.

84. B.D. Wolfe, *Three Who Made a Revolution* (Boston: Beacon, 1955), p. 253.

85. Luxemburg, *The Russian Revolution*, p. 76.

86. Ibid., pp. 66–67.

87. K. Marx and F. Engels, *Selected Correspondence, 1846–1895* (New York: International Publishers, 1942), p. 486.

88. Richta, *Civilization at the Crossroads*, p. 233; S.M. Lipset and R. Dobson, "The Intellectual as Critic and Rebel: With Special Reference to the United States and the Soviet Union," *Daedalus* 101 (1972): 137–98.

89. Bruce-Briggs, "An Introduction," p. 12.

90. J.W. Machajski, "On the Expropriation of the Capitalists," in V.F. Calverton (ed.), *The Making of Society* (New York: Random House, 1937), pp. 427–36; M. Nomad, *Aspects of Revolt* (New York: Noonday, 1961), pp. 96–117; M. Nomad, *Dreamers, Dynamics and Demagogues* (New York: Walson, 1964), pp. 103–8, 201–6; P. Avrich, "What Is Machaevism?" *Soviet Studies* 17 (1965): 66–75; M. Shatz, "Jan Waclaw Machajski: The Conspiracy of the Intellectuals," *Survey* 62 (1967): 45–57; Bruce-Briggs, "An Introduction," pp. 12–14.

91. R. Michels, *Political Parties: A Sociological Study of the Oligarchical Tendencies of Modern Democracy* (New York: Free Press, 1962), pp. 348, 355.

92. Marsh, "The Silent Revolution," pp. 29–30.

93. Michels, *Political Parties*, pp. 368–69.

94. Ibid., p. 354.

95. N. Bukharin, *Historical Materialism: A System of Sociology* (New York: International Publishers, 1925), pp. 309–11.

96. D. Lane, *The End of Inequality? Stratification Under State Socialism* (London: Penguin, 1971); F. Parkin, *Inequality and the Political Order* (London: McGibbon & Kee, 1971); M. Matthews, *Class and Society in Soviet Russia* (New York: Walker, 1972); S.M. Lipset and R.B. Dobson, "Social Stratification and Sociology in the Soviet Union," *Survey* 88 (Summer 1973): 114–85; M. Yanowitch and W.A. Fisher, *Social Stratification and Mobility in the USSR* (White Plains: International Arts & Sciences Press, 1973); G.W. Lapidus, *Women in Soviet Society: Equality, Development and Social Change* (Berkeley: University of California Press, 1978); W.D. Connor, *Socialism, Politics and Equality* (New

York: Columbia University Press, 1979); A. McAuley, *Economic Welfare in the Soviet Union: Poverty, Living Standards, and Inequality* (Madison: University of Wisconsin Press, 1979).

97. M. Djilas, *The New Class* (New York: Praeger, 1957), p. 36.
98. I. Deutscher, *The Prophet Outcast* (London; Oxford University Press, 1963), p. 467.
99. L. Trotsky, *In Defence of Marxism* (London: New Park Publications, 1966), p. 11.
100. Deutscher, *The Prophet Outcast*, p. 468.
101. Ibid., p. 467.
102. Ibid.
103. Trotsky, *In Defence of Marxism*, p. 11.

6

Radicalism or Reformism: The Sources of Working-Class Politics

From my work on my doctoral dissertation down to the present, I have been interested in the problem of "American exceptionalism."[1] That curious phrase emerged from the debate in the international Communist movement in the 1920s concerning the sources of the weakness of left-wing radical movements in the United States.[2] The key question repeatedly raised in this context has been, is America qualitatively different from other industrial capitalist countries? Or, to use Sombart's words, "Why is there no socialism in the United States?"[3]

Elsewhere, I have evaluated the hypotheses advanced by various writers from Karl Marx onward to explain the absence of an effective socialist party on the American political scene.[4] If any of the hypotheses are valid, they should also help to account for the variation among working-class movements in other parts of the world. In this article, therefore, I shall reverse the emphasis from that in my book and look at socialist and working-class movements comparatively, applying elsewhere some of the propositions that have been advanced to explain the American situation.

A comparative analysis of working-class movements in western society is limited by an obvious methodological problem; too many variables and too few cases. The causal factors that have been cited as relevant literally approach two dozen. Among them are economic variables, such as the timing of industrialization, the pace of economic growth, the concentration of industry, the occupational structure, the nature of the division of labor, and the wealth of the country; sociological factors, such as the value system (collectivist versus individualist orientations), the status systems (open or rigid), social mobility, religious differences, ethnic variations, rates of immigration, and urbanization; and political variables, such as the timing of universal suffrage, of political rights, and of freedom of organization, the electoral systems, the extent of centralization, the size of the country, orientations of conservative parties, and the nature of the welfare systems in the country concerned.

Obviously, it would be well nigh hopeless to compare systematically western countries on all of the relevant variables.[5] To limit the task to manageable proportions, I will concentrate on variations in national environments that determined what Stein Rokkan called "the structure of political alternatives" for the working class in different western countries before the First World War. Although much has changed since then, the nature of working-class politics has been profoundly influenced by the variations in the historic conditions under which the proletariat entered the political arena. Experiences antedating the First World War affected whether workers formed class-based parties and, where such parties developed, whether they were revolutionary or reformist.

Of the factors that shaped the character of working-class movements, two are particularly important: first, the nature of the social-class system before industrialization; second, the way in which the economic and political elites responded to the demands of workers for the right to participate in the polity and the economy.[6]

With respect to the first, the following general proposition is advanced: the more rigid the status demarcation lines in a country, the more likely the emergence of radical working-class-based parties. Where industrial capitalism emerged from a feudal society, with its emphasis on strong status lines and barriers, the growing working class was viewed as a *Stand*, a recognizable social entity. As Max Weber emphasized, *Staende*, or "*status groups* are normally communities" defined by particular lifestyles, claims to social honor, and social intercourse among their members; as such they provide the direct basis for collective activity. In this respect, they differ from economic classes whose members share a common market situation, for " ' classes' are not communities, they merely represent possible, and frequent, bases for communal action."[7] Nations characterized by an elaborate, highly institutionalized status structure, *combined* with the economic class tensions usually found in industrial societies, were more likely to exhibit class-conscious politics than those in which status lines were imprecise and not formally recognized. In contrast, in nations that were "born modern" and lacked a feudal and aristocratic past, class position was less likely to confer a sense of shared corporate identity.[8]

The second proposition maintains that the ways in which the dominant strata reacted to the nascent working-class movements conditioned their orientations. Where the working class was denied full political and economic citizenship, strong revolutionary movements developed.[9] Conversely, the more readily working-class organizations were accepted into the economic and political order, the less radical their initial and subsequent ideologies.[10]

This proposition subsumes a number of subpropositions: (1) The denial of political rights in a situation in which a social stratum is led to claim such rights will increase its feelings of deprivation and increase the likelihood of a favorable response to revolutionary and extremist doctrines. (2) The existence of political rights will tend to lead governments and conservative political forces to conciliate the lower classes, thus enhancing the latter's sense of self-respect, status, and efficacy. (3) The development of political parties, trade unions, and other workers' organizations permits the most politically active members of the working class to increase their income, status, and power and in the process to become a privileged group within society and a force for political moderation. (4) A capable lower-class stratum that has been allowed to develop legitimate economic and political organizations, through which it can achieve some share of power in the society and improve its social situation, is potentially less radical in a crisis situation than a comparable stratum that has been unable to develop institutionalized mechanisms for accommodating political demands.

In the remainder of this chapter, I will present the evidence that substantiates these generalizations, beginning with variations in social status.

Status Systems

The proposition that rigid status systems are conducive to the emergence of radical working-class movements may be illustrated by contrasting the development of workers' parties in North America and Europe. In countries such as the United States and Canada, which did not inherit a fixed pattern of distinct status groups from feudalism, the development of working-class political consciousness, the notion of belonging to a common "class" with unique interests, required an act of intellectual imagination. In Europe, however, workers were placed in a common class by the stratification system.[11] In a sense, workers absorbed a "consciousness of kind" from their ascribed position in the social structure. As Val Lorwin notes: "Social inequality was as provoking as economic injustice. Citizens of a country that has not passed through a feudal age cannot easily imagine how long its heritage conditions social attitudes."[12]

The early socialists were aware of the problem that the lack of a feudal tradition in the United States posed for them. In 1890, Friedrich Engels argued that Americans are "born conservatives—just because America is so purely bourgeois, so entirely without a feudal past."[13] The Austrian-born American socialist leader, Victor Berger, also accounted for the weakness of socialism as a result of the fact that "the feeling of class-distinction in America . . . has not the same historic foundation that it has in Germany, France, or England. There the people were accustomed for over a thousand years to have distinct classes and castes fixed by law."[14] In 1906, H. G. Wells, then a Fabian, explained the absence in America of two English parties, Conservative and Labour, in terms of the absence of a "medieval heritage" of socially dominant and inferior strata.[15]

The absence of feudalism in the United States and Canada, as well as in Australia and New Zealand, sharply differentiated the working-class movements in these countries from those on the European continent. In North America, socialist parties were either very weak (the United States) or emerged late and remained small (Canada), while in Australia and New Zealand, working-class labor parties have always been much less radical than most of the socialist parties of continental Europe.

Still, the early existence of a powerful Labor party in Australia may seem to challenge the hypothesis that the absence of feudalism and aristocracy undermines class-conscious politics on the part of workers.[16] The pattern of politics in Australia, however, was profoundly influenced by the fact that it was largely settled by nineteenth-century working-class immigrants from industrial Britain, who brought the strong class awareness of the mother country with them.[17]

Many Australian immigrants had been involved in Chartist and similar working-class movements in Britain.[18] Hence, Australia imported the class values of the working class of the mother country. The emergence of class politics in Australia, in contrast with the North American pattern, also reflects the fact that the rural frontier in the Antipodes was highly stratified with sharp divisions between the owners of large farms and a numerous farm labor population.[19] But despite strong class feelings, which facilitated the emergence of a powerful labor party, it was not Marxist, and hardly socialist or otherwise radical.[20]

The case of New Zealand was somewhat different. Less urbanized than Australia, with a larger proportion of small, family-owned farms, its early British-derived two-party system of Liberals and Conservatives resembled that of the United States. The Liberals appealed to the small holders and the workers. The Labour party was weak until the post–World War I period. As in Britain, anti-union legislation induced the unions to try to elect Labour candidates. After having achieved the position of a strong third party in the 1920s, the New Zealand Labour party won power in 1935, capitalizing on the discontents of the Depression. Its electoral program in that year was characterized "by the omission of socialism and the substitution of measures which revived the old Liberal tradition."[21]

In Europe, on the other hand, as Friedrich Engels noted, throughout the nineteenth century "the political order remained feudal."[22] Writing in 1892, he emphasized: "It seems a law of historical development that the bourgeoisie can in no European country get hold of political power—at least for any length of time. . . . A durable reign of the bourgeoisie has been possible only in countries, like America, where feudalism was unknown."[23]

As Joseph Schumpeter pointed out, in much of Europe, the nobility "functioned as a *classe dirigente*. . . . The aristocratic element continued to rule the roost *right to the end of the period of intact and vital capitalism.*"[24] More recently, Arno Mayer has brilliantly detailed the ways in which "the feudal elements retained a formidable place in Europe's authority systems," down to World War II.[25]

Although from the perspective of this chapter, the sharpest contrast in the political impact of varying status systems lies in the differences between the working-class movements of the English-speaking settler societies and those of continental Europe, there was great variation in the political behavior of the working classes within Europe that also may be related to differences in status systems.

Germany, whose socialist party was the largest in Europe before World War I, has frequently been cited as the prime example of an industrial society deeply influenced by the continuation of feudal and aristocratic values. Writing in the late 1880s, Engels stressed that Germany was "still haunted by the ghosts of the feudal Junker" and that it was "too late in Germany for a secure and firmly founded domination of the bourgeoisie."[26] Max Weber pointed to the continued emphasis on "feudal prestige" in Imperial Germany in explaining the behavior of its social classes.[27] As Dahrendorf has noted: "If one wants to give the social structure of Imperial Germany a name, it would be a paradoxical one of an industrial feudal society."[28]

Many historians and social analysts have placed considerable emphasis on status differentiation in explaining the existence in Germany of numerous parties, each representing a particular status group and having a distinct ideology.[29] Skilled German workers and socialist leaders exhibited a stronger hostility to the lowest segments of the population than occurred in other western countries.[30] For most European socialist parties, all depressed workers, whether urban or rural, were a latent source of support. But for the German socialists, the lowest stratum was a potential enemy. Writing in 1892, in a major theoretical work, Karl Kautsky, the leading Social Democratic theorist, described the "slum proletariat" as "cowardly and unprincipled, . . . ready to fish in troubled waters . . . exploiting every revolution that has broken out, only to betray it at the earliest opportunity."[31]

The Austrian part of the Hapsburg Empire also retained major postfeudal elements into the twentieth century, as reflected in its electoral system, similar to that of Hohenzollern Prussia. Until 1895, the Austrian electorate was divided into separate entities—the aristocracy, chambers of commerce, cities, and rural districts, with the latter two being limited by property franchise. In 1895, a fifth class, all others, was added to give the poorer strata some limited form of representation. And, as in Germany, the socialist movement was radical and Marxist.

The strong support obtained by the Social Democrats in Sweden, culminating in the formation of the most durable majority socialist government in Europe, was deeply influenced by the strength of *Staendestaat* elements in the most status-bound society of northern Europe. Comparing the three Scandinavian countries at the end of the nineteenth century, Herbert Tingsten noted that "the Swedish nobility . . . still enjoyed considerable social prestige and acted partly as a rural aristocracy, partly as a factor in the bureaucratic machinery and officers' corps, [and] was far more numerous than the Danish . . . [while] in Norway there was no indigenous nobility."[32] The social structure of Sweden in this respect resembled that of Wilhelmine Germany. Class position has correlated more strongly with party choice in Sweden than in any other European country, a phenomenon that helped generate majority support for the Social Democrats.

The strength of the Finnish Socialists, who in 1916 formed the first majority labor-based government in Europe, also can be linked to the character of the class system. The Finns were exposed to the strong emphasis on status and aristocracy that characterized both Russian and Swedish culture.[33] Finland was a Grand Duchy under the Czar from 1809 on, and a small Swedish minority was predominant within the social and economic upper classes.[34] Before 1905, the Finnish Parliament was divided "into Four Estates or Houses: the Nobility, the Clergy, the Burghers, and the Peasantry. . . . Major cleavages formed along these status dimensions and tended to co-align and reinforce each other."[35]

The political history of Great Britain, however, would seem to contradict the hypothesis that radical class consciousness was encouraged by sharp status differentiation derived from a feudal past and the continued influence of aristocracy. Marxists, such as Friedrich Engels, emphasized the importance of status factors in accounting for the fact that in England, the major capitalist nation of the nineteenth century, "the bourgeoisie never held undivided sway." As he noted, the "English bourgeoisie are, up to the present day [1892] . . . deeply penetrated by a sense of their social inferiority . . .; and they consider themselves highly honoured whenever one of themselves is found worthy of admission into this select and privileged body" of the titled nobility.[36]

The emphasis on status clearly has had an impact on British working-class politics from the outset of the Industrial Revolution down to the post-World War II period. E. P. Thompson has stressed that in the early nineteenth century, "there was a consciousness of the identity of interests of the working class or 'productive classes,' as against those of other classes; and within this was maturing the claim for an alternative *system*."[37] Such consciousness presumably facilitated the emergence of Chartism, the strongest working-class movement in the first half of the nineteenth century, which mobilized workers in a militant class-conscious struggle for the suffrage and ultimately may have helped to create the strong correlation between class position and electoral choice that has characterized British politics since World War I. As Peter Pulzer put it: "Class is the basis of British party politics; all else is embellishment and detail."[38]

But socialist movements were much weaker in Britain than in most Continental countries in the late nineteenth and early twentieth centuries. The Labour Party, allied to the Liberals, did not become a factor in British politics until 1906, when it elected 30 members to Parliament, and it only secured major-party status after the First World War. This seeming anomaly is explained by analysts of British politics by the strength of *noblesse oblige* norms among the aristocracy, who consciously served as a "protective stratum" for workers by enacting factory reforms and welfare-state legislation, activities that won the support of the workers (to be discussed in more detail below).

In Latin countries such as France, Italy, and Spain, the strength of revolutionary labor movements (anarchist, syndicalist, left socialist, and later communist) on the one hand, and ultra-reactionary political tendencies among the middle and upper classes, on the other, has been related to the failure of these societies to develop a full-grown industrial system until after the Second World War. The aristocracies in these countries had declined in power by the late nineteenth century and did little to foster *noblesse oblige* welfare policies for the workers. At the same time, their business classes in the late nineteenth and early twentieth centuries were weakly developed and resembled a semifeudal stratum whose position was tied to family property.[38] Not withstanding the Revolution of 1789, the French social structure reflected, in Stanley Hoffman's words, a "feudal hangover . . . traditional Catholic doctrines (notably concerning the evils of capitalist accumulation) left their mark . . .; the bourgeoisie in many ways imitated the aristocracy.[40] As Val Lorwin emphasizes, writing about the bourgeoisie of France and Italy, "they flaunted inequalities by their style of living. Their class consciousness helped shape the class consciousness of workers."[41] This orientation, with its emphasis on family and its concern for the maintenance of explicit status lines, was associated with a profound antagonism to collective bargaining, labor legislation, and social security.

Strikingly, efforts to account for the moderate multiclass "people's party" orientations of the Belgian, Dutch, Swiss, and Danish labor and socialist movements have pointed to the weakness of feudal elements in these societies. Carl Landauer notes that Belgium had been much less of a *Staendestaat* than its neighbors.

> Belgium is a business country, with a weak feudal tradition—much weaker than in Germany, France, or Britain. . . . In Belgium, fewer upper-class people than elsewhere think that they owe it to their pride to resist the aspiration of

the underprivileged. . . . Even less than in Britain or France and certainly less than in Germany was exploitation motivated by the idea that the humble must be kept in their places.[42]

A similar thesis has been advanced by Hans Daalder for two other small European countries, the Netherlands and Switzerland. As he notes, in both, "the position of the nobility against that of burghers and independent peasants tended always to be weak and to grow weaker as capitalism expanded."[43] And writing of his native country, the Netherlands, Daalder points out that the historic "political, social and economic prestige" of the Dutch bourgeoisie, which dates back to preindustrial times, fostered conditions which "dampened working class militancy, and eased the integration of the working class into the national political community."[44]

Preindustrial Switzerland "was one of small farms, with no considerable estates or landed aristocracy." Erich Gruner cites a comment by a Swiss writer in the late 1860s that "the poor man felt himself less oppressed, since he had the satisfaction of having his freedom in the community (*Gemeinde*) and province (*Landsgemeinde*) and the pride that, he, himself, counted for as much as the richest factory owner, which gave him self-respect and let him raise his head high."[45] Factory and welfare legislation was enacted before 1900. Unlike the large German and Austrian Social Democratic parties, the small Swiss "Socialist movement . . . was on the extreme right wing of the Second International" before World War I.[46]

The labor and socialist movements of Denmark have been the most moderate in Europe.[47] One recent analyst of the Danish case notes that although the Social Democratic Party has been "the dominant force in Danish politics for the past half century," its pragmatic reformist orientation poses the same question as that raised for the United States: "Why is there no socialism in Denmark?" a question that can only be answered by reference to its past.[48] While the explanation for Denmark, as for the United States, must be multivariate, part of it would appear to be, as Herbert Tingsten has noted, that feudalism and the nobility were much less important in Denmark than in Germany and Sweden. And in Britain, "moral responses to the miseries that existed . . . [were] sufficient to preclude any revolutionary movement."[49]

The clearest discrepancy in the relationship between status systems and working-class politics outlined here occurred in Norway. There is consensus among students of Scandinavian society that Norway was less affected by feudalism and aristocratic status norms than the other northern countries.[50] Nevertheless, the major socialist movement in Norway decided in 1919 to join the Communist International and remained affiliated until 1923.

Analysts of Norwegian politics agree, however, that this development was an historic anomaly, an event response that was out of character with the

behavior of Norwegian workers, as evidenced by the fact that the link with
the Third International lasted only a few years. Norway appears to be "the
exception that proves the rule." The Norwegian labor and socialist movements
were weak and moderate until World War I. But the war, in conjunction with
the development of cheap hydro-electric power, resulted in a period of sudden
and very rapid industrialization and social dislocation, which created a large
segment of workers without political traditions or loyalties who were prone
to support of labor militancy and radicalism.[51] The bulk of Norwegian workers
were first organized at the time of the Russian Revolution and, as in many
other countries, were swept up in the enthusiasm for the Revolution. But
Norwegian socialism and trade unionism soon returned to the characteristic
pattern of social democratic moderation.[52] Thus, Norway fits the "pattern"
up to 1914 and from the mid-twenties on. Even during the Great Depression
of the 1930s, the Communists remained a weak party, securing less than 2
percent of the vote.

The Right to Participate

As emphasized at the outset, cross-national variations in working-class
political activity were also affected by differences in the extent to which the
proletariat was legally free to form class-based organizations and participate
in the economic and political life of their societies. The greater the duration
and intensity of state repression of working-class economic and political rights,
the more likely workers were to respond favorably to revolutionary doctrines.
As Max Weber concluded in his essay on the suffrage and democracy in
Germany, "All the might of the masses is directed *against* a state in which
they are only objects and not participants."[53]

The effect of participation may best be illustrated by examining the two
principal paths by which the members of the working classes were accepted
into the fabric of societies as political and economic citizens. The first involves
their right to vote and to organize political parties that could play a constructive
role in the polity; the second refers to the way working-class economic combinations, in the form of labor unions, were accepted as formally legitimate
by the state and substantively legitimate by employers.

The absence of these rights throughout Europe for much of the nineteenth
century emphasized the inferior status of the workers and peasants.[54] The
political organization of much of premodern Europe was based on functional
representation by Estate or *Stand*.[55] The lower classes, including the emerging
proletariat, were not accepted as an Estate worthy of representation. And the
parliaments of many European countries—Austria, Finland, Prussia, and
Sweden, among others—were composed of members elected by the more
privileged *Staende*. Some eventually created a new Estate for the outcaste

groups. Thus their Constitutions legitimated the fixed hierarchical status orders. The contradiction between such patterns of hierarchical representation and the universalistic norms of capitalism and liberalism fostered efforts to secure plebiscitarian electoral systems, one man, one vote, as well as struggles for the right of free association, particularly for trade unions. The fight for the vote and the right to organize were perceived in terms of opposition to hierarchical class role, as part of a broad struggle for equality.[56]

The importance of the early granting of democratic rights for political activity has been emphasized by social analysts and historians in numerous contexts. T. H. Marshall, for one, noted that extreme ideologies initially emerged among new strata, in particular the bourgeoisie and working class, as they fought for the political and social rights of citizenship.[57] Along these lines, many writers concerned with the question of "why no socialism in America?" have pointed to the early enfranchisement of the white working class as an important causal factor. Selig Perlman made this argument in *The Theory of the Labor Movement* when he suggested that a major cause of the lack of class consciousness among American workers

> was the free gift of the ballot which came to labor at an early date as a by-product of the Jeffersonian democratic movement. In other countries where the labor movement started while workingmen were still denied the franchise, there was in the last analysis no need for a theory of "surplus value" to convince them that they were a class apart and should therefore be "class conscious." There ran a line like a red thread between the laboring class and the other classes. Not so, where the line is only an economic one.[58]

This view was shared by Lenin, who maintained that the weakness of socialism in America and Britain before World War I stemmed from "the absence of any at all big, nation-wide *democratic* tasks facing the proletariat."[59] Other countries, in which manhood suffrage and full democratic rights were secured in the nineteenth century, such as Australia, Canada, Denmark, and Switzerland, were also resistant to efforts to create strong socialist parties.

Conversely, the denial of the suffrage proved to be a strong motive for class political organization in many European nations. The first major British labor movement, Chartism, was centered on the struggle for the vote. In some countries, general strikes were called by workers to force through a change in the electoral laws (Austria, 1896 and 1905; Finland, 1905; Belgium, 1902 and 1913; and Sweden, 1902). The struggle for suffrage often had a quasi-religious fervor and was viewed by its advocates as the key to a new and more egalitarian society, since the poor outnumbered the rich and would presumably secure a radical redistribution of income and opportunity if they had the necessary political rights. The existence of a limited franchise based on property made it clear to workers that political power and economic privilege were closely related. The withholding of the franchise often became a symbol of the position of workers as a deprived and pariah group. A restricted franchise encouraged the ideologists of both unfranchised and privileged groups to analyze politics in terms of class power.

The exclusion of workers from the fundamental political rights of citizenship effectively fused the struggle for political and economic equality and cast that struggle in a radical mold. Thus, a large number of European socialist movements grew strong and adopted a radical Marxist ideology while the working class was still unfranchised or was discriminated against by an electoral system that was explicitly class or property biased. Such was the history of Austria, Germany, Finland, and Sweden, among others.

The variations in legal rights that influenced the character of working-class politics also helped to determine the relationship of trade unions to labor parties in different nations.[60] Where both trade-union rights and male suffrage existed at an early date, the unions and the workers as a social force were able to press for political objectives by working with one or more of the non-socialist parties. And even when labor parties emerged, they did not adopt radical objectives.

As Gary Marks has noted in his study of trade-union political activity:

> Where trade unions were firmly established before party-political mobilization was underway, the resulting party had to adapt itself to an already "formed" working class with its cultural ties and institutional loyalties. Unlike the parties that were established before the rise of trade unions, these parties could not integrate the working classes into a singular, inclusive, and politically oriented sub-culture of radical or revolutionary resistance against capitalism. In this important respect, then, the Social Democratic Party, the early guardian and shaper of trade unionism in Germany, stands opposite the British Labour Party, which, in Ernest Bevin's telling phrase, "has grown out of the bowels of the T.U.C."[61]

Labor unions in the English-speaking countries became legitimate pressure groups oriented to pragmatic and immediate economic goals.[62] They were involved in many of the nonideological issues of the day, such as protection versus free trade, and immigration policies. Some of the more left or liberal non-socialist bourgeois parties supported social legislation desired by labor unions.

In those countries in which the trade union movement created a labor party, such as Australia and Britain, the original radical socialist promotion groups had comparatively little influence. The dominant working-class parties were controlled by trade unions and followed a pragmatic non-Marxian ideology. Socialists remained a comparatively small pressure group within these organizations or sought to build their own parties outside the labor parties.

In nations where the state repressed economic combination, unions were faced with a common and overriding task, that of changing the rules of the game. The more intensive and longer lasting the state repression, the more drastic the consequences. Where the right to combine in the labor market was severely restricted, as it was in Germany, Austria, Russia, France, Spain, and Italy, the decision to act in politics was forced on trade unions. Whether they liked it or not, unions became political institutions; they had first to change the distribution of political power within the state before they could effectively exert power in the market. At the same time, extreme state repression or employer opposition minimized the ability of privileged groups of skilled workers to improve their working conditions in a sectional fashion. In this important respect, then, repression fostered socialist or anarchist ideologies that emphasized the common interests of all workers.

Where fundamental economic rights were denied to workers, strong radical organizations were established before unions were well developed. This meant that the parties formulated their ideologies in the absence of pressures for pragmatic policies from trade unions.

Where the working class was deprived of both economic and political rights, those who favored social change were necessarily revolutionary. The identification of state repression with privileged and powerful groups reinforced political ideologies that conceived of politics in demonological terms. Perhaps the most important example of this pattern was Czarist Russia. There, every effort to form legal trade unions or establish a democratic parliamentary regime was forcibly suppressed. This situation provided the ground for revolutionary lower-class political movements under the leadership of intellectuals or others of middle- or upper-class origin.

Although the goals of party and union tend to differ when both are tolerated by the state, under repression there is much less space for diversity. Both share the task of changing the political status quo. As Lenin observed in the context of Czarist Russia:

> . . . the yoke of the autocracy appears . . . to obliterate all distinctions between a Social-Democratic organization and trade unions, because *all* workers' associations and *all* circles are prohibited, and because the principal manifestation and weapon of the workers' economic struggle—the strike—is regarded as a criminal (and sometimes even as a political) offense.[63]

The Leninist concept of the "combat party," with its reliance on secrecy and authoritarian discipline and its emphasis on the "conquest of power," developed as a reaction to the political situation of the time.

The situation in Finland also illustrates the interrelated effect of status and political factors on working-class politics. As in other areas of the Czarist Empire, manhood suffrage and trade-union rights did not exist. The Finnish

Socialist party, formed at the end of the nineteenth century, appealed to the class discontents of the newly emerging working class and the much larger farm tenant population. The Socialists addressed themselves to the overlapping issues of class, democratic rights, cultural and linguistic identity, and national independence. This meant both that the movement was initially more revolutionary in its ideology than the parties in the other northern countries, and that it could successfully appeal for support outside the ranks of the small urban working class.[64] Once manhood suffrage was won, as a result of the General Strike throughout the Czarist Empire in 1905, the Finnish Socialists secured 40 percent of the seats in Parliament, more than any other European party up to that time. Their parliamentary support grew to 43 percent in 1910, 45 percent in 1913, and to over 50 percent in 1916.[65] The trade-union movement, however, was faced with government restrictions and with strong resistance from employers and remained very weak until the Russian Revolution.[66] The continued strength of Finnish Communism down to the present stems in large part from the commitment to radical Marxist ideology fostered by the Finnish Socialists during the period of Czarist and Swedish minority domination.[67]

In Germany, to be discussed in more detail below, the continued domination of the Reichstag by traditional conservative forces, the absence of a democratic franchise in Prussia, and the strong repressive measures taken by Bismarck against the socialists in the 1870s and 1880s, bound the socialists and the trade unions formed by them into a distinct subculture having an explicitly revolutionary ideology.[68] In practice, of course, as Robert Michels and many other contemporary observers argued, the bureaucracy of the party gradually became conservative and opposed any measures that threatened its organizational stability. Nevertheless, the position of the labor movement as a semilegitimate opposition group helped to perpetuate its use of radical terminology.[69]

In Austria, as in Germany, the intransigence of the upper class had a decisive influence on the character and ideology of the working-class movement. Anti-Socialist laws were in effect from 1866 to 1881, and a special law repressed the workers' party in many regions from 1881 to 1891.[70] The party and the unions, which cooperated closely in the struggle for the suffrage, adhered to a radical class-conscious ideology. Manhood suffrage for parliamentary elections was only attained in 1907.[71]

The achievement of this political goal, followed by a sharp increase in parliamentary representation, however, served to undermine the cohesion and radicalism of the workers' movement. As G. D. H. Cole notes, ''the very success of the Austrians in winning the vote necessarily weakened their sense of the need for close unity. The main plank in their common programme having been withdrawn, it was none too easy to find another to take its place.

Now that they had become an important parliamentary party the emphasis tended to shift to the struggle for social and economic reforms, especially for improved labour laws regulating conditions of employment and the development of social services on the German model. But these were poor substitutes because they tended to change the Socialist Party into a reformist party.''[72]

The Socialist party and the trade unions continued to make significant progress after the defeat and breakup of the Hapsburg monarchy in World War I. Such a situation should have resulted in the development of working-class political and labor movements integrated into the body politic, and a further moderation of their ideology in the direction of the British and Scandinavian patterns. In fact, this did not occur. But the responsibility did not lie with the Austrian labor movement. Rather, the Austrian conservatives, whose support was based on the rural population and business elements, and who were tied closely to the Catholic church, aristocracy, and monarchism, refused to accept the rising status of labor. Faced with rebuffs from the conservatives, the church, and the business strata, the socialists responded by adhering to Marxian class-war principles. Within the Socialist International, the Austrian party was considered to be on the far left before it was suppressed in 1934.

The political development of the working class in Switzerland contrasts sharply with that in Germany and Austria. The gradualist emphasis of the predominantly German-speaking Swiss Social Democrats not only reflects the marked difference between the status systems of Switzerland and those of Prussia and Austria, noted earlier, but also the fact that universal manhood suffrage was introduced in many cantons by 1848. Thus, as in the United States, Swiss workers never had to engage in a struggle for the vote.[73] As Christopher Hughes, emphasizes, by the last quarter of the nineteenth century, the workers ''had the fullest political rights, cantonal power was entirely within their reach. . . . The direct democracy of the referendum (or the *Landsgemeinde*) was available after 1875. . . . The normal political processes . . . seemed to place power in the hands of 'the people.' ''[74] As early as 1877, the Swiss electorate approved a referendum proposal regulating work conditions in factories.[75] Swiss trade unions, although legal, faced severe conflicts with the government in the years preceding World War I, a fact that enabled ''left-wing tendencies . . . to gain ground'' within them.[76] In this period, the unions stood considerably to the left of the party. The party, however, also briefly moved to the left during the First World War when it rejected the pro-war stance taken by the European parties in most of the war-torn countries. Both unions and party returned to their former moderate course during the 1920s.

The three Scandinavian countries, Denmark, Norway, and Sweden, varied considerably both in their status systems and the timing of the institutionalization of manhood suffrage, factors that affected the degree of radicalization of their working-class movements before World War I.[77] By 1898, the percentage of all adult males who had the right to vote was 86 in Denmark and 91 in Norway; the figure for Sweden was only 25.[78] Denmark had "moved straight into a system of nation-wide elections under a very extensive manhood suffrage in 1849" which gave almost three-quarters of men over thirty the right to vote.[79] The Social Democratic Party, established in 1871, "was born reformist and committed to the parliamentary road to power. . . . Its moderation was probably due to the comparative ease of access that the liberal franchise afforded the industrial working class in Denmark and to the availability of bourgeois parties with which it could cooperate."[80] The allegiance with the bourgeois left parties involved cooperation in Parliament to attain various economic and welfare measures. Danish labor organizations secured greater legitimation than any other in Europe when in 1899 the employers' federation and the unions "agreed to attempt, whenever possible, to settle their affairs by peaceful collective bargaining." The already strong unions continued thereafter to make economic gains and to become "among the best paid and strongly organized in Europe."[81]

In Norway, the least industrialized of the three Scandinavian countries before World War I, the Socialists were weak electorally, even following the enactment of male suffrage in 1898, and cooperated closely with bourgeois parties, first the Liberals and later the Radicals. Pre-World War I "Norwegian Socialism resembled the Danish movement. . . . It was mildly reformist in character."[82]

Unlike the situation in the other Scandinavian countries, Sweden's privileged classes resisted democratization until the first decade of the twentieth century. Although election to four Estates was abolished in 1866, the new system provided for a lower house chosen by a very restrictive income and property franchise.[83] The absence of a broad suffrage pressed the Social Democratic party, founded in 1889, to concentrate on the struggle for the vote and encouraged the use of radical class-struggle rhetoric and tactics. The partial franchise fostered an anarchist movement, syndicalism, and antiparliamentary groupings inside the Social Democratic party. As Walter Galenson notes, "contributing to early socialist radicalism was the great conservatism of the society, the late introduction of the universal franchise, and the opposition on the part of large Swedish employers to trade unionism."[84] Although the party became more moderate ideologically following the attainment of adult male suffrage for elections to the lower House in 1909, it continued to emphasize its adherence to Marxism until the First World War.[85] The

Social Democrats were welcomed as an ally and potential coalition partner by the great bourgeois party, the pro-suffrage Liberals, with whom they were to form a wartime government in 1917. But as G. D. H. Cole notes, "even then, Swedish Socialism was still far from having acquired the status as an exponent of moderate Social Democracy which it won for itself in the period between the wars."[86]

The Dutch and Belgian cases were somewhat more complicated. Although, as noted earlier, the weakness of postfeudal status structures contributed to a relatively weak emphasis on class consciousness, full male suffrage came late to both countries. The proportion of adult males eligible to vote in the Netherlands was only one-quarter in 1890, rising after a change in the law to one-half in 1900, and to two-thirds by the start of World War I.[87] The Belgians enacted male suffrage in 1894, but on a weighted basis, giving extra votes to those with property.[88] The socialist parties of the Low countries, therefore, concentrated on securing equal voting rights for all males as an essential prerequisite to securing office.

The denial of adult suffrage resulted in some support in both nations in the late nineteenth century for anarchism, syndicalism, and left-wing socialism. But the involvement of the bourgeois Liberal parties in the struggle for a wider suffrage and opposition to church schools helped move the workers' movements to the right. The socialists in each nation cooperated with the Liberals, a policy that was severely criticized by leftist parties elsewhere.[89] With the widening of the electorate and the expansion of Social Democratic representation before the Great War, the socialists in the Low countries tended toward reformism and seriously entertained proposals to form coalition governments with the Liberals.[90]

Dutch workers were in a more favorable position with respect to economic rather than political rights. The government did not oppose their right to organize unions or to strike after the repeal of an antistrike law in 1872. And as Lijphart notes, "Partly as a result of the benevolent attitude of the government, the many unions that were set up from about 1870 on, tended to be moderate in their demands and actions." The socialist union center (N.V.V.) eclipsed its anarcho-syndicalist rival and remained reformist politically in spite of considerable labor conflict in the pre–World War I and interwar eras.[91]

In analyzing the relationship between economic and political rights and working-class political behavior, I have thus far dealt primarily with formal rights, that is, whether adult suffrage existed, and whether trade unions could function without serious legal difficulties. In fact, however, legal rights were only partial indicators of the will and capacity of the upper and business classes to resist the emergence of the working class as a political force. The right to vote or organize unions did not necessarily mean that labor had acquired a legitimate place in society, or that the pressures toward radicalism flowing from the position of the worker as political outcast had disappeared.

It is possible to distinguish among three situations: total repression, legal existence but constant conflict (i.e., *de jure* but not *de facto* recognition), and *de jure* and *de facto* recognition. The existence of the first two conditions usually indicates that the business classes still desire to destroy the organized expression of the labor movement. Under such conditions, labor may be expected to react strongly against capitalism and, perhaps, the existing political system as well.

France before World War II, Spain before 1975, and pre-fascist Italy are examples of nations where unions were weak because the business and conservative classes refused to grant *de facto* recognition to them. The consequences of this for union strategy have been recognized by Fred Ridley:

> There is a close relationship between weak, unorganised labour movements and the outbreak of revolutionary or anarchist activity in Russia, Spain and Italy, as well as in France. The unions had little bargaining power when it came to across-the-table negotiations with employers; they had neither the membership nor the organisation with which to impress. Lack of funds, inability to pay strike benefits, meant that they could not hope to achieve their ends by ordinary peaceful strikes. They were thus forced to play for quick results: violence, intimidation and sabotage were the obvious weapons to choose.[92]

In much of Latin Europe, both the state and employers denied legitimacy to trade unions, i.e., their right to become the institutionalized representatives of workers, although in France manhood suffrage existed in the 1870s and in Spain from 1889. In France the Socialist party was able to gain electoral strength before unions were well developed. The party, however, had little success in fostering social legislation or trade-union organizations, given "the ferocity of bourgeois response to it."[93] In countries where a wide franchise failed to provided "an effective lever in the hands of the masses, such 'democratic' reforms could paradoxically develop into a measure of plebiscitary control over them. This could result in an enduring alienation of sizable sections of the population rather than in their permanent integration in an effectively responsive political system."[94]

The French trade-union movement continued to face strong resistance from the state and the business class, both of which refused to grant unions a legitimate role as bargaining agents in the economy. The unions required a revolutionary ideology to motivate membership and leadership participation and thus sustain their organization. They found this ideology in syndicalism. As a number of historians have suggested, syndicalism, with its faith in violence and in worker spontaneity, was not merely an impractical flight of idealism, but a response to constraints that served to limit the alternatives facing unions. Ridley has noted:

> The law forced the workers into opposition to the state; in a measure, indeed, it persuaded them to reject the state altogether. Its provisions, biased heavily in favour of the employer, excluded the worker from its benefits and left him to all intents an outcast—*hors due pays légal*. The syndicalist doctrine of autonomy, the insistence that the labour movement must develop outside the state and create its own institutions to replace it, can be understood in the light of its experience.[95]

Distrust of parliamentary government and a strong emphasis on syndicalist and revolutionary class organization developed in Spain and Italy as well. As noted, Spain introduced universal male suffrage relatively early. But the government "continued to manage elections as it pleased, to the extent of deciding centrally who were to be elected, not only for its own party, but also to represent the recognized opposition groups."[96] In the big cities, it counted the ballots; in small towns and rural areas, the "caciques," local bosses, controlled.[97] In Italy, the Liberals, who dominated the government in the late nineteenth and early twentieth centuries, rigged the election results among a more restricted electorate by a variety of corrupt practices, comparable to those used in Spain. "These practices . . . left a heritage of cynicism, highly politicized administrative machinery, corruption, and the absence of civic pride and of vital local government."[98] The expansion of the suffrage in 1912 was followed by an election in which the governing Liberals added to corrupt practices a heavy "dose of violence to ensure success."[99]

In both countries, trade union organizations were harassed by state institutions that claimed to represent the electorate democratically. Because unions were weak, the conditions for the emergence of a genuine working-class leadership were absent. Consequently, intellectuals or other upper-class radicals came to dominate the labor movement. The weakness and instability of trade unions also resulted in few achievements that could legitimate gradualist and pragmatic goals. As Juan Linz notes with respect to Spain:

> The bitterness of class conflict that ultimately led to semirevolutionary general strikes, local or regional insurrections . . . should not hide the fact that the labor movement was weak by comparison with other countries. Spanish labor lacked numbers, organizational and economic resources for strikes, success at the polls, and capacity for nationwide activities.[100]

In Italy and Spain, as in France, the business classes continually resisted coming to terms with the trade union movement. Although unions had *de jure* recognition, the history of labor in these countries was characterized by constant warfare. Revolutionary syndicalism was strong in each country.[101]

In Italy, syndicalism gained strength as a reaction to the repeated suppression of local strikes and popular protest movements that often involved the use of violence.[102] In Spain, anarchism grew in response to "alternate periods of legal toleration and savage repression."[103] This pattern culminated in the triumph of authoritarianism in both Italy and Spain and the establishment of regimes that were primarily oriented toward maintaining the economic and class status quo. And as in France, the working class and its leaders responded by supporting extremist doctrines. Thus, in Spain, moderate socialism was relatively weak, whereas doctrines such as revolutionary socialism, anarchism, and even Trotskyism were strong. In Italy, anarchism and left socialism were influential before Mussolini, and moderate socialism, even today, remains relatively weak; the bulk of the working class supports the Communist party.

It is also worth noting that both Spain and Italy were industrially backward societies in the late nineteenth century when radical working-class movements emerged. Like fascism itself, anarchism has been viewed as an antimodern doctrine, a reaction against the strains of modernity.[104] In this context, it should be noted that in France, too, syndicalism was strongest among craft workers in small-scale industries that were most threatened by industrialization and mass production.

The adoption of an anarchist or syndicalist political ideology had specific and identifiable consequences for trade-union movements. Syndicalism committed them to a loose, unstable, and relatively unbureaucratic organization. This structure, in turn, required the unions and their leaders to stress ideology at the expense of building loyalty on the basis of concrete gains achieved through collective bargaining. It also reduced those inhibitions on militant action that result from the need to protect an established structure.

In discussing the denial of legitimacy to socialists and trade unions, I have focused primarily on the influence this had on their activities and ideologies. But, obviously, the relationship is not a simple cause-and-effect one. The behavior of the left had its effect on the right. In particular, one should not ignore that France, Italy, Spain, and Austria are Catholic, which meant that the traditional struggle between the left and right was not solely, or even primarily, an economic class struggle but also was a confrontation between Catholicism and atheism or secularism. Many of the Catholic conservative leaders viewed the battle against Marxism and working-class institutions as part of the fight for their religion. To accept the legitimacy of a working-class movement that was Marxist and irreligious involved a much greater modification in their value systems than was necessary in situations where religious values were not involved, as in Britain and Australia.

In the Catholic societies of Western Europe, the church, in alliance with landed interests, attempted to establish trade unions and political organizations to counter the influence of socialism among the lower classes. The result was the "pillarization" of the working class into mutually antagonistic Catholic and socialist tendencies. In France, Italy, Spain, and Austria, socialist parties not only were rejected by the ruling powers, they were also opposed by a major segment of the working class. Both of these factors furthered the development of radical movements. Reformism tended to be more typical of working-class politics and unions in countries where labor was powerfully represented by unitary organizations that were accepted into the political and economic mainstream.[105]

Efforts at Integration: Britain and Germany

The previous discussion indicates that radical ideologies were strongest where social and political groups attempted to reduce or destroy the influence of leftist or working-class movements by refusing them legitimacy and continually fighting them. In countries in which the working class was incorporated into the body politic at an early date, the chances that workers would come to support extremist or revolutionary doctrines were considerably reduced.

The American experience clearly illustrates the consequences for working-class movements of integration into society. There the absorption occurred as a result of social structures, values, and events that predated industrial society. The European experience offers insights into the effects of deliberate efforts to win the allegiance of the working class. An examination of Great Britain and Germany is particularly informative because in both countries, sections of the ruling strata consciously sought to reduce the class antagonism of the workers by accommodating their demands; yet the attempt succeeded in Britain and failed in Germany.

The conventional explanation of why Marxism is weak in Britain suggests that the landed aristocracy and their party, the Tories, who retained considerable power in nineteenth-century Britain, sought to stem the growing power and ideology of the rising industrial business class by winning the allegiance of the "lower orders." In their opposition to the new capitalist society and in a desire to preserve past institutions and values, Conservatives, led by Disraeli, often took the same position as the spokesmen of the working classes. As Hearnshaw points out:

> The "young England" Tories [which Disraeli joined] . . . with their curious affection for an idealized feudalism and chivalry, had much in common with the Chartists and other proletarian reformers of the early Victorian days. With them they deplored and resented the operation of the new poor law of 1834; they opposed the principles of laissez-faire; they hated the new machinery and the hideous mills in which it was housed; they protested the repeal of the usury

laws and the corn laws; they distrusted the new stock-jobbers and the joint-stock bankers . . . [their] principles flowed naturally from the mainstream of the conservative tradition.[106]

The Tories, however, maintained a traditional view of the relationship between rich and poor, one that was based on an idealization of class relations as they existed in pre-industrial society. They assumed that the lower classes should remain ''dependent'' on the upper class and that the latter, in turn, should be responsible for the welfare of the lower strata.

Some of the leaders of the aristocratic upper classes were able to perceive the extent to which the new industrial workers—despite occasional violent protest actions and increasing class consciousness—shared their view of ''the good old days and the bad new days,'' and, more important, desired recognition and status within the existing order. Disraeli believed in the traditionalism of the lower classes. As Waisman notes, ''As early as 1840, he [Disraeli] had remarked: '. . . a union between the Conservative Party and the Radical masses offers the only means by which we can preserve the empire. Their interests are identical; united they form the nation.'''[107] He was able to secure the passage of the Electoral Reform Act of 1867 as well as some social legislation. To this must be added the relative freedom that British trade unions attained in the last quarter of the nineteenth century, especially through the labor laws of 1875. The facts of political life, plus the steadily rising standard of living, demonstrated to workers and their leaders that it was possible to improve their position within British society. Both the Tories and Liberals formed workingmen's associations.

The reformist policies of British politicians in the late nineteenth and early twentieth centuries helped to integrate workers into the national community, to reduce their hostility to existing political institutions (the state, the throne, and the major parties), and to adopt gradualist rather than revolutionary methods. Friedrich Engels noted that the absence of ''a separate political working-class party'' was to be expected ''in a country where the ruling classes have set themselves the task of carrying out, parallel with other concessions, one point of the Chartists' programme, the People's Charter, after another.''[108] Although a labor party gained strength in Britain in the early 1900s, following the Taff-Vale court decision that threatened the power of the trade unions, the leaders of the new movement did not view the other parties as class enemies who had to be eliminated. Rather, they conceived of a separate labor party as an electoral tactic, which would place labor in a better position to bargain with the older parties. The development of a stable, legitimate, labor movement created a stratum of working-class leaders who had secured position and power within the existing social system and consequently had close ties to it. The emergence of Fabianism as a political force in Britain is in large measure explicable by the fact that the Fabians, with their initial hope that the upper class could be converted to socialism, reflected the actual British historical experience of aristocratic intervention on behalf of the workers.

In Germany, a situation similar in certain important respects to that in Britain led to a comparable effort to integrate the lower classes into the society. The Prussian aristocracy as well as the Center Party, "which united federalist groups from all strata—aristocrats, priests, farmers and workers, most of them Catholics," sought to inhibit the influence of the rising bourgeoisie. Bismarck's refusal to "grant even the moderate demands of the liberals for more parliamentary rights" was based upon his judgement that the "bourgeoisie [was] incapable of holding its ground against the lower classes." However, Bismarck also believed "that the educated and propertied classes were the real support of the state" because the "masses were not responsible for themselves and easily fell prey to dictatorship."[109] On the other hand, Bismarck established universal suffrage in the federal empire after 1867 so that he could use the votes of the rural lower classes, and to a certain extent of the workers themselves, against the urban middle classes, who, he realized, would dominate in a restricted property-based suffrage.[110]

Unlike Disraeli and the British Tories, however, Bismarck had little confidence that the workers' organizations would become incorporated into the social order. This led him to outlaw the socialist movement in 1878 and to hope that by enacting social welfare measures advocated by the socialists he could win the loyalty of workers to the regime. The conservative *Sozialpolitik*, however, came too late. The workers had already begun to support the socialist movement; efforts to suppress it only served to undermine moderate representatives of the working class.[111] This act of repression is generally recognized to be one of the chief sources of the difference in the political development of the German and British working classes.[112]

Bismarck attempted to incorporate the proletariat by winning its loyalty to society without permitting workers to have their own organizations and leaders. By the time working-class political organization was legalized in 1890, the Social Democrats had acquired a revolutionary ideology that was difficult to discard even after the party had become a strong and stable movement, capable of antagonizing and frightening the middle and upper classes.[113]

The Bismarckian policies deeply affected the outlook and strategy of German workers. First, and most important, they placed Social Democracy in a paradoxical position. On the one hand, the party was successful: it grew steadily from one election to the next, attracted hundreds of thousands of members and employed a large bureaucracy. It gradually adapted itself to the role of a parliamentary opposition which anticipated coming to power through democratic means. On the other hand, however, the ideology that developed during and immediately following the period of repression gave it the appearance of being devoted to purely revolutionary ends and legitimized the agitation of extreme leftists within its ranks. (The party rewrote its program in 1891, after twelve years of overt repression, to emphasize its intransigence.) Until World War I, the SPD refused to repudiate its formal belief in class warfare. In large part, the subsequent strength of left-wing socialists and communists may be explained by the legitimacy the ideology of the Social Democratic party gave to such groups within the working-class.

Second, Bismarck's policies, and the socialists' ideological reactions to them, prevented the SPD from becoming a legitimate national party in the eyes of other political movements. The socialist revolutionary rhetoric may have prevented many of the middle-class, white-collar strata from supporting the party, while at the same time strengthening the potential for an alliance between the middle class and industrialists and large landowners.[114]

Third, Bismarck's "social revolution from above" included a number of welfare programs that in other countries had been the responsibility of the unions themselves and had helped to stabilize conservative unions. August Bebel, the leader of the Social Democratic party, pointed this out in a speech in 1893:

> In Germany, the state system of workingmen's insurance took away from the trade unions that branch of activity, and has in effect cut a vital nerve, as it were. For benefit systems had meant enormously in the furthering of unionism in Britain and among the German printers. Labor legislation has likewise preempted many other lines of activity which properly belong to the trade unions.[115]

The fact that the state, rather than the unions, controlled welfare funds and dictated policies, which elsewhere were handled through collective bargaining, served to increase the awareness of workers and their leaders of the need to influence state policy. The potential for a syndicalist antistatist doctrine was reduced, since conservative state intervention stimulated the belief that workers should take over and use the state system. The trade unions, far from becoming antistatist, became more statist in their orientation. But at the same time, the elimination of various trade-union functions weakened the loyalty of workers to the labor movement and reduced the stability of the unions, which denied them the role in maintaining political stability that unions in various other countries, particularly Britain, assumed.[116]

The effect of varying upper-class policies on the behavior of working-class movements can be illustrated within Germany as well as through international comparisons. As a number of political commentators have noted, the socialist movement in Prussia was quite different from that in southern Germany, especially Bavaria. In Prussia, which contained over half the population of the country, Bismarck pursued the same combination of repression and paternalism that he adopted for the federal empire. Prussia, a highly industrialized part of Germany, retained legal limits on the potential power of the workers even after the anti-Socialist laws were repealed. These restrictions were in the form of an electoral system based on three estates, which gave the middle classes and the landed nobility effective control over the Prussian legislature. The restrictions were, in large part, motivated by the fact that a purely democratic franchise would give a majority to the Socialists and the Catholic Zentrum, both anti-government parties. And as Kautsky noted in 1911, the working-class movement in Prussia gave much more emphasis to class-struggle doctrines.[117]

In the South, where governments were much less autocratic than in Prussia, in part because the old landed aristocracy was relatively unimportant and the rural and urban petty bourgeoisie proportionately stronger, the degree of political freedom was much greater. In Southern Germany, the Social Democrats cooperated with nonsocialist parties, in the process reducing their original emphasis on class struggle. The Revisionist doctrines of Eduard Bernstein were given their earliest and strongest support in the South. The Bavarian socialists, for example, broke with the tradition of the party and voted for the state budget.[118]

Bismarck failed in his effort to destroy German socialism through force. His refusal to incorporate the socialist political movement in a democratic parliamentary system helped to perpetuate revolutionary rhetoric. But the fact remains that the Social Democrats eventually became a stable, moderate, opposition party.[119] Its commitment to Marxism was largely aimed against the militarist imperial state.[120]

The failure of Bismarckian policy is evident in the rise of large movements on the left of the Social Democrats after World War I. The momentum for such movements emerged from the prewar contradiction between Social Democratic party behavior and ideology. Although support for the Communists declined in the late twenties, they made considerable headway in the early 1930s. In Britain, on the other hand, communism and fascism were weak and found no social roots.

The identification of varying British and German policies with Disraeli and Bismarck is not intended to suggest that the sharply divergent histories of the two countries may be credited to the wisdom of one and the stupidity of the other. Rather, as Barrington Moore has emphasized, the structural histories of the British and German aristocracies differed greatly. A combination of factors led the British upper classes to collaborate economically with the rising bourgeoisie and to set their peasants free. The landed aristocracy developed "bourgeois economic habits" and accepted parts of liberal political doctrine. In Germany, on the other hand, the aristocracy continued to preside over a "labor-repressive agrarian system" and to work with the monarchy and the "royal bureaucracy" rather than the business classes. This relationship produced, or rather reinforced, an emphasis on obedience and control from the top. Thus, the divergent policies of British and German upper-class conservatives reflected basic variations in their nations' social structures.[121]

Conclusion

In this chapter I have analyzed some of the ways in which the character of working-class movements has been influenced by the varying status systems of different societies and by the degree to which workers and their organizations were able to participate legitimately in the economic and political decision-making processes. In the United States, and to a lesser extent in Canada, the absence of an aristocratic or feudal past, combined with a history of political democracy prior to industrialization, served to reduce the salience of class-conscious politics and proposals for major structural change. As Walter Dean Burnham has emphasized: "No feudalism, no socialism: with these four words one can summarize the basic sociocultural realities that underlie American electoral politics in the industrial era."[122]

Conversely, in much of Europe, a "postfeudal" background was critical in shaping the political consciousness of the working class. As William Sewell, Jr. notes, "one of the most important roots of European class consciousness may have been the corporate cultural tradition of the pre-industrial European working class. This tradition made workingmen feel that their destiny was linked to that of their fellow workers, and predisposed them to collective, rather than individualistic, ideologies and modes of social and political action."[123]

The proletarian movements, born as *Staende*, adopted Marxism as their ideological cement and sought to achieve legitimation within the bourgeois order through constitutional reforms, the acquisition of citizenship. The emergence of radical politics originated as a consequence of the meshing of the hierarchical *Staende* with the inequalities of an emerging capitalist society differentiated into economic classes. Ironically, in trying to change the perception of the social hierarchy from *Stand* to class, radical working-class movements drew on and revitalized the sense of *Stand*-consciousness that they inherited. Many of the pre–World War I Social Democratic parties, as well as postwar Communist parties, also sustained corporative forms of group solidarity by creating a socially encapsulated working-class culture, in which their followers were involved in a plethora of party and union-related organizations.[124]

Where the corporate tradition broke down or never existed, what developed were interest-group organizations and ideologies. As Lenin and Perlman argued from contrary political perspectives, the orientation that stems from the class position of the proletariat is pure and simple trade unionism, or "economism,'' not revolutionary class consciousness. Against the background of Marxist theory, the outcome is paradoxical, for Marx and Engels maintained that the ''logic of capitalism'' would give rise to revolutionary movements, and that, to the degree that remnants of feudalism were removed and the victorious bourgeoisie established civic and political rights, class disparities would become the politically decisive facts engendering working-class consciousness and leading to proletarian revolution. The historical experience suggests that, with respect to the legacy of feudalism and political rights, the reasons for working-class radicalism were quite the opposite.

The impact of these variables is formalized in Table 6.1, which links the relationship between the social-class system and the rights to political and economic citizenship to the way in which workers responded in the decades before World War I. Table 6.1 illustrates both the weakness and strength of the type of comparative analysis undertaken here. The attempt to specify the kind of working-class movements that emerged under varying status systems and citizenship rights does not express the complexity of the phenomenon. Obviously, a static classification based on the dichotomization of three continuous variables cannot be expected to produce categories into which each national case fits through time. (For example, the United States and Denmark may both be classified as nonrigid status systems, although that of Denmark clearly has a greater continuity with a preindustrial corporate *Stand* tradition than the United States.)

The behavior of workers in Western societies before and after World War I was, of course, deeply affected by other variables, including the pace, extent, and shape of industrial development within their societies or how

TABLE 6.1
Outcomes of Different Combinations of Social-Class Patterns and Citizenship Rights before World War I

Economic citizenship	Political citizenship	Nonrigid	Rigid
Early	Early	Low political consciousness, weak interest-group unions (U.S.)	Low political consciousness, strong reformist unions (Britain)
Early	Late	Strong reformist parties and unions (Low countries)	Radical parties, strong pragmatic unions (Germany)
Late	Early	Weak reformist parties, radical unions (Switzerland)	Strong reformist parties, radical unions (France)
Late	Late		Revolutionary movements (Russia, Finland)

closely the objective social and economic situation "fit" the Marxist two-class model of an oppressive society. It is also important to recognize that these three factors are not independent of each other, although they may be distinguished analytically. Britain apart, the extension of postfeudal aristocratic power or values into the industrial era was associated with repressive political or economic patterns. And the British case may be explained by the fact that the aristocracy developed closer links to business than elsewhere. The emergence of democratic rights was in large measure tied to bourgeois hegemony. As Barrington Moore phrased it: "No bourgeois, no democracy."[125]

While the stress on the relationship between fundamental economic and political rights and the ideology of the labor movements is not meant to suggest that the character of contemporary movements is determined simply by their early history, the formative experiences did initiate certain trends or institutional patterns that took on a self-perpetuating character and hence affected ideology, structure, and political outcomes in later years.[126] Most of the countries in which workers found it difficult to attain economic or political citizenship before World War I were the ones in which fascist and communist movements were strong in the interwar period: Austria, Finland, France, Germany, Italy, and Spain. Currently, commitment to democratic institutions appears strong in Austria and Germany, but as Dahl notes, "it is untested by adversity."[127] Although declining in electoral strength, communist movements are still very influential among workers in Finland, France, and Italy. Spain, democratic since 1975, remains problematic.

Although formative experiences continue to have an impact on the contemporary body politic, particularly in distinguishing the European from the overseas settler societies, it is obvious that many of the differences discussed here no longer hold for present-day Europe. Apart from Britain, postfeudal elements have declined greatly or have disappeared in the industrialized countries. The economic miracle of prosperity and growth that followed World War II changed occupational structures, status systems, levels of income, and the distribution of educational attainments in ways that reduced many of the social strains characteristic of prewar industrial societies. Logically, in terms of the analysis presented here, which derives from the approaches of Max Weber and Joseph Schumpeter, the amount of class-related political conflict should be reduced as the dynamics of an industrial society undermine the status mechanisms inherited from the feudal precapitalist order. The imposition on the stratification system of capitalism's or industrial society's stress on achievement and universalism should weaken rather than increase class-linked consciousness of kind. And significantly, the correlations between class and party voting have been declining steadily.[128]

These changes, however, have given rise to new tensions reflective of an emerging postindustrial society. The new divisions can be understood as the most recent examples of the basic cleavages that structure comparative mass politics, systematically analyzed by Stein Rokkan.[129] I have discussed the character of these conflicts elsewhere and will not elaborate on them here.[130] But it is important to note that the prominence of so-called postmaterialist issues, such as quality of life, ecology, sexual equality, international relations, and ethnic rights, have changed the divisions between the left and right and have affected their bases of support. These new issues are linked to an increase in middle-class political radicalism and working-class social conservatism.

The working classes in western society no longer have to undergo repression. They have acquired economic and political citizenship. It is still possible, however, to relate the forms of present-day politics, particularly party labels and formal ideologies, to the emergence of new social strata in the formative period of modern politics. Should the western world experience a major crisis, it is likely that national politics will vary along lines that stem from the past, much as they did during the 1930s. Political scientists of the future, who seek to explain events in the last quarter of this century, will undoubtedly find important explanatory variables in earlier variations in the behavior of the major political actors.

Notes

1. S. M. Lipset, *Agrarian Socialism: The Cooperative Commonwealth Federation in Saskatchewan* (Berkeley: University of California Press, 1950 and 1968).
2. T. Draper, *American Communism and Soviet Russia* (New York: Viking, 1960), pp. 268–72; S. M. Lipset, "American 'Exceptionalism' in North American Perspective," in E. M. Adams (ed.), *The Idea of America* (Cambridge: Ballinger, 1977), pp. 107–61.
3. W. Sombart, *Why Is There No Socialism in the United States?* (London: Macmillan, 1976).
4. See S. M. Lipset, "Why No Socialism in the United States?," in S. Bialer and S. Sluzar (eds.), *Sources of Contemporary Radicalism* (Boulder, Colo.: Westview, 1977), pp. 31–149, 346–63, and chapter 4 of this volume.
5. H. Daalder, "Parties, Elites, and Political Developments in Western Europe," in J. LaPalombara and M. Weiner (eds.), *Political Parties and Political Development* (Princeton: Princeton University Press, 1966), p. 43.
6. A. Sturmthal, *Unity and Diversity in European Labor* (Glencoe: Free Press, 1953), pp. 17–33; R. A. Dahl, "Some Explanations," in R. A. Dahl (ed.), *Political Oppositions in Western Democracies* (New Haven: Yale University Press, 1966), pp. 360–67.
7. M. Weber, *Essays in Sociology*, H. H. Gerth and C. Wright Mills (eds.), (New York: Oxford University Press, 1946), pp. 186, 181.
8. L. Hartz, *The Liberal Tradition in America* (New York: Harcourt, Brace and World, 1955), pp. 3–10.

9. T. H. Marshall, *Class, Citizenship and Social Development* (Garden City: Doubleday, 1964), pp. 65–123; Dahl, "Some Explanations," pp. 364–66.
10. K. Mannheim, *Ideology and Utopia* (New York: Harcourt, Brace, 1936), p. 218.
11. L. D. Epstein, *Political Parties in Western Democracies* (New Brunswick, N.J.: Transaction, 1980), pp. 134–35.
12. V. Lorwin, *The French Labor Movement* (Cambridge: Harvard University Press, 1954), p. 37; Sturmthal, *Unity and Diversity in European Labor*, p. 18.
13. F. Engels, "Engels to Sorge," February 8, 1890 and December 31, 1892, in K. Marx and F. Engels, *Selected Correspondence, 1846–1895* (New York: International Publishers, 1936), pp. 467, 501.
14. G. Friedberg, "Comment," in J. H. M. Laslett and S. M. Lipset (eds.), *Failure of a Dream?* (Garden City: Anchor/Doubleday, 1974), p. 351.
15. H. G. Wells, *The Future in America* (New York: Harper & Bros., 1906), pp. 72–76; Hartz, *The Liberal Tradition in America*, pp. 50–64.
16. Epstein, *Political Parties in Western Democracies*, p. 137.
17. R. Ward, *The Australian Legend* (New York: Oxford University Press, 1959), p. 18; R. N. Rosecrance, "The Radical Tradition in Australia: An Interpretation," *The Review of Politics* 22 (1960): 121.
18. Ward, *The Australian Legend*, pp. 14–16; Rosecrance, "The Radical Tradition," p. 121.
19. P. F. Sharp, "Three Frontiers: Some Comparative Studies of Canadian, American and Australian Settlement," *Pacific Historical Review* 24 (1955): 371–72.
20. G. D. H. Cole, *A History of Socialist Thought*, Vol. III, *The Second International, 1889–1914* (London: Macmillan, 1956), p. 853; D. J. Murphy, "Introduction," in D. J. Murphy (ed.), *Labor in Politics: The State Labor Parties in Australia* (St. Lucia, Queensland: University of Queensland Press, 1975), p. 9; Epstein, *Political Parties in Western Democracies*, p. 137.
21. L. Lipson, *The Politics of Equality: New Zealand's Adventures in Democracy* (Chicago: University of Chicago Press, 1948), p. 230.
22. A. J. Mayer, *The Persistence of the Old Regime: Europe to the Great War* (New York: Pantheon, 1981), p. 131.
23. F. Engels, introduction to "Socialism: Utopian and Scientific," in K. Marx and F. Engels, *Selected Works* (New York: International Publishers, 1968), p. 394.
24. J. Schumpeter, *Capitalism, Socialism and Democracy* (New York: Harper & Row, 1950), pp. 136–37, emphasis in original.
25. Mayer, *The Persistence of the Old Regime*, p. 135; D. Bell, *The Coming of Post-Industrial Society* (New York: Basic Books, 1973), pp. 371–72.
26. F. Engels, *The Role of Force in History* (London: Lawrence & Wisehart, 1968), pp. 97, 103.
27. R. Dahrendorf, *Society and Democracy in Germany* (Garden City: Doubleday/Anchor, 1967), p. 50.
28. Ibid., p. 58; T. Parsons, *Politics and Social Structure* (New York: Free Press, 1969), p. 71.
29. S. Neumann, *Die Deutschen Partein: Wesen und Wandel Nach Dem Kriege* (Berlin: Junker & Dumhaupt, 1932), pp. 9–21.
30. R. Michels, "Die deutsche Sozialdemokratie. I. Parteimitgliedschaft und soziale Zusammensetzung," *Archiv feur Sozialwissenschaft und Sozialpolitik* 26 (1906): 511–14.
31. K. Kautsky, *The Class Struggle (The Erfurt Program)* (Chicago: Kerr, 1910), p. 196.

32. H. Tingsten, *The Swedish Social Democrats: Their Ideological Development* (Totowa, N.J.: Bedminster, 1973), p. 11; S. Rokkan, "The Growth and Structuring of Mass Politics," in E. Allardt et al. (eds.), *Nordic Democracy* (Copenhagen: Det Danske Selskab, 1981), pp. 60–61.
33. Rokkan, "The Growth and Structuring of Mass Politics," p. 57.
34. E. Allardt and E. Pesonen, "Cleavages in Finnish Politics," in S. M. Lipset and S. Rokkan (eds.), *Party Systems and Voter Alignments* (New York: Free Press, 1967), pp. 326–27.
35. W. C. Martin and K. Hopkins, "Cleavage Crystallization and Party Linkages in Finland, 1900–1918," in K. Lawson (ed.), *Political Parties and Linkages: A Comparative Perspective* (New Haven: Yale University Press, 1980). p. 186.
36. Engels, introduction to "Socialism: Utopian and Scientific," pp. 394–95.
37. E. P. Thompson, *The Making of the English Working Class* (London: Penguin, 1968), pp. 887–88.
38. P. Pulzer, *Political Representation and Elections in Britain* (New York: Praeger, 1967), p. 98.
39. G. Brenan, *The Spanish Labyrinth* (Cambridge: Cambridge University Press, 1950), pp. 10–15; D. S. Landes, "French Business and the Businessman: A Social and Cultural Analysis," in E. M. Earle (ed.), *Modern France: Problems of the Third and Fourth Republics* (Princeton: Princeton University Press, 1951), pp. 334–53; J. E. Sawyer, "Strains in the Social Structure," in E. M. Earle (ed.), *Modern France: Problems of the Third and Fourth Republics*, pp. 293–312; Daalder, "Parties, Elites, and Political Developments in Western Europe," pp. 56–57.
40. S. Hoffman, "Paradoxes of the French Political Community," in S. Hoffman et al., *In Search of France* (Cambridge: Harvard University Press, 1963), p. 5.
41. V. Lorwin, "Working-Class Politics and Economic Development: Western Europe," *The American Historical Review* 63 (1958): 342–43.
42. C. Landauer, *European Socialism*, Vol. I (Berkeley: University of California Press, 1959), p. 479.
43. Daalder, "Parties, Elites, and Political Developments in Western Europe," p. 55.
44. H. Daalder, "The Netherlands: Opposition in a Segmented Society," in R. A. Dahl (ed.), *Political Oppositions in Western Democracies* (New Haven: Yale University Press, 1966), p. 197.
45. E. Gruner, *Die Arbeiter in der Schweiz im 19 Jahrhundert* (Bern: Francke Verlag, 1968), p. 156.
46. Cole, *A History of Socialist Thought*, Vol. III, p. 611.
47. F. G. Castles, *The Social Democratic Image of Society* (London: Routledge & Kegan Paul, 1978), p. 14.
48. R. Cornell, "Culture, Values, and the Development of Socialism in Denmark," (unpublished paper, Department of Political Science, York University, Toronto, Canada, n. d.).
49. Ibid., p. 19.
50. V. Aubert, "Stratification," in N. R. Ramsoy (ed.), *Norwegian Society* (New York: Humanities Press, 1974), p. 111.
51. W. Galenson, "Scandinavia," in W. Galenson (ed.), *Comparative Labor Movements* (New York: Prentice-Hall, 1952), pp. 105–20; S. M. Lipset, *Political Man: The Social Bases of Politics*, expanded ed. (Baltimore: Johns Hopkins University Press, 1981), pp. 53–57.

52. H. Eckstein, *Division and Cohesion in Democracy: A Study of Norway* (Princeton: Princeton University Press, 1966), p. 15.
53. M. Weber, *Gesammelte Politische Schriften* (Tuebingen: B. Mohr, 1958), p. 279.
54. Sturmthal, *Unity and Diversity in European Labor*, pp. 20–22.
55. R. Bendix, *Nation-Building and Citizenship* (Berkeley: University of California Press, 1977), pp. 90–91.
56. Ibid., pp. 96–105, 112–22.
57. Marshall, *Class, Citizenship and Social Development*, pp. 65–123.
58. S. Perlman, *A Theory of the Labor Movement* (New York: Macmillan, 1928), p. 167.
59. V. I. Lenin, preface to the Russian translation of "Letters by J. Ph. Becker, J. Dietzgen, F. Engels, K. Marx, and others to F. A. Sorge and others," in V. I. Lenin (ed.), *On Britain* (Moscow: Foreign Languages Publishing House, n. d.), p. 51.
60. K. von Beyme, *Challenge to Power: Trade Unions and Industrial Relations in Capitalist Countries* (Beverly Hills: Sage, 1980), pp. 237–43.
61. G. Marks, *Trade Unions in Politics* (Ph.D. diss., Department of Political Science, Stanford University, 1982), p. 89; Sturmthal, *Unity and Diversity in European Labor*, pp. 37–62; L. Derfler, *Socialism Since Marx* (New York: St. Martin's, 1973), p. 73.
62. S. Pierson, *British Socialists: The Journey from Fantasy to Politics* (Cambridge: Harvard University Press, 1979), p. 16.
63. V. I. Lenin, *What Is to Be Done?* (Peking: Foreign Languages Press, 1973), p. 139.
64. Allardt and Pesonen, "Cleavages in Finnish Politics," pp. 326–29.
65. Martin and Hopkins, "Cleavage Crystallization and Party Linkages in Finland, 1900–1918," pp. 196–97.
66. C. E. Knoellinger, *Labor in Finland* (Cambridge: Harvard University Press, 1960), pp. 52–57.
67. H. Laidler, *Socialism in Thought and Action* (New York: Macmillan, 1927), pp. 447–50, 489–90; K. Deutsch, *Nationalism and Social Communication* (New York: Wiley, 1953), pp. 104–7; H. Waris, "Finland," in A. Rose (ed.), *The Institutions of Advanced Societies* (New York: Oxford University Press, 1958), pp. 211–14.
68. G. Roth, *The Social Democrats in Imperial Germany* (Totowa, N.J.: Bedminster, 1963).
69. D. Groh, *Negative Integration und Revolutionaerer Attentismus* (Frankfurt/Main: Verlag Ullstein, 1973), p. 34.
70. C. A. Gulick, *Austria from Hapsburg to Hitler*, Vol. I, *Labor's Workshop of Democracy* (Berkeley: University of California Press, 1948), pp. 21–24.
71. K. L. Shell, *The Transformation of Austrian Socialism* (New York: University Publishers, 1962), p. 11; S. Rokkan, *Citizens, Elections, Parties* (New York: McKay, 1970), p. 85.
72. Cole, *A History of Socialist Thought*, Vol. III, p. 538.
73. Rokkan, *Citizens, Elections, Parties*, p. 86.
74. C. Hughes, *Switzerland*, (London: Benn, 1975), p. 165.
75. A. Siegfried, *Switzerland: A Democratic Way of Life* (London: Jonathan Cape, 1950), p. 171.
76. Cole, *A History of Socialist Thought*, Vol. III, p. 615.
77. Rokkan, "The Growth and Structuring of Mass Politics," pp. 61–63.

78. L. Svaasand, "Democratization and Party Formation in Scandinavia," in O. Buesch (ed.), *Waehlerbewegung in der Europaeischen Geschichte* (Berlin: Colloquium Verlag, 1980), p. 403.
79. Rokkan, *Citizens, Elections, Parties*, p. 150.
80. G. Luebbert, *A Theory of Government Formation* (Ph.D. diss., Department of Political Science, Stanford University, 1983).
81. Cole, *A History of Socialist Thought*, Vol. III, p. 677.
82. Galenson, "Scandinavia," p. 151.
83. D. A. Rustow, *The Politics of Compromise: A Study of Parties and Cabinet Government in Sweden* (Princeton: Princeton University Press, 1955), pp. 18–24.
84. Galenson, "Scandinavia," p. 152.
85. Tingsten, *The Swedish Social Democrats*, pp. 166–89.
86. Cole, *A History of Socialist Thought*, Vol. III, p. 697.
87. A. Lijphart, *The Politics of Accommodation: Pluralism and Democracy in the Netherlands* (Berkeley: University of California Press, 1968), pp. 107–8; H. Daalder, "Consociationalism, Center and Periphery in the Netherlands," in Per Torsvik (ed.), *Mobilization, Center-Periphery Structures and Nation-building* (Bergen: Universitetsforlaget, 1981), pp. 202–3.
88. Rokkan, *Citizens, Elections, Parties*, p. 84; X. Mabille and V. Lorwin, "The Belgian Socialist Party," in W. F. Patterson and A. H. Thomas (eds.), *Social Democratic Parties in Western Europe* (London: Croom Helm, 1977), p. 390.
89. Cole, *A History of Socialist Thought*, Vol. III, pp. 662–63, 642–45; Mabille and Lorwin, "The Belgian Socialist Party," p. 390.
90. Cole, *A History of Socialist Thought*, Vol. III, pp. 662–63.
91. Lipjhart, *The Politics of Accomodation*, p. 108; Daalder, "The Netherlands: Opposition in a Segmented Society," p. 210.
92. F. F. Ridley, *Revolutionary Syndicalism in France* (Cambridge: Cambridge University Press, 1970), pp. 17–18.
93. Derfler, *Socialism Since Marx*, p. 78; Sturmthal, *Unity and Diversity in European Labor*, pp. 55–56.
94. Daalder, "Parties, Elites, and Political Developments in Western Europe," p. 54.
95. Ridley, *Revolutionary Syndicalism in France*, p. 23; P. N. Stearns, *Revolutionary Syndicalism and French Labor* (New Brunswick, N.J.: Rutgers University Press, 1971), p. 13.
96. S. G. Payne, *The Spanish Revolution* (New York: W. W. Norton, 1970), p. 22; Brenan, *The Spanish Labyrinth*, pp. 5–8.
97. Cole, *A History of Socialist Thought*, Vol. III, pp. 754–55; R. Carr, *Spain, 1808–1939* (New York: Oxford University Press, 1966), pp. 367–69.
98. S. H. Barnes, "Italy: Oppositions on Left, Right, and Center," in R. A. Dahl (ed.), *Political Oppositions in Western Democracies*, pp. 306–8.
99. Ibid., p. 308, quoting Gaetano Salvemini.
100. J. Linz, "A Century of Politics and Interests in Spain," in S. Berger (ed.), *Organizing Interests in Western Europe* (New York: Cambridge University Press, 1981), p. 368.

101. E. Malefakis, "A Comparative Analysis of Worker Movements in Spain and Italy," (paper prepared for delivery at the annual meeting of the American Historical Association, San Francisco, 1973), p. 5.

102. Cole, *A History of Socialist Thought*, Vol. III, pp. 733–34.

103. Carr, *Spain, 1808–1939*, p. 440.

104. Ibid., p. 444.

105. "It should also be noted that the involvement of workers in the religious parties also helped move such groups to the left in social policies, once democratic institutions were stabilized. In the Low Countries, in particular, the recognition of workers' rights by the religious groups helped to moderate the behavior of the socialists as well." Daalder, "Consociationalism, Center and Periphery in the Netherlands," pp. 207–8.

106. F. J. Hearnshaw, *Conservatism in England: An Analytical, Historical and Political Survey* (London: Macmillan, 1933), pp. 219–20.

107. Bendix, *Nation-Building and Citizenship*, p. 46; C. Waisman, *Modernization and the Working Class* (Austin: University of Texas Press, 1982), p. 47.

108. F. Engels, "The English Elections," in K. Marx and F. Engels, *On Britain* (Moscow: Foreign Languages Publishing House, 1953), p. 466.

109. Waisman, *Modernization*, pp. 52–53.

110. F. Meinecke, *Weltburgertum und Nationalstaat* (Munich: Oldenbourg, 1928), pp. 522–23; R. O. Schultze, "Funktion von Wahlen und Konstitutionsbedingungen von Wahlverhalten im deutschen Kaiserreich," in O. Buesch (ed.), *Waehlerbewegung in der Europaeischen Geschichte*, p. 129. 1980), p. 129.

111. V. L. Lidtke, *The Outlawed Party: Social Democracy in Germany, 1878–1890* (Princeton: Princeton University Press, 1966), pp. 320–32.

112. T. Buddenburger, "Das Soziologische Problem der Sozialdemokratie," *Archiv fuer Sozialwissenschaft und Sozialpolitik* 49 (1922): 164; Schumpeter, *Capitalism, Socialism and Democracy*, pp. 341, 343.

113. Schumpeter, *Capitalism, Socialism and Democracy*, p. 343.

114. Neumann, *Die deutschen Partein*, p. 164.

115. Perlman, *A Theory of the Labor Movement*, pp. 77–78, quoting August Bebel.

116. Neumann, *Die Deutschen Partein*, p. 92.

117. Buddenburger, "Das Soziologische Problem der Sozialdemokratie," p. 122.

118. P. Gay, *The Dilemma of Democratic Socialism* (New York: Columbia University Press, 1952), pp. 254–55; A. Rosenberg, *The Birth of the German Republic, 1871–1918* (Oxford: Oxford University Press, 1931), pp. 48ff.

119. Roth, *The Social Democrats in Imperial Germany*, pp. 163–71.

120. H. de Man, *The Psychology of Socialism* (London: Allen & Unwin, 1928), pp. 428–33.

121. B. Moore Jr., *Social Origins of Dictatorship and Democracy* (Boston: Beacon Press, 1967), pp. 413–50.

122. W. D. Burnham, "The United States: The Politics of Heterogeneity," in R. Rose (ed.), *Electoral Behavior: A Comparative Handbook* (New York: Free Press, 1974), p. 718.

123. W. H. Sewell Jr., "Social Mobility in a Nineteenth Century European City: Some Findings and Implications," *Journal of Interdisciplinary History* 7 (1976): 232–33.

124. Sturmthal, *Unity and Diversity in European Labor*, p. 24; Shell, *The Transformation of Austrian Socialism*, pp. 9–11.
125. Moore Jr., *Social Origins of Dictatorship and Democracy*, p. 418.
126. von Beyme, *Challenge to Power*, pp. 237–56.
127. Dahl, ''Some Explanations,'' p. 360.
128. Lipset, *Political Man*, p. 505.
129. Rokkan, *Citizens, Elections, Parties*.
130. Lipset, *Political Man*, pp. 503–21.

7

The Revolt against Modernity

The recurrent emergence of right-wing, that is preservatist, movements, which view existing political and cultural developments as corrupt, and seek to revitalize traditional, albeit declining, national traditions and social structure, is endemic in the processes labeled as development. These inherently require changes in values, in concepts of moral rectitude, as well as in the status accorded to different activities and roles. In modern society, the shifts in morality have generally been described as secularization, a decline in faith and an emphasis on rationality and pragmatism. As Max Weber has emphasized, "the fate of our times is characterized by rationalization and intellectualization and, above all, by the disenchantment of the world."[1] Building on Weber's analysis, Gino Germani has advanced "the hypothesis that *the structural tension inherent in all modern society between growing secularization and the necessity of maintaining a minimal prescriptive central nucleus sufficient for integration, constitutes a general causal factor in all authoritarian trends.*"[2]

Or as Talcott Parsons has noted, "the source of strain which is specific to our society, at least in quantitative importance, is the consequence of the rapidity of the process of rationalization, as Weber called it, the undermining of traditional patterns, symbols, by rational or pseudo-rational criticism, and the development of rationalized patterns. . . . The result . . . is to make it particularly difficult for large numbers of people to have sufficiently settled routines and modes of orientation—to have enough which they take for granted. The accompaniment of this in turn is widespread psychological insecurity and anxiety."[3] Consequently, as Parsons notes,

> Insecure people associated with the traditionalist elements of our social structure tend to react in a "fundamentalist" pattern, to attribute to these values an absoluteness and literalness which is untenable, to treat every departure from the formalistic letter of tradition as an indication of the most fundamental immorality, etc. The term "fundamentalism" is taken from the field of religion, but the same kind of reaction is observable in many fields, that of morality, of devotion to the Constitution, of patriotism, and many others.[4]

253

Industrial society has institutionalized social change. Basic to its reliance on technology are transformations of occupational structures and community organizations, with accompanying processes of integration and disintegration, of geographic and social mobility. These are invariably asynchronic.[5]

Given the pace of change since the industrial, national and democratic revolutions began, at any given period there will be many whose belief systems, derived from childhood experiences, will be at odds with those gaining dominance. Since complex societies contain diverse value-generating environments, communities ranging from rural to metropolitan, varying religious and irreligious institutions, differing levels of education, a multiplicity of occupational roles, it is not surprising that single cultures contain large groups at odds with the dominant norms.

Endemic in all postagrarian societies is conflict between the more and less modern sectors "based on the explosive tendencies of the modern sector to expand and to do so at the expense of the traditional portion of the society. . . . The conflict is perhaps most felt at the level of the elites although it is acutely felt in the lower strata as well. Certainly for the elites of the traditional sector, modernization means the eventual disappearance of the most important elements making up their world as well as their own position of privilege and power."[6]

An analytically similar tension has been identified by Stein Rokkan in "the conflict between *the central nation-building culture* and the increasing resistance of the ethnically, linguistically, or religiously distinct *subject populations* in the provinces and the peripheries." As he has noted, "the fundamental issue was one of morals, of the control of community norms. This found reflection in fights over such matters as the solemnization of marriage and the granting of divorces, the organization of charities and the handling of deviants."[7] In his native Scandinavia, "moralist-evangelical parties . . . have been primarily concerned to defend the traditions of orthodox evangelism against the onslaught of urban secularism and to use the legislative and the executive machinery of the state to protect the young against the evils of modern life."[8]

In applying the concept of modernization to political analysis, it is important to recognize that the process is not limited to the changes accompanying industrialization and urbanization. As noted in a previous chapter, the shifts from industrial to postindustrial society also involve fundamental changes in values and behavior, as well as in the sources of status and power. Various analysts of postindustrial society have emphasized the emergence of a set of postmaterialist or postbourgeois values concerning family and sex behavior, equality and participation, and environmentalism, which are divergent from those predominant in industrial society. Ironically, however, this normative complex is associated with opposition to technological innovation, and assumes the need to reduce or stop the pace of economic growth and a return to smaller production units and communities.

Malaise with the changes which accompany modernization or development has led, in Mannheim's terms, to utopias and ideologies, or, in more conventional language, to leftist and rightist politics. The former criticize the existing society from the vantage point of a belief in a future utopia, usually described as more egalitarian, more democratic, or more participatory on the part of the masses. The difficulties of the present are attributed to the exploitative power of a dominant self-serving ruling class. Rightists, on the other hand, emphasize the prior existence of the good integrated society which once characterized their nation. They argue "that the corruption of contemporary society is a result of an abandonment of the values and social relationships which characterized some earlier golden age. The past history of each society becomes the source of the myth of the golden past with which the present may be unfavorably compared."[9]

European conservative thought, particularly before World War II, has looked back nostalgically to an idealized image of a highly cohesive, stable, and cultured preindustrial society characterized by an alliance of the throne and altar, state and church, in which peoples' positions were defined by an interrelated complex of roles, and where the state, church and aristocracy fulfilled the values of *noblesse oblige* and took responsibility for the welfare of the average person. There have been national variations in this ideology, related to some extent to varying religious traditions and military resources, but there is a core myth rooted in the shared history of medieval Catholic Europe.

America has a sharply different conservative ideal. As a new society and a new nation, formed as a society by settlers who rejected the hierarchically organized churches and fixed class system of Europe, and formed as a nation in a Revolution which rejected the alliance and dominance of throne and altar, the central ideology of the United States is antistatist, individualistic, egalitarian, and democratic. It glorifies the pioneer settler and the Protestant who is morally responsible directly to God.

The antistatist individualist emphasis which defined nineteenth-century Americanism has remained important. While the European conservatives have often supported increased state power in the form of a benevolent Tory welfare state, American conservatives have stressed individualism, local rights, and *laissez-faire*, even to the extent of describing their ideology as libertarian. In Europe, right-wing extremists have fostered the authoritarian fascist corporate state, while the extreme Left has favored some form of total collectivism. Although the predominant American Left, the Democratic liberals, now advocate a welfare state, they retain a counter-commitment to traditional individualism. In the United States, welfare policies, such as the War on Poverty, are defended as means to facilitate upward mobility, to break down class, ethnic, racial and sexual barriers to individual achievement. The great concern with expanding state support of education, which has characterized the United States from the early nineteenth century on, is a reflection of this effort to foster individual success. Europeans, from the late nineteenth century, invested state resources heavily in welfare measures like unemployment insurance, old age pensions, and state-supported medical care, while Americans, as Max Weber pointed out early in this century, were more disposed to invest in schools and universities. The importance of antistatist values in America may also be observed in the strength which anarchist and near-anarchist policies have had among the more extreme Left, from the pre–World War I Industrial Workers of the World (IWW) to the New Left of the sixties and seventies.

There is increasing congruence on the American Left and Right—as against standard New Deal positions—in favor of substituting self-help programs for state-controlled social services. The individualistic position has thus reasserted itself; and indeed it is especially in America that so-called liberalism is so often at odds with itself because, as Hans Morgenthau has pointed out, "It has been unable to reconcile its original libertarian assumptions and postulates with its latter-day philosophy of the administrative and welfare state."[10]

Backlash Politics

What has been called backlash politics has characterized segments of the Right in many countries for much of modern history. Backlash politics may be defined as the efforts of groups who sense a diminishing of their importance, influence, and power, or who feel threatened economically or politically, to reverse or stem the direction of change through political means. Since their political concern has been activated by decline, by repeated defeats and failures, backlash politics is often extreme in its tactics and policies and has frequently incorporated theories of ongoing conspiracies by alien forces to undermine national traditions and strength. The more pervasive the challenge, the more extreme the reaction. Hence, extremist movements have gained most support during economic depressions or periods of severe social turmoil when powerful forces threaten the position or values of previously established groups.

The United States

In an effort at a comprehensive analysis of the role of right-wing extremism in the United States from the beginning of the Republic to the present, Earl Raab and I identified a recurrent pattern.[11] Apparently, the social changes linked to modernism, to the emergence of new values and behavior, have always constituted a challenge to those groups who remained identified with interests or values of the old order. As a result, preservatist movements have emerged which seek to put the clock back, to defend or restore threatened beliefs or interests. As Raab and I described them:

> The common grounds they find are some symbolic and effective aspects of the changing times: a disappearing way of life, a vanishing power, a diminishing group prestige, a heart-sinking change of social scenery, a lost sense of comfort and belongingness. This is status deterioration which is seen in political terms as a general social deterioration. The changing cultural impedimenta—modernism in dress, speech, religion, sexual relations—are the terms in which this deterioration is described. The emerging groups, who are bearing this modernism with them to power, are the common targets. In America these emerging groups have typically had an ethnic or racial identification.[12]

Looking over the expanse of American history, we noted the repeated emergence of backlash social movements, often linked to traditional religion, which explained changes in morality as an outgrowth of un-American or anti-Christian conspiracies. In the last century, these ranged from assorted anti-Masonic groups in the early decades to a variety of short-lived nativist and anti-Catholic organizations, particularly the mass-based Know-Nothings of the 1850s and the American Protective Association of the 1890s. The latter groups pointed to the growing waves of disproportionately Catholic immigrants as a major threat to American values and institutions.

While most of these movements have been associated with conservative political parties, it should be noted that the antibusiness Populists and Bryan Democrats of the end of the 1890s most fully expressed the antimodernist point of view. James Q. Wilson has summed up recent historical research on their sources of support:

> Bryan's appeal was as much cultural and moral as economic and political. Fundamentalist Protestants were outraged over the moral decay of urban life, the product, they supposed, of whiskey-swilling immigrants who had flooded into the tenements. Bryan called not simply for a new economic order, but for the purification of society. His appeal was as much to persons favoring temperance, blue laws, and the purging of corruption from the political parties as it was to those seeking the free coinage of silver, easy credit, and the public control of monopoly enterprises. As Richard Jensen has written in *The Winning of the Midwest*, Bryan's campaign was directed at small-town America where the voters were not only suffering farmers but also pietistic Protestants who "abhorred corruption, harbored millennial dreams, and preferred moralistic crusades to pluralistic cooperation." The pietistic view of America was not undemocratic; rather, it understood democracy in different terms from those favored by the urban political machines or the business corporations. To the pietists, democracy and social equality presupposed the acceptance of Christian morality and individual rectitude. Without these religious restraints on behavior, freedom would degenerate into license.[13]

The twentieth century witnessed the eruption of a large, powerful expression of moralist antimodernism in the form of the Ku Klux Klan of the 1920s. The record suggests that the multimillion member racially and religiously bigoted Klan, which had considerable strength in both national political parties, was a Protestant moralist movement. It was a reaction to the seeming decline in morality as exemplified in looser sexual morality, short skirts, and jazz music. As Arnold Rice put it:

> The 1920's meant "modernism." And "modernism," among other things, meant the waning of church influence, particularly over younger people; the breaking down of parental control; the discarding of the old-fashioned absolute moral code in favor of a freer or "looser" personal one, which manifested itself in such activities as purchasing and drinking contraband liquor, participating in ultra-frank conversations between the sexes, wearing skirts close to the knees, engaging in various extreme forms of dancing in smokefilled road houses, and petting in parked cars. A host of Americans were unwilling, or unable, to adapt themselves to this post-war culture. In the Klan they saw a bulwark against the hated "modernism," an opportunity to salvage some of the customs and traditions of the old religio-moralistic order.[14]

The Klan drew much of its support from adherents of fundamentalist evangelical Protestant sects. To a considerable degree it represented one side of a "sharp conflict between rural values and the changing mores of a society undergoing rapid industrialization and concentration."[15]

The 1930s also were characterized by the flowering of right-wing extremism. Reacting to the Great Depression, movements such as the Silver Shirts and the National Union for Social Justice focused on economic problems and took on a proto-fascist character. Still, it is striking to note their links to religious moralism. The most prominent leaders were Protestant evangelical ministers, Gerald Winrod, William Dudley Pelley, Gerald L. K. Smith, and Catholic priest Charles E. Coughlin.

Moreover, the social base of the Protestant-led factions strongly resembled that of the Klan and, like the Klan, their main theme was still that of moralistic fundamentalism. No cogent plan was offered for reorganization of the economy or society. Like the German Nazis, they identified the Jews as "contaminators in the moral realm as well as despoilers in the business field."[16] Winrod repeatedly discussed sexual vice. He and the other right-wing Fundamentalists also focused on Communism as symbolic of the threat to the evangelical Protestant way of life. A contemporary writer reported:

> Communism is thought of in Fundamentalist terms as something that can be foretold and exposed through a proper understanding of Biblical prophecy. . . .

They hold to an individualistic economic philosophy. They are firmly convinced that their moral standards should be accepted by the entire American people. Cities—with their polyglot and "alien" populations of Jews and recent Catholic immigrants from Southern Europe, with their multiplicity of moral philosophies—represent . . . the centers where their "fundamental Americanism" is threatened by "Communism"—as they conceive of Communism.[17]

A study of the biographies of 60 nativist leaders of the 1930s provides evidence congruent with the hypothesis that these movements appealed to those upset by challenges to traditional American values. Morris Janowitz notes:

The social careers of nativist leaders present interesting uniformities, since many of the group were born on farms or in small towns and during late adolescence drifted into large urban centers. . . . In America the agitator who seeks to address and unite the urban middle-class and working-class seems to be either of small-town origin or an alien in the metropolitan center in which he chooses to propagandize. He comes to hate the city and to dedicate his life to preaching what he believes to be its evils.[18]

Although the extremist moralistic movements based on the Fundamentalist Protestantism of the less privileged during the 1930s strongly resembled earlier backlash nativist groups, the decade produced a major addition to their ranks, lower-status Catholics, who supported the proto-fascist priest, Charles Coughlin. This development coincided with a shift in the major target of the nativists, from the Catholics to the Jews. While the earlier nativist ideologies had often posited a Catholic conspiracy to undermine the verities of Protestant America, those of the depression decade focused on the Jews and the Communists as threats to old-fashioned Christian Americanism. The Catholics, now largely native-born, devoutly religious and strongly anti-Communist, could share in being American.

Coughlin's followers, who, according to opinion polls, encompassed a quarter of the adult population in the late 1930s, were not only largely Catholic and poor, but came disproportionately from rural areas and small towns, and from the west central region of the country. A basic book in Coughlinite literature identified the supporters of socialism, the "enemies of America," as people who "advocated abolition of the laws which protected private property; advocated sensual pleasures, abjured Christianity, and called patriotism and loyalty narrow-minded prejudices. They intended to rout out all religion and ordinary morality, and break down the bonds of domestic life."[19]

Right-wing moralism reappeared after World War II in the form of Senator Joseph McCarthy's "crusade" to expose and wipe out the Communist conspiracy which had supposedly infiltrated the American government and other major institutions, particularly the opinion-molding and entertainment media. Communism in the McCarthyite ideology was not simply a revolutionary economic-political movement, it was the source of alien corruption of the American moral order. As the authors of one biography of the Wisconsin Senator comment: "The implication was clear: the campaign was religious. God and Joe, with the voters' help, would emerge victorious."[20] McCarthy himself stated it clearly: "The great difference between our western Christian world and the atheistic communist world is not political . . . it is moral."[21] The thrust was to establish anti-Communism as the religion of America, with Communism as the anti-religion.

Europe

The rightist reaction to modernism was, of course, not purely or even largely an American phenomenon. In Europe, it took the form of religious, rural and aristocratic opposition to the changes identified with the French Revolution, rationalism, liberalism, and the rise of capitalism.[22] Rightist, often Catholic, intellectuals, from Joseph de Maistre on, were proud to be know as supporters of the counterrevolution, of throne and altar.

Fritz Stern has summed up the "ideological attack on modernity, on the complex of ideas and institutions that characterize our liberal, secular, and industrial civilization," which ultimately fueled the fascist revolt.

> The conservative revolutionaries denounced every aspect of the capitalistic society and its putative materialism. They rallied against the spiritual emptiness of life in an urban, commercial civilization, and lamented the decline of intellect and virtue in a mass society. They attacked the press as corrupt, the political parties as the agents of national dissension, and the new rulers as ineffectual mediocrities. The bleaker their picture of the present, the more attractive seemed the past, and they indulged in nostalgic recollections of the uncorrupted life of earlier rural communities, when men were peasants and kings true rulers. Most of them thought that this world had been destroyed by evil hands; consequently they firmly believed in a conspiratorial view of history and society. The villain usually was the Jew, who more and more frequently came to be depicted as the very incarnation of modernity.[23]

From a similar perspective, Peter Gay has stressed the "great fear" of the nationalist Weimar intellectuals as "the fear of modernity." They "reveal a desperate need for roots and for community. . . . The hunger for wholeness was awash with hate; the political, and sometimes the private, world of its chief spokesmen was a paranoid world, filled with enemies: the dehumanizing machine, capitalist materialism, godless rationalism, rootless society, cosmopolitan Jews, and that great all-devouring monster, the city."[24]

George Mosse has analyzed the way in which the German emphasis on the "Volk," the transcendental traditional essence of a people, became the core of an anti-modernist ideology. Those who identified with a historic German essence "ultimately rejected industrial society altogether, believing it irreconcilable with national self-identification. In the end, they called for a 'German revolution' to liquidate the dangerous new developments and to guide the nation back to its original purpose as they conceived it."[25] Volkish thought concentrated on the Jew as the enemy within the gates. "He stood for modernity in all its destructiveness."[26] Hitler and the Nazis reaped support in a field that had been fertilized by these beliefs. As Henry Ashby Turner has written, the Nazis were comprehensive critics of modernization.

> In their eyes, modern industrial society was wholly and unavoidably incompatible with what they held to be the only true wellspring of social life: the folk culture. . . . While most visionary revolutionaries of modern times have looked to the future, to a new world, the Nazis sought their models in the past. . . . What they proposed was an escape from the modern world by means of a desperate leap toward a romanticized vision of the harmony, community, simplicity, and order of a world long lost. Their thinking seems best characterized as a utopian form of anti-modernism—utopian in the double sense of being a visionary panacea and unrealizable.[27]

In Italy, also, the turn-of-the-century decades were marked by the attacks of major intellectuals such as d'Annunzio, Prezzolini and Corradini, and many Catholic spokesmen, on modernist tendencies, industrialism, materialism, positivism, and liberalism.[28] Guiseppe Toniolo, the leading Italian Catholic social thinker, regarded as such by all Catholic political factions, took a theocratic and preindustrial position, advocating Florence in its period of greatness as a model. His ideal society was a rural one in which many workers would become small holders, and would be governed under a corporatist system by representatives of "crafts and social categories."[29]

It is difficult to locate the Italian Fascist Party within a coherent analytic scheme of fascism generally, since in the few years it functioned in opposition before the March on Rome in 1922, it was an extremely opportunistic movement with a limited support base. Led by a man steeped in Marxist and radical socialist thought, Benito Mussolini, the party accommodated its "doctrines" to the needs of the moment and area of the country. Still it may be said that fascism, though self-identified as revolutionary, revealed its conservatism in its "instinct for national traditions and for the restoration of personal bonds, like the family, which seemed fragmented in modern society. This conservatism was closely connected with the longing for an end to alienation, for belonging to a definite group. But the group had to be a traditional one, and it had to represent the restoration of traditional morality."[30]

Similar sentiments characterized conservative, Catholic and anti-Liberal thought in much of Europe. In France, Drumont, du Pin, and Maurras, among many, fostered anti-modernist "counter-revolutionary" views: The Jews were seen as the principal agents of materialism and various forms of moral decadence. French fascism was also to emphasize these sentiments. As Robert Soucy notes:

> Fascism disliked modernity. . . . Fascism honored the family and extolled the virtues of motherhood, of traditional motherhood. The emancipated woman was anathema, the product of the loose morality of liberalism.
>
> Certainly, one of the most striking things about fascist ideology was its moralism, its righteous indignation at all it deemed decadent and its zealous determination to root out sinfulness wherever it found it. . . . As one French fascist writer declared, there is no regime more concerned with the "moral health" of society than a fascist one and that is why fascism is devoted to "the systematic elimination of all that discourages, dirties or disgusts." Hence, the contempt of Drieu La Rochelle, the leading French fascist novelist of his day, for alcoholism, drugs, homosexuality, and other forms of physical decadence. Some fascists blamed Jews for this onslaught of immorality, associating them with hedonism, materialism, and Oriental sensualism.
>
> This corruption was seen as particularly widespread in French public education, which suffered, it was said, from a decline of obedience on the part of the young, a development both un-Catholic and un-military. One French fascist, a Catholic, commented: "We are suffering from a crisis in education. In the name of certain principles generating anarchy in the home as well as in the community, children refuse today to obey their teachers and their parents."[31]

Reviewing studies of Austrofascism, Klemens von Klemperer emphasizes that "if there is a basic trait in fascism, it is the search for wholeness and the lament over the loss of wholeness, real or imaginary. Fascism is one form or another of 'outraged tradition,' outraged authority, outraged religion in an age which has inevitably moved away from tradition, authority, religion. Fascism constitutes an attempt to recreate an irretrievably lost past and overcome an inevitable fragmentariness by magic and terror."[32]

In line with the analysis of fascism as an extreme reaction to the strains of modernization in Europe, Wolfgang Sauer notes that fascism was weakest in the countries where "the industrialization process ran relatively smoothly [as] in West European nations whose political rise concurred with the rise of modern civilization since the late Middle Ages." It was "strongest in the Mediterranean and Central European countries where the premodern traditions of the ancient Roman and the medieval German and Turkish Empires persisted. . . . In other words, fascism emerged where preindustrial traditions were both strongest and most alien to industrialism, and, hence, where the rise of the latter caused a major break with the past and substantial losses to the nonindustrial classes.''[33] Francis Carsten calls attention to a similar thesis suggested by Ernst Nolte which indicates that ''societies undergoing a rapid social and economic transformation from a preindustrial to an industrial society proved a favorite breeding ground of the fascist movements, . . . that the period of quick transition was the most difficult one: when the process of industrialization was more or less complete a new equilibrium was established.'' He cites Nolte's evidence for the existence of a curvilinear relation between the degree of industrialization and the strength of fascist movements:

> The agrarian population . . . in Albania and Yugoslavia around 1930 comprised around 80 per cent of the total but in England counted for hardly more than 10 per cent. It could obviously be held that in the former group the social preconditions for fascism did not yet exist, while in the last group they existed no longer, that only in the centre of Central Europe fascism found the preconditions for a full development.[34]

Or as Hans Rogger sums up the findings of a set of studies of the radical Right in eleven countries:

> It was in those countries where the tensions created by industrialization, by social protest, by the novelty of political combat, or by defeat in war had not yet been mastered, practically or psychologically, that the Right found its characteristic expression. . . . Where the old and the new, parliamentary politics and a paternalistic social structure, a modern industry and a feudal or near-feudal agriculture, lived uneasily side by side, there the Right arose to furnish answers to problems that new institutions and processes were not yet, and old ones no longer, able to handle effectively.
>
> In the final reckoning, . . . and in spite of some shrewd appreciations of the needs of the contemporary world, the Right represents . . . a nihilistic hostility to modernity, a fear of the unfamiliar, and an infantile yearning for protection (through nation, race, boundless power, or aimless activism) against dark and only dimly comprehended forces that lurk and threaten on all sides.[35]

The thesis that fascism and Nazism were antimodernizing movements has been countered with the evidence that in power they sought to further industrialize their societies to add to their military potential.[36] But the actual behavior of parties as governments does not necessarily shed light on the nature of their appeal; it does not help to explain how they developed a mass following. Analyses of the social base of the parties in both Italy and Germany indicated that it was disproportionately drawn from preindustrial strata, farmers, artisans and small business.[37] As Wolfgang Sauer points out:

> Fascism can be defined as a revolt of those who lost—directly or indirectly, temporarily or permanently—by industrialization. Fascism is a revolt of the *declassés*. The workers and industrialists do not fall under this definition; it

applies mainly to most of the lower middle class . . . peasants who opposed the urbanizing aspects of industrialism; small businessmen and those engaged in the traditional crafts and trades that opposed mechanization or concentration; white-collar workers (at least as long as they felt the loss of economic independence); lower levels of the professions, especially the teaching profession, which opposed changing values; and so forth.[38]

Any effort to generalize about the support or even the ideology of fascist movements must acknowledge that these varied somewhat from country to country. Basic to fascism everywhere was nationalism. Each movement was a reaction in part to a sense that its particular nation was denied its proper place in the sun, that its strength had been corrupted by bourgeois materialism, permissive liberal values and the internationalist class politics of the Marxists. It is thus no accident that, as Juan Linz has pointed out, "the defeated nations or those like Italy which considered themselves cheated by the victorious powers were those where fascism made its greatest gains and emerged earliest: Italy, Germany, Hungary, Austria."[39]

In some countries, such as Italy, where religious parties had "developed as a response to the strains of modern society in the process of liberal democratization and the secularizing policies of liberals and socialists" and had incorporated in their following "a large part of the population, particular pre-industrial sectors . . .," the fascists "encountered a serious competitor that had pre-empted much of . . . [their] political space."[40] Under these conditions, the fascist appeal was tailored more to anticlerical nationalist elements.

Efforts to locate a consistent class base of support for fascist parties fail because all those movements which drew large-scale support did so in periods of drastic social crisis, from those in every segment of society whose socioeconomic position or values were threatened. Fascist movements, as Linz has noted, were "in their ideological and pragmatic eclecticism and their effort to appeal to all strata, . . . a prefiguration of the post-second world war catchall party."[41] An early analysis in 1923 by a German Communist leader, Clara Zetkin, noted, in contradistinction to later Communist literature, that fascism appealed across class lines to the socially displaced of all strata: "The carrier of fascism is not a small caste, but broad social groups, large masses which reach far into the proletariat. . . . Masses of many thousands flocked to fascism. It became a refuge for those without a political home, for the socially uprooted, for those without an existence and the disappointed."[42]

Along similar lines, Gino Germani has generalized that "the human basis of fascism was provided by a process of displacement, caused by the deterioration of the capitalist system and accentuated by the upsetting conditions of the war. . . . Even in the popular image in Italy, for instance, we find a word which clearly describes such conditions: fascists were seen as *spostati*, literally 'displaced' persons."[43] He described the phenomenon as "disequilibration'' which resulted in ''loss of status [in terms of prestige as well as in terms of power and wealth] . . .''[44]

The varying national traditions and levels of development, the unique characteristics of the crises which spawned fascist movements, and the differing political structures involved, particularly the existing patterns of mobilization into political parties of diverse strata and groups, gave right-wing authoritarian movements heterogeneous followings. At the core of all these movements, however, lay an effort to restore threatened values and to rebuild the nation by reestablishing institutions and structures identified with the premodern, glorious past.

In Europe, in the decades immediately following World War II, the linkage of right-wing extremism and leading conservative antimodernist intellectuals with discredited fascism and Nazism undoubtedly played a major role in dampening the possibilities for a radical rightist revival. Neofascist parties did badly wherever they attempted to contest elections, with the partial exception of Italy, where neofascist and monarchist groups were able to secure around a tenth of the vote. In France, antisystem, right-wing movements led by Pierre Poujade and Charles DeGaulle had some success in elections in the fifties. The Poujadists, who were open critics of the democratic electoral system, appealed to the preindustrial strata, the petty bourgeoisie, the artisans, and peasants, inveighing against the dire effects of a modern industrial society. They strongly identified with religious values. They differed from the traditional right and the fascists, however, by identifying with the revolutionary republican tradition of 1789. Combined with attacks on big business, left parties, and unions were criticisms of the Jews, and a nationalist defense of colonialism. Appealing to populist sentiments—the idea that the people rather than the parties should control the government—Poujade proposed the revival of various revolutionary institutions like the *Estates-General,* to which would be presented lists of grievances submitted by local citizens in the fashion of 1789. As Peter Campbell noted:

> In its various forms the traditional anti-democratic Right has held that the Republic has betrayed France: according to Poujadism it is the politicians and the administrators who have betrayed the Republic and the honest folk it ought to protect.
>
> Nevertheless, its psychology is very near to that of Fascism. . . . In Poujadism there is the same fear of being merged into the proletariat . . . , desire for scapegoats (domestic and foreign), and hostility towards culture, intellectuals, and non-conformists.[45]

Poujadism turned out to be an unstable movement which quickly disappeared. But Gaullism, which was oriented to restoring French greatness, was able to overthrow the postwar French Republic on the bayonets of the French army, disheartened by the lack of support it received in the Indochinese and Algerian wars. Those behind DeGaulle's return to power found in the weakness of the Third and Fourth Republics evidence that the selfish bourgeois materialism of liberal democracy had brought France and themselves down. However, they rejected the notion of returning to a preindustrial France, in favor of rapid economic development to enable France to regain her place as a major power and the leader of Europe. But such a France should also be solidaristic, communitarian and hierarchical.

Postindustrial Society

Although west European, North American and Japanese societies are now regarded as developed, industrially, culturally, and politically, they continue to be characterized by asynchronistic processes of "modernization." Hence, they remain subject to the political and social tensions inherent in "disequilibration," quite apart from any specific crises they may undergo. As noted in a previous chapter, a variety of commentators have suggested that these societies are passing into a new stage, postindustrialism.[46] And postindustrial society too has given rise to protests against evils associated with economic development, but in this case, the opposition comes from political tendencies identified as leftist, as well as from more traditional and conservative forces.

These societies are seen as postindustrial because the dominant technological trends of industrial systems—increasing involvement of the labor force in the industrial productive apparatus, the growth of factories, large farms, etc.—have declined or ended. Tertiary service occupations are growing more rapidly than production jobs. The proportion (and, in some countries, the absolute number) of manual workers is declining, while the occupations which are expanding are white-collar, technical, professional, scientific, and service-oriented. The class structure now resembles a diamond bulging at the middle much more than a pyramid. High levels of education are needed for such economies and the number of students has increased many times. Education, science, intellectual activities have become more important.

The emerging strata of postindustrialism—whose roots are in the university, the scientific and intellectual worlds, and particularly in the public sectors, spread out in the professions and bureaucratic environments—have developed their own values. According to Ronald Inglehart, these "postmaterialist" values (labeled "postbourgeois" in his original formulation) are related to "self-actualization" needs (aesthetic, intellectual, belonging and esteem). These values manifest themselves in a desire for a less impersonal, cleaner, more cultured society, a freer personal life, and democratization of political work and community life. Such concerns run counter to those which are dominant in the traditional classes of industrial society, who are more concerned with satisfying material needs, i.e., sustenance and safety. For people with these objectives, the most salient concerns are a high standard of living; a stable economy; economic growth; an enduring family life; fighting crime, and maintaining order.[47] Another student of postindustrial value change, Scott Flanagan, has reconceptualized and broadened these distinctions. He suggests that advanced technology has led to a change from traditional consciousness to libertarian consciousness, shifting ''along four dimensions: frugality versus self-indulgence, pietism versus secularism, conformity versus independence and devotion to authority versus self-assertiveness.''[48] Inglehart has also noted that these value changes are related to a general climate of affluence and the absence of major wars. The generations who came of age during the post– World War II era hold vastly different values from previous cohorts, who were reared in economic scarcity and experienced severe economic depressions and international conflicts. While there is a generational effect, clearly postbourgeois values are much more common among better educated and wealthier individuals.

The concept of the revolt against modernism may be applied to the changing issues and divisions of postindustrial society. In the United States, where the new issues and conflicts emerged earlier and stronger than elsewhere in the advanced industrial world, postindustrial ideology has criticized the dominant economic trends of bureaucratized industrial society and has advocated policies that are in accord with the Jeffersonian antiurban, antiindustrial ideal of a relatively egalitarian society of small producers in small communities. If economic growth and bureaucratic rationality are viewed as aspects of modernity, these new tendencies are antimodern. But postindustrial ideology is rooted in the educated scientific strata, and involves a comprehensive attack on the moral values associated with evangelical Protestantism, traditional Catholicism, and uncritical patriotism, which are still located disproportionately in the less urbanized, less economically developed areas, among those working in small economic units, and in the less educated strata. From the perspective of the latter groups, the postbourgeois values represent the sharpest onslaught against their belief systems that has occurred since the rationalist humanism of the Enlightenment era.

The New Politics

Regardless of how we label the new conflicts, they have profoundly affected the political arena. The basic political division of industrial society was a materialist one involving a struggle over the distribution of wealth and income, supplemented, of course, by religious, ethnic and regional conflicts between the preindustrial and industrial worlds. Postindustrial politics is increasingly concerned with *noneconomic* or *social issues*—a clean environment; a better culture; equal status for women and minorities; the quality of education; more cooperative international relations; greater democratization; and a more permissive morality, particularly with regard to familial and sexual issues. But as Wolfgang Zaph has stressed, major new postindustrial political forces in the form of "regional/ethnic movements on the one hand, and . . . the anti-technocratic movements on the other (ecologists, anti-nuclear power, feminists and many single-issue groups)" are reacting against "the very achievements of modernization."[49] The reform elements concerned with postmaterialist or social issues derive their strength not from the workers and the less privileged, the social base of the Left in industrial society, but from segments of the well educated: students, academics, journalists, professionals and civil servants. The New Left, the New Politics, the Green parties, all receive their support from such strata. Most workers, on the other hand, remain concerned with material questions. Less educated, less cosmopolitan, less affluent, less secure, they are also more traditional, discernably more conservative in their social or moral views.[50]

Strikingly, therefore, the new postmaterialist Left represents in part a protest against the values of industrial society. Concerned with the quality of life, its affluent supporters regard the emphasis on economic growth, the quintessence of industrial society, as having led to assorted social morbidities, in the environment, in levels of democratic participation, and in the quality of life generally. Hence, the postmaterialist Left proclaims that "small is better," that economic growth or increased speed of transportation should be halted where it results in pollution or in overcrowding areas. Many in the movement condemn mass popular culture as uncouth.

An analysis of American New Left ideology points up its similarities to mid-nineteenth-century transcendental critiques of capitalist-industrial society as "ugly, repressive, and dehumanizing." As Martin Schiff notes:

> New Left radicals seek a change in the quality of life where humanism abounds and consciousness expands, where the human spirit is liberated from materialist concerns, where man returns to nature for new life styles, meaningful social participation and relationships, and organic community.

> The post-industrial socioculture values posited by the New Left, however, bear striking resemblances to the pre-industrial values glorified by the transcendentalists and other nineteenth-century utopians. In fact both groups in many respects echo Rousseau's call in the eighteenth century for a restoration of the values of man as they presumably existed in the state of nature. . . . Similarly, the mainstream of transcendentalist thought epitomized by Emerson dealt with such problems as capitalist exploitation of labor by condemning the industrial society that produced capitalists and laborers. Emerson saw the solution to social ills in a return to the Jeffersonian values of individual labor and self-reliance, particularly on one's own plot of land.

The New Left shares the transcendentalist repugnance for the scientific technology characteristic of industrial society. Technology is viewed as stultifying and dehumanizing with people treated as cogs in the industrial machine and human needs subordinated to industrial profits and technological programs.

Both the transcendentalists and the New Left professed disdain for materialism and conformity to materialist goals and standards. Such disdain was evident in their lack of involvement and identification with those groups, less well-situated economically, seeking to improve their condition within the existing capitalist-pluralist system.[51]

Although much of the effort to curtail growth may be seen as adversely affecting the chances of the less privileged to secure a higher standard of living from their share of an ever-growing pie, or limiting their opportunities for inexpensive housing or leisure facilities, the postindustrial Left also identifies the interests of the poor with opposition to big institutions. For example, the New Left has defended the values and social organization of the slum dwellers against bureaucratic planning which is supposedly only interested in good housing. New Leftists criticize the destruction of neighborhoods to facilitate urban renewal as undermining local autonomy and culture.

Postindustrial society has precipitated a conflict between two Lefts, the materialist and the postmaterialist, which are rooted in different classes, related to their varying attitudes to growth. The materialist Left favors continued or enhanced economic development, while the postmaterialists focus on the social evils accompanying expansion.

Both Lefts are often in the same party (Democratic, Social Democratic, even Communist, as in Italy), but they have different views and interests. The New Politics intelligentsia do not like trade unions which, like business, they consider "materialistic" rather than "public interested." The debate over the use of nuclear power has divided the Left in many countries. The well-educated postmaterialists have been antinuclear, while the trade unions and the majority of the workers have favored building more nuclear plants.[52]

Minority Nationalism

The most dramatic form of resistance to modernizing trends in postindustrial society has been the reemergence of ethnic or linguistic nationalism in many countries. These movements object to the centralization of power, economic strength, and cultural dominance in the majority regions of their country. They seek, either through gaining independence or autonomy, to control educational and cultural facilities and to build up the economy of their areas.[53]

Such movements, as Jeffrey Alexander has emphasized, run counter to the assumptions associated with "the twin revolutions of political nationalism and industrialization . . . [which] have been rationalistic in the extreme, sharing a utilitarian distaste for the non-rational . . . and the illusion that a truly modern society will soon dispense with such concerns.'' Both Marxists and non-Marxists assumed that industrialization, urbanization, and the spread of education would reduce ethnic consciousness, that universalism would replace particularism.[54]

National minority movements existed in many of the same countries before World War II. At that time, most of them were identified with rightist socioeconomic politics, sometimes fascist ones, and often had strong links to the church. They were almost totally eclipsed in the immediate post-war era. They revived during the mid-1960s, in tandem with the other protest waves of that period.[55] This time, ethnic consciousness surfaced in alliance with left-wing ideologies in countries ranging from Canada to Britain, Spain, and France. The Left, in turn, has dropped its traditional Marxist and liberal disdain for ethnic loyalties as obstacles to class consciousness. The new postindustrial Left, in particular, has come to identify the cause of the minority cultures as akin to those of colonial peoples.[56]

The ethnic revival has been linked by Erik Allardt with the larger sources of protest against centralization and bigness which characterize New Left politics. As he suggests, it is part of a more general reaction to "tendencies toward economic, military and political concentration [which] have led to protest movements of different kinds . . . ."[57] The anti-modern aspect of the ethnic movements may be seen not only in their demand for the dispersal of factories in the various regions, rather than concentration in efficient large units, but also in their support for the revival of "folkloristic elements."[58]

In a case study in Brittany, Edgar Morin points out "that modernization has preserved and added new substance to archaism. The processes of centralization and modernism that produce cultural homogeneity and national political integration *also* produce ethnic consciousness and a growing desire for identification and membership in a community less distinct and impersonal than national society. As television, travel, education, and occupational mobility brought Bretons into greater contact with other Frenchmen, they became increasingly aware of their differences. The villager who in the past had identified only with others in the little region where his own dialect of Breton was spoken, and whose only contact with France was in regard to taxation, conscription, and education, has learned from the mass media that he is a *Breton*."[59]

James Jacob notes that a typical ethnic movement, the Occitan struggle for autonomy or independence of linguistically distinct regions of southern France, is in alliance with groups subscribing to "postindustrial" values. "Its coalition partners include ecologists, pacifists, women's groups and those devoted to the concept of self-management, whether at the level of the workplace or of the entire region."[60]

Reporting on a study of Belgian ethnic-nationalist movements, Ronald Inglehart notes:

> Among those with Post-Materialist value priorities the ethnic nationalists are heavily over-represented. They are more than three times as prevalent among Post-Materialists as among Materialists. This tendency is more applicable to the Flemish than the Walloon nationalists, but it holds true for both groups. The latter are over-represented among the Post-Materialists by a ratio of two to one; the former by a ratio of *five* to one![61]

A tie to these other forms of postindustrial protest may be seen in the fact that the leadership and a disproportionate amount of the support for such ethnic movements now comes from the well-educated professional strata among those minority groups, that the less educated, more traditional elements, such as the farmers and small business people who predominated in the prewar movements, are currently underrepresented.[62]

The revolt of the ethnic periphery against the cultural and political center constitutes another example of the opposition to growth and bigness which marks the politics of postindustrialism. The relative lack of enthusiasm for autonomy and separation among the minority ethnic working-class and business people may result from the same factors which differentiate supporters of the old and new politics in the majority population.

The Reemergent Backlash

Ironically, postindustrial processes have also brought in their wake the reemergence of deep-rooted conflict over issues strongly resembling those dividing traditionalists and modernists in industrializing societies. The spread of education, science, and cosmopolitan values has not only resulted in a moral challenge to traditional religion and patriotism, but has also enlarged the rights of minorities, women, and homosexuals, and has altered concepts of morality as they affect sexual behavior, marriage, abortion, relations between generations, the treatment of criminals, the use of drugs, dress codes and manners, and unconventional behavior generally. The postmaterialists generally have supported more egalitarianism, personal freedom, and permissiveness.

These trends, of course, are not new. They resemble the changes identified with modernism, which offended traditionalists and right-wing extremists in the decades before World War II. But now such developments are much more pervasive and dominant than they were in earlier eras. The challenges to conventional morality manifested in freer sexual behavior, variant forms of dress, widespread use of drugs, and the militant tactics of the 'youth revolt', are seemingly much greater than those which disturbed the Klansmen, fascists, and adherents of fundamentalist religion in the interwar years.

Not surprisingly, these changes have produced backlash phenomena. In America and Europe, extreme right-wing, religious and populist movements have arisen to counter the new immorality and decline of patriotism.

Europe

Backlash reactions to modernism have appeared in northern European countries in the relatively recent formation of religious parties such as the Christian Peoples' Party of Denmark, the Christian League of Finland, the Christian Peoples' Party of Norway, and the Christian Union of Sweden. John Madeley has emphasized that the condition which triggered "the latent and long-standing cleavage between the religiously active and the rest of society . . . into a political cleavage" was the changes in conceptions of morality, which occurred in the sixties and seventies.

> This trend has been the rise in the political salience of issues relating to family and personal morality, narrowly conceived—divorce, homosexuality, pornography, abortion, drug control, etc. The overriding salience of these issues for the religiously active and the lack of satisfactory leadership from the established political parties have provided the occasion for the emergence of the new parties. "Permissive society" legislation represents perhaps the last stage in the establishment of a programmatically liberal social order, removing the last important statutory support of a sectional ethical ideal; its effect has been to call forth a reaction leading to the development of a new type of political party.[63]

The oldest and strongest of these Scandinavian parties, the Norwegian Christian Peoples' Party, is clearly a provincial party seeking to resist the new cosmopolitanism. It is based on the lower middle-class of the rural and smaller communities.[64] Support for the other religious parties in northern Europe, however, has remained small, five per cent or less. They have "found it difficult to formulate a general, i.e., secular political platform."[65] Resistance to social change has also been evident in opposition to participation in the European community and in the emergence of "populist" groups such as the Finnish Rural Party and Poujadist antitax Progress Party in Denmark, and in protest in various countries against the large-scale influx of foreign workers. The latter has been most vividly expressed in the large segments of the Swiss electorate who voted against immigrant labor in four referenda placed on the ballot by nativist groups in the 1970s, and the formation of two anti-immigrant parties, National Action and the Republicans.[66] None of these groups, however, shows any sign of playing an important role in the politics of their countries.

An effort to analyze the nature of recent "populist" protest movements generally, in the context of a discussion of the Finnish Rural Party and the Poujadist movement in France, notes their "opposition to the products of modernization, namely urbanization and industrialization . . . [as well as their] strong stress on religiosity . . . distinct primitivism . . . isolationism, particularly on foreign policy issues, and . . . localism with respect to domestic politics." Their support base "is primarily made up of small farmers and small businessmen" in small communities and of persons in cities "who have lived there only a short time."[67] The largest of the parties, the Danish Progress Party, whose vote hovered around 15 percent of the total in elections in 1973, 1975 and 1977, dropping to 11 percent in 1979, is also disproportionately supported by persons living in rural areas and provincial towns, the less educated, the self-employed, and farmers.[68]

Studies of the supporters of the antiimmigrant parties in Switzerland arrive at similar conclusions. David Schweitzer emphasizes the similarities between them and those who have backed small ultra-right postwar movements elsewhere. "The Swiss National Action and Republican movements, very much like their counterparts in other countries, appeal especially to the marginal insecure groups in the population who are reacting to the modern ways of big business, big government, large-scale organizations, and an increasing complexity in the social order that is vaguely, if at all understood."[69]

A survey of behavior in the 1970 referendum reveals a strong relationship between size of community in which people grew up and the way they voted, with the percentage opposed to immigration decreasing from farm to village to large city and suburbs.[70] Opponents of immigration tended to agree with items grouped under the categories of "traditionalism" and "moral rigidity," and to be opposed to social change.[71] As Janet Martin concludes, "The immigrant workers apparently symbolized to these conservative Swiss a trend towards economic and social modernization, a trend they feared and hoped to reverse by halting immigration."[72] But it should be noted that by 1979, the combined vote for the two antiimmigrant parties had fallen to two per cent.

The best publicized European radical rightist tendency of the 1970s was the French "New Right." This movement, largely an expression by a number of intellectuals and journalists of frustration at the decline in power and prestige of France as a nation and culture, like the intellectual right of pre-World War I France, focused its criticism on "alien" anti-European forces, foreign immigrants, and radical and liberal forces. Supported by press lord Robert Hersant, owner of three major Paris newspapers, *Le Figaro, L'Aurore, and France-Soir,* plus many provincial organs, and once an overt anti-Semite and youthful collaborator with the Germans in World War II, the views of the New Right reach wide circles of the population, and may have helped stimulate widespread anti-Semitic violence in 1980.

These intellectuals reject world-wide modernization because they see it as a source of cultural homogeneity, a threat to the ancient cultures of Europe. Hence, like the New Left, they support the growth of regionalist minority tendencies. As Alain de Benoist, a key figure in this movement, puts it:

> The principal menace today . . . is the gradual disappearance of diversity from the world: the leveling of individuals, the reduction of all cultures to a "world civilization" founded on what is most common. . . . From Holiday Inn to Howard Johnson, the outlines of a uniformly gray world are emerging.[73]

Louis Pauwels, the editor of *Figaro Magazine*, emphasizes that to be part of the New Right one must "admit the fact of inequalities among men, the necessity of elites . . . from birth."[74] According to the New Rightists, inequality has a racial dimension. Yvan Blot, in a document drawn up for their central study center, Grece, writes: "Ethnic identity is the factor that establishes preferential differentiations on the scale of biological potentials. . . . The more evolved a society is, the more it is hierarchically ordered. The very existence of the human species is bound to racial differentiation."[75]

The United States and the Soviet Union, communism, liberalism and capitalism, must be opposed as the sources of egalitarianism and economic materialism. Europe must be rebuilt on its traditional "Indo-European" (they eschew the term Aryan) values which they contrast to the corruption fostered by "Judeo-Christianity" and "Freudo-Marxism."

Unlike their radical forebears, the New Right intellectuals do not seek to build a new mass movement. Rather they have a conscious strategy of first seizing "cultural power" and of penetrating the political and administrative elites.

It is difficult to account for the flowering of such doctrines within a segment of the well educated and highly placed in French society, and to evaluate their power potential. The movement's appeal appears related to the relative decline of France as a cultural and political force, and to the desire manifest in Gaullism, to revive her position by making France the leader of a Europe which opposes both the Soviet Union and the United States. Many French people look on their nation and her values as a victim of worldwide developments, a country which is oppressed by the new international order.

Evidence of the widespread feeling that France has declined may be found in a 1971 opinion survey which asked samples of the entire population and of elite groups to evaluate the position of France in the world on a scale from one (high) to six (low). The majority of the population placed her at 3.5, while the elites ranked their country even lower at 5.1, close to the very bottom.[76] The character of the complaint about the decline of French culture may be seen in a book by a leading Gaullist intellectual on *Colonized France,* which was favorably reviewed in *Le Monde Diplomatique.* Jacques Thibau pessimistically analyzes the cultural colonization of France by the United States, and concludes with the question: "Does France have a future?"—a question he is unable to answer in the affirmative.[77]

The influential and unique position of "New Right" intellectuals is probably related to the same factors which have made Gaullism a major factor in French political life. As Jeane Kirkpatrick states:

> At the core of the Gaullist vision of France is nationalism . . . , a conception of history that sees peoples rather than classes as creative historical actors, a conception that celebrates the national character and emphasizes the distinctive identity and destiny of France, a conception expressed in Charles de Gaulle's conviction that France can only be herself when she is great.[78]

Yet, it should be noted that these ambitions for France are not strongly supported outside the ranks of the Gaullists. In the 1971 opinion poll, which asked: "In the international realm, should France try to become a world power, or should she be satisfied with a more modest role?" a majority, 52 percent, chose the modest option, compared to 36 percent for the world power one. The Gaullists were the only political group a plurality of whose supporters (47 to 44 percent) favored an effort to return to world power status.[79]

The New Right has extended the Gaullist conception to its own racial belief that the French and the old "pure" Europeans are biologically superior to the mongrelized Americans and Soviets and the nonwhite peoples. This doctrine appeals outside the rightist intelligentsia and helps fuel "neutralist" nationalism.

No other European nation has maintained as intense an image of the superiority of its culture as the French have. Other national elites are not as frustrated by their place in a world system in which their country or culture has become less important. There is, therefore, little support among European intellectuals generally for French-type New Right thought. For the most part, the extreme Right outside of France draws its support from the more traditionalist strata and regions which object to the dominant structural and cultural trends within their own society.

Italy is the only country in Europe in which a neo-fascist party, the Italian Social Movement (MSI), has visible electoral support, around 5 percent. But this level represents a considerable decline from the vote which it and the Monarchist party, absorbed by the MSI in 1972, obtained in the first postwar decade (12.7 percent in 1953). In recent years, segments of the MSI have adopted as their own ideas taken from the New Left and the French New Right. Fascist youth camps "are springing up in Italy dedicated to the purity of nature and opposed to nuclear power. The new fascists base their theories of racial difference on the 'new genetics.' '' Like the French New Right, MSI leaders reject ''materialism, American- or Russian-style, in favour of 'spiritual values.' ''[80]

A review of the evidence dealing with the support of political tendencies in Italy and France, as of the mid-1960s, notes ''that, on the electoral level at least, Neo-Fascism, Poujadism, and the 'activism' of Extreme Rightists are—as were German Nazism, Belgian Rexism, French *Croix de Feu*, Romanian Iron Guard of the 1930's—the expression of the petty bourgeoisie.'' And Mattei Dogan goes on to emphasize that ''surveys on the most diverse problems—economic, social, cultural, religious, and moral—show that the [main supporters of such movements] the so-called independent petty bourgeoisie manifest more sectarian, more 'misoneistic' (anti-novelty) opinions than the middle bourgeoisie, who in turn appear somewhat less liberal, less tolerant, than the upper bourgeoisie. And this is a fact not only in France and Italy, but in many other countries as well.''[81]

The pattern is similar in Germany, where neo-nazism, in the form of the National Democratic party, dropped from a high point of close to 5 percent in the 1969 parliamentary elections to one per cent in 1980. Analyses of its support in state and national elections in the late 1960s indicate that the ''appeal of the right-wing National Democratic party was chiefly in small towns among older people of low educational attainment and with traditional middle-class occupations.''[82]

The United States

Ironically, the most frequent examples of recent rightist revolts against modernity have occurred in the most developed nation, the United States, where a variety of large-scale movements, social, religious, and single-issue groups, have arisen to oppose social changes.[83] These run the gamut from the John Birch Society, through the George Wallace Presidential candidacies, single-issue movements to oppose busing for school integration, legalized abortion, the Equal Rights Amendment, and, most recently, widespread efforts to mobilize fundamentalist Christians to actively support arch-conservative candidates at the ballot box and to influence the curriculum in the public schools.

These efforts cannot be considered unimportant. George Wallace, who received considerable support in opinion polls and primary elections, as well as in the 1968 Presidential contest, for his opposition to policies benefiting the black population, also served as a ''general duty'' protest candidate, blaming the educated elites for undermining the American way of life. His disproportionately Southern and lower-status supporters were most likely of all to oppose the changes in moral values and practices which had occurred from the mid-sixties on.

Survey research indicates that support for Wallace correlated with racist and traditionalist attitudes.[84] And Wallace's strength, in conjunction with the electoral victories by racist candidates in local elections and the various protests launched by antiintegrationist groups, made an impact upon the rhetoric and policies of major-party spokespeople. The opposition to reforms associated with gay rights and feminism has also been effective in affecting legislative and administrative policy.[85]

At the beginning of the 1980s, a new moralistic and antimodernist movement, the effort to politicize the sentiments of fundamentalist Protestants and Catholics, has received widespread attention in the press. Yet a detailed examination of the evidence relating to the electoral impact of this effort suggests that it is not much more significant than similar attempts in Europe.

There can, of course, be no doubt that a host of evangelical ministers who broadcast regularly, together with organized ''pro-family'' opponents of legalized abortion and the Equal Rights Amendment, have attempted to unite religious traditionalists in a political movement.[86] They have formed ''a loose alliance of groups attempting to enlist strict Bible adherents—mostly Baptist and independent evangelical sects, but also theological conservatives within Catholic, Mormon and Protestant denominations—as the new troops of political conservatism.''[87] Although this movement may be located within the historic stream of right-wing backlash, and is based on the same social categories as earlier efforts, it is tactically more moderate, devoting its efforts largely to propaganda and electoral action within the mainstream parties. It does, however, resemble the previous movements in its evocation of supposed elitist conspiracies in the form of the Trilateral Commission, the Bilderbergers, and the Council on Foreign Relations as the sources of a cosmopolitan internationalist attack on American values and sovereignty.

The evangelical political movement has supported strongly conservative policies on a long list of domestic and foreign-policy issues: the Equal Rights Amendment, homosexual rights, legalized abortions, a federal Department of Education, socialized medicine, an anti-communist foreign policy, military spending, balancing the budget, and enforcement of laws against pornography and drug-selling. Nevertheless, its ''most concerted lobbying efforts . . . have been the battle for voluntary school prayer and passage of an amendment restricting federal intervention in private [mainly Christian] schools to stop racial discrimination.''[88] According to a review of the movement in *The National Catholic Reporter,* ''at the core of the current conservative religious movement is Senator Paul Laxalt's Family Protection Act. The bill supports school prayer, parental review of textbooks, eliminates tax laws requiring married couples to pay more than singles living together and includes conservative provisions on gay rights and abortion."[89]

The political evangelicals are part of a larger New Right which has imitated the tactics developed by New Politics liberals in building a variety of single-issue groups. At the heart of the movement, in Richard Sennett's words, is "a collage of programs whose followers feel dislocated in America now, who fear that the society they were brought up to believe in is disappearing or has disappeared. . . . Along with this sense of dislocation the new-right rhetoric contains a search for magical solutions that will put "us" back on the map. Everything has to change; we must destroy the present to regain the mythic past."[90]

What has given evangelical movements associated with the New Right their mass audience is access to television on a national scale and the application of sophisticated computerized systems which make it possible to send "personal" letters to large numbers of persons who have shown interest in related causes. The *New York Times* reports that Reverend Jerry Falwell, the Fundamentalist leader of the explicitly rightist Moral Majority, has an audience of six million people for his weekly television program.[91]

It is difficult to estimate the strength and impact of this movement. Seemingly motivated by family, sexual morality, and religious concerns, its followers may be more easily mobilized for action on specific issues falling under these categories than for the complete collection of more secularized domestic and foreign-policy programs which characterize the right-wing agenda. Many less affluent religious persons, particularly Catholics, who back single-issue groups concerned with abortion or homosexual rights, belong to trade unions and support welfare-state policies.

Conservative politicians generally face severe criticism whenever they compromise tactically; the right-wing moralists apparently insist on the absolute application of moral principles, a requirement which if met is an almost certain guarantee of electoral defeat. The Fundamentalists also stringently evaluate the personal behavior of politicians, including conservatives. William Billings, the head of the National Christian Action Coalition, "revealed that after Reagan used the word 'damn' in public, he was swamped with phone calls and letters from anguished evangelicals. Christians don't swear, he was told."[92] Joseph Coors, the owner of a major brewery, and an important financial contributor to assorted right-wing causes, was vigorously denounced by the Reverend Jerry Falwell when the Coors Company advertised in a newspaper for homosexuals and noted in its ad that the company "does not discriminate on the basis of sexual preference."[93]

Public opinion data also cast doubt that fundamentalist Christianity can form the basis for an effective right-wing political movement in the 1980s.

An extensive investigation of the evangelical movement, conducted in a national survey taken by the *Los Angeles Times* between September 2nd and 7th, 1980, classified 25 percent of the American population as evangelicals on the basis of their responses to three questions used by evangelicals to define their basic creed: whether people "believe that preaching the Gospel is the way to encourage others to accept salvation through Jesus Christ," "believe that the Bible is the actual word of God and is to be taken literally," and have "personally experienced a religious awakening that can be described as being born again." Using the same three questions, Gallup reported that 19 percent are evangelicals.[94] The Gallup Poll also indicates that the evangelicals are more likely to be Southerners, to live in nonmetropolitan cities (under 50,000), small towns (under 2,500), and rural areas, to be women, and less educated than the population as a whole.[95]

The one-fifth to a quarter of the population who may be classified as evangelicals, however, are quite disparate in their political allegiances and beliefs. The 1979 Gallup survey of religious belief found "that Democrats outnumber Republicans among Evangelicals better than three to two. Forty-two percent are Democrats and 27 percent are Republicans. Republicans are slightly overrepresented and independents are slightly underrepresented but in general they conform to the national pattern."[96] According to the September 1980 *Los Angeles Times* survey, they divided on the 1980 presidential race much like the sample as a whole: 40 percent Reagan, 39 percent Carter, 13 percent Anderson. Variation among them may be explained in part by demographic factors. The 16 percent of the evangelicals who are black preferred Carter, giving him 66 percent of their choices, compared to Reagan's 14 percent and Anderson's 11 percent. The choices of white Protestant evangelicals differed by region. In the South, Reagan led Carter by 44 percent to 36, with 15 percent for Anderson. The white evangelical preference for the more conservative candidate showed up more strongly in the rest of the country, where the G.O.P. nominee dominated with 52 percent compared to 26 percent for Carter and 12 percent for Anderson.

The core group of evangelical conservatives, whites who listen regularly to evangelical preachers on television and/or send them financial contributions, constituted 13 percent of the *Los Angeles Times* national sample. Although disproportionately Southerners, only half of them were for Reagan, compared to 29 percent for Carter and 12 percent for Anderson. The white evangelicals who said they did not watch the ministers regularly were overwhelmingly for Carter.

Clearly, the public opinion data suggest that potential support for a political backlash by white Protestant evangelicals is largely limited to a small segment of the population, namely those who watch the evangelical preachers on television. But, as is evident from their presidential preferences, even they are not homogeneous politically. They are also far from unanimous in their opinions on moral issues. Gallup queried as to the acceptability of abortion under varying conditions and found that less than a third, 31 percent, of evangelicals felt that it is unacceptable in all circumstances compared to 19 percent of the general public. Over three-fifths, 63 percent, however, are willing to approve of abortion under certain specified circumstances, as is 62 percent of the population.[97] The *Los Angeles Times* poll indicates that they agree by only a 3–2 margin with the proposal for a constitutional amendment to ban abortions and the statement that the Equal Rights Amendment ''is an attack on the American family.''

The ABC News-Harris Survey, reporting on all white evangelicals among likely voters, found them favoring a ''constitutional amendment . . . to ban legalized abortion'' by 55 to 42 percent, but opposing the statement ''Most sex education courses in the schools are little more than pornography'' by 37 to 46 percent, and rejecting the opinion, ''It is impossible to be a liberal politically and also a good Christian,'' by 30 to 61 percent.[98]

A detailed report on the politically active evangelical movement in a series of articles in the *New York Times* emphasized the differences among them even with respect to the Equal Rights Amendment and civil rights for homosexuals. It concluded that they only ''unite on two specific issues, their opposition to abortion and their assertion that the nation is spiritually adrift.'' Basically, they seek ''a spiritual revival'' more than any particular institutional change. For many ''a loss of religious faith is linked to the Supreme Court decisions against Bible reading and mandatory prayer in the schools. Public schools are intensely criticized on the ground that 'God has been removed from the classroom.' As the meeting ground and processing center for American children, the schools are given great importance. . . . From that standpoint, what they see as a takeover of schools by 'secular' forces alarms them.''[99] Beyond the divisions among them, the potential impact of the Fundamentalist moralists is further reduced by the fact that they are disproportionately drawn from the less educated strata and as a result polls ''show this group to be one of the least politically active segments of the electorate.''[100] The evangelicals' lack of interest in politics is furthered by their deep dedication to religion rather than to society. By two to one, they ''consider involvement in groups and causes that strengthen the entire community less important than strengthening the local church,'' according to the Gallup Poll. A majority, 53 percent, place ''world evangelization'' as the prime Christian priority, while personal and family spiritual growth is put first by 27 percent, and ''help strengthen the church'' by 14 percent. Few feel influencing public legislation should be emphasized. When asked what should be the Christians' second most important priority, only 4 percent of the evangelicals rate the latter activity that high compared to 11 percent of the general public.[101]

The politicized evangelicals were clearly on the side of a variety of Republican candidates, including Ronald Reagan, in the 1980 elections. It is doubtful, however, that the G.O.P. victories can be credited to a sizable increase in the Republican vote among white fundamentalists. A detailed analysis of past evangelical voting by Albert Menendez, based on election results in precincts predominantly inhabited by specific religious groups, indicates that in every election from 1956 on, with the single exception of Lyndon Johnson's 1964 electoral sweep, the majority voted Republican, although most continued to identify themselves as Democrats. Menendez finds in an analysis of predominantly evangelical voting precincts that, in 1968 and 1972, Hubert Humphrey and George McGovern secured at most about one third of the white evangelical ballots. Jimmy Carter improved the Democratic showing in 1976, but even he did not secure a majority of the vote of his fellow white evangelicals. A poll taken at "Wheaton College (sometimes called the evangelical Harvard) . . . just before Election Day found students and faculty for Ford by about 67% to 30%," while Carter had a wide lead among students and professors in the nation generally.[102]

Given the magnitude of the change between 1976 and 1980, it is clear that the Democrats lost heavily among all religions, strata, and ideological groups, including those such as liberals and Jews who were unlikely to have been affected by the movement. Thus, according to *The New York Times*/CBS News Election Day poll, the G.O.P. presidential vote among trade union family members increased from 39 to 44 percent between 1976 and 1980, and from 24 to 36 percent among Hispanics. Reagan's backing among Jews was 39 percent, up from 34 for Jerry Ford four years earlier. His Catholic support was 40 percent, 6 percent more than Ford's vote, while among all white Protestants, Reagan gained six points, from 56 to 62 percent. The 1976 poll did not deal with the "born-agains" separately, so that no direct comparison between the two elections is possible. In 1980, the G.O.P. nominee secured 61 percent of the votes of "born-again white Protestants," compared to 63 percent among other white Protestants. Reagan seemingly did slightly less well among the born-again whites than among other white Protestants.[103]

The 1980 Election Day survey did inquire how respondents voted in 1976, but as is usual in postelection inquiries, it found a larger proportion reporting they had supported the victor than he in fact received. Still, a comparison of the weighted 1976 vote, as reported in 1980, with the actual 1980 candidate choice, indicates that Carter retained a slightly larger proportion of his supporters, 83 percent among the white born-again Protestants, than among other white Protestants, 79 percent. The drop-off in Carter's support among Catholics and Jews was also somewhat more than among the born-agains. These results do not attest to the efficacy of groups such as the Moral Majority.

Similar conclusions have been reached by Arthur Miller, a study director of the University of Michigan's Survey Research Center. Based on interviews with 10,000 people, Miller believes the impact of fundamentalist groups on the election outcome was exaggerated. As he notes, "Our data suggest that it wasn't values or life styles or social issues, but the economy and defense—the state of our prestige abroad, and not abortion, women's rights or drugs" that affected the vote.[104]

Louis Harris even argues that the right-wing moralists hurt rather than helped the G.O.P. cause.

> Conservative Republicans have been hurt not helped, however, by their right-wing supporters who advocate a constitutional convention to ban abortions (opposed by a 62–30 percent majority), oppose the ERA (favored by 56–36 percent), oppose registration of handguns (favored by 78–20 percent), and oppose affirmative action programs (assistance, not quotas) for minorities (favored by 67–17 percent). The country has moved slightly to the conservative side in opposing nearly all new government regulatory measures on economic matters, but has not moved at all to the right on the social issues that are such an emotional concern to the die-hard right-wing conservatives.[105]

The results of the 1980 Senate elections also cast doubt on the assumption that the New Right and the politicized evangelical groups had much impact on the election results. They targeted five Northern liberal Democratic Senators—Bayh, Church, Cranston, Culver, and McGovern. All, except Cranston, were defeated for reelection. But the decline in their vote *was almost identical* with that of the Democratic Senatorial candidates in eighteen non-targeted states in the North. The average vote of the five liberal Senators fell from 54.5 percent in 1974 to 48 in 1980; the Democratic Senatorial vote in the eighteen other Northern contests declined from 55 to 48 percent.

Strikingly, each of the four northern Republican victors, who were supposedly aided by the New Right's targeting their very liberal opponents for defeat, has publicly declared that his campaign was not helped, and may have even been harmed, by these allies. One, James Abnor of South Dakota, who trounced George McGovern, has even complained to the Federal Election Commission about the use of his name by a New Right group without his authorization. An aide to Steven Symms, victor over Frank Church in Idaho, told the press that Symms probably lost votes because of "erroneous charges" made by New Rightists against Church.[106]

The indications that the efforts to mobilize a religious constituency in America had no measurable effect are congruent with the results of a survey taken among "likely voters" by NBC News and the Associated Press in early

October 1980. They found that when asked whether an election recommendation by a member of the clergy would "make you more likely to vote for that candidate, less likely to vote for that candidate, or wouldn't it make a difference," that only 3 percent replied more likely, 8 percent said less likely, and 88 percent answered, "no difference." Only 3 percent reported having "been asked by a member of the clergy to vote for a specific candidate in this fall's election."

The available evidence bearing on the 1980 elections would appear to sustain the thesis that the emergence of a political evangelical movement and the electoral swing toward conservatism were parallel developments, which may have been mutually-reinforcing, rather than related in a cause and effect fashion. That is, the politicization of the evangelicals did not contribute much to the G.O.P. victories, except possibly in the South, where it may have helped to increase electoral participation. Economic and foreign-policy reversals pressed all segments of the American electorate to shift toward the Republicans, while challenges to traditional religious-linked values activated the political concerns of many fundamentalists.

The white South, the stronghold of the evangelicals, has been moving away from the Democratic party ever since 1948, first on the presidential level, and more recently in Senatorial and House contests. The first candidate to win a Senatorial contest running on the G.O.P. line in a Confederate state was Strom Thurmond in 1962. By 1981, the Republicans held 11 out of the 22 seats in the states which had seceded before the Civil War. These changes reflect a process of party realignment by the Southern whites, as they react to the conflict between their dominant, racial, economic and cultural values and those of the national Democratic party. But it should be noted that the weighted results of the *New York Times*-CBS News 1980 Election Day Exit Poll indicate that in the South Carter retained a larger proportion of those who said they voted for him in 1976 among white, born-again Protestants, 88 percent, than he did among other white Protestants, 76 percent, or Catholics, 64 percent.

If the right-wing evangelicals were not effective in seriously influencing their co-religionists' voting behavior, what is the import of their activity? Perhaps they are best thought of not as evangelical groups, but as right-wing political groups which happen to have an evangelical bent. Perhaps, organizationally, they should be seen as a part of—perhaps a tail to—the so-called New Right network.

That "network" includes Richard Viguerie with his famous computer in Falls Church; Paul Weyrich with his Committee for the Survival of a Free Congress; Terry Dolan with his National Conservative Political Action Committee and Howard Phillips with the Conservative Caucus. According to one journalistic history, this network began to see the usefulness of the "moral issues" to their right-wing cause before the evangelical preachers seriously got into political activity. It was Weyrich who helped form the Christian Voice with one of his close associates as its legislative consultant. Then Weyrich, an Eastern-rite Catholic, along with Howard Phillips, a Jew, helped to establish the Moral Majority, with the Reverend Jerry Falwell at its head. The Reverend Robert Billings was at one time both the executive director of the Moral Majority, and Weyrich's deputy at the Committee for the Survival of a Free Congress. [107]

The prime senatorial targets were named by Terry Dolan of NCPAC, and indeed by the Republican Party, before the Moral Majority did so. Those Senators were named not only because they were hated liberals, but because in most cases their records on defense and inflation seemed out of step with substantial sentiments in their districts; in other words, they were vulnerable to begin with.

The sheer amount of time and money which the New Right and the politicized evangelicals expended on some target areas may have had some practical political effect—especially in congressional districts where name recognition was a factor. Philip Sheldon, of Christian Voice, reported his belief that the political evangelical groups did not so much *start* new waves of political activity, as they did *service* those emerging on their own. "Something was happening out there," he said. Groups like his found a "sense of outrage," and, indeed, the initiative to call for his agency's services often came from the churches themselves. It is important to recognize the significance of churches as natural places of social contact, where the "sense of outrage" became naturally converted to political activity. Sometimes meetings were held after church. Often, agencies like Christian Voice were called for literature and political advice. "We found that people were waiting for us," Sheldon said, but basically, he felt, local church groups did it on their own.

Therefore, while the role of the culturally conservative impulses, and of the religious institutions which harbored them, must be acknowledged, the country's political swing was present before the New Right went into action; and the change was recorded around the nation in districts which were not targeted by the New Right. And, most of all, it should be noted that the swing turned around neither the evangelical population nor the support for evangelical issues.

Conclusion

What is most striking about the right-wing backlash movements in Europe and the United States during the last decade is not the fact that they exist, but their weakness, particularly when compared to the electoral and membership strength of comparable tendencies in the interwar years generally or the immediate postwar era in the United States and France. Certainly the stimulus for such movements has existed. The challenge to the status, power and cultural influence of traditionalist elements has been great. Urbanization and industrialization have continued at a rapid pace. Left-wing politicians have held office in many countries since World War II. Legislation threatening the power of private business through nationalization and government regulation has been enacted in most nations. Communism has continued to expand on an international scale. From the mid-sixties on, a veritable cultural revolution has occurred with respect to relations between the sexes and the generations. The kinds of behavior characterized as "loose" by the rightists of the interwar years are now much more common than ever before.

Yet, relatively little support has developed for extremist movements designed to counter these developments. The interesting problem, therefore, is not to account for the revival of backlash rightist politics, but rather its failure. The explanation for the apparent political weakness of traditionalist forces would seem to lie in structural changes which have undermined their social base. The proportion of the population remaining in agriculture has declined greatly, as has that residing in small towns. Conversely, the occupational and educational trends which have been identified with the emergence of a post-industrial society indicate the extent to which there has been a rapid growth in the numbers engaged in pursuits which require advanced education.

Religion also has lost considerable support; there are simply fewer people living in the environments which produce its adherents. There has been a decline in the proportion of those who attend church regularly. According to the Gallup Poll, the percentage who attended church in a typical week in the United States was 58 percent in 1944, 49 percent in 1955, falling gradually to 40 percent in 1973, a figure which has remained fairly constant through to 1979. The proportion of American adults who report themselves as church members has fallen from 73 percent in 1965 to 68 in 1979.[108] Gallup also reports as of the end of 1979, "the percentage of persons who have religious training has declined sharply over the last quarter-century. In addition, the proportion of persons who say they have no religious preference has increased from two percent in 1966 to eight percent in our latest surveys. . . . An increase in secularity: Far fewer today than in earlier years, for example, believe religion can answer all or most of today's problems."[109]

The trend in replies to the question: "How important would you say religion is in your own life—very important, fairly important, or not very important?" also reveals a steady decline from 1952 to 1978, with 75 percent reporting "very important" in 1952, down to 70 in 1965, and falling to 52 in 1978. There has, however, been a slight reversal in 1980, up to 56 percent. The recent increase, however, was much greater among Catholics, from 51 in 1978 to 56 in 1980, than among Protestants, from 60 in 1978 to 62 in 1980.[110]

Similar patterns have occurred in other western nations. The Institute for Demoskopie reports that the proportion of Germans who take communion at least once a year has declined greatly between 1953 and 1979, from 66 to 48 percent among Catholics, and from 41 to 28 percent among Protestants. Only 8 percent of all Germans attended church "regularly" in 1980, down from 15 percent in 1963. In France, the percentage who regularly attend mass on Sunday has fallen from 23 in 1966 to 19 in 1970 to 13.5 in 1975.[111]

But, if traditional religion has lost support in many countries, it should be noted that the United States is still the most religious country in the Western world, with the exception of Ireland.[112] In 1977, youth between the ages of 18 and 24 were asked by Gallup affiliates in a number of countries whether religion is "very important" in their lives. Over 40 percent of American youth answered in the affirmative, against less than 10 percent of those in each of Japan, France, Germany and Great Britain.[113] Gallup surveys of the entire adult population also reveal that Americans generally are more likely to hold this view of religion's importance (58 percent do so) than the citizens of 12 other developed countries. A much larger proportion of Americans (94 percent) report a belief in God than in the other nations. Most noteworthy is the finding that among these 13 states, the only ones in which a majority say that they "believe in life after death" are the United States (71 percent) and Canada (54 percent). Less than two-fifths of the French, West Germans and Scandinavians share this faith.[114]

Moreover, the character of religion in both Europe and America has changed. The Catholic Church in particular is no longer a homogeneous source of antimodernist conservative thought. In many countries, large numbers of the clergy and lay people identify with liberal-left socioeconomic doctrines. Most Catholics in the United States practice birth control, and half of them favor legalized abortion. Similar shifts have occurred among the Protestant denominations as well. Although membership in evangelical churches increased somewhat during the 1970s, these denominations form a much smaller proportion of the population than during the 1920s and 1930s. And a recent report in *Christianity Today* notes that the Southern Baptists, the "largest predominantly conservative denomination in the United States, with 13 million members, not only faces a decline in the number of baptisms, but is now also losing 1,000 pastors from the ministry annually."[115]

In line with the thesis that the activization of backlash politics is a response to a decline in the strength of a group, John Madeley has argued that it is the weakness of religion in Scandinavia (less than 10 percent are church attenders in a given week) that "facilitated the emergence of the Scandinavian species of Christian Democracy. The narrowing of the religious constituency by the decline of traditional norms of religious observance and belief has facilitated the growth among the religiously active of an awareness of a common distinctive heritage of social and moral values.[116]

Efforts to revive right-wing extremist movements flounder because of the absence of a social base and the fact that, France apart, their views are rejected by the educated strata. Ironically, the most effective attacks on "modernist" tendencies associated with growth, bigness and cultural integration have come from elements identified with the rationalist, culturally radical Left.

The failure of militant protest, both on the Right and the Left, may also be linked to the general prosperity of the post–World War II years. The 30 years after the war ended witnessed the longest period without a serious depression since the start of the Industrial Revolution. It was a period of sustained growth in most Western industrialized countries (Britain is a conspicuous exception), which brought about a sizable increase in the per capita national income and an expanded opportunity for upward social mobility. There have, of course, been downswings and periods of inflation, but these have been milder and of shorter duration than before the last war. Although many have suffered economic reverses, these have not been so severe nor so widespread as in previous eras. Thus economic discontent has not served to fuel the fires of militant political discontent. It is noteworthy that the rise of a large-scale nativist reaction to the presence of foreign workers in Switzerland occurred in the seventies during a severe economic recession.

Major national political reverses, particularly the Algerian War in France and the Vietnam War in the United States, have led to periods of internal political instability marked by massive protest on the Left and the Right. The opposition to the Vietnam war not only brought about a crisis of authority in the United States, it spread to stimulate the growth of left-wing opposition among the educated and younger postindustrial strata in other countries. As noted, traditional elements sought to resist the changes in morality associated with these developments, as well as to oppose the claim of ethnic-racial minorities and foreign migrants to economic and social rights.

There seems little possibility that right-wing backlash movements will re-emerge as major threats to the democratic process in developed countries in the absence of severe economic crises or major international challenges to national security. To repeat, what is most notable about such efforts since the 1960s is their inability to mobilize influential followings. Right-wing extremist parties rarely secure more than 5 percent of the vote. And no matter how the politics of the various New Rights are evaluated, their supporters can rarely be accused of engaging in extremist tactics, small groups of neofascists and terrorists apart. For the most part, the backlash moralistic reactions are contained within the conservative or religious parties and some churches. The New Politics and New Left tendencies, based on a sizable segment of those involved in the expanding occupations of postindustrial society who have considerable influence in the opinion-molding institutions, including the universities and the media, have had an impact on the politics and cultural life of their societies. Like the New Right, they are committed to working within the framework of democratic institutions, again excepting tiny extremist and terrorist groups. Functioning for the most part as factions inside the mass left-of-center parties, they have influenced policies on issues such as the environment and energy and have constituted influential allies for minority, ethnic and national movements.

Still, it should be emphasized that the most important measurable effect of recent antimodernist reactions on the western political systems has been the reduction of correlation between social class and support of Left and Right politics. Postmaterialist tendencies have generated new sources of support for the Left from a segment of the more affluent and better educated, while reactive social conservatism has helped recruit support to right-of-center parties from less privileged and less educated strata.

Notes

1. M. Weber, *Essays in Sociology* H. H. Gerth and C. Wright Mills (eds.), (New York: Oxford University Press, 1946), p. 155.
2. G. Germani, *Authoritarianism, Fascism, and National Populism* (New Brunswick, N.J.: Transaction, 1978), p. 7, emphasis in original.
3. T. Parsons, *Politics and Social Structure* (New York: Free Press, 1969), p. 110.
4. Ibid., p. 115.
5. Germani, *Authoritarianism, Fascism, and National Populism*, p. 16.
6. A. F. K. Organski, "Fascism and Modernization," in S. J. Wolf (ed.), *The Nature of Fascism* (New York: Random House, 1968), pp. 24–25.
7. S. Rokkan, *Citizens, Elections, Parties* (New York: David McKay, 1970), pp. 102–103.
8. Ibid., p. 106.
9. E. K. Scheuch, "Right Wing Radicalism in Western Industrial Societies," (unpublished paper, Department of Sociology, University of Cologne, 1967), p. 5.
10. H. Morgenthau, *The Restoration of American Politics* (Chicago: University of Chicago Press, 1962), p. 29.
11. S. M. Lipset and E. Raab, *The Politics of Unreason: Right-Wing Extremism in America, 1790–1977*, 2d ed. (Chicago: University of Chicago Press, 1978).
12. Ibid., p. 429.
13. J. Q. Wilson, "Reagan and the Republican Revival," *Commentary* 70 (October 1980): 28; Lipset and Raab, *The Politics of Unreason*, pp. 94–95.
14. A. Rice, *The Ku Klux Klan in American Politics* (Washington D.C.: Public Affairs Press, 1962), p. 16.
15. C. Alexander, *The Ku Klux Klan in the Southwest* (Lexington: University of Kentucky Press, 1965), pp. 26–27.
16. G. Myers, *History of Bigotry in the United States* (New York: Capricorn, 1960), p. 366.

17. D. S. Strong, *Organized Anti-Semitism in America* (Washington D.C.: American Council of Public Affairs, 1941), pp. 76–77.
18. M. Janowitz, "Black Legions on the March," in D. Aaron (ed.), *America in Crisis* (New York: Knopf, 1952), p. 318.
19. G. Cougan, *Money Creators* (Chicago: Sound Money Press, 1955), pp. 280–81.
20. J. Anderson and R. W. May, *McCarthy, the Man, the Senator, the Ism* (Boston: Beacon, 1952), p. 364.
21. *Congressional Record,* "Communists in Government Service," 81st Congress, 2d session, 20 February 1950, p. 1954.
22. A. J. Mayer, *Dynamics of Counter-revolution in Europe, 1870–1956: An Analytic Framework* (New York: Harper & Row, 1971).
23. F. Stern, *The Politics of Cultural Despair: A Study in the Rise of the Germanic Ideology* (Berkeley: University of California Press, 1961), pp. xviii–xix. See also Z. Sternhell, "Fascist Ideology," in W. Laqueur (ed.), *Fascism: A Reader's Guide* (Berkeley: University of California Press, 1976), pp. 321–22.
24. P. Gay, *Weimar Culture: The Outsider as Insider* (New York: Harper, 1968), p. 96.
25. G. L. Mosse, *The Crisis of German Ideology: Intellectual Origins of the Third Reich* (New York: Grosset & Dunlap, 1964), p. 4.
26. Ibid., p. 7.
27. H. A. Turner Jr., "Fascism and Modernization," *World Politics* 24 (1972): 550.
28. E. Nolte, *Three Faces of Fascism* (New York: Holt, Rinehart & Winston, 1966), pp. 149–50.
29. R. A. Webster, *The Cross and the Fasces: Christian Democracy and Fascism in Italy* (Stanford: Stanford University Press, 1960), pp. 10–11.
30. G. L. Mosse, "Introduction: The Genesis of Fascism," in W. Laqueur and G. L. Mosse (eds.), *International Fascism, 1920–1945* (New York: Harper, 1966), p. 16.
31. R. Soucy, "French Fascism as Class Conciliation and Moral Regeneration," *Societas: A Review of Social History* 1 (1971): 293, 294–95.
32. K. von Klemperer, "On Austrofascism," *Central European History* 11 (1978): 315.
33. W. Sauer, "National Socialism: Totalitarianism or Fascism," *American Historical Review* 73 (1967): 420.
34. F. L. Carsten, "Interpretations of Fascism," in Laqueur (ed.), *Fascism: A Reader's Guide,* pp. 426–27. The Nolte quote is from E. Nolte, *Die Faschistischen Bewegungen* (Munich: Deutscher Taschenbuch-Verlag, 1966), pp. 189–90.
35. H. Rogger, "Afterthoughts," in H. Rogger and E. Weber (eds.), *The European Right: A Historical Profile* (Berkeley: University of California Press, 1965), pp. 577, 587–88.
36. A. J. Gregor, "Fascism and Modernization: Some Addenda," *World Politics* 26 (1974): 370–85.
37. S. M. Lipset, *Political Man: The Social Bases of Politics,* expanded and updated, ed. (Baltimore: Johns Hopkins University Press, 1981), pp. 144–46; A. Szymanski, "Fascism, Industrialism and Socialism: The Case of Italy," *Comparative Studies in Society and History* 15 (1973): 395–404.
38. Sauer, "National Socialism: Totalitarianism or Fascism," p. 417.

39. J. Linz, "Some Notes Toward a Comparative Study of Fascism in Sociological Historical Perspective," in Laqueur (ed.), *Fascism: A Reader's Guide,* p. 15.
40. Ibid., pp. 26–27.
41. Ibid., p. 5.
42. Clara Zetkin, "Der Kampf gegen den Fashismus," protocol of the Enlarged Executive of the Communist International, as quoted in Carsten, "Interpretations of Fascism," p. 418. Carsten cites latter-day dissident Communists, August Thalheimer and Paul Serrine, as making similar points, p. 419.
43. Germani, *Authoritarianism, Fascism, and National Populism,* p. 47.
44. G. Germani, "Fascism and Class," in S. J. Woolf (ed.), *The Nature of Fascism* (New York: Random House, 1968), p. 89.
45. P. Campbell, "Le Mouvement Poujade," *Parliamentary Affairs* 10 (1957): 363–65, See also J. Meynard, "Un essai d'interpretation du mouvement Poujade," *Revue de l'institut de sociologie* 1 (1956): 5–38, and S. Hoffman, *Le Mouvement Poujade* (Paris: Librairie Armand Colin, 1956).
46. D. Bell, *The Coming of Post-Industrial Society* (New York: Basic Books, 1973); A. Touraine, *The Post-Industrial Society: Tomorrow's Social History: Classes, Conflicts, and Culture in the Programmed Society* (New York: Random House, 1971); J. Gurshuny, *After Industrial Society? The Emerging Self-service Economy* (London: Macmillan, 1978); B. Gustafsson (ed.), *Post-industrial Society* (New York: St. Martin's, 1979).
47. R. Inglehart, "The Silent Revolution in Europe: Inter-Generational Change in Post-Industrial Societies," *American Political Science Review* 65 (1971): 991–1017; *The Silent Revolution: Changing Values and Political Styles Among Western Publics* (Princeton: Princeton University Press, 1977); "Value Priorities and Socioeconomic Change," in S. H. Barnes and M. Kaase (eds.), *Political Action: Mass Participation in Five Western Democracies* (Beverly Hills: Sage, 1979), pp. 305–42.
48. S. C. Flanagan, "Value Change and Partisan Change in Japan: The Silent Revolution Revisited," *Comparative Politics* 11 (1979): 274.
49. W. Zaph, "Political and Social Strains in Europe Today," (unpublished paper, Department of Sociology, University of Mannheim, 1980), p. 5.
50. S. M. Lipset, "The Industrial Proletariat and the Intelligentsia in Comparative Perspective," chapter 5 in this volume.
51. M. Schiff, "Neo-transcendentalism in the New Left Counter-culture: A Vision of the Future Looking Back," *Comparative Studies in Society and History* 15 (1973): 132, 139, 140.
52. These ideas are elaborated and documented in S. M. Lipset, "The Industrial Proletariat and the Intelligentsia in Comparative Perspective" in chapter 5 in this volume.
53. C. R. Foster (ed.), *Nations Without a State: Ethnic Minorities in Western Europe* (New York: Praeger, 1980).
54. J. Alexander, "Core Solidarity, Ethnic Outgroup and Social Differentiation: A Multidimensional Model of Inclusion in Modern Societies," in J. Dofny and A. Akiwowo (eds.), *National and Ethnic Movements* (Beverly Hills: Sage, 1980), p. 6.
55. A. Lijphart, "Political Theories and the Explanation of Ethnic Conflict in the Western World: Falsified Predictions and Plausible Postdictions," in M. J. Esman (ed.), *Ethnic Conflict in the Western World* (Ithaca: Cornell University Press, 1977), pp. 46–78; S. M. Lipset, "Racial and Ethnic Tensions in the

Third World,'' in W. S. Thompson (ed.), *The Third World: Premises of U.S. Policy* (San Francisco: Institute for Contemporary Studies, 1978), pp. 123–48; N. Glazer and D. P. Moynihan (eds.), *Ethnicity: Theory and Experience* (Cambridge: Harvard University Press, 1975), pp. 6–7.

56. R. Lafont, *La Révolution régionaliste* (Paris: Gallimard, 1967) and *Décoloniser en France* (Paris: Gallimard, 1971); M. Hechter, *Internal Colonialism: The Celtic Fringe in British National Development* (Berkeley: University of California Press, 1975).

57. E. Allardt, ''Implications of the Ethnic Revival in Modern Society'' (colloquium paper, Woodrow Wilson International Center for Scholars, 22 May 1979), p. 28.

58. Ibid., pp. 9–12.

59. E. Morin, *Commune en France: La métamorphose de Plodémet* (Paris: Fayard, 1967), pp. 61, 276 ff., as summarized in S. Berger, ''Bretons and Jacobins: Reflections on French Regional Identity,'' in Esman (ed.), *Ethnic Conflict in the Western World*, p. 176.

60. J. E. Jacob, ''Ethnic Mobilization and the Pursuit of Post-Industrial Values: The Case of Occitanie,'' *The Tocqueville Review* 2 (1980): 77–78. For comparable tendencies in other French regional movements, see Berger, ''Bretons and Jacobins,'' pp. 168–76.

61. Inglehart, *The Silent Revolution*, p. 237.

62. M. J. Esman, ''Perspectives on Ethnic Conflict in Industrialized Societies,'' in Esman (ed.), *Ethnic Conflict in the Western World*, pp. 374–75; W. Beer, ''The Social Class of Ethnic Activists in Contemporary France,'' in Esman (ed.), *Ethnic Conflict in the Western World*, pp. 143–58.

63. J. T. S. Madeley, ''Scandinavian Christian Democracy: Throwback or Portent?'' *European Journal of Political Research* 5 (1977): 270; M. N. Pedersen, ''Denmark: The Breakdown of a Working Multiparty System'' (unpublished paper, Odense University, Odense, Denmark, 1979), p. 21.

64. S. Rokkan and H. Valen, ''The Mobilization of the Periphery,'' *Acta Sociologica* 6 (1962): 111–41.

65. Pedersen, ''Denmark: The Breakdown of a Working Multiparty System,'' p. 21.

66. J. L. R. Martin, *Swiss Policy on Immigrant Workers and the Uberfremdung Initiatives: A Study in Consociational Democracy and Direct Democracy* (Ph.D. diss., Department of Political Science, Yale University, 1979), pp. 3, 196–229.

67. R. Sankiaho, ''A Model of the Rise of Populism and Support for the Finnish Rural Party,'' *Scandinavian Political Studies* 6 (1971): 41.

68. Pedersen, ''Denmark,'' p. 51.

69. D. R. Schweitzer, ''Status Politics and Conservative Ideology: A French-Swiss Case in National and Comparative Perspective,'' *European Journal of Political Research* 5 (1977): 398.

70. Martin, *Swiss Policy on Immigrant Workers*, p. 338.

71. Ibid., pp. 339–44.

72. Ibid., ''Abstract,'' p. iii.

73. Quoted in R. Kaplan, ''France's New Right,'' *Commentary* 69 (March 1980): 51. For a detailed exposition of New Right ideas and a bibliography of relevant writings, see E. Weber, ''Dextrogyrations in Paris,'' *The Times Literary Supplement*, 10 October 1980: 1133–34.

74. Kaplan, ''France's New Right,'' p. 51.

75. Quoted in J. Block-Michel, ''Anti-Semitism and the French 'New Right,' '' *Dissent* 27 (Summer 1980): 296.

76. V. J. Charlot, "Les élites et les masses devant l'indépendance nationale d'après les enquêtes d'opinion," in *Les conditions de l'indépendance nationale dans le monde moderne* (Paris: Editions Cujas, 1977), p. 45.
77. J. Thibau, *La France colonisée* (Paris: Flammarion, 1980); Y. Florenne, " 'La France Colonisée' de Jacques Thibau," *Le Monde diplomatique* (April 1980): 22.
78. J. A. Kirkpatrick, "Patterns of Partisanship in Post-Gaullist France," in H. R. Penneman (ed.), *The French National Assembly Elections of 1978* (Washington D.C.: American Enterprise Institute, 1980), p. 212.
79. Charlot, "Les Élites et les masses," p. 48.
80. *The Economist* (London), "Gollum and Friends," 11 October 1980: 56.
81. M. Dogan, "Political Cleavage and Social Stratification in France and Italy," in S. M. Lipset and S. Rokkan (eds.), *Party Systems and Voter Alignments* (New York: Free Press, 1967), p. 159.
82. G. Loewenberg, "The Development of the German Party System," in K. H. Cerny (ed.), *Germany at the Polls: The Bundestag Election of 1976* (Washington, D.C.: American Enterprise Institute, 1978), p. 23.
83. Lipset and Raab, *The Politics of Unreason.*
84. Ibid., pp. 525–35.
85. A. Crawford, *Thunder on the Right: The "New Right" and the Politics of Resentment* (New York: Pantheon, 1980), pp. 144–55.
86. Ibid., pp. 159–64.
87. B. Keller, "Lobbying for Christ: Evangelical Christians Move from Pews to Polls, But Can They Sway Congress?," *Congressional Quarterly Weekly Report,* 6 September 1980: 2627.
88. Ibid., p. 2633.
89. J. W. Michaels, "Conservative Christians Spread Influence, Attract Political Attention," *National Catholic Reporter*, 15 August 1980: 8.
90. R. Sennett, "Power to the People," *The New York Review of Books,* 25 September 1980: 24, 27; L. J. Davis, "Conservatism in America," *Harper's* 261 (October 1980): 21–26.
91. D. Clendinen, "Rev. Falwell Inspires Evangelical Vote," *New York Times*, 20 August 1980, p. 822.
92. Keller, "Lobbying for Christ," p. 2634.
93. Crawford, *Thunder on the Right,* p. 216.
94. *Christianity Today*, "The Christianity Today–Gallup Poll: An Overview," 21 December 1979: 1666–69.
95. *Christianity Today*, "Who and Where Are the Evangelicals?" 21 December 1979: 1671–72.
96. T. Clancy, "Fundamental Facts about Evangelicals," *America,* 31 May 1980: 456.
97. Ibid., p. 456.
98. L. Harris, "The Evangelical Vote," *ABC News-Harris Survey*, 6 October 1980: 3.
99. K. A. Briggs, "Evangelicals Turning to Politics Fear Moral Slide Imperils Nation," *New York Times*, 19 August 1980, p. 10.
100. Keller, "Lobbying for Christ," p. 2632.
101. C. F. H. Henry, "Henry on Gallup: Faith and Social Concerns," *Christianity Today*, 10 October 1980: 1136–37; D. O. Moberg, "Do the Properly Pious Really Care?," *Christianity Today*, 19 September 1980: 1047.

102. A. J. Menendez, *Religion at the Polls* (Philadelphia: Westminster, 1977), pp. 138–40, 197–98, 217–18.
103. The results of this poll are reported in T. Smith, "Carter Post-Mortem: Debate Hurt, But It Wasn't Only Cause of Defeat," *New York Times,* 9 November 1980, pp. 1, 18, and the *National Journal,* "Carter's Collapse: The Anatomy of Reagan's Victory," 8 November 1980: 1878.
104. W. E. Barnes and C. Irving, "Why Reagan Won: He Played upon Nation's Frustrations," *San Francisco Chronicle,* 9 November 1980, p. 28.
105. Harris, "The Evangelical Vote," p. 2.
106. B. Keller, "New Right Wants Credit for Democrats' Nov. 4 Losses But GOP, Others Don't Agree," *Congressional Quarterly Weekly Report,* 15 November 1980: 3372–73.
107. Davis, "Conservatism in America."
108. G. Gallup, *The Gallup Poll, Public Opinion 1935–1971,* Vol. 1 (New York: Random House, 1972), p. 473; "40% Attend Church in Typical Week," *Princeton Religion Research Center Emerging Trends,* January 1980: 1; "68% of Adults Are Church Members," *Princeton Religion Research Center Emerging Trends,* February 1980: 1.
109. G. Gallup, "10 Key Trends in Religion in U. S.," *Princeton Religion Research Center Emerging Trends,* January 1980: 3.
110. G. Gallup, "More Today See Religion Important," *Princeton Religion Research Center Emerging Trends,* October 1980: 1.
111. F. A. Isambert, "Le Sociologue, le prêtre et le fidèle," in H. Mendras (ed.), *La sagesse et le désordre France 1980* (Paris: Gallimard, 1980), p. 228.
112. For an analysis of the structural sources of American religiosity see S. M. Lipset, *The First New Nation: The United States in Historical and Comparative Perspective,* 2d ed., (New York: Norton, 1979), pp. 140–69.
113. G. Gallup, *The International Gallup Polls: Public Opinion 1978* (Wilmington: Scholarly Resources, 1980), p. 399.
114. "Opinion Roundup," *Public Opinion* 2 (March/May 1979): 38–39.
115. C. F. H. Henry, "Evangelicals: Out of the Closet but Going Nowhere?," *Christianity Today,* 4 January 1980: 18.
116. Madeley, "Scandinavian Christian Democracy," p. 270.

8

Values and Political Structure:
Moralism, Movements, and Violence
in American Society

Events during the late 1960s and early 1970s gave rise to considerable distress both at home and abroad concerning the state and future prospects of the American political system. The political parties were under intense attack from the Right and the Left for their seeming inability to respond quickly to changes in popular sentiment about issues of war, poverty, and race. The Democratic and Republican parties were charged with being unrepresentative, and many Americans gave their energies and support to third, even fourth, party efforts. Further, there arose over the issues of race and war movements dedicated to achieving their ends through militant and often violent political action outside the party system—actions ranging from demonstrations to illegal acts of civil disobedience. The operations of major universities were halted and sections of major cities were burned to the ground. Punctuating this turmoil, and perhaps most distressing of all, were a series of political assassinations.

Given the popular conception of America as a conservative and stable nation characterized by consensus politics, these events suggested to many that the American system was breaking down, that the two-party system that seemingly functioned well in the past was no longer adequate to deal with "modern" problems. It is useful to put matters such as these into some historical and comparative perspective. Even a cursory review of American political history suggests the conclusion that the protests of the 1960s, at the very least, were thoroughly precedented—that moralistic mass movements characterized by the politics of conscience and extreme commitment, which on occasion have encouraged violence, have emerged on past occasions.

The conservative image of American politics has been fostered by the fact that all efforts to create radical "third" parties, whether of the Left or Right, have failed. The United States remains one of the few countries without any socialist representation in its legislative bodies. The Democratic Party claims correctly to be the oldest party in the world with continuous existence. And although its opposition has changed format over the years, it is possible to trace a line of continuity among the more elitist-based Federalist, Whig, and Republican parties.

Partisan continuity in two broad electoral coalitions, which include groups that are often in conflict with each other, however, has not prevented the enactment of important changes. The clue to the flexibility of the American two-party system in policy terms has been the relative ease with which a variety of "social movements," some of which have also been third parties, have arisen and had a significant impact. These movements have included the large-scale anti-Masonic party of the 1820s and early thirties, abolitionism, which rose to strength in the forties and fifties, the large nativist and anti-Catholic organizations that rose and fell with considerable support during the nineteenth century and the early 1900s, the prohibition movement that existed for over a century before its success in enacting the Eighteenth Amendment, the various radical agrarian movements of the second half of the nineteenth century, the suffragette movement in the nineteenth and early twentieth century, the multimillion-member Ku Klux Klan of the 1920s, the pro-fascist mass-based movements of Father Coughlin and others of the 1930s, the various socialist and other liberal-left organizations of this century, the McCarthyite syndrome of the 1950s, the assorted white segregationist groups of the post–World War II era, their opponents in the rising civil rights and black nationalist movements, the campus-based movement against the Vietnam war, and, finally, the feminist, environmental, antinuclear power and freeze movements.

The politics of social *movements* as distinct from that of *parties* creates a sharply divergent image of the degree of stability and instability and of the ability of dissident groups to foster change in America. If we contrast the American political system with that of a number of affluent European nations (e.g., Great Britain and Scandinavia) with respect to the frequency and importance of major mass movements, the United States would clearly appear to be less stable, i.e., it gives rise to more movements.

The implications of the distinction between movement and party may be pointed out by a comparative look at Canada and the United States.[1] Since World War I, Canadian politics has witnessed a growth of many "third parties." These include the Progressives in the 1920s who became the second largest party for a brief period and controlled the government in a number of provinces; New Democracy, a third party that secured their 10 percent of the vote in the mid-1930s; the socialist Cooperative Commonwealth Federation (CCF), now renamed the New Democratic Party (NDP), and Social Credit, both formed during the 1930s; and a host of French Canadian parties that have had transient but significant electoral success in various provincial and federal elections in the Province of Quebec. If one examined a statistical table that reports on Canadian and American federal, provincial, and state elections between 1916 and the present, one would have to conclude if he or she had no other information, that the Canadians have been among the world's most unstable and tension-ridden people, while the U.S. electorate is relatively quite conservative and unmovable, except in terms of switches between the two major parties. The only significant third-party vote cast during the same period was that received by Senator Robert La Follette in his Progressive campaign in 1924.[2] But such a conclusion could only derive from the evaluation of political stability and conservatism in terms of the rise and fall of ideological parties to the right and left of the two major moderate ones; and it would clearly, in our view, be in error.

The equivalent of new minor parties in the American context has been extraparliamentary social movements. Not being part of the normal partisan political game, they are all the more likely to be extremist in their tactics. They are not subject to the discipline inherent in the need to win the support of moderate voters which parties face. Rather, as minority-based movements they try to force the leaders of the two broad-based electoral coalitions to respond to their demands. Lacking the discipline of parties seeking to elect people to office, many of them have appealed openly to racial and religious tensions. Some of them have sought to label their opponents as agents of foreign conspiracies; or like the abolitionists, the two Ku Klux Klans, the Southern segregationists, or the current antiwar movement, they have engaged in civil disobedience, employing tactics that violate what they have held to be "immoral law," even if enacted by democratically elected governments. Some of these movements, whether extremist or not in tactics, have been radical in their objectives, e.g., seeking to upset existing concepts of property rights.

A view of American history that focuses on the role and tactics of movements, as distinct from parties, must produce the conclusion that reliance on methods outside of the normal political game has played a major role in affecting change throughout most of American history. While most of the movements mentioned here have not engaged in violence as such, it is important also to recognize that some of the major changes in American society have been a product of violent tactics resulting from the willingness of some of those who have felt that they had a morally righteous cause to take the law into their own hands in order to advance it. And by extreme actions, whether violent or not, the moralistic radical minorities have often secured the support or acquiescence of some of the moderate elements, who have come to accept the fact that change is necessary in order to gain a measure

of peace and stability. To some extent, also, the extremists on a given side
of an issue have lent credence to the arguments presented by the moderates
on that issue. Extremists, whether of the Right or Left, have often helped the
moderates in the center to press through reforms.

The most striking example of this sort of behavior in American history has
been the successful movement to abolish slavery. The radical abolitionists
were willing to violate congressional law and Supreme Court decisions to
make their case before the public and to help black slaves escape to Canada.
Some of them were even ready to fight with arms in order to guarantee that
the western territories would remain free of slavery. John Brown's armed
raid on Harper's Ferry played a major role in convincing both Southerners
and Northerners that the slavery debate had to be ended, either by secession
or by some form of manumission. Conversely, the violence of the first Ku
Klux Klan after the Civil War helped convince the North that it had to desist
in its effort to prevent white domination of the South. The guerrilla actions
of the Klansmen played a major role in reestablishing white Bourbon power
and in securing the end of Reconstruction.

The women's suffrage movement, as it gained strength, also manifested
the depth of its commitment by various forms of civil disobedience such as
efforts to disrupt the orderly operation of government by illegal demonstrations, women chaining themselves to buildings, and so forth. Some prohi-
bitionists also showed the intensity of their feelings against liquor by efforts
to ridicule and ostracize those patronizing saloons, and even on occasion by
violent attempts to prevent dispensers of liquor from doing business.

The violence often exercised by various anti-Catholic movements both
before and after the Civil War, continuing into the twentieth century, had
considerable effect on local authorities in determining their policies in the
schools.[3] They also activated opposition to mass immigration. The violence
of the second Ku Klux Klan following World War I played an important role
in intimidating opposition to nativism and Protestant fundamentalism, and
helped pass legislation against non-Protestant immigration.

During the Great Depression, illegal efforts were also important. Agrarian
movements brought about moratoriums on mortgage-debt collection and changes
in various banking laws by their armed actions designed to prevent the sale
of farms for nonpayment of debt. In the cities, also, the labor movement won
its right to collective bargaining in industries that had traditionally opposed
it by illegal "sit-ins" in factories in Akron, Detroit, and other places. State
governments found themselves helpless to remove workers from factories,
and antiunion employers were often forced to accept unions in their plants
by these actions.

Following the Supreme Court school desegregation decision in 1954, the
issue of black rights in the South stimulated both sides to engage in civil

disobedience to attain their opposing moral ends. The Southern white up-holders of segregation initiated such tactics when organizations like the White Citizens' Councils and the Klan, and various elected officials, including governors, police chiefs, and judges, deliberately disregarded the law as enunciated by the Supreme Court and Congress. Ross Barnett of Mississippi, George Wallace of Alabama, and Lester Maddox of Georgia essentially told their followers that it was right to disregard immoral law, that they should do all in their power to prevent the enforcement of integration.

It is important to recognize that the tactics of civil disobedience and even of violence in the black-white struggles in the South were introduced by Southern conservative whites, a point made many years ago by Gunnar Myrdal in his classic study of the black problem in the United States, *An American Dilemma.*[4] Myrdal pointed out in the forties that the conservative white up-holders of segregation endorsed law violation and engaged in what we now call civil disobedience. The blacks and their white supporters learned from firsthand experience with those in authority in the South that the most effective tactic in their struggle was civil disobedience, that this was necessary to counter the illegal actions of their opponents. The use of ''sit-ins'' arose in the South in the context of the civil-rights activities and then spread to the North to struggles within universities as in Berkeley, and later in the protest movement against the Vietnam War. The resort to armed violence by some of the most extreme black groups paralleled in a real sense, comparable earlier efforts by Klansmen and other white segregationists.

The politics of our social *movements* as distinct from that of our *parties* suggests not stability but instability, and emphasizes the power of dissident groups to foster change in America. If we compare the American political system to that of a number of affluent European nations with respect to the frequency, tactics and importance of mass movements, the United States would clearly appear to be *less* stable. It gives rise to more militant moralistic mass movements—but these do not result in institutionalized forms of radicalism.

The paradoxical character of American politics is not disclosed by a reading of *The Federalist* or the Constitution. It emerges, rather, from the historical experience of a people which, if not ''chosen,'' is in many respects quite peculiar.

The ''Dissidence of Dissent''

Moralism is an orientation Americans have inherited from their Protestant past. This is the *one* country in the world dominated by religious traditions of Protestant ''dissent''—the Methodists, Baptists, and other sects. The teachings of these denominations called on people to follow their conscience, with an unequivocal emphasis not to be found in those denominations which evolved from state churches (Catholics, Lutherans, Anglicans, and Orthodox Christians). The American Protestant religious ethos has assumed, in practice if not in theology, the perfectibility of humanity and their obligation to avoid sin, while the churches whose followers predominate in Europe, Canada, and Australia have accepted the inherent weakness of people, their inability to escape sinning and error, and the need for the church to be forgiving and protecting. This basic observation was made by Edmund Burke two centuries ago:

> The People are Protestants; and of that kind most averse to all implicit submission of mind and opinion. . . . Everyone knows that the Roman Catholic religion is at least coeval with most of the governments, where it prevails; that it had generally gone hand in hand with them. . . . The Church of England too was formed from her cradle under the nursing care of regular government. But the dissenting interests have sprung up in direct opposition to all the ordinary powers of the world. All Protestantism, even the most cold and passive, is a sort of dissent. But the religion most prevalent in our northern colonies is a refinement of the principles of resistance; it is the dissidence of dissent, and the Protestantism of the Protestant religion.[5]

The fact of disestablishment—that is, the absence of a state church in America—meant that a new structure of moral authority had to be created to replace the link between Church and State. The withdrawal of government support made the American form of Protestantism unique in the Christian world. Ideological and institutional changes which flowed from the Revolution led to forms of church organization analogous to popularly-based institutions: The United States became the first nation in which religious groups were viewed as purely voluntary organizations, which served to strengthen the introduction of religious morality into politics. Many ministers and laymen consciously recognized that they had to establish voluntary organizations to safeguard morality in a democratic society which lacked an established church. Associations for domestic missionary work, for temperance, for abolition, for widespread education, for peace, for the reduction of the influence of the Masons or the Catholics, and more recently for the elimination of communists, were organized by people who felt these were the only ways they could preserve and extend a moral society.

The need to assuage a sense of personal responsibility has made Americans particularly inclined to support movements for the elimination of evil—by illegal and even violent means, if necessary. A key element in the conflicts that culminated in the Civil War was the tendency of both sides to view the other as essentially sinful—as an agent of the Devil. And more recently, the resisters to the Vietnam War reenacted a two-century-old American scenario in which a "Protestant" sense of personal responsibility led the intensely committed to violate the "rules of the game." This moralistic tendency in a more secular America has been generalized far beyond its denominational or even specifically religious base. During the (Joe) McCarthy era, a distinguished French Dominican, R. L. Bruckberger, criticized American Catholics for having absorbed the American Protestant view of religion and morality. He noted that American Catholics resemble American Baptists and Presbyterians more than they resemble European or Latin American Catholics: "One often has the impression that American Catholics are more Puritan than anybody else. . . . [An] instance of the same thing was the enthusiasm whipped up by McCarthy among certain American Catholics for 'either virtue or a reign of terror.'"[6] Presumably, the emergence of a Catholic Left, which has supported civil disobedience, adds weight to this observation. But agnostic and atheistic reformers in America also tend to be utopian moralists who believe in the perfectibility of man and of civil society and in the immorality, if not specifically sinful character, of the opposition. Like Bruckberger, who reflected a more traditionally Catholic orientation, Russell Kirk has noted that the purist conservatism of his colleagues on *The National Review* also embodies an American utopian moralistic stance which differs greatly from that of European conservatism, which is much more pessimistic about human nature and society.

Moralistic politics and movement politics clearly continue today. It is not easy to be a nation which takes morality seriously. Each wave of moralistic protest and reform is necessarily followed by an era of institutionalization in which the inspired utopian hopes become the daily work of bureaucrats, and thus the passion which aroused them is left unsatisfied. Further, it becomes obvious that the problems are much more complex than assumed in the simple solutions proposed by protest movements, whether for emancipation, civil service reform, prohibition, conservation, women's suffrage, control of trusts and monopolies, intervention for economic and welfare purposes, or war against reactionary foreign states. What is often worse is the realization that what Robert K. Merton has termed the "unintended consequences of purposive social action" have brought new evils.[7]

And even when the reforms accomplish their manifest purpose, they still leave a society which is highly immoral from the vantage point of those who take seriously the constantly redefined and enlarged ideals of equality, democracy, and liberty. Corruption is perhaps endemic in a competitive meritocratic society, whether capitalist or communist, and periods of prolonged prosperity in which many become visibly wealthy generally witness the spread and institutionalization of corruption. Privilege, too, always seeks to entrench itself, and is generally able to do so in such times. Thus it is not surprising that new generations of Americans recurrently respond to some event or crisis which points anew to the gap between the American ideal and reality by supporting a new protest wave premised on the assumption that a corrupt and morally sick America must be drastically reformed.

The United States has been in such a period since the mid-1960s. As in the past, the moralistic reformers have thrown a wide net of criticism over American institutions and behavior. Not surprisingly, those most motivated to support these criticisms place them in a traditional Protestant context—of good versus evil, God versus Satan, progress against reaction—and define American society as totally evil in much the same terms as abolitionist William Lloyd Garrison did when he tore up the Constitution as a compact with the Devil. The rhetoric of American politics, as Will Herberg noted many years ago, normally goes far beyond the substantive content of the issues: Franklin Roosevelt denounced his opponents as "Copperheads"—i.e., as the equivalent of traitors to the Northern cause during the Civil War—while his rivals identified Roosevelt's New Deal as communist-inspired.

Moralism and Foreign Policy

The strength of moralistic pressures may be seen most strikingly in reactions to foreign policy issues. There have been three uniquely American stances: conscientious objection to unjust wars, nonrecognition of "evil" foreign regimes, and the insistence that wars must end with the "unconditional surrender" of the Satanic enemy. Linked to Protestant sectarianism, conscientious objection to military service was until recently largely an American phenomenon. To decry wars, to refuse to go, is at least as American as apple pie. Sol Tax of the University of Chicago, who attempted to compare the extent of antiwar activity throughout American history, concluded that as of 1968 the Vietnam War rated as our *fourth* "least popular" conflict with a foreign enemy.[8] Widespread opposition has existed to all American wars, with the possible exception of World War II, which began with a direct attack on United States soil. Large numbers refused to go along with the War of 1812, the Mexican War, the Civil War, and the Korean War. They took it as self-evident that they must obey their conscience rather than the dictates of their country's rulers.

The supporters of American wars invariably see them as moralistic crusades—to eliminate monarchical rule (the War of 1812), to defeat the Catholic forces of superstition (the Mexican War), to end slavery (the Civil War), to end colonialism in the Americas (the Spanish-American War), to make the world safe for democracy (World War I), and to resist totalitarian expansionism (World War II, Korea, and Vietnam).[9] Unlike other countries, we rarely see ourselves as merely defending our national interests. Since each war is a battle of good versus evil, the only acceptable outcome is "unconditional surrender" by the enemy.

George Kennan has written perceptively of the negative consequences of the "carrying-over into the affairs of states of the concepts of right and wrong." As he notes, when moralistic "indignation spills over into military context, it knows no bounds short of the reduction of the law-breaker to the point of complete submissiveness—namely, unconditional surrender." Ironically, a moralist "approach to world affairs, rooted as it unquestionably is in a desire to do away with war and violence, makes violence more enduring, more terrible, and more destructive to political stability than motives of national interest. A war fought in the name of high moral principle finds no early end short of some form of total domination."[10]

The stalemated struggle with communism is, of course, a blow to this sense of a moralistic contest which must end with the defeat of Satan. America's initial reaction to communism was one which implied no compromise. After each major communist triumph—Russia, China, Cuba—we went through a period of refusing to "recognize" this unforgivable, hopefully temporary, victory of Satan. (This behavior contrasts with that of Anglican conservatives such as Churchill, or Catholic rightists such as de Gaulle or Franco, whose anticommunism did not require "non-recognition.") Ultimately, the facts of power, and in the 1930s the rise of another even more belligerent enemy, Nazism, pressured the United States to deal with communism. During World War II, we were even forced to ally ourselves with the Soviet Union and communist partisan movements. Our initial reaction to this necessity is indicative of the way in which moralism affects the national purpose: The Soviet Union was quickly transformed into a beneficent, almost democratic state. Eddy Rickenbacker wrote in glowing terms in the *Reader's Digest* that the Soviet Union had practically become a capitalist society. Both Stalin and Tito were presented as "progressive" national leaders and heroes comparable to classic American figures. Franklin Roosevelt, for a time, allowed himself to see Stalin as a leader of anti-imperialist forces with whom the United States could cooperate in planning the postwar world, even against the French and British imperialists.

Subsequent Soviet behavior in Eastern Europe and Berlin during the latter years of the war and the early postwar years destroyed this effort to transform the image of communism. The Communist victory in China, reinforced by the events of the Korean War, produced a reaction comparable to that directed against the Soviets after 1917. The United States refused to recognize evil in China (and later in Cuba). It engaged in an internal heresy hunt seeking to find and eliminate the traitors at home responsible for the inefficacy of our anticommunist efforts abroad. The McCarthyite period, of course, coincided with a hot war against communism, the Korean War, and thus also represented an effort to repress critics of the war, corresponding to previous waves of wartime repression.

The reaction to the Vietnamese War also revealed the extent to which the need for moralistic politics, particularly in foreign policy and wartime, affects the behavior of Americans. For this conflict was the first war waged by the American political elite which did not include a moralistic crusade designed to gain total victory. From the start, an unwillingness to get involved in a major war in Asia, a desire to avoid provoking Chinese and/or Soviet direct military intervention and—not least—a fear that an anticommunist crusade would reawaken a right-wing McCarthyist reaction led John F. Kennedy and Lyndon Johnson to underplay deliberately the anticommunist ideological crusade as a justification for the war. It was defined as a limited war in which the United States would do as little as was required to prevent North Vietnam from taking over the South. There was almost no government-inspired propaganda designed to portray the repressive character of the North Vietnamese state.[11] Pro-war journalists, seeking information about communist atrocities or pictures such as those of the heads of village leaders on spikes, were actually denied them by the Defense Department to avoid inflaming public opinion. For some years after the antiwar movement reached mass proportions, Lyndon Johnson was quoted by intimates as worrying much more about right-wing "hawkish" opposition than that arising on his left.

Given the unwillingness of the government to motivate a crusading atmosphere, the obvious breakdown in the monolithic image of a totalitarian communist empire in the wake of de-Stalinization in the Soviet Union— revolts and nationalist regimes in eastern Europe and the Sino-Soviet split— and, finally, the inability of hundreds of thousands of U.S. troops to defeat the Viet Cong and the North Vietnamese, the rise of a moralistic mass opposition to the war was inevitable. An unengaged morality shifted to the side of the antiwar forces, and as the war was prolonged, it was inevitable that they would win.

The Dilemmas of Detente

Whether the failure of the spirit of a moralistic crusade to emerge during the Vietnam War represents a basic change in popular thinking is, of course, difficult to answer. It may be that efforts to appeal to a purist patriotism are no longer possible, that acceptance of simplistic moralism is much reduced by the greater awareness of the complexities of modern politics which results from higher education and the more sophisticated mass media. Although I doubt that such a basic change has occurred, it is true that the proliferation of nuclear weaponry—of atomic deterrents—means that future wars cannot be fought through to "unconditional surrender." Hence the only alternatives are cold wars, limited wars, and détente. In a situation in which total war means mutual annihilation, both policy makers and the public alike are pressed to define international conflict in nonmoralistic terms and to seek evidence that the other side is not impossibly evil. The absence of significant public support for the moralistic right-wing program for total war in Vietnam, as compared to that which rallied around Joe McCarthy during the Korean War, attests to a major change in attitudes.

The same dilemma posed by Vietnam was replayed in a less-sanguine context of the United States's detente policy. The Nixon-Ford-Kissinger policy which sought detente with the Peoples Republic of China and the Soviet Union inevitably undermined efforts to sustain strong American defense and foreign alliance programs, as well as intelligence activities premised on the need to resist expansionist communist systems and movements.

This situation is an illustration of the well-known political principle, "You cannot have your cake and eat it too." To the moralistic posture, communism is or is not evil; it is or is not a threat to democracy at home and abroad. If it is, it must be resisted—a feeling many Americans still have. If it is not, then it makes little sense to assign a major share of our limited resources to anticommunist defense and alliance efforts. And in this context, many noncommunist American leftists "understand" a strong defense program as being little more than self-interested efforts by those who seemingly gain from such a policy, the "military-industrial complex."

This is, of course, a vastly oversimplified description of the nature and sources of the American reaction to Vietnam and detente. Obviously, from the perspective of policymakers in the White House and in the State and Defense departments, United States intervention in Vietnam was in the national interest. The issue of American credibility in supporting noncommunist SEATO allies concerned President Kennedy at the beginning of American involvement and continued to affect President Ford and Secretary Kissinger at the end. Once direct involvement had begun, president after president indicated that he did not want to be the first one to preside over an American defeat. Henry Kissinger seemingly was affected by the Weimar analogy, by the consequences of an American defeat for the legitimacy of the regime, particularly with regard to the loyalty of the military.

The destructive effects of the failure of Vietnam on the American sense of its world responsibility are reinforced by the concomitant rejection of American AID and alliance policies by much of the Third World and many Europeans. Regardless of the economic consequences of such efforts, most Americans supported these in the spirit of missionary efforts to improve and uplift the way of life of oppressed foreigners. Rejection by those we are trying to help is a blow to this self-conception. As Gabriel Almond has emphasized in his analysis of *The American People and Foreign Policy*, "If generous actions, motivated by moral and humanitarian considerations, are accepted without gratitude, are misinterpreted, or are unrequited, a 'cynical' rejection of humanitarianism may follow, resulting from the humiliation of having been 'played for a sucker.' ''[12]

The Depression following the failure of a supposedly humanitarian foreign policy after World War I resulted in a wave of isolationism and cynicism about the motives of other peoples and their leaders. We seemingly are in a comparable period today, as reflected in the popular unwillingness to continue our military involvement in Lebanon and Central America.

Moralism and Domestic Policy

An even more striking consequence, however, of the loss of the moralistic self-image has been the drastic decline in confidence in American domestic institutions, in the American way of life itself. Twenty years ago, Yale political scientist Robert Lane reviewed the comprehensive evidence from a large number of opinion surveys with respect to attitudes toward the American system, government, and political leadership. On every indicator, the trends revealed sizable majorities—often over three quarters—giving positive responses. As we all know, with the benefit of hindsight, Lane's article appeared just as the era he described as an "age of consensus" was ending. From 1965 on, the answers of the American public and leadership groups to comparable questions went steadily downwards until only 30 percent or so were responding positively to the questions about the system to which over 70 percent had been favorable a decade earlier.[13]

The survey evidence, as reported in detail by William Schneider and myself in *The Confidence Gap*, revealed a sharp decline of public faith in government, business, and labor since the mid-1960s.[14] The marked parallelism of the confidence trends indicates that the loss of faith occurred most rapidly between 1966 and 1971 and that it applied very broadly to all three institutions and their leaders. And they continued on a slight but steady downward slope through the seventies and early eighties. The business recovery and the election of Jimmy Carter in 1976–77 seemed to lift public spirits slightly, but only temporarily. Negative feelings resumed at the end of the decade as hyperinflation set in. By 1983, antigovernment, antibusiness, and antilabor sentiment had all reached record high levels. These then declined slightly in 1983–1984, in tandem with economic recovery.

Although the events stemming from Vietnam and the moralistic protest it sustained clearly were the catalytic events which stimulated the crisis of confidence and the growth of alienation, they were of course, strongly reinforced by the Watergate exposés, and inflation and unemployment. These changes in popular feeling about basic institutions and leaders reflect a declining self-confidence by many Americans that their country still is the *good society*, that it is on God's side. For the deviations in behavior which accompanied protests against the Vietnam War involved acceptance of practices, once totally repugnant to the traditional morality—drugs, easy sex, abortion, pornography, no prayers in schools, less stringent punishments for severe crimes, etc.—which in turn engendered the feeling in many Americans that their own children were not acting morally. For those who still wanted to believe in the Manifest Destiny of America, there was the evidence that anticommunism, nonrecognition and boycotts of the enemy, and support for anticommunist forces simply did not work in dealing with China, Cuba, and North Vietnam.

Yet from another perspective, these reactions—the decline in confidence in institutions and leaders—may be perceived as the other side of moralism, much as the historic American penchant for antiwar activity is the reverse image of a belief in Manifest Destiny. As a myriad of articles on foreign reaction to Watergate and CIA revelations have emphasized, Europeans, Israelis, Japanese, and others have frequently expressed bewilderment at what looks to them to be an ''over-reaction'' of Americans to types of government behavior which foreigners take for granted as inherent in the relation of politics to society. Here is another illustration of the differences in outlook between societies which assume some natural wickedness of men, and one whose ethos is premised on a utopian, religious belief in human perfectibility. Americans retain both the capacity to be shocked by evil and the motivation to resist it.

Moralistic Backlash

The construction of electoral coalitions on a national level is an extremely delicate task, and often requires that party leaders deemphasize ideological (moralistic) appeals and focus on either ''throwing the rascals out'' or keeping them out. Critical change periods—e.g., the slavery issue and the Civil War, the rise of agrarian populism in tandem with the industrialization at the end of the nineteenth century, the Great Depression—have witnessed realignments of party supporters into new coalition systems. And such periods of realignment have usually produced coalitions that have persisted for some decades. They break down, however, as groups find themselves out of step with their party on specific new issues, while the alternative party is not prepared to make their causes its own.

Thus, extraparty ''movements'' arise to press for moralistic causes, which are initially not electorally palatable. These extra-major-party movements have taken various forms, most often emphasizing a single special issue, but sometimes cohering around a broader ideology. Among their central themes have been anti-Masonry, nativism (particularly focusing around the sins of Catholics), abolitionism, feminism, prohibition, peace, socialism, clean government, conservation, and the environment.

Such movements are not doomed to isolation and inefficacy. If mainstream political leaders recognize that a significant segment of the electorate feels alienated from the body politic, they will readapt one of the major party coalitions. But in so doing, they temper much of the extremist moralistic fervor. Sometimes this may be done by accommodations in rhetoric, but the results are often actual changes in policy. The protestors are absorbed into a major party coalition but, like the abolitionists who joined the Republicans, the Populists who merged with the Democrats, or the radicals who backed the New Deal, they contribute to the policy orientation of the newly formed coalition.

Among the many moralistic strands that have affected the American polity for well over a century, two stand out: one grew out of intergroup tensions in multiethnic America, which were reflected in a variety of mass-based movements dedicated to nativist, religious, or racist intolerance; the other was the outcome of a persistent strain between the values of segments of the highly educated intellectual elite and those of a materialistic economic system. The first, though massively present in such earlier movements as the Anti-Masons (1828–1832), the Native Americans (1840s), the Know-Nothings (1852–1857), and the American Protective Association (1890–1897), and continuing as a major tendency today, had its most important impact in the 1920s. Movements stemming from the intelligentsia, on the other hand, reached their high point of influence in the late 1960s but may be even more important in the future.

The decade of the 1920s witnessed political repression (the Red Scare, the Palmer Raids), moralistic intolerance (prohibition, the antievolution teaching laws), and racial and religious bigotry (the rise of the multimillion member Ku Klux Klan, the diffusion of Henry Ford's mass circulation, anti-Semitic paper, the *Dearborn Independent*, and the passage of racist-inspired immigration legislation). Henry Ford, viewed as a possible presidential candidate, led in opinion polls in 1923 and was offered third-party nominations. Defenders of the Klan had close to half the delegates at both the Democratic and Republican Conventions in 1924.

This massive protest wave may be seen as a backlash reaction to the fact that as a result of broad structural changes American society was becoming cosmopolitan, secular, and metropolitan—with negative consequences for evangelical values. Traditional Protestantism was well on its way to becoming a minority culture, given the growth of the disproportionately Catholic, Jewish, and secularist cities as centers of communications and power. As historian Arnold Rice noted: "The 1920's meant 'modernism.' And 'modernism,' among other things, meant the waning of church influence . . . the discarding of the old-fashioned absolute moral code in favor of a freer or 'looser' personal one, which manifested itself in such activities as purchasing and drinking contraband liquor, participating in ultra-frank conversations between the sexes, wearing skirts close to the knees, engaging in various extreme forms of dancing . . . and petting in parked cars."[15] As one Klan leader put it poignantly, "We have become strangers in the land of our fathers."

In reaction to this growth of "modernism," the 1920s produced a Dixiecrat-Republican coalition, in which the evangelical Protestant nonmetropolitan Republicans of the North joined with the Protestant Democrats in the South against the big-city Catholic Democrats. And it was this Dixiecrat-Republican coalition that put across measures like prohibition and immigration restriction. Given the identification of the northern Republican party with these issues, it is not surprising that the G.O.P. gained considerably in Presidential voting. The rise of the Klan, the appeal of Henry Ford, and the massive increase in Republican support each reflected in a different way the desire of many Americans to restore an America which had been changed by war, urbanization, and heavy waves of non-Nordic immigration to reflect once more the values of a rural, moralistic Protestant society. Conversely, emerging Catholic, Jewish, and ultimately, black Americans were drawn to the Democratic party coalition, which in the 1930s became a majority when the Depression and the growth of organized labor gave it significant strength among urban Protestants, particularly the trade unionists among them.

Nativism and the New Ethnicity

Backlash politics, however, was to continue to provide the basis for new forms of nativism which upset party loyalties. Ironically, nativism began to attract support from the ranks of the more recently established Catholic population—who themselves had been the chief victims of such moralistic sentiments before 1930. As the blame for the moral threat to American values shifted from persons of alien *origin* and *religion* to persons of alien *ideas* and *values*, particularly communists, non-WASP elements could become partisans of the new nativism. Thus, segments of the Catholic population briefly broke with the Democratic coalition to support two rightist Catholic spokesmen, Father Charles Coughlin in the 1930s, and Senator Joseph McCarthy in the early 1950s. Both had a clear impact on public policy. Coughlin (and Huey Long) ironically helped push Franklin Roosevelt to the left on economic issues by emphasizing the plight of the poor and the need for government action. McCarthy contributed to the increased intensity of the United States cold war posture.

In a curious way, developments in recent decades comparable to those which produced the backlash movements of the 1920s have led members of some of the very groups whose presence and growing influence inspired racist reaction in the earlier period to engage in comparable behavior today. A combination of the ''invasion'' of the central cities by blacks and Hispanic Americans and the cultural changes in sexual morality, patriotism, religious beliefs, law and order, and the nature of education revived backlash cultural and ethnic politics. Many lower-middle-class and working-class whites began to feel that a large segment of the Democratic party leadership, of the newly emboldened liberal Protestant and Catholic clergy, and of the WASP and Jewish ''suburban elites'' had lost interest in them, that they were concerned solely with the plight of the blacks, middle-class women, and with ''permissive'' changes in the cultural arena.

Moralism in the 1980s

In evaluating the conservative political revival of the 1980s, we must bear in mind that religious fundamentalism and cultural conservatism have long gone together in this country. Religious identity is, after all, bound up with cultural tradition as part of a total way of life. When the security and status of that way of life appear threatened, its religious and moral content typically become rallying points of defense. Political figures who seem indifferent or hostile to these values will be seen as messengers of wickedness, while those politicians who appeal to them are likely to be invested with an aura of moral goodness.

The group most vulnerable to changes in moral values has been the fundamentalist Protestants—not because they are fundamentalist, but because they are by region, history, and education the group most rooted in the past, the one with the least capacity for adjusting to change. More significant than their religion and morality is their traditionalism. They are taking a stand against the whole sweep of modernity itself, and all the changes it signifies, and in doing so they speak for many other traditionalists who did not share their particular religious beliefs.

In different forms and under varying circumstances, this reaction has occurred over and over again in American history. It suggests that political orientation is not just an economic question, but is also a matter of mood. Negative political sentiment has often been generated by a sense of imminent deprivation, or diminishing status on the part of a substantial segment of the population.

Clearly, it was while in such a mood that many Americans, most of them not evangelicals, made their election choices in 1980. Even if their own status was not in question, many voters were registering displeasure at the diminishing status of America itself in the world. They were protesting American humiliation, and not even by another superpower but by a group of petty Middle Eastern despots, Khomeini and his followers.

Even the economic issues which dominated the campaign can be seen in this light. For most of us, inflation is more than just a pocketbook issue. It erodes the household budget but it also, more subtly, undermines past achievements. In the same way, the decline in American productivity and the growing superiority of foreign imports over our own products may be seen as issues of national status as much as of economics.

Actually, these issues of status far outweigh the factor of moral backlash that has been the subject of so much worried speculation since the election. Voters in 1980 were certainly expressing revulsion at what they perceived as an assault on traditional moral values. That particular beachhead, however, had been established over a decade before, and the evangelical preachers had been fighting ever since to enlarge it, with no great success. Not until a general backlash mood swept the country, precipitated by such matters as the Persian Gulf and the inflation rate, did the moral issue become an election factor, symbolizing for many the whole downward drift of the nation.

Today's evangelical groups have made it a point to avoid hatemongering. Though there is no denying that many evangelicals today are still wary of the Catholics, and have great theological problems with the Jews, and though one may argue further that the Moral Majority's focus on "Christian" values undermines the healthy pluralistic tone of the nation, nevertheless that organization has never even come close to incorporating in its platform the nativism and overt bigotry central to earlier groups. For the Reverend Gerald Winrod to have accepted an award from a national Jewish conclave, as Jerry Falwell did, is unimaginable. Indeed, so sensitive is the Moral Majority to Jewish fears that it has requested a "dialogue" with representatives of every major Jewish organization "to make the Jewish community aware that we are not an anti-Semitic group and that we probably are the strongest supporter of Israel in this country."

But it is not just in the absence of overt bigotry that today's evangelical Right has been more moderate than its predecessors. Though its public agenda calls for action on a whole range of domestic and international questions— from socialized medicine to relations with Taiwan and Zimbabwe—its real goals seem to be more limited. One observer, writing in the *Congressional Quarterly*, reported the movement's most concerted lobbying efforts to have been the battles for voluntary school prayer and for an amendment restricting federal intervention in private, mainly Christian, schools[16]—important issues, but hardly global in their scope. Another observer, writing in the *National Catholic Reporter*, noted that the real core of the platform is Senator Paul Laxalt's Family Protection Act.[17] This bill, too, confines itself to fairly narrow questions—prayer in the schools, parental review of textbooks, elimination of tax laws requiring married couples to pay more than singles living together, and a number of other sections concerning gay rights and abortions.

In other words, thus far at least, the activity of right-wing evangelical political groups has centered on moral issues rather than on general political ones. These are the only matters on which the positions of the evangelical political groups have reflected the opinions of the general evangelical population. Whenever attempts have been made to stretch the Christian dimension beyond these specific religion-linked issues, they have provoked internal dissension. When, for example, the Harris Poll of 6 October 1980 asked whether it is impossible to be both a political liberal and a good Christian, both the general population and the white evangelical population disagreed overwhelmingly, as did a number of evangelical leaders.

Some, if not all, of these leaders have themselves been careful to make a distinction between moral questions and political ones. Thus, Carl Henry, a leading evangelical theologian, warned against making the jump from "individual spiritual rebirth to assuredly authentic and predictable public policy consequences. . . ." He reminded his hearers that "equally devout individuals may disagree over the best program for achieving common goals."[18] Making the same point, an editorial in the most widely read evangelical journal, *Christianity Today*, said: "We get the impression that some evangelical lobbies on the political Right as well as liberal lobbies on the Left want us to believe that theirs is the only true Christian position on all issues. How can a policy board of evangelical Christians without access to vast amounts of intricate political data emerge from a meeting and announce that it has arrived at *the* Christian or moral position on lifting sanctions against Zimbabwe, for example?"[19]

To fail to acknowledge that the growth of support for the GOP and conservatism is a consequence of general social processes is to give groups like the Moral Majority more credit than they deserve and to run the risk of a self-fulfilling prophecy. If politicians become convinced that the Moral Majority is a decisive force in American life, they are more likely to treat it as such, just to be on the safe side. A more important danger of overestimating the Moral Majority's role is that it can serve to blur the meaning of what *has* happened. For many liberals, who cannot quite believe that the American people, blue-collar and all, have turned conservative of their own free will, it would seem preferable to believe that some sinister manipulative force is at work which has turned large segments of the population into robots. But this is self-delusion—the facts state otherwise.

In attempting to keep the Moral Majority in perspective, it may be useful to acknowledge that moral backlash is not necessarily a pejorative term. If it "belongs" to the evangelicals, this is because other organized religious groups have not claimed it, which may explain why fundamentalist churches, in recent years, have been growing at a 2-percent annual rate while mainstream churches have been declining at 1 percent per annum. Only 40 percent of the adult population attends church regularly as of 1980, the lowest figure recorded since pollsters started inquiring about this subject.

The Americans who "turned Right" in the 1980 election did not by any means agree with the Moral Majority or New Right programs. These Americans were not supporting specific political solutions any more than they usually do. They wanted a government that would more demonstrably reflect their *mood*: a more assertive America on the world scene, and on the domestic front a serious campaign to fight inflation and refurbish American industry. That is the extent of their political conservatism.

Left-Wing Moralism

The adequacy of the two-party system to produce effective coalition government has also been undermined in the past 20 years by another element in the polity: the well-educated, affluent, cosmopolitan elites who have become a major force in contemporary America. This is clearly not a new tendency. Segments of these strata have sought to "clean up" and to purify America for almost as long as the nativists, and have been repeatedly frustrated by the nonmoralistic, compromise character of the two-party system. Historians have traced a pattern of continuity in the leadership and activist core of "antimaterialistic" reform movements from the pre–Civil War abolitionists, through the clean government "mugwump" (antiparty) movement of the late nineteenth century, to the antimachine and antitrust Progressives of the pre–World War I era. More recently, these themes have been revived by assorted segments of the protest "movement" of the 1960s and early 1970s, which have emphasized clean environments, clean government, clean business, honesty in advertising, and equal rights for women and minorities, opposed America's effort to impose its political will abroad, and sought to eliminate the remnants of ascetic Protestant morality concerning sex and the behavior of youth.

Writing in 1873 about the situation before the Civil War, Whitelaw Reid, abolitionist activist and editor of the New York *Tribune*, noted that "exceptional influences eliminated, the scholar is pretty sure to be opposed to the established. . . . As our politics settled into the conservative tack in the pre–Civil War decades a fresh wind began to blow about the college seats, and literary men, at last, furnished inspiration for the splendid movement that swept slavery from the statute book. . . ."[20] And commenting on the rise of "mugwump" opposition to the party system in the 1880s, James Bryce described the role of intellectuals, academics, and their college-educated followers in terms not dissimilar from those used to analyze their impact on the massive protest wave of the 1960s:

> The influence of literary men [on politics] is more felt through magazines than through books. . . . That of the teachers tells primarily on their pupils and indirectly on the circles to which those pupils belong, or in which they work when they have left college. One is amused by the bitterness—affected scorn trying to disguise real fear—with which "college professors" are denounced by professional politicians as unpractical, visionary, pharisaical, "kid-gloved," "high-toned," "un-American," the fact being that a considerable impulse towards the improvement of party methods, towards civil service reform, and towards tariff reform, has come from the universities, and has been felt in the increased political activity of the better educated youth. The new generation of lawyers, clergymen, and journalists . . . [has] been inspired by the universities, particularly of course by the older and more highly developed institutions of the Eastern States, with a more serious and earnest view of politics. . . . Their horizon has been enlarged, their patriotism tempered by a sense of national shortcomings, and quickened by a higher ideal of national well-being. The confidence that all other prosperity will accompany material prosperity, the belief that good instincts are enough to guide nations through practical difficulties—errors which led astray so many worthy people in the last generation, are being dispelled. . . . The seats of learning and education are at present among the most potent forces making for progress . . . in the United States.[21]

Similar views were expressed concerning the role of the academy in fostering opposition to the Spanish-American War and to its aftermath, the struggle against Filipino guerrillas. A historian of academe, Laurence Veysey, notes that "faculty opposition to imperialism during the 1890s was observed as general all over the country." While the short war against Spain was still on, Oliver Wendell Holmes, Jr., commented to a friend, "I confess to pleasure in hearing some rattling jingo talk after the self-righteous and preaching discourse which has prevailed to some extent at Harvard College and elsewhere." An article in the *Atlantic Monthly* in 1902 reported that college professors had acquired a reputation for taking obstructionist political positions: "Within a twelve-month college teachers have been openly denounced as 'traitors' for advocating self-government for Filipinos. In many a pulpit and newspaper office . . . it was declared that the utterances of college professors were largely responsible for the assassination of President McKinley."[22]

Following World War II, the intellectual elite shifted the focus of its moralistic critique from political and economic institutions to a corrupted culture and environment. It found its prototypical leader in Adlai Stevenson, a man who deemphasized economic and class issues in favor of a stress on the decline of moral, cultural, and ecological standards. Many sought to reform and clean up American politics, and Democratic reform movements, which centered in the west side of Los Angeles, Hyde Park in Chicago, Cambridge, and the west side of Manhattan, attracted considerable support among the growing intellectualized professional strata. The linkage of cultural-academic concerns to party politics in the 1950s made possible the intense politicization of the intellectuals in the ensuing decade. But it is interesting to note that the cultural-political folk hero of that subsequent period, John F. Kennedy, initially was not popular among intellectuals when he ran for president in 1960: They were repelled since his record revealed no great political passions and he had sat out the fight against McCarthy, while other members of his family, including his brother Robert, had actively supported McCarthy. Stevenson and, to a lesser extent, the erstwhile academic, Hubert Humphrey, were the preferred candidates of the politicized intellectuals.

"Movement" Politics

During the mid-1960s, American intellectuals once again assumed the role of "moralists" with respect to political criticism, denouncing the system for betraying its own basic democratic and antiimperialist beliefs. Beginning with the faculty-initiated teach-ins against the Vietnam War in 1965, intellectuals played a major role in sustaining a mass antiwar movement out of which a large radical constituency emerged. Given the identification of both major parties with the war, the antiwar agitation contributed to a decline in partisan identification, and added to the growing number of "independents" on the left, much as Wallace-linked sentiments produced large numbers of independents on the right. There can be little doubt of the efficacy of this protest movement of the intelligentsia. A variety of statistical data validates Galbraith's 1971 boast that "It was the universities . . . which led the opposition to the Vietnam War, which forced the retirement of President Johnson, which are leading the battle against the great corporations on the issue of pollution, and which at the last Congressional elections retired a score or more of the more egregious time-servers, military sycophants, and hawks."[23] The "movement" was, of course, able to impose its will on the Democratic party nomination in 1972, but in the process it drove out of the party a sizable segment of the less affluent, many of whom had voted for George Wallace in the primaries.

Moralism and Polarization

Each ideological strand is looking for a political home which will give expression to its particular form of moralistic politics. The air rings with code words like busing, crime in the cities, welfare frauds, Watergate, Secret Police repression, business corruption, ecology, and the like. But the very intensity of these beliefs makes difficult the kind of compromise which has sustained the two-party system.

The breakdown of parties and the political disorganization which appears to characterize the contemporary scene are far from unique. In the past, dislocations of the great party coalitions have also been accompanied by the process of "polarization." This term generally describes the condition whereby significant sections of the population move to the left and right of normal two-party politics. In the 1820s and 1830s the rise of the Anti-Masons was paralleled by the Workingmen's parties; the nativists of the 1840s and 1850s by the Free Soilers, Liberty Party, and Abolitionists; the anti-Catholic American Protective Association of the 1890s by the Populists; the massive Klan of the 1920s by the Progressive and Farmer-Labor movements; the Coughlinites of the 1930s by significant, active, leftist radical movements; and in the last decade, George Wallace and his followers by the "movement" encompassing the New Left, the New Politics, the Black Revolution, and the opposition intelligentsia.

This polarization process always involves two forces which react not only to specific issues but to each other. And as this occurs, politics increasingly comes to be perceived in purely moralistic terms, as involving a struggle between good and evil forces rather than as a series of collective bargaining issues.

The increased commitment to extrapartisan moralism in the 1960s produced the most serious breakdown of political restraint since the early 1920s. Civil disobedience often verging on violence became an accepted tactic among leftist militants, civil rights advocates, and opponents of school busing alike. Governor Wallace, the editors of the *New York Review of Books*, and John Ehrlichman all justified illegal acts that were intended to defeat enemies of the republic.

Why Violence?

Thus far we have discussed some of the reasons for the prevalence of militant extraparty movements in American political history. The willingness of those involved in American social movements to resort to violent, often illegal, tactics requires explanation. The drive toward moderation within two broad coalition parties seeking support from the center creates the need for dramatic action on the part of those who feel themselves to be unrepresented or unspoken for. But why do Americans who wish to be politically dramatic so often resort to violence? It is worth noting, in this context, that political violence appeared in advance of the firm establishment of the American party system. The nation was founded in an act of violent revolution. The American Revolution was followed by Shays Rebellion in 1786 and the Whisky Rebellion in 1794. An important event in the founding of the first party system itself was resistance to the Jay Treaty, which peaked with mass disorders and rioting in Boston in September 1795.[24]

Comparison with the Canadian experience is instructive. Both nations share similar positions on scales of industrialization, urbanization and social mobility, as well as comparable ecological and demographic conditions. However, on virtually any scale of political and related violence, ranging from ratios of those concerned with maintaining law—police or lawyers—to population, homicide and other crime rates, and industrial violence or political assassinations, the United States would appear to be a significantly more violent society.[25] This difference is related to different national experiences with respect to political origins, religious traditions, and frontier settlement, all of which resulted in differences of degree with respect to shared value systems.

Unlike Canada, the United States is a result of a successful revolution. The ideology of the revolution, as spoken in the Declaration of Independence, is one of equalitarianism. This has been a most salient and pervasive American value ever since. It is to be seen in our emphasis upon education for all, in our relatively unauthoritarian parent-child relationships, and in the preponderance of elective rather than appointive civic offices in this country. A theme running through our history has been the notion that "the people" are the ultimate source of wisdom and decision and a complementary mistrust of established elites and expertise. Naturally enough, this populist ethos has led to impatience with legal due process and even disrespect for the law.

In America, unlike more status-oriented societies, generalized deference is not accorded to those at the top. Popular derision of public servants is a very old tradition in this country. Our civic discourse has always been distinguished by intemperate rhetoric coming both from those in power and those outside, which often stands in sharp contrast to the grinding reality of party processes. Canada, by contrast, had her political origins in a counter-revolution. Status distinctions have had greater legitimacy there as have more traditional mechanisms of social control—what Russel Ward refers to as "deferential respect for the squire."[26]

An interesting aspect of the background for these differences is the varying experiences that these two nations have had with frontier settlement. In Canada, fear of American expansionist tendencies resulted in the early extension of the power of civil authority to the frontier. The Royal Canadian Mounted Police are interesting in this context, for they clearly were representative of central authority, and their presence greatly increased the respect for legal institutions on the frontier.[27] Even in mining camps—notorious in American lore as centers of volatile behavior—the Queen's peace prevailed in a fashion. On the American frontier, law and order were enforced by local authorities, who themselves embodied the distinctive values of the frontier. Respect for legal processes was by no means the rule in frontier towns. A good measure of this phenomenon is the persistent glorification of frontiersmen and outlaws like Jesse James in American folklore. Canadians have always had a somewhat more ambivalent attitude toward these rough and ready men of the West and have made heroes of the frontier police, the Mounties.

Another pervasive value in American society has been that of achievement—a strong emphasis on an "open society," on "getting ahead." This has been linked by analysts of American society (especially the sociologist Robert K. Merton) with making it an "ends-oriented" culture as distinct from a "means-oriented" one.[28] In the former type, winning is what counts, not how one wins. Conversely, social systems with a more rigid status system, with a greater emphasis on the norms of elitism, are more likely to be concerned with appropriate means; the norms place greater stress on conforming to the proper code of behavior. The comment by Leo Durocher that "nice guys finish last" may be counterposed against the old Olympic motto that "it matters not who wins the game, it matters how you play." The latter, of course, is the aristocratic code of a ruling class that "won" some generations back and in effect, is seeking to prevent the "outs" from pressing too hard to replace it. The differences between an achievement- and "ends-oriented" culture as distinct from a "means-oriented" one are subtle and hard to demonstrate in any rigorous fashion, but they are real and, in our view, contribute to many aspects of social life, including the crime rate and general willingness to rely on militant political tactics. American extremism may be seen as another example of the propensity to seek to attain ends by any means, whether legitimate or not.

This propensity is related to the equalitarian ethos discussed previously, i.e., upon the emphasis in America for achievement for all.[29] We can see this at work in the greater degree of union militancy in America compared with most of Europe, or even Canada.[30] In an open-class system, resentment of disparities of income is more deeply felt than in a more avowedly status-bound system where labor is regarded, in the words of Winston Churchill, as "an estate of the realm." Americans eschew the notion of estates and blame individuals, should their status be low, and by implication encourage individuals to improve their status and alleviate their resentment in self-interested and narrowly defined terms. Thus we find Americans accepting conflict as a "normal" method of resolving labor disputes, and violation of rules and laws as merely an unfortunate by-product of such conflict. Strikes in northern Europe and Canada have typically been accompanied by less violence than in the United States. "The use of professional strike breakers, labor spies, 'goon squads,' 'vigilante' groups, armed militia, and other spectacular features of industrial warfare in the United States in previous decades has been absent from the Canadian scene—again with several notable exceptions."[31]

Moralism is also a source of violence. Americans have been utopian moralists who press hard to attain and institutionalize virtue or to destroy evil people and wicked institutions and practices. They tend to view social and political dramas as morality plays. This moralistic tendency in America generalizes beyond its Protestant sectarian origin. Again the contrast with Canada is dramatic. There, religion has an ecclesiastic character and strong ties with the state.[32] Thus, rather than giving encouragement to egalitarianism and complementary trends of fundamentalism and experimentalism, the Canadian Catholic and Anglican churches, with which a majority of the population are affiliated, have provided the society with hierarchical models and tradition-rooted control mechanisms which are noticeably stronger than in America. The connection with the state is of particular importance. Churches with an experience of having been established have been by definition churches of the whole society and, as such, tend to be more tolerant of people who deviate on ostensibly nonreligious matters. Being securely rooted in the society, they can afford such tolerance and in general avoid a fundamentalist orientation. They also, of course, have firmer connections with the "established order" and some degree of historical responsibility for the moral tone of the present social order. For these reasons as well, established churches—and the general moral environment that they promote—are less likely to encourage extremist behavior.

Why Assassination of Presidents?

There is one final topic that has been dealt with only indirectly so far—the extent to which American presidents, and potential presidents, have been the targets of assassination attempts. It is important at this point to make quite clear at what level this problem should be discussed. In the final analysis, most acts of assassination are more psychological than sociological or political events. When one asks, "Why did he do it?" the relevant answer ultimately must focus upon the psychopathology of the assassin rather than on what might be construed as the social pathology of the society in which the event took place. However, rates of assassination and attempted assassinations are sociological facts. If many more assassinations have been committed in the United States than Canada or Britain, the explanation must focus upon what kind of societies they are. The fact that a man is deranged is a psychological fact. But the fact that in one society such a man is tempted to kill a president, while in another he might be more tempted to commit suicide is a sociological fact admitting a sociological explanation. This distinction between psychological and sociological facts was most cogently advanced in Durkheim's classic work *Suicide*.[33] There can be no more individual and personal act than the taking of one's own life, but, as Durkheim indicated, an explanation of the fact that, for instance, more Germans commit suicide than Frenchmen must be a sociological one.

It is impossible to offer anything as grandiose as an explanation of America's tragic experience with assassinations. Certain factors that might be related to such an explanation, however, may be suggested. There is no need to repeat the obvious relevance of some of the more general factors contributing to political violence in America, which have already been discussed. Beyond these is the effect of the American political system, which is unique among the stable democracies.

The American political system can be viewed as made up of two subsystems—the federal system and the presidential one. The former is indeed marked by decentralization and elaborate checks and balances. However, within this federal system the key elections held at the national, state, and local level are for only one person—the president, governor, or mayor. As a result, government tends to be *personalized* in the individual who holds the key executive office. For instance, the American cabinet is responsible to the President, not to party or parliamentary colleagues.

A related factor is the nature of the parties. Most students of party systems are immediately struck, when comparing the American with, say, the English or Canadian cases, by the loose structure of American political parties. In Europe parties are more tightly disciplined ongoing organizations. In America, at the national level, they are loose electoral coalitions coming together once every four years to nominate and then to elect a president. In the European case, parties have long-term strategies that go beyond the personality or policies of any particular leader of the moment. In America such strategies are less prominent, and the general emphasis is reversed; it rests precisely upon the qualities of the leader. This emphasis is a realistic one, since the less coherence the party has, the more important the leader in fact is. This emphasis is present at all levels of government but is obviously felt most intensely at the national level with respect to the president. It is also significant to note here that the relative importance of the presidency in this sense has increased progressively through the course of American history. An interesting measure of the importance placed upon the particular individual who occupies that office is the fact that in the sixty-year period from the presidency of Jackson to that of McKinley only two out of ten presidents—Lincoln and Grant—were elected to a second consecutive term in office. From McKinley to the present only four out of fourteen living presidents—Taft, Hoover, Ford, and Carter—have failed to be reelected.

The phenomenon described here is not limited to political parties but is a generalized consequence of certain organizational dynamics. A similar example is provided by Harrison in his book *Authority and Power in the Free Church Tradition*—an analysis of the organization of the Baptist Church.[34] The Baptists are congregationalists and hence deemphasize hierarchical systems of authority. The church's organization, on paper, is highly decentralized. But the philosophy and organizational reality of congregationalism in no way eliminates the necessity of organizational coordination, or of some basis for effective authority within the organization. As Harrison depicts it, these needs are met by a heavy emphasis upon personal leadership—upon what Weber called "charismatic authority." This kind of authority emanates from the personal qualities of leaders rather than the bureaucratic power of office.

The analogy between the organization of the Baptist Church and that of the American political system is fairly clear. There are two prominent consequences for the problem of leadership. One, already mentioned, is an intense emphasis upon the office of the president and upon the specific characteristics of the one who occupies that office. It is significant here that the development of the media of communication in recent decades has served to increase dramatically the intensity of this emphasis and, some might claim, distort our view of the office and its holder. Contributing to this is the tendency discussed earlier of the parties to deprecate the ideological differences between them and stress, among other things, variations in the ability, character, and personality of leaders. All these factors have the effect of increasing the intensity of feelings about the president, be they positive or negative.

The other consequence is that in this kind of system it does in fact matter who is president and that the departure of a president, whether the agent of that departure is the voter at the ballot box or an assassin's bullet, does make a difference. Neither of these consequences makes the assassination of a president a rational action. However, they do increase the probability that an irrational mind might be tempted to commit such an action.

Conclusion

We have seen that extremism, in act, if not objective, is (to paraphrase Rap Brown) "as American as cherry pie." Though reliance on civil-disobedience tactics by the civil-rights and antiwar movements clearly placed a severe strain upon the operation of a democratic system, the American system survived such efforts in the sixties, much as it did in the past. Movements have often played a dynamic role within the system. There was, then, little reason to fear or hope that such waves of unrest would topple the established order.

It is important to emphasize, however, that a review of the themes of this chapter should not result in a complaisant or calm feeling for anyone concerned about the country. The message is most decidedly not "all will work out in the end." We must recognize that those who have engaged in civil disobedience and confrontation tactics have not always achieved their objectives. By resorting to such tactics, they run the risk of turning many moderates against them, of creating a "backlash" that strengthens their opponents, and not only defeats them but helps to reverse social trends which they favor. Inherently, civil disobedience weakens the respect for the rule of law, which guarantees the rights of all minorities, of all whose opinions or traits are considered obnoxious by the majority. Hence, the use of civil disobedience as a political tactic is only justified as an extreme last-ditch measure, to be employed when there are no democratic means available to realize deeply held moral values. Indiscriminate use of confrontationist tactics can only result in the undermining of the rule of law and the encouragement of all groups (including the military) to take the law and general power into their hands whenever they feel frustrated politically.

Ultimately, of course, it is not enough to say that the established order will survive. We must always ask, "At what price?" The word "violence" has been used rather casually in this chapter, but it is not a casual phenomenon. While the political system has been reorienting itself, many have suffered and some have died. The American political system emerged from the turmoil of the sixties and early seventies intact. But is the loss of leaders of the caliber of John F. Kennedy, Medgar Evers, Martin Luther King, and Robert F. Kennedy a price we must periodically be prepared to pay?

Though violence has been discussed as, in effect, a subtheme of the operation of the American political system, it goes far beyond that. It involves, as indicated, some of the central values and traditions of American society itself. Perhaps we must begin to question some of these. In doing so, however, we must keep in mind that everything discussed here as a precipitant of violence—a plurality electoral system, the values of equalitarianism and achievement, the "nonconformist" moralistic religious ethos, the personalized presidency, etc.—are also precipitants of some of the best and noblest aspects of our society.

Freedom, the underlying principle of a democratic society, requires a commitment to restraint, a willingness not to do anything to undermine the basic set of conventions which enable men of different values and interests to live together. In an effort to avoid or to end the law of the jungle, men set up constitutional and legal curbs on what they may do to one another to attain desired ends. It is no accident that the Bill of Rights is worded not positively, but largely in the language of restraint: "Congress shall make no law. . . ."

Yet the chief bulwark against a breakdown in restraint is not the Constitution as such but the American two-party system. James MacGregor Burns has described well the role of the party system:

Majority rule in a big, diverse nation must be moderate. No majority party can cater to the demands of any extremist group because to do so would antagonize the great "middle groups" that hold the political balance of power and hence could rob the governing party of its majority at the next election. A democratic people embodies its own safeguards in the form of social checks and balances—the great variety of sections and groups and classes and opinions stitched into the fabric of society and thus into the majority's coalition. . . . Moreover, the majority party—and the opposition that hopes to supplant it—must be competitive; if either one forsakes victory in order to stick to principle, as the Federalists did after the turn of the century, it threatens the whole mechanism of majority rule. Majoritarian strategy assumes that in the end politicians will rise above principle in order to win an election.[35]

The two-party system has served to moderate the moralistic passions that are inherent in what Lincoln called the American "political religion." That system, however, is finding this task of moderation increasingly difficult. The factors making for moralistic extremism, and the need for compromise politics have not declined in two centuries of American independence. The sixties and seventies have demonstrated that. It clearly has been difficult to govern America in the past. It is not likely to be easier in the third century.

Notes

1. This chapter is an elaboration of various themes analyzing violence and extremism in the context of studies of American values and structures in my earlier work. Particularly relevant are S. M. Lipset, "On the Politics of Conscience and Extreme Commitment," *Encounter* (August 1968): 68–71, and analyses in S. M. Lipset, *The First New Nation* (New York: Basic Books, 1963; New York: Norton, 1979); *Revolution and Counterrevolution* (New York: Basic Books, 1968; rev. ed., Garden City: Doubleday/Anchor, 1970); and, S. M. Lipset and E. Raab, *The Politics of Unreason* (New York: Harper, 1970; rev. ed., Chicago: University of Chicago Press, 1978). The following are a number of relevant works on Canada: S. D. Clark, *The Canadian Community* (Toronto: University of Toronto Press, 1962); Kaspar D. Naegele, "Canadian Society: Some Reflections," in Bernard Blishen et al. (eds.), *Canadian Society* (Toronto: Macmillan, 1961), pp. 1–53; Frank Underhill, *In Search of Canadian Liberalism* (Toronto: Macmillan, 1960); Dennis Wrong, *American and Canadian Viewpoints* (Washington D.C.: American Council on Education, 1955).

2. George Wallace made a substantial showing in the 1968 election but did not create a viable third party, or rather a movement that called itself a party to go to the polls. It is interesting to note in this context that Wallace's "party" offered no candidates at the state and local level. For a discussion of this and other points relating to Wallace see S. M. Lipset, "George Wallace and the U.S. New Right," *New Society* 12 (3 October 1968): 477–83; Lipset and Raab, *Politics of Unreason*, chaps. 9 and 10; and Carl A. Sheingold, *Third Party Politics in America: A Social Structural Analysis of the Rise and Fall of the Wallace Vote in 1968* (Ph.D. diss., Harvard University, 1971).

3. With respect to movements on the right, Lipset and Raab, *Politics of Unreason*. Detailed sources for many of the statements presented here can be found in this volume.

4. G. Myrdal, *An American Dilemma: The Negro Problem and Modern Democracy* (New York: Harper & Row, 1944).

5. E. Burke, *Selected Works*, edited by E. J. Payne (Oxford: Clarendon Press, 1904), pp. 180–81.

6. R. L. Bruckberger, "The American Catholics as a Minority," in T. T. McAvoy (ed.), *Roman Catholicism and the American Way of Life* (Notre Dame: University of Notre Dame Press, 1966), pp. 45–47.

7. R. K. Merton, *Social Theory and Social Structure* (Glencoe: Free Press, 1957), chapter 1.

8. Conscientious objection to military service could also be found on a less wide-spread scale in other English-speaking countries, where, however, it has been less prevalent since a much smaller proportion adhere to the "dissenting" sects. Sol Tax, "War and the Draft," in Morton Fried, Marvin Harris, and Robert Murphy (eds.), *War* (Garden City: Doubleday, The Natural History Press, 1968), pp. 199–203.

9. Both abolitionists and others objected to fighting Mexico, and the Mexican army actually formed units manned by deserters from the U.S. forces.

10. G. Kennan, *Realities of American Foreign Policy* (Princeton: Princeton University Press, 1954), pp. 3–50.

11. French expert on Vietnam, Jean LaCouture, described North Vietnam as the most Stalinist regime in the communist world. North Vietnam continued to include Stalin in its pantheon, and was led by a die-hard Stalinist, Ho Chi Minh, who had been a major Comintern representative in internecine communist battles for many decades, and who engaged in a bloodbath against Trotskyists and other radicals after taking power in Hanoi.

12. G. Almond, *The American People and Foreign Policy* (New York: Praeger, 1960), p. 52.

13. R. E. Lane, "The Politics of Consensus in the Age of Affluence," *American Political Science Review* 59 (December 1965): 874–75; "The Decline of Politics and Ideology in a Knowledgeable Society," *American Sociological Review* 31 (October 1966): 649–62.

14. S. M. Lipset and W. Schneider, *The Confidence Gap: Business, Labor, and Government in the Public Mind* (New York: Free Press, 1983).

15. A. Rice, *The Ku Klux Klan in American Politics* (Washington D.C.: Public Affairs Press, 1962) p. 16.

16. B. Keller, "Lobbying for Christ: Evangelical Conservatives Move from Pew to Polls, But Can They Sway Congress?" *Congressional Quarterly Weekly Report*, 6 September 1980, p. 2627.

17. J. W. Michaels, Jr., "Conservative Christians Spread Influence, Attract Political Attention," *National Catholic Reporter*, 15 August 1980, p. 8.

18. "Evangelists Out of the Closet, but Going Nowhere?" *Christianity Today*, 4 January 1980, p. 21.

19. "Getting God's Kingdom into Politics," *Christianity Today*, 19 September 1980, p. 11.

20. W. Reid, "The Scholar in Politics," *Scribners Monthly* 6 (1873): 613–14.

21. J. Bryce, *The American Commonwealth*, Vol. III (London: Macmillan, 1888) pp. 77–78.

22. L. Veysey, *The Emergence of the University* (Ph.D. diss., Department of History, University of California Berkeley, 1962), p. 160; F. Freidel, "Dissent in the Spanish-American War and the Phillippine Insurrection," in S. E. Morrison et al., *Dissent in Three American Wars* (Cambridge: Harvard University Press, 1970), pp. 77; B. P., "College Professors and the Public," *Atlantic Monthly* 89 (February 1902): 286.

23. J. K. Galbraith, "An Adult's Guide to New York, Washington and Other Exotic Places," *New York*, 15 November 1971: 52.

24. P. M. Downing, *Acts of Civil Disobedience in American History: Selected Examples* (Washington D.C.: Library of Congress Legislative Reference Service, 1967).

25. For some examples see Lipset, *Revolution and Counterrevolution*, pp. 45–47.

26. R. Ward, *The Australian Legend* (New York: Oxford University Press, 1959), p. 27.

27. See E. W. McInnis, *The Unguarded Frontier* (Garden City: Doubleday, Doran, 1942); P. F. Sharp, "Three Frontiers: Some Comparative Studies of Canadian, American and Australian Settlement," *Pacific Historical Review* 24 (1955): 373–74. See also S. D. Clark, "The Frontier and Democratic Theory," *Transactions of the Royal Society of Canada* 48 (1954), Series 111, Section 2.

28. Merton, *Social Theory and Social Structure*, pp. 185–214.

29. Lipset, *The First New Nation*; R. Williams, *American Society* (New York: Knopf, 1970).

30. Lipset, *The First New Nation*, pp. 193–236; L. Adamic, *Dynamite: The Story of Class Violence in America* (New York: Viking, 1934); B. C. Roberts, *Unions in America: A British View* (Princeton: Industrial Relations Section, Princeton University Press, 1959), p. 95; A. M. Ross and P. T. Hartman, *Changing Patterns of Industrial Conflict* (New York: Wiley, 1960), pp. 141–45, 161–62.

31. S. Jamieson, *Industrial Relations in Canada* (Ithaca: Cornell University Press, 1957), p. 7.

32. Clark, *The Canadian Community*, p. 388.

33. E. Durkheim, *Suicide*, (Glencoe: Free Press, 1951).

34. P. M. Harrison, *Authority and Power in the Free Church Tradition* (Princeton: Princeton University Press, 1959).

35. J. M. Burns, *The Deadlock of Democracy: Four-Party Politics in America* (Englewood Cliffs: Prentice-Hall, 1963) pp. 40, 41.

PART III

EPILOGUE

9

Predicting the Future: The Limits of
Social Science

As a graduate student and a young sociologist in the late forties and early fifties, I shared the sense of excitement about the future of social science and its implications for human betterment. We and our teachers saw ourselves as part of a social movement that would raise social science to the standards achieved earlier by the natural sciences. We would play a role in reshaping society, both nationally and internationally. We were convinced that social science had finally broken through the methodological and theoretical barriers that had kept it in a prescientific stage; it was ready to take off intellectually to make breakthroughs that would transform society. Four decades later that promise is largely unfulfilled.

Policy makers, particularly since the 1930s, have called on social scientists to be social engineers, to tell them how to accomplish their objectives. This demand has not only distorted scholarly imperatives, but it has subjected social science to evaluations of its ability to anticipate specific outcomes. Social science cannot possibly meet these expectations.

This refusal to engage in long-range futurology represents a deliberate conclusion: social scientists are not in a position to make such predictions with any degree of certainty that their anticipations are likely to be accurate. The reasons for this are simple. It has become increasingly evident that for good methodological reasons we are still in a situation comparable to that of the meteorologists—they can describe what is happening to produce a cold wave or a drought; they can look at yesterday's weather and predict tomorrow's; but they do not understand enough about the complex relations among the many forces that produce diverse weather to make reliable long-term predictions.

It seems clear that social scientists also can explain only a small part of the variance, of the causal factors, involved in dealing with the major societal or worldwide issues that concern them. To a considerable degree, scholars, like other people, tend to react to what are often short-term changes in mood when defining the major problems that require analysis and understanding. Many changes, initially perceived as secular, structural ones, occur in waves that ebb and flow, though not necessarily in any regular cycle. In this chapter I would like, therefore, to point up some of the problems faced by the different social sciences in predicting major developments, and to look in more detail at the discussions of possible sources of limits to growth, or of continued growth.

Awareness of the difficulties in making projections is evident in the writings of the futurologists themselves. Rudolf Klein has noted that the dominant concerns of the young field of futurology, itself, have changed dramatically. "Indeed, just to glance at some recent products is to realize how quickly intellectual fashions now oscillate: man's future (if one is to believe the professional social prophets) is changing almost on a year to year basis." In the 1960s, futurologists were concerned with the ways to secure growth, with the negative implications of automation, with the problems of nuclear destruction:

> Now . . . it appears that the world's long-term future has suddenly changed. We no longer live under the shadow of nuclear war. We no longer live under the threat of enforced idleness brought on by automation. We are no longer faced by the danger of domination by an all-knowing because all-computerized bureaucracy or by a military-industrial power elite (to quote some other prophetic visions of the recent past). Instead we are told that we are living in the shadow of an overpopulated, overexploited, overproducing, and overconsuming world.[1]

Social scientists, working on more specialized topics, cannot boast of a better record. Our standard operative procedure seems to be to account for a current trend, or current definition of the mess that we are in, by looking for other concomitant structural trends. Since the structural tendencies associated with the trend we are trying to explain or find solutions for generally continue, while more often than not the trend or problem that concerns us disappears or ebbs away, much of our interpretive analysis turns out to be inadequate. This can be seen by looking back at some of the kinds of analyses and predictions made by social scientists and economists over the past three decades, that is, since World War II. An examination of this record suggests that we should be exceedingly modest about using our status as experts to draw conclusions that call for major policy changes. I would like to briefly mention some of these.

The first misprediction is the depression that never arrived. As we all know, the Great Depression of the 1930s was not ended by the natural play of economic forces or, in most countries, by deliberate government action. Rather, mass unemployment and low prices were eliminated by World War

II. Many economists generally assumed, therefore, that once the war ended, large-scale unemployment would recur, particularly in those industries and areas that had concentrated heavily on defense work.

Scholars were so certain of this development that a number of research projects were planned that involved studying the impact of unemployment on people who had been employed during the war. Detailed interviews were made with people whose jobs were certain to disappear with the end of the war. The call by Henry Wallich and others for government planning to guarantee 60 million jobs was dismissed as utopian. In fact, as we know, there was no postwar depression of any major consequence. The developed world has sustained three decades of relatively high levels of employment. Most of the recessions resulted in lower rates of unemployment than were experienced in some prewar periods, such as the 1920s, which had been considered times of prosperity.

It is now almost forgotten that continued depression consciousness in the late 1950s and early 1960s led many economists to pay considerable attention to finding ways to speed up growth both within the United States and on a world scale. As Henry Wallich has noted:

> There can be little doubt that, particularly following the recession of 1957–58, economists began to go overboard in their glorification of growth. In part this was a political response to the slow growth of the late 1950s, in part a reflection of the impact of Sputnik. The interest of less-developed countries in catching up helped to cast growth in the role of an all-absorbing goal at that time.[2]

The record of economists in anticipating major developments during the 1970s does not lend support to any argument that their theory adequately accounts for the working of the economy. For example, they did not anticipate the postwar recessions of 1973–75. Brookings economist Arthur Okun has pointed out that "most economic forecasters, including me, saw . . . a strong but well-balanced expansion in 1973 accompanied by an imperfect but hardly alarming record of price performance. Rarely has such a broad, bi-partisan professional consensus been so wrong."[3]

Economists, on the whole, also failed to anticipate the change in relationship between unemployment and inflation. It had always been assumed that inflation was negatively related to increases in unemployment. This assumption has not held up for various periods in the postwar epoch, particularly the recession of the seventies, from which we are just emerging. As George Katona indicates:

> Before 1973, the doctrine embodied by the Philips curve was generally accepted, and inflation and unemployment were viewed as opposites. When the one increased or accelerated, the other was expected to decline or slow down.

Economic policy was based on that doctrine and inflation was fought by attempting to slow down economic activity and reduce employment. But in 1974–75, at a time of unprecedented two-digit inflation, unemployment rose sharply. In 1976–77 unemployment remained high in spite of sizable inflation.[4]

Norman Macrae has also pointed to the inadequacies of economic forecasts. He notes:

Over the first 20 postwar years, a majority of important decision-influencing people at one time or another forecast coming famines in six main particular products. The world then progressively created unsaleable and unprofitable surpluses in every one of them: temperate foodstuffs after 1947, raw materials after 1951, more ''manufactured goods than could conceivably ever be sold to the United States and bridge the dollar gap'' after about 1954, fuels (especially coal after 1945, and oil after Suez), orthodoxly trained university students (especially in the science faculties) after 1960.[5]

It is with good reason that Robert Heilbroner has emphasized the difficulties faced by economists in predicting the future of a national economy, saying that ''the maze of interconnections in modern society is so vast and complex that it requires a Laplacean intelligence to predict the consequence of any action. An industrial economy utilizes and creates volumes of data that are beyond the capacity of the vastest computer. It is an information-generating system that can only be controlled by its interior cybernetic devices—the crude stimuli of the price mechanism—which, alas, give rise to the very problems that require policy in order to be corrected.''[6]

Wassily Leontief is even more pessimistic about the ability of economics to formulate generalizations that withstand change. As he put it in his presidential address to the American Economic Association in 1971:

In contrast to most physical sciences, we study a system that is not only exceedingly complex but also in a state of constant flux. I have in mind not the obvious changes in the variables . . . that our equations are supposed to explain, but the basic structural relationships described by the form and the parameters of these equations. In order to know what the shape of the structural relationships actually are at any given time, we have to keep them under continuous surveillance.[7]

Monetarist economists may be in no better shape. I was present at a meeting in which Allen Greenspan, then head of the Council of Economic Advisors and sympathetic to the approach, discussed inflationary pressures, and in so doing failed to mention the money supply. When asked why not by a monetarist present, Greenspan replied that unfortunately for his and the questioner's theory, the available data simply did not show a relationship.

In citing these problems of economic analysis, I am not suggesting that economics is not able to explain or understand what has happened since 1945. Economists, like the rest of us, are good historians. That is, they are able to find the factors that explain and retrospectively predict what occurred. Somehow, however, they have not been very good forecasters. Robert Solow has emphasized the problems that economists' "predictions are often wrong" poses for their role as policy advisors: "Why should anyone who forecasts so badly be expected to have worthwhile opinions on other questions?"[8]

Demography, a borderline discipline falling between sociology and economics, also cannot boast of its record. Extrapolating from the history of Western countries, demographers formulated the "theory of the demographic transition," which projected a steady decline in the rate of population growth in advanced societies characterized by "the achievement of general literacy, urbanization, and industrialization" and the diffusion of knowledge of birth control methods. But as Dudley Kirk noted in the mid-1960s, the theory seemed to break down around World War II:

> It is ironic that demographers developed the techniques for projecting certain long-standing trends in the components of population growth, especially in natality, just at a time when these trends were about to dissolve. New attitudes favoring earlier marriage and more children appeared in the very societies where the great majority of families had been practicing birth control. The recovery of the birthrate in Western countries just before, during, and especially after World War II violated the projection of previous trends and those formulations of the demographic transition that considered Western countries to be approaching a stationary or declining population.[9]

As we all know, this period did not last either. Kenneth Boulding concludes that

> fertility seems to be subject to quite unpredictable shifts. Thus, in the United States we had a period of high fertility (1947–1961) which was quite unpredicted, now we are in a phase of low fertility which was equally unpredicted. . . . It would be a rash prophet, however, who would assert that there could not be an equally unexpected rise in the future, or even a further unexpected drop, to the point where one country or another would exhibit the 'fertility shock' which Rumania went into in 1969, when it apparently hit the Rumanian government that Rumanians might simply die out.[10]

The same concern has recently been voiced in Australia, which has reached the zero population growth level. The slogan "populate or perish" has been revived, as students of demographic trends warn Australians that "they may be a dying race." A television program in West Germany presented in 1978 was titled: "Are the Germans Dying Out?" since Germany now has more deaths than births annually. The French began a major campaign designed to increase the birthrate and avert a population decline in 1979.

This decline in the birth rate has affected both developed and underdeveloped countries. Demographers Donald J. Bogue and Amy Ong Tsui note this "worldwide fertility decline comes as a major surprise to many demographers, who anticipated no change or only very gradual declines in fertility. For example, the United Nations population projections made in 1973 predicted levels of fertility for 1975 that were, for almost all nations, substantially above that actual fertility of these countries in 1975. Indeed, the decline seems to have been two-and-a-half times greater than these projections!"[11]

As Charles Westoff has effectively noted:

> I must now admit that the record of population projections has not been a happy one. A 1947 projection of the 1970 U.S. population fell 65 million short of the 205 million actually enumerated. . . . The major variable determining such estimates is fertility, and fertility has changed considerably since the early 1960s. . . . To develop more accurate population forecasts, demographers would have to know a lot more than they now do about the social and economic determinants of fertility. Even assuming such theoretical understanding, one would then have to predict the future course of the appropriate social and economic indexes, and there is no evidence that the relevant social-science disciplines have developed any such capacity.[12]

Economists and demographers, of course, do not have the worst record. Other social scientists are equally inefficient. Problems, anticipated by a considerable amount of social science literature, that society would face in reabsorbing the veterans of World War II simply did not occur, for the most part, either on the level of collective or individual behavior. The sociological literature of the 1950s addressed itself in some part to explaining what seemed to be major basic changes in the American national character. Those who agreed that the conservative fifties reflected increased secular pressures for conformism in American society ranged in political point of view from Erich Fromm and C. Wright Mills to William White and David Riesman. They sought to explain structurally the increased prevalence of other-directed or market-oriented personalities, which had replaced the once dominant inner-directed or producer-oriented types. The change was related to the shift from an economy of small producers, a labor force a major segment of which was self-employed in agriculture or business, to one in which the majority worked within large-scale bureaucracies. The analyses suggested that the latter environment tended to produce conformists, for people within bureaucracies advanced by selling themselves, by impressing superiors and colleagues. In the earlier society people succeeded by working hard and intensively, with much less concern for the opinions of others. The logically predictable conformist decade of the fifties was followed, as we know, by the nonconformism of the late sixties and early seventies. Yet, the same structural environment, the factors that allegedly produced conformist trends, were present in a more intensive fashion in the late 1960s.

Sociologists also erred in their anticipations about the class structure of American society. Leftist students of stratification such as Robert Lynd and C. Wright Mills and conservative sociologists such as August Hollingshead and W. Lloyd Warner suggested that the high level of social mobility that characterized American society was a consequence of economic growth and geographical expansion, trends that could not continue indefinitely. The growth of large-scale corporations, the decline of self-employment, were also logically expected to reduce opportunity. Many anticipated the emergence of hard, fixed class lines and conflict as a result. Such assumptions also turned out to be erroneous. What the experts failed to evaluate properly was the change in the occupational structure. The proportion of lowly, unskilled positions has steadily declined—it is now under 10 percent, while middle- and upper-level jobs, requiring more education, have increased. Where we once had a pyramidal structure with many menial jobs at the bottom, we now have shifted to a diamond one, which bulges at the middle. Social mobility on a mass level remains as high or higher than ever.

The analysts of stratification also failed to anticipate that the combination of a rapid expansion of higher education facilities, which permitted persons from relatively deprived backgrounds to go to universities, and the end of family capitalism, the concomitant growth of large-scale corporate bureaucracies, together with the increase in government, would create new possibilities for the lowly to rise within the corporate ladder of industry and the bureaucratic hierarchy of government. A much larger proportion of the heads of major companies now come from poor social origins than ever before in American history.[13]

As a result of these developments, there appears to be less rather than more emphasis on status (family class) background, more social egalitarianism. The technological revolution, computerization, and increased automation have reduced the proportion of people in the lower class. Increased mechanization has led to greater equality. Comparable structural trends may be found throughout the developed world.

The most striking example of a generalized failure of sociologists to anticipate developments may be found in the area of ethnicity. Until recently, Marxist and non-Marxist scholars agreed on a standardized set of generalizations about ethnic and national minorities. These assumed that ethnicity reflected the conditions of traditional society, in which people lived in small communities isolated from one another, and in which mass communications and transportation were limited. Most scholars anticipated that industrialization, urbanization, and the mass spread of education would operate to reduce ethnic consciousness, that universalism would replace particularism. Marxists were certain that socialism would mean the end of ethnic tension and consciousness on the levels that existed in presocialist societies. Non-Marxist sociologists in Western countries assumed that the processes of industrialization and modernization would do the same. Assimilation of minorities into a larger integrated whole was viewed as the inevitable future. As two scholars of the subject, Nathan Glazer and Daniel P. Moynihan, note, it was generally believed that "divisions of culture, religion, language," and race

> would inevitably lose their weight and sharpness in modern and modernizing societies, that there would be increasing emphasis on achievement rather than ascription, that common systems of education and communication would level differences, that nationally uniform economic and political systems would have the same effect. Under these circumstances the "primordial" (or in any case antecedent) differences between groups would be expected to become of lesser significance. The "liberal expectancy" flows into the "radical expectancy"— that class circumstances would become the main line of division between people, erasing the earlier lines of tribe, language, religion, national origin, and that thereafter these *class* divisions would themselves, after revolution, disappear. Thus Karl Marx and his followers reacted with impatience to the heritage of the past, as they saw it, in the form of ethnic attachments.[14]

As we all know, the opposite has occurred, both in the Western and Communist worlds, and in the less developed world as well. The Achilles' heel of communism has turned out to be nationalism, not only the consciousness of Poles and Czechs vis-à-vis the Soviet Union, but also of the various national groupings within Yugoslavia and the Soviet Union. Most of the multilingual, bi-national or bi-religious states that have persisted for many decades, if not centuries, have faced turmoil in recent years. Canada, Belgium, Malaysia, and Lebanon all face crises of national existence in which minorities press for autonomy if not independence. Pakistan and Cyprus have divided. Nigeria suppressed an ethnic rebellion. In the classic Swiss case, tension has risen within multilinguistic cantons. France faces difficulties with its Basques, Bretons, and Corsicans. In Spain, Basques and Catalans have demanded linguistic rights and greater autonomy.

In seeking to explain, after the fact, the disintegration of previously united societies, some social scientists have in characteristic fashion inverted the causal process, that is, they identify the processes that once were supposed to be leading to a decline in differences as the cause of their increase. As Eugene Skolnikoff notes:

> The old belief that growing *interdependence* among nations would breed at least a sense of common purpose, and more hopefully a genuine community

of values, has proven a weak reed at best. Unexpectedly rapid growth in the relations and dependencies across national borders has not reduced strife but rather has sharpened divisions and distinctions. Much of the change can be traced to the more rapid development and application of technology than was or could have been predicted, a phenomenon that still appears to be accelerating. . . . Increased openness and interconnectedness has led to new areas of dispute [and the] breakdown of consensus within nations.[15]

Sociological generalizations about the necessary functional requirements for the stability of family relationships, which supposedly affected relationships between men and women, also have turned out to be contradicted by developments. One may find many references, including in my own writings, to the proposition that sex cannot be a source of major political difference, that the members of the same family unit must have similar social-political attitudes. Role differentiation between men and women, husbands and wives, fathers and mothers, was perceived as fulfilling functional needs. Affective, that is emotional, relationships and instrumental ones were seen as being dealt with by different sexes because they could not be handled well by the same persons. Biological sex differences led to sex being used as a way of differentiating roles within families and societies. Once again, the events of recent years require some serious modification of these standard assumptions and predictions.

Political analysis is in no better shape. During the early fifties in the United States, I was one of a group of scholars who attempted to explain the phenomenon of McCarthyism.[16] Most of us linked it to the tensions of a prosperous society, which produced heightened status concerns and anxieties, increased competition among groups and individuals who were rising or falling in status. Status politics, rather than class politics, seemingly characterized such periods. The underlying trends that supposedly produced increased status tensions have continued, but McCarthyism disappeared with the end of the Korean War. There are, of course, other continuing forms of group tension, such as the rise of white racist movements, which may be properly linked to status threats. It is clear, however, that the broad predictive power of the theory of status politics is nowhere near as strong as was suggested in the early fifties.[17]

As noted in an earlier chapter, the post–McCarthy era found many people analyzing "the end of ideology," or as in my own case, its "decline."[18] The reduction in ideological tensions within advanced industrial societies was related in large measure to growing affluence, to the incorporation of previously excluded strata into the body politic, to the spread of education, and to the seeming reduction of many of the extreme morbidities of industrial society through the institutionalization of the planning and welfare state. Although many of the analysts of the end of ideology excluded intellectuals and young people from their generalizations about the decline of ideology, it is generally true that few anticipated the emergence of the forms of protest that characterized the growth of the New Left and minority movements in the late sixties and early seventies.

The New Left and the New Politics of the sixties and seventies, which drew their strength heavily from the universities and from the ranks of the intelligentsia, the educated professional strata, were in turn subjected to scholarly analysis. In this country and elsewhere, the student revolt was explained in part by changes in the situation of the students, particularly within the university. It was argued that the growth of large massive bureaucratic universities, of a mass student and faculty population, all made the experience of being a student much less pleasant, and offered fewer prospects for the future than ever before. The Berkeley Revolt and its successors were seen in some considerable degree to reflect a protest against bureaucracy and impersonality, and the pressures on students to prepare for materialistic careers.[19] The seventies and eighties, however, have been characterized by a "calm," a period of political quiescence on campus, although the structural conditions that supposedly produced student protest still continue, and if anything, have intensified. Pressures on students to conform to educational authority, to devote their education to preparing themselves for a niche in the economy are stronger than ever, yet few protest.

Two political scientists, Gabriel Almond and Stephen Genco, after citing many other comparable failures, conclude about political science:

> The regularities we discover are soft. They are soft because they are the outcomes of processes that exhibit plastic rather than cast-iron control. They are imbedded in history and involve recurrent "passings-through" of large numbers of human memories, learning processes, human goal-seeking impulses, and choices among alternatives. The regularities we discover appear to have a short half-life. They decay quickly because of the memory, creative searching, and learning that underlie them. Indeed, social science itself may contribute to this decay, since learning increasingly includes not only learning from experience, but from scientific research itself.[20]

Speaking more generally to the effort to apply engineering concepts of systems analysis to "a vast array of social problems," Berkeley sociologist Ida Hoos points out that what works in the controlled system of the engineer is not applicable to society. As she states: "Although the term 'system' can be applied to both space hardware and social problems, the inputs are vastly different, as are the controls and objectives. In the engineered system, the components are tangible, the variables controlled, and the outputs identifiable. In the social sphere, the crucial elements often defy definition and control and do not behave according to a set of rules."[21]

Some who adhere to Marxism or other revolutionary doctrines may react to this brief survey of the inadequacy of social science analysis by concluding that it demonstrates the failure of bourgeois or nonradical social science. But if one looks at Marxism, it is certainly in no better shape. Marxist economists and sociologists made the same errors as non-Marxists in evaluating economic developments, ethnicity, and the prospects for political tensions in Western industrialized societies. A major figure in radical sociology, Alvin Gouldner, has pointed out that the record of "academic sociology" has been superior to that of the Marxist sociologists in anticipating various recent changes, that the non-Marxists were more sensitive than the Marxists.[22] Marxist economists also have been repeatedly disconfirmed in their anticipations of economic breakdown in the West and lack of growth in less developed societies.

On a broader scale, however, it may be said that Marxism's major assumptions and predictions about the transition to socialism bear little or no relationship to actual developments. Capitalism's progressive role, according to Marx, is to create a level of production that would enable people to live in genuine freedom for the first time in history, that would permit everyone to have enough and thus make possible a much more egalitarian if not a totally egalitarian society. Marxists, until World War I, assumed that the United States would be the first socialist country because it was the most advanced capitalist country. Marx wrote categorically that the most developed society presents to others the image of their future. Social superstructures, political systems, were supposed to follow in the train of economic development.[23]

The Russian Bolsheviks regarded their seizure of power in a less developed country as an historic anomaly, which could not and would not last. They anticipated that the only possibility for a progressive advance in the Soviet Union lay in its being tied up to advanced socialist industrial countries in the West. They looked forward eagerly to the outbreak of the revolution in Western countries. No crueler joke has been played by history than the phenomenon of Marxism becoming the banner of the revolutionary movements to totally nonindustrial societies, of communism holding power in China, Cambodia, Albania, and many other poor, largely agrarian, nations. Conversely, of course, revolutionary Marxism is weakest in the countries with the highest level of industrial development, those which have the largest working class, which have the highest standard of living. Literally, no relationship exists between Marx's anticipations about the links between economic structure, technological development, and social and political development, and what has actually happened. Marxism as a system of sociological, economic, and political analysis has been negated, not only by events in the Western industrial countries that have seemingly overcome the anticipation that their contradictions would produce massive economic crises, but even more fundamentally by the coming to power of socialist statist movements in less developed countries. Socialism in a total sense seems to be a phenomenon of less developed, non-industrial societies, the precise opposite of Marx's forecast.

In citing the failures or, more accurately, inadequate predictions of the assorted social sciences, it is not my intention to suggest that social science is unable to deal with social and economic phenomena. Clearly, all the disciplines have done much to explain the ways in which economy, society, and individuals behave. Social science, however, is still at its best in advancing what Robert K. Merton has called middle-level theories and in explaining specific time- and place-limited developments.[24] It can best handle interrelationships between two or more variables within specific delimited structures. As social science moves out to deal with macroscopic systemic trends and tendencies, it accounts for smaller and smaller parts of the variance. Economists escape some of this problem theoretically by dealing with analytically closed systems, based on limited sets of assumptions. They, however, are no more able than other social analysts to fully comprehend total system behavior. Our enduring analyses tend to be historical. There is nothing wrong with this. In many ways our best work resembles that of physicians who analyze the behavior of specific individuals rather than of biologists specifying the characteristics of a total system.

A leading psychologist, Lee Cronbach, discusses precisely the same difficulties faced by his supposedly more experimental and scientific field. Cronbach cites many examples of experimentally validated generalizations that no longer hold up. He notes:

> Generalizations decay. At one time a conclusion describes the existing situation well, at a later time it accounts for rather little variance, and ultimately it is valid only as history. The half-life of an empirical proposition may be great or small. The more open a system, the shorter the half-life of relations within it are likely to be. . . . Though enduring systemic theories about man in society are not likely to be achieved, systematic inquiry can realistically hope to make two contributions. One reasonable aspiration is to assess local events accurately, to improve short-run control. The other reasonable aspiration is to develop explanatory concepts that will help people use their heads.[25]

This emphasis on middle-range theory and on historical case studies does not mean that we should not try to deal with macroscopic developments or predict future trends. Sociologists analyze consequences of changes in the proportion of the population who reach varying levels of education, differences in the distribution of occupations, e.g., the decline in the number of manual or skilled positions and the increase in professional or technical employment discussed earlier. We know that higher education is associated with certain kinds of values and behavior, while different occupations are conducive to varying life-styles and patterns of social organization and have specific orientations to competition, work, and the like, associated with them. Presumably, then, a systematic change in the composition of the work force or of the age levels of the population should have determinate though not necessarily predictable effects on the body politic.

Yet it should be noted that we cannot predict secular changes on a system level, or the probability of events resulting from changes in the composition of a population, or the relative weight of the same factor in different systems. Thus, there is abundant evidence that the more education people have the more tolerance they have for ambiguity, the more likely they are to be free of bigotry, to support civil liberties and civil rights. From this fact, it ought to follow that as the population of a country becomes better educated, it should be more protective of minority rights. In fact, as we know, this is not true. The McCarthyite America of the 1950s was the best educated America up to that time. Periods of massive intolerance have recurred frequently over the two centuries of American history although education and wealth have increased secularly. On a comparative scale, we may point to the fact that some of the best educated nations have fallen victim to persecution manias, such as Germany in 1933. Clearly unpredictable combinations of specific events or factors frequently negate the weight of the most powerful structural factors.[26]

An interesting example, discussed earlier in a different context, of such a reversal upsetting a structural prediction may be taken from political science. In 1965, Robert Lane published two articles in the *American Political Science Review* and the *American Sociological Review* reporting on evidence from opinion polls and other sources that indicated a steadily growing degree of satisfaction with the body politic and economic among the population from 1938 until 1965.[27] The changes included an increase in commitment to values and norms sustaining tolerance, free speech, and participation in the democratic political system. Lane attributed such changes to the steady growth in affluence and in education of every stratum in the population. The opinion polls showed that the better educated and the more well to do a person is, the more tolerant he is of others, and the more satisfied he is with his own situation and the body politic. Yet, as we all know, 1965 was the end of an epoch. From 1965 to the early seventies almost every indicator that Lane used of satisfaction, tolerance, and participation declined rapidly. The reaction to the Vietnam War followed by Watergate and the revelations about activities of various American security agencies plus, in the latter years of the period, economic recession, brought about a steady reduction in confidence in the American polity and increased intolerance.[28] Yet, until 1972 all the structural trends that Lane had identified as concomitants of the growth in positive attitudes in behavior continued.

The relationship between education, affluence, occupation, and political participation presents a somewhat similar phenomenon. All studies agree higher education, higher economic position, and wealth correlate with increased participation.[29] And it would appear that as education, wealth, and occupations of Americans improve, participation should increase; but as we know, the highest rates of voting occurred in the late nineteenth century. We are better educated than ever before, a higher percentage of college graduates are in professional jobs, yet from 1972 to 1982 we had the lowest turnout rates ever.

The low turnout figures occurred in the context of a situation in which the politicians had listened to the political scientists' recommendations for increasing participation. President Kennedy had appointed a commission under an important elections expert, Richard Scammon, to inquire why the United States voting rate, then 63 percent, was so low compared to other countries and lower than in the nineteenth century. The Scammon Commission reported that much of the problem was caused by electoral registration laws, which were much more rigorous than in other countries, or in our past, i.e., the need to personally register to vote months before an election, residential requirements, and so on.[30] As a result, registration was made easier, permanent registration was extended, residency requirements were reduced sharply. But the percentage voting declined further so that a decade later it hit a low of 53 percent in a presidential contest: with increased education and easier registration, still fewer voted.

I am not suggesting that the research on which the Scammon recommendations were based was faulty. The problem is that education, class background, and ease of voting are only some of the factors that determine propensity to vote; other factors and event effects are seemingly more important.

To repeat, this discussion is not meant to imply that we should not try to analyze and predict. Quite obviously in economic, as in political or other forms of social behavior, more knowledge and systematic thinking are better than less knowledge. But when one is involved in making major policy recommendations and decisions for the future of nations, or, in the case of the Club of Rome, for the world, it is necessary to be humble, to be cautious, to know much more than we do, before being able to state conclusively, as the Club of Rome did, that humankind's commitment to growth should stop. Clearly, the less precision in an analysis or prediction, the more unexplained variance, the more likely the conclusions that people reach from the available data reflect what they want to find, whether the "what" stems from political ideology, an academic or intellectual theoretical commitment, self-interest, or something else.

As political scientist James Q. Wilson has stressed, social science can test (predict) the relationship among factors only when it can isolate them from other variables, and when the factors and their effects are unambiguous and easily measurable. But the most significant effects on a societal level rarely meet these criteria:

> Either the effects to be studied are hard to measure (as with educational attainment or true crime rates) or the possible effects are hard to define and detect (as with most habits of mind and of personality), or the possible explanatory factors are hard to disentangle (as with race, class, and education), or the act of studying the situation alters it.[31]

This means that with almost any complex problem, people who disagree about the consequences of a given policy will rarely resolve their disagreement by reference to research. The improvement in research techniques—made possible by use of the computer, for example—has not increased the likelihood of reliable, unambiguous results.

In raising these questions about the ability of social scientists to predict macroscopic trends, to systematically understand contemporary problems so that they can recommend specific solutions, i.e., a change in a causally relevant variable to deal with a complex problem, I am not simply engaged in a purely academic exercise irrelevant to policy. The assumptions politicians derive from scholarly analysis can have consequences for good or ill.

The Limits to Growth Discussion: A Case Study

Many politicians, such as former governor of California Jerry Brown and many New Politics Democrats, believe that there must be an end to growth. They accept the assumptions of E.P. Schumacher and of the Club of Rome report, *The Limits of Growth*, of the neo-Malthusians, that the pattern of steady growth that characterized the Western world since the Industrial Revolution began must come to an end.[32] This approach also assumes that the dreams or aspirations underlying the efforts of less developed countries to dramatically increase their productive systems are utopian. They cannot aspire to become wealthy industrialized societies. The underlying assumptions for these pessimistic conclusions are fairly simple. The neo-Malthusians point to the considerable increase in the population of the world, one that will continue to the point where we will inevitably have many more billions than we now have. Second, they note that the resources that have sustained industrial development in the West, particularly those that have contributed energy and raw materials for industry and transportation, are not inexhaustible.

Western industrialized countries, until recently the principal claimants for such materials, absorb an inordinate proportion of them. Immediately after

World War II it was estimated that the 6 percent of the world's population living in the United States consumed about 50 percent of the raw materials used for industrial purposes. With the postwar growth of other Western economies and also of demands from less-developed countries, the proportion of an increased world supply now used by the United States is one-third. In any case, the developed countries of North America, Europe, Japan, and Australasia clearly consume considerably over half of these resources, while they have less than a quarter of the world's population. Beyond these two main structural considerations, some advocate the cessation of growth in the foreseeable future because of value judgments that insist that growth has brought with it various negative or dysfunctional consequences for humankind. These negative effects lie mainly in the area of ecology. Industrial growth has dirtied the world in a variety of ways, which make conditions of life less good, or less healthful. It has also adversely affected social relations—as a consequence of the fact that the pace of life in large-scale industrial society is highly competitive, ultramaterialistic, and bureaucratic. The critics argue that the advanced industrial societies have not produced human happiness but rather a variety of social, psychological, and biological morbidities. Thus, it is argued on one hand that growth will have to stop because of the changing ratio of available resources to the population, and on the other that it should stop because it produces a bad world.

These pessimistic views are countered by other economists and social thinkers who believe that a Malthusian perspective today is as erroneous as it was when Malthus first contended that the inevitable growth in population would prevent an increase in wealth. The counter-view holds that just as Malthus underestimated the resources that could be located and the inventive ingenuity of the human race, his contemporary disciples make the same error, and the scarcity-bound trends they emphasize will not continue.

The most optimistic version of this position has been argued by the deputy editor of the *Economist*, Norman Macrae, one that is about as diametrically opposite to the views assumed by the report of the Club of Rome as is conceivable. Macrae anticipated in 1972 that within the next 80 years the poorer "two-thirds of mankind should be raised from intolerable indigence to something better than the comfortable affluence which the other one-third of us already enjoy." In fact, he contends that much of the needed increase in the less developed countries will occur by 2012. Among other reasons for such optimisim is his belief that scientific knowledge and technological development have been proceeding exponentially and that continuing even more rapid advances will solve the problems of pollution and limited resources. He suggests that it is "probable that during at least our children's lifetimes the eventual breakthrough to widespread and intelligent use of computers will add totally new dimensions to all of man's traditional powers of deduction and induction and serendipity . . . that this will drive human invention and innovation through a growing ability to put together matter molecule by molecule, through extraordinary new abilities to control natural phenomena (the weather, drawing all the energy we need from the fusion process that will utilize the waters of the oceans as their limitless reservoir of fuel). . . ."[33]

An equally optimistic view is contained in *The Next 200 Years*, written by Herman Kahn, William Brown, and Leon Martel of the Hudson Institute. Their thesis "can be summarized with the general statement that 200 years ago almost everywhere human beings were comparatively few, poor, and at the mercy of the forces of nature, and 200 years from now, we expect, almost everywhere they will be numerous, rich, and in control of the forces of nature."[34]

The Next 200 Years points to a number of factors that make this scenario plausible. These include evidence that the birthrates are declining in many less developed countries, and that a variety of population experts agree that the maximum rate of growth will soon be reached. Kahn et al. point to the fact that those who are pessimistic about the potentiality for growth in less developed countries have been wrong, since the UN's original goal for the decade of development, 5 percent growth, has not only been met but has been considerably exceeded. Further, they agree with Macrae that long-term energy prospects are good, that these rest in fact on "sources that are inexhaustible." Sources of raw materials are great and are continuing to grow, e.g., there are various sources such as ocean nodules, which will in fact increase the supplies of many materials needed by industry. As the world moves to postindustrial economies, it will become increasingly less dependent on many metals. Recycling as an economic factor has only begun to play a role that will contribute much to the raw material potential in the future. Kahn et al. argue that the anxiety about the availability of food to feed whatever size population of the world comes into existence is much exaggerated, that at the moment the problem is not production but inadequate distribution systems. This clearly can be remedied. In addition, agricultural technology can increase food production enormously in countries that today are not food surplus countries.

Here we see two diametrically opposed views as to what the actual structural trends are by reputable scholars. And, as in the past, some of the conditions defining the problem are beginning to change.

A survey dealing with *World Population Trends* by Lester Brown issued in October 1976 reported that worldwide "the rate of growth has slowed so dramatically over the past five years that a long-predicted doubling of the population may not occur." Brown stated: "I would not be surprised if the world population never again doubled." The worldwide population growth rate dropped from 1.9 percent to 1.64 between 1970 and 1975, the first such decline in world history. In the most populous country, China, the birthrate declined sharply from 32 to 19 births per thousand people. And in 1979, two demographers, Bogue and Tsui, whose work was discussed earlier, have extrapolated recent trends as suggesting that the effectiveness of international family-planning efforts may result in "zero world population growth" in the foreseeable future.[35]

A number of research publications point to sharp declines in population growth rates in developed countries, many of which are below the fertility rate for zero growth. It is anticipated that the rate for Europe will reach 1.5 by 1986, while the United States will stop growing by 2015. The Chinese growth rate, according to R.T. Havenholt, dropped from 2.05 percent in 1971 to 0.95 in 1978. In Mexico, which has had one of the highest growth patterns, according to the Population Reference Bureau, the rate fell from 3.5 percent in 1973 to 2.9 in 1978. In the fifth most populous nation, Indonesia, it dropped from 2.9 percent in 1969 to 2.1 percent ten years later.[36]

An international group of economists headed by Nobel Laureate Wassily Leontief, who had been commissioned by the United Nations Department of Economic and Social Affairs to investigate the problems of growth, reported in 1976 after three years of research that "world resources will be sufficient to support a growing population and higher living standards, without inevitable environmental damage." The existing limits to growth, according to them, are not scarce resources, but political and institutional deficiencies. They call for accelerated rates of development in the less-developed countries.[37]

Concerns about Growth

The recent increase in the number of people writing about the negative consequences of growth, of affluence, of industrialization, of urbanization, revives to some degree recurrent intellectual and political concerns. Periodically Americans have voiced anxieties comparable to those of the present. As literary historian Daniel Aaron has pointed out, throughout American history:

> The preachers of lay or secular jeremiads feared what the phenomena of growth (wealth, progress, power) might do to unregenerate Americans. Had not this surfeit of success, this obsession with progress, induced them to connive with the devil in stealing land from Mexico, condoning slavery, cheating Indians, exploiting workers, tolerating slums?
>
> In recent years the critique of growth has not altered much, although it has taken a different tack. American literature is full of statements rating quality over quantity. . . . Most important of all . . . for writers and artists is the identification of size and growth with pollution in all of its forms—economic, political, moral.[38]

In the political arena one of the steady syndromes has been the "Mr. Clean" one. Since the late nineteenth century, groups of Americans, usually affluent reformers, have seized on some aspect of American society as dirty and have sought to clean it up and reform it. The government, the civil service, was one of the first such areas to be cleansed. Civil service reform secured its main support base from the "Mugwumps," from members of educated old families and academe, who saw in corrupt politics a destructive force in American life. The concern with corrupt politics was followed by the criticisms of the pre–World War I Progressives, recruited heavily from the same sources as the Mugwumps, who, seeking to clean up the environment, fostered the conservation movement. They also were disturbed by the destructive effect on American cultural values and way of life of the vulgar materialism fostered by the *nouveaux riches* of the decades about the turn of the century. These "Mr. Clean" elements have revived in our time in the form of concerns about pollution, ecology, and the influence of money on politics. Organizations like Common Cause, Nader's Raiders, the Sierra Club, and the Urban Coalition reflect this tendency. These groups have constituted the reform movement of the affluent in an affluent society. Dirt, ugliness, corruption, vulgarity, disturb those dedicated to the higher life, involved in intellectual activities or coming from privileged families, who have not had to dirty themselves in order to become well to do or get a good education.

Other advocates of an end to growth argue that advanced technological society with its emphasis on division of labor has also led, in the words of E.J. Mishan, to "a decline . . . in the satisfactions that men once derived from their daily tasks, [and] who is to say that the loss has been fully compensated by the consequent proliferation of goods and gadgetry and the transformation to a mechanized environment? . . . Economic growth depends, among other things, on extreme specialization that dulls the spirit, narrows the sympathies, and cuts one off from the largeness of life."[39] But black political scientist Willard Johnson contends that Mishan "is guilty of debating the issues in terms of values that, for all their humaneness, ignore the concerns of the poor. . . . No doubt his concerns feed on a genuine consideration for the quality of life, but they seem to me mistaken about the contribution material goods can make to it."[40] Or, as the late Anthony Crosland, Cabinet member in various British Labour governments, argued, those who seek to limit growth to protect the environment are "kindly and dedicated people. But they are affluent; and fundamentally, though of course not consciously, they want to kick the ladder down behind them."[41]

Conversely, the advocates of growth, those who would down-play the consequences of pollution, those who are less concerned about beauty in the environment, tend to come from groups involved in the productive process who want to get more for themselves through material advancement. They include well-to-do businessmen, together with workers and poor people who are more interested in increasing their economic circumstances, enhancing chances for mobility for their children, getting more education, securing access to leisure facilities, and so on.

Defining or locating the groups supporting varying points of view does not, of course, say anything about the validity of a given proposition or opinion. Growth may be good or bad, possible or impossible, in the long run, regardless of who likes it or dislikes it, or benefits or is harmed by it. Since I am not an economist and I have not done first-hand research on the conditions of growth or on the limits to growth, I do not intend to take a position based on the evaluation of the evidence. Rather, I would like to spend the remainder of this chapter discussing some of the consequences of the no-growth scenario. It is possible to bring together some of the evaluations or hunches that have been advanced to describe what will happen to the human race as a result. I should note, however, that like Herman Kahn, I tend to be an optimist about growth and innovation. I believe—or perhaps more accurately I should say I hope—that we will be able to find substitutes for resources that are being depleted, to recycle or, more probably, to innovate in various ways that will enable the race to continue toward a more affluent and I hope more egalitarian and freer future. I favor the growth scenario in part because, as I shall indicate, I think the possibilities for much of what I would like to see occur, namely, the expansion of freedom and greater equality, are linked to abundance and to growth. I believe that a no-growth society would be a more authoritarian and more intensely stratified social system.

The Consequences of Growth and No-Growth

Abundance, as David Potter has told us in his brilliant book, *The People of Plenty*, lies at the center of efforts to explain American exceptionalism.[42] Countless European observers of the American national scene, such as Tocqueville and Carlyle, stressed the extent to which the richness of the American continent with a limited population made possible a new social structure, a new man, a new set of social relationships that emphasized equality. Most of the articles and books written to explain the absence of socialism as a political force and class-consciousness in the European sense in the United States have also stressed abundance. Werner Sombart put it well in his classic work, *Why Is There No Socialism in the United States of America?:* "All Socialist Utopias come to nothing on roast beef and apple pie."[43]

Historians and sociologists have agreed that abundance reduces the potential for class tensions. As David Potter stated, compared with the class societies in other countries and other times, the United States has a "new kind of social structure in which the strata may be fully demarked but where the bases of demarcation are relatively intangible. The factor of abundance has exercised a vital influence in producing this kind of structure, for it has constantly operated to equalize the overt differences between the various classes and to eliminate the physical distance between them, without, however, destroying the barriers which separate them.''[44]

It is obvious, of course, that the United States is not an egalitarian country, if by egalitarianism one means anything that approaches equality of results. In fact, comparative studies completed under the auspices of the Organization for Economic Cooperation and Development indicate that income distribution is more skewed, more unequal, in the United States than in the Netherlands, Sweden, Norway, Japan, the United Kingdom, and Australia, although the differences among these relatively affluent countries are not very great.[45] It may be argued, however, that the way in which people *perceive* the distribution of income linked to the distribution of different kinds of consumer goods they use for immediate gratification is more important in affecting their feelings about equity than the actual distribution of income as such. The distribution of consumer goods has tended to become more equitable as the size of national income has increased. This relationship between wealth and the distribution of consumer goods has been commented on by Gunnar Myrdal: ''It is, indeed, a regular occurrence that the poorer the country, the greater the difference between the poor and the rich.''[46]

This, of course, does not mean that an increase in GNP automatically results in a narrowing of the income gap among the classes. In less developed countries, such an increase initially may largely go to increasing the wealth of the affluent and the standard of living of the middle class, without improving the lot of the large mass of the poor. The extent of income inequality in these countries also varies greatly with the policies followed by their governments, e.g., the variation in spread of education, land distribution, population control, production, and regional sectors emphasized, and the like.[47] In addition, it should be noted that a number of recent studies of income distribution find relatively little change in income inequality accompanying growth since World War II in the wealthy non-Communist countries.[48] Yet, a conclusion that the proportion of the national income received by different segments of the population does not change much in a given period does not imply that the standards of living of the less privileged may not rise considerably, enabling the *consumption gap* among the classes to decline.

In the United States, the average per capita income has increased eight times during the course of the century, and this dramatic growth has brought about a wide distribution of various social and economic benefits, greater than that which exists in almost all other countries except for a few of the wealthiest ones in Europe. Thus, in America a much larger proportion of the population graduates from high school (over 80 percent), or enters college (close to 45 percent) than in any other country. The greater wealth of the

United States also means that consumer goods such as automobiles and telephones are more evenly distributed here than elsewhere. An evaluation by the (London) *Economist*, using twelve social indicators to assess the relative advantages of different countries as places to live, placed the United States far in the lead over eight other industrialized non-Communist states.[49]

Sociologist Gideon Sjoberg has traced the implications of such developments historically in America. He suggests that the emergence of mass production during the twentieth century has caused such a redistribution of highly valued prestige symbols that the distinctions between social classes are much less visible now than they were in nineteenth-century America, or in most other less affluent countries. Sjoberg argues that the status differences between many blue-collar workers and middle-class professionals have become less well defined, since working-class families, like the middle-class ones, have been able to buy goods that confer prestige on the purchaser—clothing, cars, television sets, and so on. Such improvements in style of life help to preserve a belief in the reality of the promise of equality.[50]

Economic growth is also associated, of course, with the upgrading of the occupational structure, discussed earlier. Where Western societies once had many menial jobs at the bottom, a pattern that still characterizes less-developed nations, including most Communist ones, they have now changed and the proportion of reasonably well-rewarded positions has increased so that, like the United States, they bulge at the middle. One of the conditions for an increased sense of equality and greater opportunity is increased mechanization. The most advanced technological societies, such as the United States, Sweden, and Germany, have reduced onerous work to a greater degree than others. It should be evident that those who foresee or advocate no growth, who oppose technological expansion either because they do not believe available resources will sustain growth or because they feel that a more mechanized system will be a dirtier society, in a variety of meanings of that term, must anticipate a future in which the possibilities for progress toward greater equality will also decline. If we have to stop technological development, if we have to move into a no-growth age, then instead of moving toward greater equality, toward upgrading the situation of the poor, we will experience intense struggles in which those who control power resources, whether through ownership or capital or control of the state, will be at a considerable advantage.

As Kenneth Boulding has pointed out:

> One reason why the progressive [steady growth] state is "cheerful" is that social conflict is diminished by it. In a progressive state, the poor can become richer without the rich becoming poorer. In the stationary state, there is no escape from the rigors of scarcity. If one person or group becomes richer, then the rest of society must become poorer. Unfortunately, this increases the payoffs

for successful exploitation—that is, the use of organized threat in order to redistribute income. In progressive societies exploitation pays badly; for almost everybody, increasing their productivity pays better. . . . One can get ten dollars out of nature for every dollar one can squeeze out of a fellow man. In the stationary state, unfortunately, investment in exploitation may pay better than in progress. Stationary states, therefore, are frequently mafia-type societies in which the government is primarily an instrument for redistributing income toward the powerful and away from the weak.[51]

Robert Heilbroner, who expresses the belief that growth will cease, notes that a no-growth America will not simply involve increased conflict with the upper class and the rich, for "the top 5 percent get only 15 percent of all income." The working class and the poor cannot improve their situation without coming into conflict with the middle class. Thus, he says, "when growth slows down, we must expect a struggle of redistribution on a vast scale—a confrontation not just between a few rich and many poor, but between a relatively better-off upper third of the nation and a relatively less well-off slightly larger working class. And fighting against both will be the bottom 20 percent—the group with most to gain, the least to lose."[52] This intensification of the class struggle, of course, will go on everywhere.

In the United States, rising demands for quotas, for affirmative action, with special advantages for underprivileged groups like blacks, Hispanics, and women, may be portents of the future that Boulding and Heilbroner anticipate. The premise of the argument for such quotas, in part, is that the only way these hitherto deprived groups can move up is at the expense of other groups, that they cannot take advantage of the economic expansion of society in the way in which white male and Oriental immigrant groups did in the past. But the more privileged, who are more powerful, will seek to resist such demands in a non-expanding economy.

Richard Zeckhauser also emphasizes that a "no-growth society would work most severely against the interests of the poorer members of society. . . . If zero economic growth were imposed on the current structure of the American economy, Lester Thurow has calculated 'the distribution of family income would gradually become more unequal, blacks would fall farther behind whites, and the share going to female earnings would fall below what it would otherwise be.'"[53]

For those who believe that the good society is a democratic and free one, it is also necessary to recognize that democracy requires abundance, or at least that nations in which opposition parties, contested elections, and a free press exist are largely well to do. Currently, with the exception of a limited group of poor countries, the only democratic regimes are located in the prosperous regions of Europe, North America, Australasia, and Japan. Those nations that have maintained stable democratic regimes longest, and in which antidemocratic parties are very weak, are the cluster of countries that are the wealthiest by far.

Classic democratic theory stemming from Aristotle suggests that free societies are most likely to be found in nations with a preponderant middle class. Societies with a large lower-impoverished stratum tend either to be oligarchies (ruled by a self-perpetuating traditional elite) or tyrannies (popular-based dictatorships).

Sometime ago, in discussing the conditions of the democratic order in *Political Man*, I elaborated on some of the ways in which affluence is related to democracy, noting that increased wealth changes the stratification structure, particularly by increasing the size and role of the middle class:

> A large middle class tempers conflict by rewarding moderate and democratic parties and penalizing extremist groups. The political values and style of the upper class, too, are related to national income. The poorer a country and the lower the absolute standard of living of the lower classes, the greater the pressure on the upper strata to treat the lower as vulgar, innately inferior, a lower caste beyond the pale of human society. The sharp difference in the style of living between those at the top and those at the bottom makes this psychologically necessary. Consequently, the upper strata in such a situation tend to regard political rights for the lower strata, particularly the right to share power, as essentially absurd and immoral. The upper strata not only resist democracy themselves; their often arrogant political behavior serves to intensify extremist reactions on the part of the lower classes.

> The general income level of a nation also affects its receptivity to democratic norms. If there is enough wealth in the country so that it does not make too much difference whether some redistribution takes place, it is easier to accept the idea that it does not matter greatly which side is in power. But if loss of office means serious losses for major power groups, they will seek to retain or secure office by any means available. A certain amount of national wealth is likewise necessary to ensure a competent civil service. The poorer the country, the greater the emphasis on nepotism—support of kin and friends. And this in turn reduces the opportunity to develop the efficient bureaucracy which a modern democratic state requires.

> Intermediary organizations which act as sources of countervailing power seem to be similarly associated with national wealth. Tocqueville and other exponents of what has come to be known as the theory of the "mass society" have argued that a country without a multitude of organizations relatively independent of the central state power has a high dictatorial as well as revolutionary potential. Such organizations serve a number of functions: they inhibit the state or any single source of private power from dominating all political resources; they are a source of new opinions; they can be the means of communicating ideas, particularly opposition ideas, to a large section of the citizenry; they train men in political skills and so help to increase the level of interest and participation in politics. Although there are no reliable data on the relationship between

national patterns of voluntary organization and national political systems, evidence from studies of individual behavior demonstrates that, regardless of other factors, men who belong to associations are more likely than others to give the democratic answer to questions concerning tolerance and party systems, to vote, or to participate actively in politics. Since the more well-to-do and better educated a man is, the more likely he is to belong to voluntary organizations, the propensity to form such groups seems to be a function of level of income and opportunities for leisure within given nations.[54]

The assumption that abundance is a necessary condition for a good society is not limited to the example, or the writing, of people who prefer the kinds of societies that have emerged in the so-called Western world. At the root of the Marxist theories of progress and of the condition required for a free socialist society is a similar assumption. Marx fervently believed and sought to demonstrate that inequality, the exploitation of people by each other, reflected the necessary social conditions imposed on societies by scarcity. As I noted earlier, the one major precondition for socialism is abundance. Socialism, according to Marx and Engels, must be a highly prosperous, what we now call postindustrial, society. They assumed that as long as there are not sufficient goods available to enable all people to live in comparative luxury, inequality of income and power is necessary. They believed, as Trotsky pointed out, that efforts to create socialism, a more egalitarian society, before an era of overwhelming abundance would inevitably fail, that intense stratification must recur.[55]

Marxist theory places an even greater emphasis on the relationship between abundance and political and social structure than does democratic theory. For according to the Marxist fathers, coercive social systems, that is, stratified ones, are a product of the division of labor inherent in the need to produce goods and services in societies characterized by scarcity. For people to become totally free and equal, they must have complete control of their own destiny. They must be able to choose and control their own work and their conditions of life. Economies based on the division of labor also require power relationships. Engels, in his essay "On Authority," wrote that over the entrance of every factory should be written, "He who enters here gives up his freedom."[56] It is clear from reading the essay that Engels was not just talking about factories in capitalist society, that he meant this generalization to hold under all conditions in which factories and the division of labor existed. Marx, on one of the few occasions in which he described socialist societies, portrayed them as societies in which men would be free to hunt in the morning, fish in the afternoon, and criticize or read poetry in the evening.[57] It seems evident that Marx and Engels looked forward to a society in which all the onerous, menial work is done by machines.[58] Socialism would be a free society because work would be handled by inanimate slaves, in which no one lacked for what he required in the way of food, clothing, or shelter, and in which people enjoyed the luxuries that only the well to do have in a precommunist world.

Marx strongly rejected Malthusian arguments that abundance is not possible, that the relationship among productivity, raw materials, and the growth of population would prevent continued increases in the per capita income, not only because these arguments seemed wrong to him, but clearly because if they were true, then socialism is impossible. Communist theorists, like Lenin, Trotsky, and Gramsci, all wrote in exuberant terms about American mass production because they believed that advanced techniques made socialism possible. Henry Ford, in spite of his reactionary political views and industrial practices, was a hero to the Russian Communists of the 1920s because of his development of the assembly line and mass production. Soviet factories contained pictures of Lenin and Ford.[59] And, of course, this worship of the god of productivity and abundance continues in the Soviet Union and China today. Authoritarianism and inequality are justified as leading to increased productivity, which will ultimately make an egalitarian communist society possible.[60]

The revival in different ways of doctrines of neo-Malthusianism, the "limits to growth" thesis, the concern for the relationship of limited natural resources to growing populations, must be seen, therefore, not only as matter of analytic and policy concerns with respect to deciding whether there are effective limits to growth and, if so, what the social consequences of a world in which productivity will no longer increase would be. It is also necessary to recognize that the end of the dream of universal abundance, of a world in which all nations will be richer than contemporary America or northern Europe, is an end also to the dream of a democratic world, or of an egalitarian socialist world, at least in terms of the assumptions of the classic theorists of democracy and of socialism. This does not mean, of course, in terms of these theories and of our own experience, that a socialist or communist world, as exemplified by countries that now describe themselves by these labels, is impossible. State-dominated societies, total government economies, are possible at any level of productivity or abundance. Communism exists in countries that range in economic levels from totally agrarian societies like Cambodia to industrialized ones like East Germany.

From a Marxian perspective, Trotsky argued that low productivity systems must be authoritarian and inegalitarian, that they would be failures from the point of the communist objectives.[61] The argument, in fact, has been made by Karl Wittfogel and others that the statist communist societies of today are actually forms of the type of social system that Marx called Asiatic. Asiatic societies in the Marxist framework existed in the ancient world, mainly in Asia and North Africa. They were characterized by state-dominated economies. The state was the central economic and power institution because of the need to control elaborate systems of irrigation and waterworks over large territories. They were statist, highly inegalitarian, and tyrannical. Wittfogel in his book *Oriental Despotism* contends that contemporary communism is a revival of Asiatic society in the Marxian sense, that it is an intensely stratified one and cannot lead to any social order that might resemble communism in the Marxist sense.[62] Leninism-Stalinism-Maoism have collectivized scarcity, and inequality and tyranny are necessary concomitants of such a system.

The dangers involved in increased state power are not limited to less-developed communist societies. As Mancur Olson has noted:

> Another characteristic that no-growth societies have is an extraordinary degree of governmental or other collective action. This would be true whether growth ceased through ZEG and ZPG policies now or because growth had someday proceeded to the point where it was obviously and immediately impossible to grow any further. Whether it became so by choice or by necessity, a no-growth society would presumably have stringent regulations and wide-ranging prohibitions against pollution and other external diseconomies, and thus more government control over individual behavior than is now customary in the Western democracies. . . . Thus there is reason to ask how well democracy as we know it would fare amidst the ubiquitous controls that would be involved either in stopping growth now or in adjusting ultimately to the inescapable environmental constraint.[63]

Those who support "no growth" in order to secure a more moral and cleaner society, of course, reject these pessimistic scenarios on value grounds. They, too, favor a more egalitarian and freer society. It is not possible for any of us to say categorically that our preferences are unattainable under either conditions of growth or no growth. Obviously, growth societies like the United States have not avoided major dysfunctions, severe inequality, poverty, racial tensions, and the like. But conversely, the best single example of a developed no-growth economy, albeit involuntarily, Great Britain, suggests problems even greater than those that accompany growth and affluence. The British people have shown in a variety of ways that they want the kinds of changes that are dependent on growth. As British political scientist Rudolf Klein noted in 1972, they want more:

> Resentment of continuing inequalities is compounded by resentment of unemployment and of the failure of living standards to rise. For poverty is not just relative. Rising standards can and do mean better food, better housing, and better clothes for people. And at the current British standard of living—the "standard" for the future, let it be remembered—these sorts of improvements still matter very much. Although Britain probably has better housing conditions than most Western European countries, 13 percent of households still lack private bathrooms and 12 percent still live in houses or flats officially classified as unfit for human habitation. More than a third of households have no refrig-

eration or cooling machine, 55 percent have no car, 65 percent have no telephone, and 70 percent have no central heating.[64]

Most of those who believe that we must or should move into a no-growth era do not want consciously to condemn those living in abysmal poverty, particularly in the less developed nations, to remain at that level. Rather, they see the need to reduce the standard of living of the affluent nations, to transfer access to resources to the less well-to-do so that they can at least partially catch up. Ignoring the question of how this can be done politically, it is unfortunately necessary to point out that the wealth of the former is not primarily a function of their control of resources. Nathan Keyfitz has noted that "natural resources account for only 5 percent of the value of goods and services produced in the U.S. and other developed countries." Thus, cutting back on American consumption will not enable other nonindustrialized nations to increase sharply their level of productivity. As he also points out: "The trouble is that goods, as well as jobs that require materials, fit into other social activities in an interlocking scheme that is hard to change; social configurations are as solid a reality as raw materials."[65]

These disagreements among eminent economists and social scientists concerning the constraints or lack of constraints that affect the potential for growth and increased affluence on a national as well as on a world scale are not, of course, unique to that discussion. The academic's easy out is to say that they point up the need for further research to test the validity of the different assumptions made by advocates on each side. It is not likely, however, that this debate will be resolved in the foreseeable future by more data, better theory, or more sophisticated arguments.

Who is right in these sharply divergent anticipations? If we run out of resources, fuel, energy, etc., the world will suffer major social upheavals, to put it mildly. But if we sharply reduce growth, we will condemn most of the world to continued poverty, we will probably curtail movements toward greater equality within nations, we will probably see more severe class struggle over division of the general economic pie and, as Robert Heilbroner and others anticipate, a greater prospect for dictatorships. The assumption that necessity is the mother of invention, that demand will provide the impetus for new discovery in the future as in the past, made by Kahn, Macrae, and many others offers a more beneficent prospect for the future of both the developed and underdeveloped worlds.

If we ask what determines the conclusions of different "experts," at least some of the factors are political. Well-to-do leftists, many intellectuals, the oppositionist intelligentsia tend to favor no growth, to think small. Trade unionists, workers, businessmen, social democrats, communists, conservatives are more likely to still see growth as both possible and desirable.

Is all this a counsel of despair, a confession of failure or inadequacy by a social scientist? I do not mean it to be. Rather, it may be viewed as a declaration of independence, of autonomy, of insistence that people can still feel free to make their own history, that the future is not so determined that we should feel helpless about our ability to affect it. We are still far from having a Calvinist social science, from having to accept predestination. Social science can help us, can trace relations, but the future still remains an uncharted sea waiting for the venturesome.

Notes

1. Rudolf Klein, "Growth and Its Enemies," *Commentary* 53 (June 1972): 38–39.
2. Henry C. Wallich, "Economic Growth in America," in Chester L. Cooper (ed.), *Growth in America* (Westport, Conn.: Greenwood, 1976), p. 62.
3. Arthur M. Okun, "What's Wrong with the U.S. Economy? Diagnosis and Prescription," *Quarterly Review of Economics and Business* (Summer 1975): 26.
4. George Katona, "Behavioral Economics," *Challenge* 21 (September–October 1978): 17–18; see also Milton Friedman, "Nobel Lecture: Inflation and Unemployment," *Journal of Political Economy* 85 (June 1977): 451–71.
5. Norman Macrae, "The Future of International Business," *Economist*, 22 January 1972, p. v.
6. Robert L. Heilbroner, "The Missing Link(s)," *Challenge* 21 (March–April 1978): 17.
7. Wassily Leontief, "Theoretical Assumptions and Nonobserved Facts," *American Economic Review* 61 (1971): 3.
8. Robert M. Solow, "The Public Discussion of Economics: Some Pitfalls," *Challenge* 21 (March–April 1978): 39.
9. Dudley Kirk, "The Field of Demography," in David L. Sills (ed.), *International Encyclopedia of the Social Sciences* 12 (New York: Macmillan and Free Press, 1968): 345.
10. Kenneth E. Boulding, "The Shadow of the Stationary State," *Daedalus* 102 (Fall 1973): 93.
11. "Population Drop Worries Australia," *New York Times*, 3 October 1976, p. 16; Donald J. Bogue and Amy Ong Tsui, "Zero World Population Growth?" *The Public Interest* 55 (Spring 1979): 100, and Peter C. Stuart, "Undoing Malthus: Developing Asia's Countryside," *The New Leader* 62 (March 12, 1979): 8–10.
12. Charles F. Westoff, "Marriage and Fertility in the Developed Countries," *Scientific American* 239 (December 1978): 51–52.
13. For a review of the evidence on social mobility, see S. M. Lipset, "Equality and Inequality," in Robert K. Merton and Robert Nisbet (eds), *Contemporary Social Problems*, 4th ed. (New York: Harcourt Brace, Jovanovich, 1976), pp. 305–53.
14. Nathan Glazer and Daniel P. Moynihan, "Introduction" to their *Ethnicity: Theory and Experience* (Cambridge, Mass.: Harvard University Press, 1975), pp. 6–7 (emphasis in original).
15. Eugene B. Skolnikoff, "The Governability of Complexity," in Cooper (ed.), *Growth in America*, p. 78. For a sophisticated critique of scholars who failed to anticipate the renewed importance of ethnicity, see Walker Connor, "Nation-Building or Nation-Destroying?" *World Politics* 24 (April 1972): 319–55. See

also S. M. Lipset, "Racial and Ethnic Tensions in the Third World," in W.S. Thompson (ed.), *The Third World* (San Francisco: Institute for Contemporary Studies, 1978), pp. 123–48.

16. See the essays in Daniel Bell (ed.), *The Radical Right* (Garden City, N.Y.: Doubleday-Anchor Books, 1963).

17. I still find it a useful analytic concept. See S. M. Lipset and Earl Raab, *The Politics of Unreason: Right-Wing Extremism in America, 1970–1977* (Chicago: University of Chicago Press, Phoenix edition, 1978).

18. For a review of the original writings and various critical commentaries see chapter 3 in this volume.

19. For a discussion of the literature seeking to explain the student revolt, see S. M. Lipset, *Rebellion in the University* (Chicago: University of Chicago Press, Phoenix edition, 1976), pp. 3–38.

20. Gabriel A. Almond and Stephen J. Genco, "Clouds, Clocks, and the Study of Politics," *World Politics* 29 (July 1977): 494.

21. Ida R. Hoos, *Systems Analysis in Social Policy* (London: The Institute of Economic Affairs, 1969), pp. 20–24.

22. Alvin Gouldner, "Toward a Radical Reconstruction of Sociology," *Social Policy* 1 (May–June 1970): 21.

23. S. M. Lipset, "Why No Socialism in the United States?" in S. Bialer and S. Sluzar (eds.), *Sources of Contemporary Radicalism*, Vol. 1 (Boulder, Co.: Westview, 1977), pp. 31–149, 346–63.

24. Robert K. Merton, *Social Theory and Social Structure* (New York: Free Press, 1957), pp. 9–10, 280, 328.

25. Lee J. Cronbach, "Beyond the Two Disciplines of Scientific Psychology," *American Psychologist* 30 (February 1975): 122–23, 126.

26. S. M. Lipset, *Political Man* (Garden City, N.Y.: Doubleday, 1960), pp. 100–101.

27. Robert E. Lane, "The Politics of Consensus in an Age of Affluence," *American Political Science Review* 59 (1965): 874–95, and "The Decline of Politics and Ideology in a Knowledgeable Society," *American Sociological Review* 31 (1966): 649–62.

28. See James D. Wright, *The Dissent of the Governed* (New York: Academic Press, 1976), pp. 168–200; S. M. Lipset and William Schneider, "How's Business? What the Public Thinks," *Public Opinion* 1 (July–August 1978): 41–47; S. M. Lipset and W. Schneider, *The Confidence Gap: Business, Labor and Government in the Public Mind* (New York: Free Press, 1983).

29. Lester Milbrath and M. L. Goel, *Political Participation* (Chicago: Rand McNally, 1977), pp. 90–106; S. M. Lipset, *Political Man*, pp. 182–84, 190–200, 214–15.

30. President's Commission, *Registration and Voting Participation* (Washington, D.C.: Government Printing Office, 1963).

31. James Q. Wilson, "On Pettigrew and Armor: An Afterword," *The Public Interest* 30 (Winter 1973): 133.

32. Donella H. Meadows et al., *The Limits to Growth* (New York: Universe Books, 1972); E. P. Schumacher, *Small is Beautiful* (London: Blond and Briggs, 1973). A comprehensive summary of the growth and no-growth positions as well as a detailed presentation of various scenarios related to different assumptions can be found in Edison Electric Institute, *Economic Growth in the Future* (New York: McGraw-Hill, 1976).

33. Macrae, "Future of International Business," pp. v–vi, x.
34. Herman Kahn, William Brown, and Leon Martel, *The Next 200 Years: A Scenario for America and the World* (New York: William Morrow, 1976), p. 1.
35. Lester R. Brown, *World Population Trends* (Washington, D.C.: Worldwatch Institute, 1976) and Bogue and Tsui, "Zero World Population Growth?" pp. 99–113.
36. U.S. Bureau of the Census, *World Population: 1977—Recent Demographic Estimates for the Countries and Regions of the World* (Washington, D.C.: 1978); Patrice Wingert, "Chinese Birthrate for '78 Down, Says Population Expert," *Houston Chronicle*, 13 December 1978, p. 8, Section 7; "Study Shows Drop in Mexico's Growth," *San Francisco Chronicle*, 14 December 1978, p. 11; Westoff, "Marriage and Fertility," pp. 51–57; "Indonesia Stressing a Lower Birth Rate," *New York Times*, 18 February, 1979, p. 31.
37. Peter Grose, "Report at U.N. Says Rich-Poor Gap Can Be Narrowed by the Year 2000," *New York Times*, October 14, 1976, p. 1; Wassily Leontief et al., *The Future of the World Economy* (New York: Oxford University Press, 1977).
38. Daniel Aaron, "Reflections on Growth and Literature in America," in Cooper (ed.), *Growth in America*, pp. 152–53.
39. E. J. Mishan, "Ills, Bads, and Disamenities: The Wages of Growth," *Daedalus* 102 (Fall 1973): 74–75.
40. Willard R. Johnson, "Should the Poor Buy No Growth?" *Daedalus* 102 (Fall 1973): 165.
41. As quoted ibid.
42. David Potter, *People of Plenty: Economic Abundance and the American Character* (Chicago: University of Chicago Press, 1954).
43. Werner Sombart, *Why Is There No Socialism in the United States of America?* (White Plains, N.Y.: International Arts and Sciences Press, 1976).
44. Potter, *People of Plenty*, p. 102.
45. Malcolm Sawyer, "Income Distribution in OECD Countries," *OECD Economic Outlook* (July 1976): 3–36.
46. Gunnar Myrdal, *An International Economy* (New York: Harper, 1956), p. 133. See Simon Kuznets, *Modern Economic Growth* (New Haven, Conn.: Yale University Press, 1966), p. 207.
47. See particularly the essays in Hollis Chenery et al., *Redistribution with Growth* (London: Oxford University Press, 1974).
48. For a review of the findings relevant to different aspects of inequality in the United States, see S. M. Lipset "Equality and Inequality," in Merton and Nisbet (eds.), *Contemporary Social Problems*, pp. 305–53.
49. "Where the Grass Is Greener," *Economist*, December 25, 1971, p. 15.
50. Gideon Sjoberg, "Are Social Classes in America Becoming More Rigid?" *American Sociological Review* 16 (December 1951): 775–83.
51. Boulding, "Shadow of the Stationary State," p. 95.
52. Robert L. Heilbroner, "Middle-Class Myths, Middle-Class Realities," *Atlantic* 238 (October 1976): 41.
53. Richard Zeckhauser, "The Risks of Growth," *Daedalus* 102 (Fall 1973): 103.
54. Lipset, *Political Man*, pp. 66–67.
55. Leon Trotsky, *The Revolution Betrayed* (Garden City, N.Y.: Doubleday, 1937).
56. Friedrich Engels, "On Authority," in Karl Marx and Friedrich Engels, *Basic Writings in Politics and Philosophy*, Lewis S. Feuer (ed.), (Garden City, N.Y.: Doubleday, 1959), pp. 482–84.

57. Karl Marx and Friedrich Engels, *The German Ideology* (New York: International Publishers, 1947), p. 22.
58. See Joachim Israel, *Alienation from Marx to Modern Sociology* (Boston: Allyn & Bacon, 1971), p. 25.
59. For discussion of the Communist attitude to American productivity, see Lipset, "Why No Socialism in the United States?" pp. 78–79; Warren L. Susman, "Comment 1," in J. H. M. Laslett and S. M. Lipset (eds.), *Failure of a Dream? Essays in the History of American Socialism* (Garden City, N.Y.: Anchor/Doubleday, 1974), pp. 450–51.
60. G. R. Barker, "La Femme en Union Soviétique," *Sociologie et Sociétés.* 4 (November 1972): 180–81.
61. Trotsky, *Revolution Betrayed*, esp. p. 56.
62. Karl Wittfogel, *Oriental Despotism* (New Haven, Conn.: Yale University Press, 1957).
63. Mancur Olson, "Introduction," *Daedalus* 102 (Fall 1973): 8–9.
64. Klein, "Growth and Its Enemies," p. 43.
65. Nathan Keyfitz, "World Resources and the World Middle Class," *Scientific American* 235 (July 1976): 32, 34.

Bibliography

Books and Monographs
by Seymour Martin Lipset

Authored Works

Agrarian Socialism (1950; 1968; 1971).
(with Martin Trow and James S. Coleman), *Union Democracy* (1953; 1977).
(with Reinhard Bendix), *Social Mobility in Industrial Society* (1959; 1961).
(with Earl Raab), *Prejudice and Society* (1959).
Political Man: The Social Bases of Politics (1960; 1981).
The First New Nation: The United States in Historical and Comparative Perspective (1963; 1967; 1979).
Estudiantes universitarios y politica en el tercer mundo (1965).
Revolution and Counterrevolution (1968; 1970).
(with Earl Raab), *The Politics of Unreason: Right-Wing Extremism in America 1790–1977* (1970; 1978).
Group Life in America (1972).
Rebellion in the University (1972; 1976).
(with Everett C. Ladd), *Professors, Unions, and American Higher Education* (1973).
(with Everett C. Ladd), *Academics, Politics, and the 1972 Election* (1973).
(with Everett C. Ladd), *The Divided Academy: Professors and Politics* (1975; 1976).
(with David Riesman), *Education and Politics at Harvard* (1975).
(with Irving Louis Horowitz), *Dialogues on American Politics* (1978).
(with William Schneider), *The Confidence Gap: Business, Labor and Government in the Public Mind* (1983).

Edited Works

(with Walter Galenson), *Labor and Trade Unionism* (1960).
(with Neil Smelser), *Sociology: The Progress of a Decade* (1961).
(with Leo Lowenthal), *Culture and Social Character* (1961).
(with Sheldon Wolin), *The Berkeley Student Revolt* (1965).
(with Reinhard Bendix), *Class, Status and Power: Social Stratification in Comparative Perspective* (1966).
(with Neil Smelser), *Social Structure, Mobility and Development* (1966).
(with Aldo Solari), *Elites in Latin America* (1967).

(with Stein Rokkan), *Party Systems and Voter Alignments* (1967)
Student Politics (1967).
(with Richard Hofstadter), *Turner and the Sociology of the Frontier* (1968).
(with Richard Hofstadter), *Sociology and History: Methods* (1968).
Politics and the Social Sciences (1969).
(with Philip Altbach), *Students in Revolt* (1969; 1970).
(with David Bell and Karl Deutsch), *Issues in Politics and Government* (1970).
(with John Laslett), *Failure of a Dream? Essays in the History of American Socialism*
        (1974; 1984).
Emerging Coalitions in American Politics (1978).
The Third Century: America as a Post-Industrial Society (1979; 1980).
Party Coalitions in the 1980s (1981).

Index

West Germany. *See* Germany
Westoff, Charles, 334
Weyrich, Paul, 283–84
Wilson, James Q., 257, 343
Winrod, Gerald, 258
Wittfogel, Karl, 206–7, 354–55
Wolff, Robert, 88
Worker-employer cleavages, 135–40. *See also* Industrial revolution; Name of country
Working class, 48–52, 187–217; and historical materialism, 188–93; and politics, 219–52; and postindustrial society, 193–205; and religion, 251n105; and social integration, 238–40, 242–43; and socialism, 205–12. *See also* Class, social; Industrial revolution/Industrialization; Marx, Karl; Socialism; Unions; Worker-

employer cleavages; Working class movements
Working class movements: causal factors of, 219, 220; and European party system model, 164–68; and feudalism, 243, 244, 245. *See also* Class, social; Electoral game, rules of the; Industrial revolution; Unions, Working class

Youth, rebellion of, 25, 26, 28. *See also* Alienation; Student revolts

Zaph, Wolfgang, 268
Zeckhauser, Richard, 351
Zetkin, Clara, 264
Zetterberg, Hans, 200